Monetary and Currency Policy Management in Asia

Monetary and Currency Policy Management in Asia

Edited by

Masahiro Kawai

Dean and CEO, Asian Development Bank Institute, Tokyo, Japan

Peter J. Morgan

Senior Consultant for Research, Asian Development Bank Institute, Tokyo, Japan

Shinji Takagi

Professor, Graduate School of Economics, Osaka University, Japan

A JOINT PUBLICATION OF THE ASIAN DEVELOPMENT BANK INSTITUTE AND EDWARD ELGAR PUBLISHING

Edward Elgar
Cheltenham, UK • Northampton, MA, USA

Published by
Edward Elgar Publishing Limited
The Lypiatts
15 Lansdown Road
Cheltenham
Glos GL50 2JA
UK

Edward Elgar Publishing, Inc.
William Pratt House
9 Dewey Court
Northampton
Massachusetts 01060
USA

A catalogue record for this book
is available from the British Library

Library of Congress Control Number: 2011934816

MIX
Paper from
responsible sources
FSC® C018575
FSC
www.fsc.org

ISBN 978 0 85793 334 8

Typeset by Servis Filmsetting Ltd, Stockport, Cheshire
Printed and bound by MPG Books Group, UK

Contents

Contributors

Joshua Aizenman, Professor, Economics Department, University of California, Santa Cruz, CA and Research Associate, National Bureau of Economic Research, Cambridge, MA, USA.

Menzie D. Chinn, Professor, Economics Department, University of Wisconsin, Madison, WI and Research Associate, National Bureau of Economic Research, Cambridge, MA, USA.

Andrew Filardo, Head of Economics for Asia and the Pacific, Bank for International Settlements, Hong Kong, China.

Shin-ichi Fukuda, Professor, Graduate School of Economics, University of Tokyo, Tokyo, Japan.

Hans Genberg, Assistant Director, Independent Evaluation Office, International Monetary Fund, Washington, DC, USA.

Hiro Ito, Associate Professor, Economics Department, Portland State University, Portland, OR, USA.

Masahiro Kawai, Dean and CEO, Asian Development Bank Institute, Tokyo, Japan.

Soyoung Kim, Professor, Economics Department, Seoul National University, Seoul, Korea.

Yoshifumi Kon, Assistant Professor, Aoyama Gakuin University, Tokyo, Japan.

Peter J. Morgan, Senior Consultant for Research, Asian Development Bank Institute, Tokyo, Japan.

Ila Patnaik, Professor, National Institute of Public Finance and Policy, New Delhi, India.

Ajay Shah, Professor, National Institute of Public Finance and Policy, New Delhi, India.

Shinji Takagi, Professor, Graduate School of Economics, Osaka University, Osaka, Japan.

Doo Yong Yang, Associate Professor, College of International Studies, Kyung Hee University, Seoul, Korea.

Fan Zhai, Managing Director, Department of Asset Allocation and Strategic Research, China Investment Corporation, Beijing, People's Republic of China.

Preface

In most Asian economies, the global financial crisis is increasingly becoming a thing of the past. By mid-2009 recovery was already evident in much of the region; in 2010 it was by far the fastest growing region of the world. Among the most impressive performers have been the dynamic economies of the People's Republic of China and India, each of which registered growth approaching or exceeding 10 percent for the year. The performance of several other economies, notably Singapore and Taipei,China, was more impressive, and the Association of Southeast Asian Nations (ASEAN) member countries also registered healthy growth rates in 2010. While advanced economies remain sluggish, the Asian region is once again leading the way.

The legacy of the crisis, however, will be long lasting. The diagnosis and the lessons of the crisis – including whether or not Asia's policy mix had contributed to the crisis and how to reform the international financial architecture to prevent another crisis of the same kind – will no doubt be debated over the coming years. An important post-global financial crisis agenda for the Asian region involves building a consensus on appropriate macroeconomic policies over the medium term. Should a country pursue a more flexible exchange rate policy? Should it target both price and financial stability as objectives of monetary policy? Should it continue to accumulate foreign exchange reserves as an insurance against a sudden outflow of capital? These are some of the critical issues for the region's policymakers.

This volume brings together both theoretical and empirical studies that address aspects of the macroeconomic policy issues noted above. The studies were originally prepared for two international conferences on the global financial crisis hosted in 2009 by the Asian Development Bank Institute (ADBI). Most of the empirical works have a specific focus on Asia. But the issues they discuss are by no means region-specific. The volume pays particular attention to monetary and exchange rate policy issues, though fiscal policy is also discussed in one chapter as it relates to broader issues of macroeconomic policy management. The Asian region's recovery ahead of other regions, together with ultra-low interest rate policies and quantitative easing in advanced economies, has led to a resumption of large capital inflows and attendant currency appreciation pressure, thus presenting a set of challenges for macroeconomic policy management. In this respect, the topics discussed in this volume are both urgent and timely.

The volume consists of nine chapters, including an overview chapter. The eight analytical chapters are organized into five parts. Part I deals with monetary policy issues, including the effectiveness of unconventional policies and medium-term policy frameworks. Part II is devoted to exchange rate policy and foreign exchange reserve management issues. Part III discusses policy choices related to the 'impossible trinity', the proposition in the economic literature that no economy can simultaneously achieve all three objectives of (i) exchange rate stability; (ii) capital mobility; and (iii) monetary policy independence. Part IV models the impact of the global financial crisis and policy responses on Asian economies. Finally, Part V proposes a framework for regional exchange rate cooperation. All of these chapters, though initially prepared in 2009, were subsequently updated for inclusion in this volume.

As co-editors, we are first and foremost grateful to the authors of the individual chapters for providing high-quality analyses of the macroeconomic policy issues that are so relevant to the Asia region today. Our thanks are also due to many others whose assistance has made the production of this volume possible. Mario Lamberte, as one of the architects of the 2009 ADBI project on the global financial crisis, provided intellectual inputs at each stage of the production process. Nimesh Salike assisted with the final preparation of the manuscript. Ainslie Smith was responsible for ADBI's internal editing. Last but not least, able ADBI support staff, especially Hideki Miura, Kazumi Hasegawa, Tomoko Doi and Yuzuru Nagai, provided invaluable logistical support to the 2009 conferences where the chapters were initially presented. It is our sincere hope that this volume will contribute to the ongoing debate on post-crisis macroeconomic policy management and become part of our collective efforts to make Asia and the world a more stable and resilient place.

Masahiro Kawai
Peter J. Morgan
Shinji Takagi

Abbreviations

ABMI	Asian Bond Markets Initiative
ACU	Asian currency unit
ADBI	Asian Development Bank Institute
AMCF	Asian monetary cooperation fund
AMLF	Asset-Backed Commercial Paper Money Market Fund Liquidity Facility
AMRO	ASEAN+3 Macroeconomic Research Office
AREAER	IMF's Annual Report on Exchange Arrangements and Exchange Restrictions
ASEAN	Association of Southeast Asian Nations
ASEAN+3	ASEAN member countries plus the PRC, Japan and Korea
ASW	Ahsan, Skully and Wickramanayake (2008)
BBC	band, basket and crawl
BoE	Bank of England
BoJ	Bank of Japan
BoK	Bank of Korea
BOP	balance of payments
CAB	current account balance at central bank
CAR	capital adequacy ratio
CBC	Central Bank of Taipei,China
CBGI	central bank governance and independence
CE	credit easing
CES	constant elasticity of substitution
CHF	Swiss franc
CMI	Chiang Mai Initiative
CMIM	CMI Multilateralization
CMP	commodity price
CNY	Chinese yuan
CP	commercial paper
CPFF	Commercial Paper Funding Facility
CPI	consumer price index
CR	call rate (or interbank rate)
DC	developing countries

DEM	Deutsche mark
DFS	domestic financial sector
ECB	European Central Bank
ECU	European currency unit
EEA	emerging East Asia
EMCF	European Monetary Cooperation Fund
EMG	emerging market countries
EMP	exchange rate market pressure
EMS	European Monetary System
ERM	exchange rate mechanism
ERPD	Economic Review and Policy Dialogue
ERS	exchange rate stability
FDI	foreign direct investment
Fed	US Federal Reserve
FFR	Federal funds rate
FX	foreign exchange
G20	Group of Twenty
GEM	Global Economy Model
GDP	gross domestic product
GIMF	global integrated monetary and fiscal model
GNI	gross national income
GTAP	Global Trade Analysis Project
HP	Hodrick–Prescott
IDC	industrialized countries
IFS	*International Financial Statistics*
IMF	International Monetary Fund
INR	Indian rupee
IP	industrial production
IR	international reserves
IT	inflation targeting
JGB	Japanese government bond
JPY	Japanese yen
KA	capital account
KAOPEN	capital account openness
LDC	less-developed countries
LIBOR	London Interbank Offered Rate
M	monetary aggregate
MI	monetary independence
M0	monetary base
M2	broad money
MMIFF	Money Market Investor Funding Facility
NBR	non-borrowed reserves

OA	other assets
OECD	Organisation for Economic Co-operation and Development
OLS	ordinary least squares
PBC	People's Bank of China
PDCF	Primary Dealer Credit Facility
PRC	People's Republic of China
QE	quantitative easing
RBI	Reserve Bank of India
RES	foreign exchange reserves
ROW	rest of the world
SDR	Special Drawing Right
TAF	Term Auction Facility
TALF	Term Asset-Backed Securities Loan Facility
TOT	terms of trade
TSLF	Term Securities Lending Facility
UK	United Kingdom
US	United States
VAR	vector autoregression
ZIRP	zero-interest-rate policy
ZLB	zero lower bound

Glossary of selected abbreviations

AMLF: Asset-Backed Commercial Paper Money Market Fund Liquidity Facility. A lending facility that provides funding to United States (US) depository institutions and bank holding companies to finance their purchases of high-quality asset-backed commercial paper (ABCP) from money market mutual funds under certain conditions.

CABs: Current account balances – that is, reserve deposits of a central bank.

CE: Credit easing describes policies aimed at affecting the composition of a central bank's balance sheet.

CPFF: Commercial Paper Funding Facility. A facility that complements the US Federal Reserve's existing credit facilities to help provide liquidity to term funding markets.

MMIFF: Money Market Investor Funding Facility. A facility to support a private sector initiative designed to provide liquidity to US money market investors.

PDCF: Primary Dealer Credit Facility. A lending facility to improve the ability of primary dealers to provide financing to participants in securitization markets.

TAF: Term Auction Facility. Auction for Federal term funds from the discount window.

TALF: Term Asset-Backed Securities Loan Facility. A facility that will help market participants meet the credit needs of households and small businesses by supporting the issuance of asset-backed securities collateralized by student loans, auto loans, credit card loans, and loans guaranteed by the Small Business Administration.

TSLF: Term Securities Lending Facility. Access to Fed discount window for primary dealers.

1. Monetary and currency policy issues: an overview

Shinji Takagi

1.1 INTRODUCTION

The global financial crisis severely affected Asia, with the sharpest contraction of output occurring from late 2008 to early 2009. Although the initial impact of the crisis appeared limited, the region was hard hit when the crisis spread to the real sector and caused the volume of world trade to collapse. The hardest hit was Japan, whose real gross domestic product (GDP) growth fell from 2.4 percent per year in 2007 to –1.2 percent in 2008 and further to –5.2 percent in 2009 (Figure 1.1). The region's other

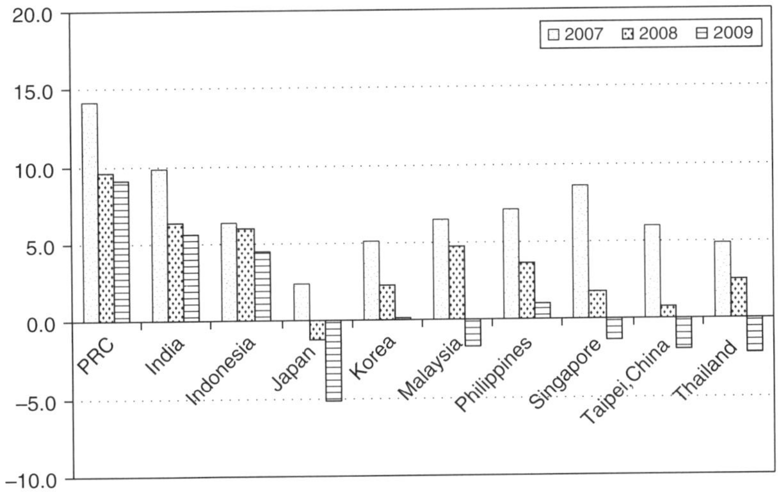

Note: PRC = People's Republic of China.

Source: IMF, World Economic Outlook database, October 2010, available at http://www.imf.org/external/pubs/ft/weo/2010/02/weodata/index.aspx.

Figure 1.1 GDP growth in selected Asian economies (% per year)

exporters of manufactured goods were adversely affected in early 2009, but they pulled themselves out of severe economic contraction by mid-2009. For the year as a whole, real GDP declined only moderately in these countries (for example, −1.7 percent for Malaysia; −1.3 percent for Singapore); the Republic of Korea (henceforth Korea) even managed to escape negative economic growth for the year. The People's Republic of China (PRC), India and Indonesia continued to grow at a steady pace in 2009 (ranging from 4.5 percent to 9.1 percent), but even in these countries the negative impact of the crisis was evident.

In responding to the sharp contraction of output from late 2008 to early 2009, countries in Asia substantially eased monetary and fiscal policies. Although it is difficult to quantify the precise impact of these policies on growth, they appear for the most part to have succeeded in preventing these economies from contracting further. By mid-2009, most of the region was well on its way to recovery. In fact, Asia was by far the fastest growing region in 2010 when economic recovery remained fragile in the rest of the world. It is therefore appropriate to reflect on the macroeconomic policy issues that came out of the crisis experience. Asia's strong recovery ahead of other regions presents a different set of challenges for macroeconomic policy management, especially as monetary tightening could trigger an increase in capital inflows into the region. Thus, it is also important to consider forward-looking issues related to macroeconomic policy.

This volume is a collection of eight chapters that address aspects of the macroeconomic policy issues raised above. The chapters were originally presented as papers at conferences that focused on the global financial crisis hosted in 2009 by the Asian Development Bank Institute (ADBI). Most had a specific focus on Asia. But the issues they discussed are by no means country- or region-specific. This volume pays particular attention to monetary and currency (that is exchange rate and reserve management) policy issues, in light of their close relationship, and covers fiscal policy issues briefly. Chapter 8 of this volume discusses the role of fiscal policy as it relates to broader issues of macroeconomic policy management.

This overview chapter presents the main thrust of the individual chapters, and puts them in the context of the ongoing debate on macroeconomic policy issues. Section 1.2 reviews the monetary policy measures taken by Asian and other economies in response to the crisis, and draws on Part I to discuss their lessons and policy implications. Section 1.3 covers the range of issues discussed in Part II and Part III, namely, the choice of exchange rate regime, costs and benefits of foreign exchange reserve accumulation, the trade-off between exchange rate stability and capital account openness, and how to manage capital inflows. Section 1.4 is a summary of the fiscal policy measures taken by the region's authorities and places the fiscal policy issues discussed in Chapter 8 in a broader context. Section 1.5 addresses the need and prospects for regional policy cooperation discussed principally in Chapter 9 but also in other chapters, while section 1.6 concludes.

1.2 MONETARY POLICY ISSUES

1.2.1 Monetary Policy Measures in Asia

Although all economies in the region eased their monetary policies in the latter part of 2008, most came into the onset of the crisis with a tight monetary policy stance. Their pressing concerns in mid-2008 were about the inflationary consequence of overheating and rising commodity prices. When the real impact of the crisis was felt, however, all central banks shifted to monetary easing. The softening of energy and commodity prices allowed the monetary authorities to cut policy interest rates aggressively. The response of the People's Bank of China (PBC) was particularly quick. On 16 September 2008, it reduced the benchmark lending rate by 27 basis points; it would cut the rate by an additional 189 basis points by the end of 2008. Other central banks took similar actions. As a result, market interest rates in Asia edged downward in late 2008 and early 2009, though the levels of interest rates remained high in Indonesia, India and the Philippines (Figure 1.2).

Some Asian central banks not only cut interest rates but also attempted to increase the flow of credit through conventional tools. For example, the PBC removed limits on credit growth, which led to an extraordinary expansion of bank lending in the first quarter of 2009. At the end of March 2009, broad money (M2) was higher by 25.5 percent from a year earlier, while bank credit was higher by 27.0 percent, and the pace of growth continued. With a drying up of capital inflows and the associated rise in demand for credit from the domestic banking system, the initial response of the Reserve Bank of India (RBI) on 16 September 2008 was to raise the ceiling on deposit rates. Though Bank Indonesia did not begin to cut the policy interest rate until December, it immediately responded to the onset of the global crisis by lowering the overnight repo rate on 16 September 2008 to maintain liquidity. The Bank of Japan (in October 2008) and the Bank of Korea (in December 2008) began to pay interest on excess reserves and required reserves, respectively.

A number of central banks also cut statutory reserve or cash requirements. For example, the PBC reduced reserve requirements four times from September to December. The RBI made a one-time cut in liquidity

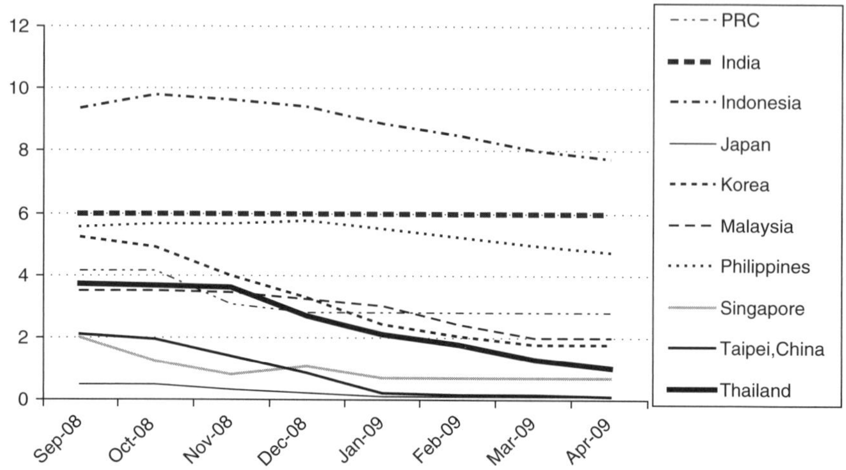

Note: PRC = People's Republic of China.

Source: International Monetary Fund, International Financial Statistics, online database (http://www.imfstatistics.org/imf/), accessed October 2010; for Taipei,China only, Central Bank of Taipei,China, Financial Statistics (http://www.cbc.gov.tw/mp2.html), accessed October 2010.

Figure 1.2 Market interest rates in selected Asian economies, September 2008–April 2009 (% per year)

requirements in November. Similar actions were taken by the central banks of Indonesia; Malaysia; the Philippines; and Taipei,China. Some countries used exchange rate policy as another tool of monetary easing. In the second half of 2008, the PRC abruptly halted the policy of allowing the yuan to appreciate gradually against the United States (US) dollar. In October 2008, Singapore shifted to a 0 percent appreciation of the nominal exchange rate, reversing a policy of graduate appreciation it had followed since April 2004. In a further move, in April 2009, the Monetary Authority of Singapore, while keeping the zero appreciation policy, recentered the policy band to the prevailing level of the nominal exchange rate, which represented an effective depreciation of the currency.

For the most part, monetary policy appears to have worked reasonably well for countries with sufficient policy space. With the level of interest rates sufficiently high at the onset of the crisis, the conventional monetary policy transmission channel was largely intact, allowing a substantial reduction in market interest rates. On the other hand, in countries where interest rates were low to begin with, the interest rate transmission mechanism was impaired by the zero lower bound, requiring the use of 'unconventional' monetary policies. Even in countries where the level of interest rates was sufficiently high, some use was also made of unconventional policies when, in an extraordinary environment of global deleveraging, rising risk premiums loosened the relationship between the policy rate and long-term lending rates (for example, India, Korea and Taipei,China).

1.2.2 Unconventional Monetary Policies

The effectiveness and utility of unconventional policies, used not only in Asia but also more importantly in the US and Europe, is perhaps the single most important monetary policy issue that came out of the crisis experience, a topic addressed in Chapter 2 and Chapter 3. Broadly two types of unconventional policies are identified in the literature. First, quantitative easing refers to policies that aim to increase free reserves of the banking system, through open market operations or foreign exchange market intervention. During the crisis, the Bank of England (BoE) adopted this type of measure when it set a target for reserve deposits in March 2009. In the case of quantitative easing, it is apparent that the term 'unconventional' applies mainly to economies with advanced markets where the interest rate is the 'conventional' tool of monetary policy, although it is applicable to emerging economies that face foreign currency liquidity shortages as well.

Second, credit easing (or qualitative easing) refers to policies aimed at affecting the composition of a central bank's balance sheet leaving the size unchanged, for example through an exchange of government bills for government bonds or purchases of private sector assets. Although credit easing includes direct lending to market participants and therefore, like quantitative easing, generally involves an increase in the size of a central bank's balance sheet, the focus is on the composition of assets, not the size of liabilities. Many of the measures used by central banks in Asia fell into this category, including bilateral currency swap agreements with the US Federal Reserve (the Fed). To the extent that central banks purchased private sector assets, they assumed significant credit risk.

Credit easing was actively used by the central banks of advanced economies. For example, the Fed created a number of new credit facilities to mitigate stresses in various market segments, including the Term Auction Facility, the Term Securities Lending Facility, the Primary Dealer Credit Facility, the Asset-Backed Commercial Paper Money Market Fund Liquidity Facility, the Commercial Paper Funding Facility and the Term Asset-Backed Securities Loan Facility. The Bank of Japan downgraded the credit rating of corporate bonds acceptable as collateral from A− to BBB, and accepted debt instruments issued by real estate investment corporations as collateral. The BoE accepted as collateral commercial paper, corporate bonds, bonds issued under the United Kingdom's (UK) credit guarantee scheme, syndicated loans and asset-backed securities created in viable securitization structures.

Peter Morgan (Chapter 2) discusses the effectiveness of unconventional monetary policies by reviewing the empirical literature and recent experience. First, he cites empirical evidence to show that, among the several channels through which unconventional policies might operate, the commitment or duration effect (whereby verbal commitments by central banks to maintain very low interest rates for a certain period affect market expectations) seems to work. In fact, most studies of the commitment effect in Japan and the US suggest that central bank statements do lower market interest rates, though the impact is mainly limited to short-term rates.

Second, evidence on quantitative easing is less conclusive. Morgan observes that, after the announcement of a target for reserve deposits by the BoE in March 2009, the spread between the three-month sterling London Interbank Offered Rate (LIBOR) and the base rate narrowed. Third, as to credit easing, the impact of outright purchases of government bonds on bond yields looks limited. Morgan notes that the recent experience of the Fed and the BoE was not encouraging, though Andrew Filardo and Hans Genberg (Chapter 3) claim that government bond purchases did reduce the term premiums. In contrast, credit easing successfully relieved credit-related stresses in other market segments; the Fed's Term Auction Facility and currency swaps with foreign central banks seem to have achieved their intended objectives, as did the BoE's move to provide unlimited dollar liquidity to the banking sector.

1.2.3 The Exit Policy and Medium-Term Issues

Even though the types of unconventional policies used in Asia were modest compared to those used in the US and the UK, credit easing measures nonetheless represented a more intrusive intervention of the public sector in the allocation of credit, which during normal times should best be left to the market. Filardo and Genberg (Chapter 3) argue that a central bank, by taking on credit risk, runs the risk of having to ask the government for additional capital in case a significant portion of its portfolio underperforms. This could compromise a central bank's political independence and lead to a deterioration of its ability to carry out its mandate. Sooner or later the exit policy must be considered, though it may not be straightforward to unwind the holding of illiquid assets, such as asset-backed securities, in a timely manner.

Filardo and Genberg, after describing monetary policy regimes (including policy objectives and instruments, governance and independence) in

12 Asia and Pacific economies, discuss medium-term issues for monetary policy, including the type of regimes Asia's central banks should adopt going forward. Prior to the global financial crisis, almost all central banks in Asia had aimed for price or exchange rate stability as the overarching objective of monetary policy. Empirical evidence suggests that inflation rates in Asia were well anchored for both inflation-targeting and non-inflation-targeting central banks. Moreover, both the inflation-targeting and non-inflation-targeting central banks saw considerable improvement in independence and other aspects of governance. It is thus clear that as long as there is a right policy focus, inflation targeting is not the only way to achieve price stability.

Much less consensus exists on the extent to which central banks should take account of asset prices in the conduct of monetary policy. The conventional wisdom until recently was that central banks should not lean against possible financial imbalances as they build up, but should respond aggressively once they collapse. This view was based on the assumption that significant imbalances are nearly impossible to detect with confidence in real time, and the costs of cleaning up the impaired financial sector are expected to be low and manageable. But the crisis has opened up the debate regarding 'leaning versus cleaning'. There is now a widely held view that too narrow a focus by central banks on price stability created a speculative bubble in the asset market and led to excessive risk-taking in financial markets, and monetary policy therefore should give greater attention to financial stability.

According to Filardo and Genberg, assigning a central bank the responsibility for financial stability would be difficult because there is no agreed definition of financial stability, let alone a single numerical indicator (such as the rate of inflation) that could serve as a measure of success or failure. Financial instability can take many forms, so that there is no model that can link the absence of it with a central bank's policy instruments. Stabilizing asset prices would be a mistake as it requires such large adjustments in the policy interest rate that it would be destabilizing for inflation, output and employment. Financial stability should not come at the expense of price and macroeconomic stability.

The point that Filardo and Genberg emphasize, however, is that the two objectives need not be incompatible. To the extent that a central bank's objective is to minimize fluctuations in inflation around a target value, and fluctuations of output around its natural level, all relevant information, including asset prices, should be factored in. Then, it should be possible to pursue medium-term price stability while taking account of a sustained one-way movement in asset prices. Filardo and Genberg conclude that as central banks lack a direct instrument to achieve financial stability, it is useful to develop mechanisms to limit the procyclicality of a market-based financial system.

1.3 CURRENCY POLICY ISSUES

1.3.1 Exchange Rate Policies

Asian economies entered the onset of the crisis with considerable diversity in exchange rate arrangements. The Japanese yen was the only bona fide freely floating currency. In the rest of the region, some currencies (such as the Korean won and the Indonesian rupiah) appeared to be floating with some flexibility, while others (such as the Chinese yuan) remained tightly managed with respect to the US dollar. Soyoung Kim and Doo Yong Yang (Chapter 4) confirm this observation. They applied several classification schemes, including the International Monetary Fund's (IMF) de facto classification, to show that several economies in Asia (namely, Indonesia; Korea; Philippines; Singapore; Taipei,China; and Thailand) moved toward greater exchange rate flexibility after the Asian crisis, while the PRC and Malaysia continued to manage the nominal value of their currencies tightly against the US dollar.

This diversity, however, masked the continued tendency of the Asian monetary authorities to limit the fluctuations of their currencies against the US dollar. Ila Patnaik and Ajay Shah (Chapter 7) applied the Frankel–Wei regression to 11 Asian currencies (where the US dollar, the euro, the British pound and the Japanese yen enter the equation as the explanatory variables)[1] to conclude that the degree of exchange rate flexibility in Asia increased only marginally at best after the Asian crisis; even for the Korean won, they obtained the Frankel–Wei weight of 1.25 for the US dollar between 1995 and 2009.

Kim and Yang approached this issue from the point of view of monetary independence. If a country pursues a fully flexible exchange rate policy, it should be able to pursue a fully autonomous monetary policy, such that domestic interest rates should not be significantly affected by monetary developments abroad. Building on this line of reasoning, they obtained evidence that before the global financial crisis most Asian economies had been limiting the flexibility of their currencies against the US dollar. In particular, their structural vector autoregression (VAR) model shows that from 1999 to 2007, domestic interest rates in all presumed free and managed floaters (Korea; Singapore; Philippines; Taipei,China; and Thailand) responded strongly to US interest rate changes, while those in the PRC and Malaysia did not. They interpreted this result to mean that the de jure floaters actually gave up monetary autonomy by limiting exchange flexibility while the de facto US dollar peggers restricted their capital account.

With the onset of the global financial crisis, this divergence became even more pronounced. The two presumed floating currencies (the Indonesian rupiah and Korean won) utilized their flexibility to depreciate sharply, while the PRC and Singapore terminated the policy of allowing their currencies to appreciate gradually against the US dollar. As most other currencies also softened against the US dollar, these developments meant that the Japanese yen, which remained flexible, became virtually the only currency in the region to appreciate against the US dollar. These exchange rate movements placed a huge burden of adjustment on the Japanese economy, while allowing the other Asian economies to benefit from depreciation. From the onset of the global financial crisis to its height, the divergence between the most appreciated currency in Asia (the Japanese yen) and the most depreciated currency (the Korean won) amounted to nearly 80 percent.

1.3.2 Reserve Management Policies

The propensity of Asian countries to manage exchange rates under appreciation pressure meant that they accumulated large balances of foreign exchange reserves following the Asian crisis. The rise in Asia's balance of international reserves was spectacular indeed: the balance for ten major economies (which excludes Japan but includes Hong Kong, China) rose from a mere US$560 billion at the end of 1998 to over US$3 trillion at the end of 2007 (Figure 1.3). Much of the increase was accounted for by the PRC whose balance of international reserves rose from less than US$150 billion to over US$1.5 trillion over the same period (and nearly US$2 trillion at the end of 2008). Among the crisis-hit Asian countries, Korea's gains were most noticeable, with the balance rising from US$52 billion to over US$260 billion (though this amount proved insufficient once the full effect of the global crisis was felt in late 2008). With Japan included, Asia's balance of international reserves amounted to over US$4 trillion at the end of 2008.[2]

Joshua Aizenman, Menzie D. Chinn and Hiro Ito (Chapter 6) argue that emerging market economies use foreign exchange reserves to mitigate the binding constraints of the 'impossible trinity' (that is, difficulty of simultaneously attaining monetary independence, exchange rate stability and full financial integration). By using what they call 'trilemma indices', they observed that Asian emerging market economies achieved the intermediate levels of monetary independence, exchange rate stability and financial

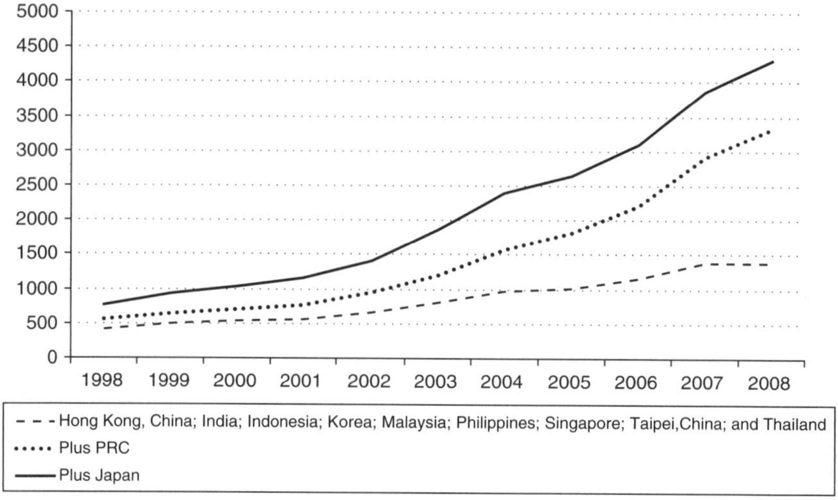

Note: PRC = People's Republic of China.

Sources: IMF, International Financial Statistics on-line database (http://www.imfstatistics.org/imf/), accessed October 2010; for Taipei,China only, Central Bank of Taipei,China, Financial Statistics (http://www.cbc.gov.tw/mp2.html), accessed October 2010.

Figure 1.3 Foreign exchange reserves in selected Asian economies (in billions of US dollars; end-of-year data)

integration in the 2000s. Patnaik and Shah (Chapter 7) concurred with this assessment but noted that the combination of exchange rate stability and moderate financial integration created procyclicality in monetary policy in much of Asia prior to the global financial crisis.

Foreign exchange reserves seem to carry the following benefits. First, they can act as an insurance against a sudden reversal of capital inflows as countries partially open their capital accounts, increase exchange rate flexibility somewhat and attempt to retain some monetary independence. According to Aizenman, Chinn and Ito (Chapter 6), there is evidence to show that countries holding large reserves are less likely to experience large output loss during a crisis (defined as a period of significant economic underperformance). Second, evidence suggests that a country can offset the volatility of investment and output that comes from keeping the exchange rate stable (by virtue of loss of monetary independence) by holding large foreign exchange reserves (of more than 12 percent of GDP).

There are, however, costs to holding foreign exchange reserves. Shin-ichi Fukuda and Yoshifumi Kon (Chapter 5) argue that holding reserves, by reducing liquidity risk, would allow a country to borrow from abroad by issuing lower-cost, more liquid (short-term) debt. But private agents would change their behavior. Fukuda and Kon present a model in which a utility-maximizing representative agent decides consumption, capital stock, labor input and the amounts of liquid and illiquid debt, subject to the amount of foreign exchange reserves. Comparing steady-state values, the authors show that an increase in reserves leads to a permanent decline in consumption (through lower interest rates on reserves) and a transfer of labor from the non-tradable to the tradable sector (to generate net exports). These predictions are broadly supported by data for some 130 countries from 1980 to 2004.

Whatever the benefits of holding large international reserves may be from the point of view of individual countries, the outcome was problematic from a more global standpoint. It allowed large US current account deficits to be financed at low cost and contributed to the global imbalance, the unwinding of which was in part a triggering cause of the global financial crisis. As Kim and Yang (Chapter 4) argue, as long as Asian countries restrict the flexibility of exchange rates, it might lead to the resurgence of another global imbalance problem. The choice of exchange rate policy by one economy could therefore have regional and global implications. Given the costs involved, the region's economies would benefit from having an alternative safeguard mechanism as they liberalize their capital accounts while maintaining reasonable intraregional exchange rate stability.

1.3.3 Managing Capital Inflows

Managing capital inflows is an important aspect of the strategy to ensure macroeconomic stability while facilitating the required global rebalancing. This is especially important because Asia has emerged from the crisis as the fastest-growing region. As Asian economies continue to tighten their monetary policies, they are bound to face a surge in capital inflows. If countries maintain the policy of stabilizing their exchange rates with respect to the US dollar in face of these inflows, they will experience an accumulation of international reserves, which not only is contrary to the requirements of global rebalancing but also, if unchecked, may lead to inflationary pressure. The policy of stabilizing nominal exchange rates in order to maintain international price competitiveness may then prove counterproductive as inflation will cause the real exchange rates to appreciate over the medium term.

Developing and emerging Asia was a significant recipient of international capital flows in the mid-2000s until the onset of the global financial crisis, receiving around US$300 billion of net inflows in 2007 and 2008

Table 1.1 *Net capital flows to developing and emerging Asia, 1990–2008 (US$ billion; annual averages)*

	1990–1996	1997–2002	2003–2006	2007	2008
Current account balance	–23	40	154	406	422
Private capital flows, net	59	11	82	165	128
Direct investment, net	32	59	83	138	223
Private portfolio flows, net	17	–3	–23	11	–66
Other private capital flows, net	11	–45	23	15	–29
Official flows, net	0	1	–19	–37	–13
Change in reserves	–37	–80	–309	–673	–634

Note: Negative sign indicates increase in reserves.

Source: International Monetary Fund, World Economic Outlook database, April 2009.

(Table 1.1). As a percentage of GDP, Asia's gross private capital inflows and outflows were also significant (peaking at 16 percent and 13 percent, respectively, in 2007), although they were smaller than the percentages recorded prior to the Asian crisis, as well as compared to some other regions of the world. The significant net private inflows, despite the large current account surplus that Asia has recorded against the rest of the world, correspond to the accumulation of large international reserves over the period.

Large capital inflows can pose various risks, including the macroeconomic risk of creating overheating and inflation, and the financial stability risk of pushing up asset prices excessively and reducing the quality of assets (Kawai and Takagi 2010). Because capital inflows can reverse quickly, they can also create a risk of currency crisis. Managing these risks is not easy, short of allowing exchange rates to appreciate. The empirical and policy literature suggests that there is no single solution to the problems posed by capital inflows, and that authorities need to use all the available instruments, among which are sterilized intervention, capital controls and fiscal tightening.

Sterilized intervention has been the favorite tool applied by many emerging Asian economies to prevent nominal and real exchange rate appreciation and economic overheating in face of large capital inflows. As the supply of government debt is limited, a large number of central banks in the region, including in the PRC; Indonesia; Korea; Malaysia; the Philippines; Taipei,China; and Thailand, have issued central bank securities for sterilization purposes. The RBI in 2004 introduced an innovation in the form of a market stabilization scheme for this purpose (Mohan and Kapur 2009). Sterilized intervention has associated costs, the most important of which is the quasi-fiscal cost that comes from the difference between the domestic interest rates paid on sterilization bonds and the foreign interest rates earned on international reserves. Sterilization is not a sustainable policy tool for large and persistent capital inflows.

Capital controls can be effective for countries that have not substantially liberalized the capital account. In fact these countries, notably the PRC and India, fared better when they experienced a surge in capital inflows. In India, for example, access norms to external commercial borrowings were tightened in August 2007 in the wake of heavy inflows (which were relaxed in 2008); interest rate ceilings on non-resident deposits with the banking system were reduced during 2006–2007 to moderate the inflows (which were raised again in 2008). For countries with more open capital accounts, however, capital controls can entail significant side-effects. When Thailand introduced unremunerated reserve requirements in December 2006, it met an immediate and extremely adverse equity market reaction and was forced to withdraw the measure with respect to equity flows. The empirical literature on the effectiveness of temporary capital controls is at best mixed, as noted in Chapters 4 and 7.

Fiscal tightening may be the only viable tool to mitigate the effect of large and sustained capital inflows, short of allowing the exchange rate to appreciate. In Asia, fiscal policy has not yet been explored thoroughly as an instrument for managing large capital inflows. Although there is no theoretical presumption on the impact of fiscal policy on capital flows, evidence suggests that countries that use fiscal tightening tend to perform better than others in managing the adverse consequences of large capital inflows (Schadler 2010). Tightening fiscal policy in the face of a surge in capital inflows has been found to help reduce the risk of an overheating economy and the appreciation pressure on the domestic currency. Although fiscal policy is not a flexible policy instrument, fiscal tightening should receive serious consideration from the region's policymakers.

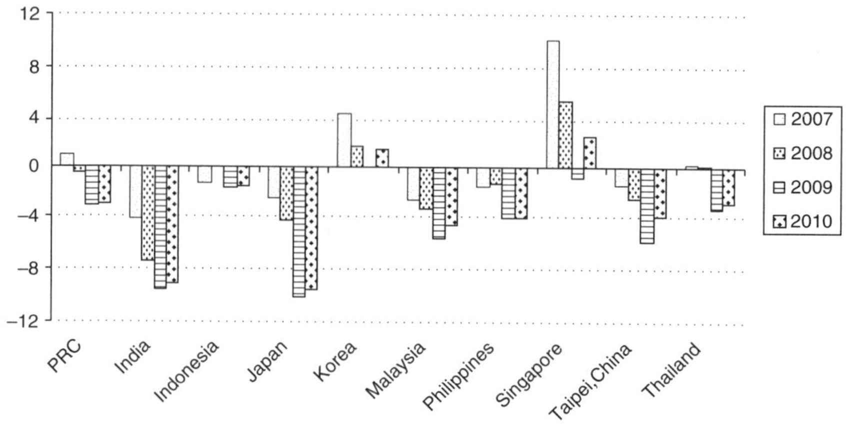

Notes: The figures for 2010 are projections. PRC = People's Republic of China.

Source: IMF, World Economic Outlook database, October 2010, available at http://www.imf.org/external/pubs/ft/weo/2010/02/weodata/index.aspx.

Figure 1.4 Fiscal balances in selected Asian economies, 2007–2010 (% of GDP)

1.4 FISCAL POLICY ISSUES

1.4.1 Fiscal Policy Measures in Asia

Given the unprecedented collapse of real economic activity, and the awareness in some countries that further monetary easing might be limited, many governments in the region, as elsewhere, resorted to aggressive easing of fiscal policy. The fiscal positions deteriorated sharply throughout Asia from 2007 to 2008, and further in 2009 (Figure 1.4). The sharpest deteriorations from 2008 to 2009 were experienced by Japan (a rise in the deficit of 6.2 percent of GDP) and Singapore (from a surplus of 5.2 percent of GDP to a deficit of 0.8 percent measured in terms of net borrowing). Except in Japan, such an active use of countercyclical fiscal policy was a radical departure from the fiscal conservatism that had characterized the economic policymaking of most Asian economies.

Of course, not all fiscal deterioration was due to the introduction of a crisis-related fiscal stimulus package, as automatic stabilizers also kicked in (though automatic stabilizers in emerging Asia are not as well developed as in advanced countries). It is not easy to estimate the size of the fiscal packages, net of the automatic stabilizers as well as the spending or tax reduction measures that had already been planned; the announced spending increase in some cases, moreover, also included prospective contributions from the private sector and may even include an amount which will never be implemented in the end. With this caveat, the announced fiscal stimulus packages ranged widely across the region, from less than 1 percent to over 10 percent of GDP.

It was the relatively healthy state of government finances that allowed the aggressive use of countercyclical fiscal policy in many Asian economies. With the exceptions of India and Japan, public debt-to-GDP ratios were significantly lower in Asia than in many countries in other parts of the world. Years of fiscal discipline had created a significant space to expand fiscal policy in the PRC, Indonesia and Korea; Singapore's large fiscal reserves provided ample scope to use fiscal policy to counter adverse external shocks. Japan and India, despite the limited fiscal space, nonetheless expanded their fiscal policies substantially. Coinciding with the election-related increase in spending, and a surge in subsidies associated with the rise in international oil prices, the stimulus measures implemented in India in 2008 eliminated all the gains made in fiscal consolidation since 2004 (Kumar and Soumya 2010).

A close look at the individual stimulus packages adopted in Asia reveals that the share of capital spending on infrastructure was considerable in most countries. Such spending was particularly large in the PRC, Korea, the Philippines and Thailand, accounting for more than 60 percent (Doraisami 2011). In the PRC, for example, more than 85 percent of the CNY4 trillion stimulus package announced in November 2008 was accounted for by investment spending. An important exception to this observation was Thailand's first fiscal package, which included cash payments (stimulus checks) to a large number of households. Such cash transfers were also included in the packages adopted by Japan and Taipei,China. Japan's stimulus packages predominantly included public consumption and transfers to households.

1.4.2 Fiscal Policy Implementation and Effectiveness

What Asia's crisis experience has revealed about fiscal policy is the lag in implementation. This was particularly true of public spending on infrastructure. The amount was sometimes too large for the absorptive capacity of the governments concerned; in several countries delays in parliamentary approval and problems with disbursements were reported (Park et al. 2010). As to effectiveness, while the experience has led to a number of empirical attempts to estimate fiscal multipliers, no consensus has yet emerged. The experience of Asia does seem to suggest that general transfers did not work as intended. Japan's Cabinet Office, based on a survey of households, concluded that only 33 percent of the cash paid out by the government as part of the emergency fiscal measures was actually spent on consumption (Cabinet Office of the Government of Japan 2010). Likewise, according to a survey conducted by the Thai National Statistical Office in May 2009, only 20 percent of those who cashed the stimulus checks actually used the money for extra spending (Jitsuchon 2009).

Emerging empirical evidence suggests that the effectiveness of countercyclical fiscal policy is related to the perception of debt sustainability. IMF (2009), for example, shows that fiscal stimulus in economies that have low levels of public debt has a higher impact on the strength of the recovery relative to economies that have higher levels of public debt. Although debt sustainability is not a serious concern in most of Asia, the importance of debt sustainability nonetheless points to the medium-term need to build institutions, such as legally binding fiscal rules, to secure a government's commitment to fiscal prudence. Several governments in Asia already have legal frameworks for fiscal policy, including Singapore, the Philippines, India and Indonesia. It may be necessary to introduce such frameworks for some of the economies that do not have them at the present.

Another important aspect of fiscal policy effectiveness, especially for small open economies of Asia, is the need for coordinated action. Masahiro Kawai and Fan Zhai (Chapter 8), built a multi-country dynamic general equilibrium model of the world economy (consisting of the US, Japan, emerging Asia, and the rest of the world) to analyze the impact on Asia of various negative shocks affecting the US and the global economy. Calibrating the model to fit the Global Trade Analysis Project (GTAP) database in 2004, Kawai and Zhai, among others, show the disastrous consequence for Asia of a free fall of the US dollar. Fiscal policy, anchored against fiscal sustainability, is effective against such negative shocks especially when accommodated by monetary easing. But fiscal policy implemented by emerging Asia alone would not be very effective, given the large leakage of demand through trade openness. The authors conclude that globally coordinated action is the only effective tool of fiscal policy for smaller individual Asian countries. In one specification of globally coordinated fiscal expansion, the authors argue that the multiplier of fiscal stimulus (sustained over two years) could be as high as 0.75, and that emerging Asia would experience the largest rise in consumption because of the high share of liquidity-constrained households in the region.

1.5 REGIONAL MONETARY COOPERATION ISSUES

While the usefulness of fiscal policy coordination for small open economies was noted, regional macroeconomic policy coordination must ideally cover monetary cooperation as well. Masahiro Kawai and Shinji Takagi (Chapter 9) note that Asia has seen a rise in intraregional trade in recent years and macroeconomic interdependence has strengthened as a result. This means that the actions of policymakers in one economy to pursue their own interests could more frequently come in conflict with those in the region's other economies, with exchange rates constituting a critical link. Yet, exchange rate policy has so far been the least developed aspect of regional economic cooperation initiatives. Admittedly, no country in Asia is likely to give up sovereignty over exchange rate policy any time soon, but there are steps the region's economies can take to strengthen cooperation in the monetary area. An immediate step would be to incorporate exchange rate issues into the existing policy dialogue process.

An obvious area of policy cooperation would be to devise a system whereby countries no longer have incentives to continue accumulating foreign exchange reserves as a buffer against adverse shocks. A reform at the global level has been progressing since early 2009 in order to improve the global system of providing financial support to countries in need. The IMF augmented its resources; it also modernized conditionality in an attempt to remove the stigma attached to IMF borrowing. The newly established Flexible Credit Line, for pre-qualified strong-performing economies, has done away with conditionality. For other existing lending facilities, the IMF now relies 'more on pre-set qualification criteria (ex ante conditionality) rather than on traditional (ex post) conditionality'. Structural reforms are monitored in the context of program reviews, and the use of structural performance criteria was discontinued in all arrangements.[3]

Despite these global efforts to remove the stigma of IMF borrowing, the prognosis for Asia is not encouraging. Some regional economies lost reserves and many more experienced a decline in the pace of reserve accumulation during the height of the global financial crisis (Table 1.2). Yet, none of the economies in East Asia sought IMF assistance but they all sought an alternative source of liquidity. Korea, for example, secured swap arrangements with the US Federal Reserve, followed by similar arrangements with the PRC and Japan; Indonesia likewise received credit lines from Australia, Japan, the Asian Development Bank and the World Bank.

Now that capital inflows are recovering, some countries, notably Korea

Table 1.2 Changes in the stock of foreign exchange reserves in selected Asian economies, June 2007–June 2009 (US$ billion)

	June 2007–June 2008	June 2008–June 2009
People's Republic of China	476.2	322.8
India	96.2	–48.2
Indonesia	7.9	–1.9
Japan	80.7	15.1
Korea	7.4	–26.9
Malaysia	27.4	–34.6
Philippines	9.3	2.0
Singapore	32.6	–3.6
Taipei,China	25.3	26.2
Thailand	31.9	14.9

Sources: International Monetary Fund, International Financial Statistics, online database (http://www.imfstatistics.org/imf/), accessed October 2010; for Taipei,China only, Central Bank of Taipei,China, Financial Statistics (http://www.cbc.gov.tw/mp2.html), accessed October 2010.

and Indonesia, have resumed accumulating foreign exchange reserves. This only represents a return to the pre-global crisis regime. If countries in Asia are reluctant to approach the IMF, a regional support mechanism can assume part of its function. In this respect, a welcome development is the decision in May 2009 of the ASEAN+3 Finance Ministers to multilateralize the Chiang Mai Initiative (CMI) and to create an independent surveillance unit called the ASEAN+3 Macroeconomic Research Office (AMRO) to support the decision-making process in the management of the pooled reserves.[4] Asia's economies must make this scheme user-friendly and cooperative in nature, to minimize the incentive to accumulate more reserves for insurance purposes.

Such a scheme is desirable both for macroeconomic management and for global rebalancing. By providing an alternative insurance mechanism, the regional system of mutual financial assistance, in the form of the CMI Multilateralization (CMIM), could potentially play a role in encouraging the region's economies to allow greater exchange rate flexibility. In this context, countries with a large holding of US dollar reserves may be reluctant to allow a significant appreciation of their currencies against the US dollar because it would entail a significant capital loss. This strengthens the case for a globally and regionally cooperative solution, which ensures an orderly adjustment of exchange rates and the composition of reserve assets over time. Kawai and Takagi (Chapter 9) discuss issues involved in the choice of exchange rate regime for the region, emphasize

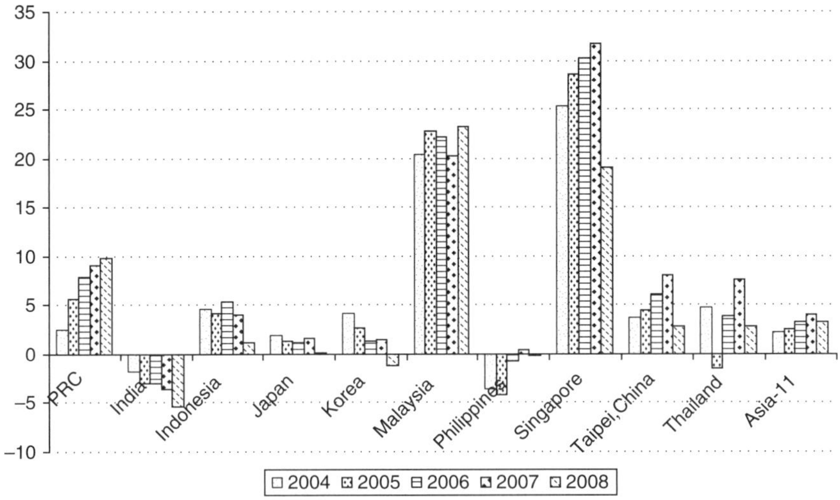

Note: PRC = People's Republic of China.

Sources: IMF, International Financial Statistics, online database (http://www.imfstatistics.org/imf/), accessed October 2010; for Taipei,China only, Central Bank of Taipei,China, Financial Statistics (http://www.cbc.gov.tw/mp2.html), accessed October 2010.

Figure 1.5 Current account balances in selected Asian economies, 2004–2008 (% of GDP)

the importance of intraregional exchange rate stability for an integrated region, and explore alternative modalities of exchange rate cooperation in order to achieve the dual objectives of intraregional stability and increased flexibility with respect to currencies outside the region.

The role Asia can play in the global rebalancing of demand is significant indeed. In terms of imbalances as a percentage of GDP, considerable policy adjustments are required of Singapore, Malaysia and the PRC whose current account surpluses equaled 10 percent–30 percent of GDP in 2008 (Figure 1.5). Given the absolute size, however, the PRC must clearly lead the way in making the desired adjustment. In 2008, the PRC's current account surplus of over US$400 billion was equivalent to more than half of the US deficit of over US$600 billion. In contrast, the combined surpluses of Japan and other Asian economies were relatively small. In addition to allowing greater flexibility for its currency, which would facilitate a shift of demand from external to internal sources (Kawai and Zhai, Chapter 8), the PRC must also raise the share of consumption, which stood only at 55 percent of GDP during 2003–2007.[5] Building better social safety nets as a way of promoting consumption must go hand in hand with exchange rate action in much of emerging Asia.

As another area of cooperation, the region's economies could coordinate their response to capital inflows. The stigma of capital controls is minimized if they are used as part of collective action. Moreover, the same argument applies to managing capital inflows as to exchange rate cooperation. At the heart of the capital inflow problem ultimately lies the reluctance of governments to allow their currencies to appreciate. Available measures, including sterilized intervention and capital controls, may be effective in the short term but many of them cannot be permanent solutions to large and sustained capital inflows. Sooner or later, the economies in the region must address the issue of how much longer they should continue to limit the nominal appreciation of their currencies. Regional cooperation, designed to coordinate a collective appreciation of their currencies against the US dollar, is also useful in this respect, as it would allow the governments to overcome the fear of losing price competitiveness through unilateral appreciation.

1.6 CONCLUSION

The experience of implementing macroeconomic policies in the Asia and Pacific region suggests the importance of securing adequate monetary and fiscal policy space during good times by maintaining sufficiently high interest rates and by keeping public debt-to-GDP ratios sufficiently low. The experience of Korea and Indonesia also suggests that substantial currency depreciation is helpful in stimulating aggregate demand, but this cannot be a lesson to be learned from the recent crisis experience. Against each depreciating currency is an appreciating currency. As a country with the only Asian currency that has seen significant appreciation during the crisis, Japan has assumed an exorbitant share of the burden of adjustment. Rather, the world and the region should strive to create a system in which exchange rate policy does not serve as an instrument of countercyclical policy, especially when the whole world finds itself in recession.

The monetary policy of most central banks in the region has almost fully exited from the crisis mode. Central banks must now rely on the robust institutions they have built in the past to pursue price stability. At the same time, in view of the conditions that had contributed to the crisis, they should also give greater attention to financial stability (though whether or not financial stability should be made part of the explicit mandate of the central bank remains an open issue). Price stability considerations may call for greater exchange rate flexibility as capital inflows are expected to resume. Keeping the exchange rate stable in terms of the US dollar under these circumstances may create inflationary pressure, given the de facto capital account openness of most economies in the region irrespective of their de jure openness.

It is here that informal regional cooperation can be helpful. Such cooperation can foster a collective appreciation of the region's currencies against the US dollar, allowing the governments to overcome the fear of losing price competitiveness through unilateral action while retaining intraregional exchange rate stability. It may take years to achieve formal exchange rate cooperation in a region that is diverse and lacks political will. Even so, there are additional steps the region's economies can take to formalize cooperation in this area. The immediate step is to incorporate exchange rate issues into the existing policy dialogue process, the ASEAN+3 Economic Review and Policy Dialogue (ERPD). For this, agreement must be made on the choice of indicators for surveillance, including how to identify currency misalignment and rules for corrective action.

In order to help prevent another similar crisis, it is urgent that the region devise a system in which countries no longer have the incentive to maintain the costly practice of accumulating foreign exchange reserves for precautionary purposes. Asia has emerged from the global financial crisis as the fastest-growing region in the world. As capital inflows into the region are expected to pick up, they cannot go on keeping their exchange rates stable against the US dollar and piling up international reserves. This would be the same recipe that led to unsustainable global imbalances, the unwinding of which in part contributed to the global financial crisis. Providing an alternative insurance scheme for a sudden reversal of capital is therefore helpful for encouraging greater exchange rate flexibility against the US dollar.

In this respect, the CMIM, with the newly established surveillance mechanism in the form of AMRO, should be strengthened further as a way of reducing the insurance role of foreign exchange reserves. To make it truly a regional financing facility, the CMIM, as a self-managed reserve pooling facility, may need to evolve over the longer term into an Asian Monetary Fund. This requires not only augmenting the available resources of the CMIM but also enhancing the effectiveness of regional surveillance, not least to remove the requirements of an IMF program from granting access to regional mutual support. The relationship between AMRO and the existing policy dialogue processes (such as the ASEAN+3 Economic Review and Policy Dialogue process) must be clarified in coming years. The macroeconomic issues addressed in this book are components of this grand vision for the region.

NOTES

1. The 11 countries are: PRC; Hong Kong, China; India; Indonesia; Korea; Malaysia; the Philippines; Singapore; Taipei,China; Thailand; and Viet Nam. The Frankel–Wei methodology is a linear model in which changes in the value of a national currency (expressed in terms of a chosen numeraire) is regressed against changes in similarly valued major currencies that are considered a priori as important determinants of the exchange rate policy of the country concerned. The idea is to capture the extent to which the national currency in question is linked to each of the currencies included in the regression. See Frankel and Wei (1994).
2. Although the Japanese authorities in principle allow the yen to be determined freely by market forces, they have at times intervened in the foreign exchange market. The foreign exchange market intervention conducted from January 2003 to March 2004 was especially large. As a result, the balance of foreign exchange reserves increased from US$450 billion at the end of 2002 to over US$820 billion at the end of 2004. They subsequently refrained from intervention entirely until September 2010.
3. See 'modernizing conditionality' at www.imf.org.
4. The Joint Media Statement of the 12th ASEAN+3 Finance Ministers' Meeting in Bali, Indonesia on 3 May 2009. ASEAN+3 comprises the ten member countries of the Association of South East Asian Nations (ASEAN) plus the PRC, Japan and Korea.
5. The PRC share is comparable to that of Singapore. The share of consumption in India, Korea and Thailand was almost 70 percent of GDP, while it was about 75 percent in Japan.

REFERENCES

Cabinet Office of the Government of Japan (2010), 'Teigaku Kyufukin ni kanrenshita Shohito ni kansuru Chosa no Kekka ni tsuite', in Japanese.

Doraisami, A. (2011), 'The global financial crisis: countercyclical fiscal policy issues and challenges in Malaysia, Indonesia, the Philippines, and Singapore', ADBI Working Paper 288, Tokyo: ADBI, available at http://www.adbi.org/working-paper/2011/06/06/4581.gfc.countercyclical.fiscal.policy.issues.challenges.

Frankel, J. and S.J. Wei (1994), 'Yen bloc or dollar bloc? Exchange rate policies of the East Asian countries', in T. Ito and A. Krueger (eds), *Macroeconomic Linkage: Savings, Exchange Rates, and Capital Flows*, Chicago, IL: University of Chicago Press, pp. 295–355.

International Monetary Fund (IMF) (2009), *World Economic Outlook: Crisis and Recovery*, Washington, DC: IMF.

Jitsuchon, S. (2009), 'Fiscal policy issues in Thailand after the current economic crisis', paper presented at the ADBI conference on Global Financial and Economic Crisis: Fiscal Policy Issues after the Crisis, Tokyo, 19 January.

Kawai, M. and S. Takagi (2010), 'A survey of the literature on managing capital inflows', in M. Kawai and M.B. Lamberte (eds), *Managing Capital Flows: The Search for a Framework*, Cheltenham, UK and Northampton, MA, USA: Edward Elgar Publishing, pp. 46–72.

Kumar, R. and A. Soumya (2010), 'Fiscal policy issues for India after the current crisis', paper presented at the ADBI conference on Global Financial and Economic Crisis: Fiscal Policy Issues after the Crisis, Tokyo, 19 January.

Mohan, R. and M. Kapur (2009), 'Liberalization and regulation of capital flows: lessons for emerging market economies', paper presented at the

ADBI Conference on Financial Sector Reforms and Regulations, Tokyo, 21–23 July.
Park, D., S. Hur, S. Jha and P. Quising (2010), 'Did fiscal stimulus lift developing Asia out of the global crisis? A preliminary empirical investigation', ADB Economics Working Paper Series 215, Manila: ADB.
Schadler, S. (2010), 'Managing large capital inflows: taking stock of international experiences', in M. Kawai and M.B. Lamberte (eds), *Managing Capital Flows: The Search for a Framework*, Cheltenham, UK and Northampton, MA, USA: Edward Elgar Publishing, pp. 105–28.

PART I

Monetary Policy Issues

2. The role and effectiveness of unconventional monetary policy

Peter J. Morgan

2.1 INTRODUCTION

The global financial crisis of 2007–2009 was perhaps unique in that it saw short-term interest rates fall to nearly zero in a number of countries. Countries with policy rate targets of 0.5 percent or less included the United States (US), Japan, the United Kingdom (UK), and Canada. Although Japan was the only Asian country with official rates this low, short-term money market rates sank to nearly zero in a number of other economies, including Hong Kong, China; Singapore; and Taipei,China (Figure 2.1).

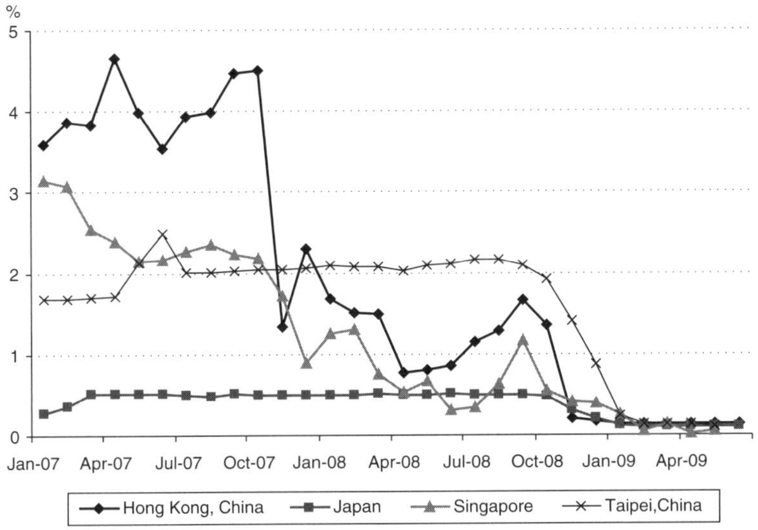

Source: CEIC Data Co. Ltd Database (accessed 16 July 2009).

Figure 2.1 Asian economies with overnight interbank rates near zero (monthly average)

Because conventional monetary policy operates mainly by setting interest rate levels, this meant that the limits of conventional policy had been reached in these economies, and that any further monetary stimulus must be obtained from 'unconventional' means.

The global financial crisis was also characterized by a breakdown in the normal transmission mechanism of monetary policy. Reflecting a sharp increase in the perceived risk of insolvency of financial institutions and other firms, spreads widened sharply in a number of markets, including those for interbank deposits, commercial paper, corporate bonds and bonds in emerging economies. Some markets stopped functioning altogether, especially those related to asset-backed securities. As a result, a reduction of policy rates often failed to be reflected in a commensurate decline in market rates, while in some cases a credit crunch developed where credit was not forthcoming at all. This situation can occur even when short-term rates are above zero, but still calls for unconventional policy responses.

Section 2.2 of this chapter reviews the range of unconventional monetary policy tools available to central bankers and summarizes their theoretical strengths and weaknesses. Section 2.3 reviews available empirical studies of their effectiveness and other recent evidence. Section 2.4 reviews issues related to exit strategies and other risks. Section 2.5 assesses the applicability of unconventional monetary policy measures to the current situation of Asian economies and other emerging markets. Section 2.6 concludes.

2.2 UNCONVENTIONAL POLICY TOOLS

Once regarded as an historical relic of the Great Depression, the significance of the zero lower bound (ZLB) on interest rates as a constraint on the effectiveness of monetary policy has received much attention as a result of Japan's experience with deflation between 1999 and 2006 and concerns about the risk of deflation in the US following the collapse of the information technology bubble in 2000. Ironically, the seeds of the current recession in the US could partly be traced to the concerns of the US Federal Reserve (henceforth the Fed) about avoiding deflation in the early part of the 2000s, which led it to adopt a very easy monetary stance. Although this bias toward easing was aimed at stabilizing the consumer price index (CPI), it contributed to a destabilization of housing and other asset prices, which contributed to the development of the US housing bubble. The US and much of Western Europe fell into liquidity traps as well. This was seen most obviously by the breakdown of the traditional relationship between the monetary base and broad money. In other words, the money multiplier broke down.

Much of the current literature on unconventional monetary policy can be traced back to Krugman et al. (1998), which focused on the problem that deflation prevents the real interest rate from falling enough to achieve full employment. Krugman and others argued that, in principle, a central bank must offset this by trying to raise the market's expectations about future inflation in order to bring down the real interest rate sufficiently to stimulate aggregate demand.

Bernanke and Reinhart (2004) divided unconventional monetary policy tools into three main categories:

1. providing assurance to investors that short rates will be kept lower in the future than they currently expect (commitment effect);
2. increasing the size of a central bank's balance sheet beyond the level needed to set the short-term policy rate at zero (quantitative easing); and
3. changing the relative supplies of securities in the marketplace by altering the composition of a central bank's balance sheet (qualitative easing or credit easing).

A central bank has another powerful option, namely, buying foreign currency assets in order to depress the value of the country's foreign exchange rate and thereby stimulate export demand. This effect, analyzed by Svensson (2001) among others, could be particularly powerful for a small open economy. However, the stigma associated with adopting 'beggar-thy-neighbor' policies appears to have effectively discouraged central banks from adopting such policies during economic downturns. There are many recent examples of central banks intervening to maintain a stable exchange rate or to slow currency appreciation during an expansion phase, but no obvious examples of intervention to engineer currency depreciation as a macroeconomic stabilization tool during an economic downturn. In the remainder of this section, I examine the first three categories of unconventional measures described above.

2.2.1 Commitment Effect

A large amount of literature has developed around the commitment effect or policy duration effect. The basic idea is simple: even though a central bank may set the very short-term rate (normally the overnight interbank rate) at zero, the market still has considerable uncertainty about the future development of monetary policy. This is reflected in the yield curve, since longer-term rates essentially reflect the market's expected future path of short-term rates plus a risk premium. Therefore, if a central bank can persuade the market that it will keep the policy rate lower than the market would expect otherwise, this should cause longer-term rates to fall, thereby stimulating the economy. This type of policy has been analyzed theoretically by a number of authors, including Svensson (2001) and Eggertsson and Woodford (2003).

Typically, a central bank commits to maintain its policy interest rate at zero for a certain period. This commitment could be conditional or unconditional, but normally is conditional because a central bank cannot reasonably be expected to ignore future developments. In particular, it would be normal for the central bank to start raising interest rates once the economy has recovered and inflation has begun to pick up, so the central bank might commit to keep rates at zero until these conditions were achieved. The first instance of such a commitment in recent times was the declaration by the Bank of Japan (BoJ) in April 1999 that it would maintain its zero-interest-rate policy until 'deflationary concerns were dispelled' (Okina and Shiratsuka 2004: 75–6). In May 2001, the Bank of Japan took a more refined approach by promising that it would keep its policy rate at zero until consumer price inflation 'stably' registered 0 percent or positive year-on-year growth (Bank of Japan 2001). It further clarified its definition of what the end of deflation meant in October 2003 (Bank of Japan 2003). In the US, the August 2003 statement of the Federal Open Market Committee that 'policy accommodation can be maintained for a considerable period' is another example of a commitment by policymakers (US Federal Reserve Board 2003). Indeed, the Fed more recently used similar language: its policy statement in December 2008 noted 'economic conditions are likely to warrant exceptionally low levels of the federal funds rate for an extended period' (US Federal Reserve Board 2008).

Many scholars, including Reifschneider and Williams (2000), have proposed that a commitment to keep rates at zero should be maintained well beyond the time when inflation turns positive. This would effectively lower the market's expectation of real interest rates, thereby imparting a greater stimulus to the economy. Many variations of 'backward-looking' policy rules for the inflation target price-level target or modified Taylor rules have been proposed to minimize output losses, for example Benhabib et al. (2002) and Wolman (2005). (The Taylor rule for monetary policy, which determines the policy interest rate as a function of the size of the output gap and the gap between actual and target inflation, was originally described in Taylor 1993). They generally have the feature that the greater the cumulative loss in output due to deflation, the more the policy target must adjust, in terms of higher target inflation rate or price level, in order to compensate for this. However, there are no recent examples of central banks implementing such rules, so they will not be examined in this study.

2.2.2 Quantitative Easing

Another form of easing is to expand the size of a central bank's balance sheet by increasing the size of reserve deposits – current account balances (CABs) – beyond the level that is required to bring the overnight funds rate to zero. (The monetary base consists of both cash in circulation and reserve deposits, but a central bank can only directly affect the level of reserve deposits.) This is referred to as 'quantitative easing' (QE) and, as defined by Bernanke and Reinhart (2004), focuses on the liabilities side of a central bank's balance sheet. Possible channels of impact of such a policy include: (i) the portfolio balance effect; that is, if money is an imperfect substitute for other financial assets, the rise in money holdings leads investors to shift toward other assets, thereby raising their value and stimulating final demand; (ii) providing a clearer signal of a central bank's commitment to keep the policy rate low; and (iii) a permanent increase in the money supply could reduce the expected value of government debt servicing costs, thereby reducing the expected value of future tax payments. The first effect was investigated by Goodfriend (2000) in detail. The third effect was investigated by scholars including Auerbach and Obstfeld (2005).

The magnitude of the portfolio balance effect can be influenced significantly by the interest rate that a central bank pays to banks on their reserve deposits at the central bank. If a central bank pays a positive interest rate on reserve deposits, this will discourage banks from shifting out of excess reserves into other assets such as loans. Paying interest on reserve deposits is very close to sales of bills by a central bank as a funds-absorbing operation to tighten money market conditions. On the other hand, if a central bank pays a zero or even a negative interest rate, this would encourage re-intermediation. Goodfriend (2000) analyzed how a central bank could push nominal interest rates below zero throughout the economy by paying negative interest rates on reserve deposits. On 1 July 2009, the Swedish Riksbank cut the interest rate on reserve deposits to minus 0.25 percent, the only recent instance of a central bank doing so. US Federal Reserve Chairman Bernanke observed that recent US legislation to allow the Fed to pay interest on reserve deposits gives the Fed greater flexibility to reduce its balance sheet when it needs to implement its 'exit strategy' for tightening monetary policy (Bernanke 2009b). The last point is discussed further below.

The main theoretical objection to quantitative easing is that at zero interest rates, money and short-term paper are perfect substitutes, so changes in the level of current account balances simply represents shifts in holdings of assets that are essentially the same, and hence should have no real economic impact. However, there is some evidence in favor of the portfolio balance effect, which is discussed below.

The main example of quantitative easing was by the Bank of Japan in April 2001, when it shifted its policy target from the overnight call rate to the level of CABs. This policy was maintained until March 2006. Most recently, the Bank of England adopted quantitative easing on 5 March 2009, although the bank rate remained positive.

One drawback of quantitative easing and, indeed, of a zero-interest-rate policy (ZIRP) is the distortion of the functioning of the money market due to the very low level of interest rates resulting from the fact that money market brokers cannot cover their costs. Indeed, balances in Japan's call market dropped dramatically by almost half during the operation of the QE policy, while balances in the euroyen market fell almost 90 percent. As a result, the Bank of Japan has kept the overnight call rate at around 0.1 percent since January 2009, just high enough to cover the costs of the money market brokers. Other central banks have tended to keep the policy rate sufficiently above zero to preserve the functioning of money markets as well.

2.2.3 Qualitative Easing

The third set of policies is aimed at varying the mix of assets held by the central bank, and is referred to as 'qualitative easing' or 'credit easing'. The basic idea is that operations to change the shares of various kinds of assets held by the private sector will lead to changes in their relative prices, and thereby have implications for real economic activity. For example, if a central bank increases its outright (or permanent) purchases of long-term government bonds, this could be expected to reduce long-term bond yields and stimulate the economy. Qualitative easing also includes direct lending to market participants in cases where the normal transmission mechanism breaks down. In such cases, policies are focused on reducing credit market spreads and improving the functioning of private credit markets more generally. Like quantitative easing, qualitative easing generally involves an increase in the size of a central bank's balance sheet, but the focus is on the mix of assets, not the level of bank reserves (or liabilities). This was particularly relevant during the global financial crisis, where credit spreads had been much wider and credit markets more dysfunctional in the US and other countries than was the case in Japan during Japan's experiment with quantitative easing from 2001 to 2006.

In a recent speech (Bernanke 2009a), US Federal Reserve Chairman Bernanke distinguished between three kinds of qualitative easing activity:

1. a central bank's traditional role of provision of short-term liquidity to sound financial institutions, that is, 'lender of last resort' activity;
2. provision of liquidity directly to borrowers and investors in key credit markets; and
3. purchase of longer-term securities for the Fed's portfolio.

All of these measures could be seen as responses to malfunctioning of credit markets due to severe market concerns about capital adequacy and bankruptcy risk.

The first category starts with traditional borrowing at the discount window, which is not unconventional, although it has long played a secondary role to open-market operations. The most straightforward kinds of easing involve relaxing the criteria for the kinds of borrowers or types of collateral that qualify for open-market operations, or extending the period of such operations. Financial market stresses led to the creation of a number of new programs in this category. In the US, this included a number of new credit facilities for auctioning credit that were responses to stresses in the interbank funding market: the Term Auction Facility (TAF), Term Securities Lending Facility (TSLF), Primary Dealer Credit Facility (PDCF) and bilateral currency swap agreements with 14 other central banks, including the Bank of England, the European Central Bank, the Bank of Japan, the Bank of Korea, the Monetary Authority of Singapore and the Swiss National Bank (see Glossary for a brief description of some of these programs and Appendix Table 2A.1 for a chronology of announcements by the Fed and other central banks). The TAF was aimed at solving the stigma problem related to banks borrowing from the Fed, while the TSLF and PDCF provided comparable facilities for primary dealers. The swap agreements were aimed at easing shortages of US dollars in overseas markets. These loans were viewed as having very low risk, since they were generally overcollateralized and with recourse. Also, the foreign exchange swap agreements were made with other central banks, where there is a high degree of mutual trust.

The second category of policies was aimed at other markets besides the interbank market, including the commercial paper market, the asset-backed securities market and money market funds, which also showed increased signs of stress. In the US, these new programs included the Asset-Backed Commercial Paper Money Market Fund Liquidity Facility (AMLF), Commercial Paper Funding Facility (CPFF), Money Market Investor Funding Facility (MMIFF) and Term Asset-Backed Securities

Loan Facility (TALF). The measures for asset-backed securities were aimed at AAA-rated securities collateralized by student loans, auto loans, credit card loans and loans guaranteed by the US Small Business Administration (jointly with the US Treasury to cover risk). Again, credit risk was seen as very low in both programs. In particular, the TALF program required that loans be overcollateralized and was further protected by capital provided by the US Treasury.

Under the third category, the Fed announced on 18 March 2009 that it would purchase cumulative amounts of up to US$1.25 trillion of agency mortgage-backed securities, up to US$200 billion of agency debt by the end of 2009, and up to US$300 billion of longer-term Treasury securities over the following six months (US Federal Reserve Board 2009). The principal goal of these programs was to lower the cost and improve the availability of credit for households and businesses. On 19 January 2009, the UK Treasury specified the following types of sterling-denominated assets as eligible for purchase under the Bank of England's Asset Purchase Facility: commercial paper, corporate bonds, bonds issued under the UK's credit guarantee scheme, syndicated loans and asset-backed securities 'created in viable securitization structures' (Her Majesty's Treasury 2009).

During the earlier period of its quantitative easing policy, the Bank of Japan progressively increased the level of outright Japanese government bond (JGB) purchases from ¥400 billion per month to ¥600 billion on 14 August 2001; to ¥800 billion on 19 December 2001; to ¥1000 billion on 28 February 2002; and finally to ¥1200 billion on 30 October 2002. This level was maintained until 19 December 2008, when the Bank of Japan announced that the amount of outright purchases of JGBs would be increased to ¥1.4 trillion yen, and then finally to ¥1.8 trillion yen on 18 March 2009. It also expanded the range of JGBs accepted in outright purchases (30-year bonds, floating-rate bonds and inflation-indexed bonds were added to the list of eligible JGBs). In addition, in order to prevent the remaining maturities of JGBs purchased from becoming too short or too long, it introduced a scheme to purchase JGBs from specific maturity segments (maturity segments are defined as one year or less, more than one year through ten years, and more than ten years). Following the global financial crisis, the Bank of Japan announced on 19 February 2009 that it would commence outright purchases of corporate bonds (Bank of Japan 2009).

Table 2.1 shows a comprehensive list of qualitative easing measures adopted by various central banks during the global financial crisis. The breakdown follows that of Bernanke (2009a) mentioned earlier. Measures aimed at easing conditions in interbank markets were more numerous than those aimed at influencing credit markets, while those aimed at influencing

Table 2.1 Qualitative easing measures during the global financial crisis

Objective	Measures adopted	Fed	ECB	BoE	BoJ	BoC	RBA	SNB
(i) Influence wholesale interbank market conditions	Modification of discount window facility	X		X				
	Exceptional long-term operations	X	X	X	X	X	X	X
	Broadening of eligible collateral	X	X	X	X	X	X	X
	Broadening of counterparties	X		X	X	X	X	
	Inter-central bank FX swap lines	X	X	X	X	X	X	X
	Introducing or easing conditions for securities lending	X		X	X	X		
(ii) Influence credit markets	CP funding/ purchase/ collateral eligibility	X		X	X	X	X	
	ABS funding/ purchase/ collateral eligibility	X	X	X			X	
	Corporate bond funding/ purchase/ collateral eligibility			X	X	X		X
(iii) Influence broader financial conditions	Outright purchase of public sector securities	X		X	X			
	Outright purchase of other non-public sector securities				X			X

Notes: ABS = asset-backed securities; BoC = Bank of Canada; BoE = Bank of England; BoJ = Bank of Japan; CP = commercial paper; ECB = European Central Bank; FX = foreign exchange; RBA = Reserve Bank of Australia; SNB = Swiss National Bank.

Source: Adapted from Bank for International Settlements (2009).

broader financial conditions were less common. This most probably reflects the relative unconventionality of the three stages, as central banks, being conservative, tended to favor modest steps in the direction of unconventionality. All banks conducted exceptional long-term operations, broadened eligible collateral, and participated in foreign exchange (FX) swap lines with the Fed. For example, on 2 December 2008 the Bank of Japan announced that it would ease the criterion on credit ratings from 'A-rated or higher' to 'BBB-rated or higher'. The Bank of Japan also introduced, as a measure to enhance flexibility in funds-supplying operations collateralized by corporate debt, a new operation that provided funds over the fiscal year-end at an interest rate equivalent to the target for the uncollateralized overnight call rate. It also included the Development Bank of Japan Inc. as a counterparty in operations such as commercial paper (CP) repo operations. On 22 January 2009, it announced acceptance of debt instruments issued by real estate investment corporations as eligible collateral as well. On 19 February, government guaranteed dematerialized commercial paper was included in eligible collateral, and the range of Japanese government securities offered in the security lending facility was broadened. On 7 April 2009, it also accepted loans on deeds to municipal governments as eligible collateral.

Among the steps taken to influence credit market conditions, the most common were aimed at CP funding, followed by asset-backed securities and corporate bonds. Only the Bank of Japan and the Swiss National Bank purchased other non-public sector securities such as equities. Among steps to influence broader market conditions, only three central banks (US Fed, Bank of England and Bank of Japan) made outright purchases of public sector securities, while only two (Bank of Japan and Swiss National Bank) bought private sector securities.

2.3 EVIDENCE OF EFFECTIVENESS OF UNCONVENTIONAL POLICIES

Although the theoretical literature on unconventional monetary policy has grown extensively over the past 20 years, empirical analysis of the impacts has been much more limited. This is not surprising, given that until recently only Japan between 1999 and 2006 provided data on the experience of monetary policy at zero interest rates, at least since the Great Depression, and on quantitative easing between 2001 and 2006. Some analyses of the US experience with zero interest rates and unconventional policy are beginning to emerge, for example McAndrews (2009). Unfortunately, this means that the bulk of the empirical analysis of unconventional monetary policies has been conducted with various kinds of macroeconomic models such as vector autoregression (VAR) models. This raises questions about the validity of the results, as they depend critically on the extent to which the models capture the underlying behavior of the economy. Given the complexity and non-linearity of the economy, one has to approach the results of this literature with a good deal of skepticism. This section reviews the evidence for the effectiveness of different kinds of unconventional monetary policies.

Analyses of the impact of unconventional monetary policy face a number of other methodological problems. First, a number of different policies may have been adopted at the same time, making it difficult to separate their effects. Second, one has to identify the counterfactual, that is, what would have happened in the absence of such policy steps? Third, it is necessary to identify the extent to which a specific announcement may have been a surprise to the market. Fourth, spillover effects may be important, that is, market conditions in one country may be influenced by easing measures in another country.

2.3.1 Commitment Effect

There is a lot of evidence that announcements by central banks do affect market expectations about future policy, since market participants regard the direction of monetary policy to be an important influence on the path of interest rates and markets. Table 2.2 shows the results of a number of empirical studies of this effect. Most studies focused on the impact on the yield curve, which is the first and most obvious link in the transmission mechanism. Other studies looked at the impacts on credit spreads (which may be more relevant for the recent crisis), real output and inflation.

Early studies such as Fujiki et al. (2001) and Kuttner and Posen (2001) relied on casual inspection and came up with opposite conclusions regarding impacts on the yield curve in Japan. Later studies adopted more formal approaches. Japanese authors all found significant impacts of the commitment effect on the yield curve using a variety of methodologies, including time series and/or cross-section modeling of the yield curve and combinations of macro models with either a Taylor rule decision function for monetary policy or an econometric model of the yield curve. Perhaps the most thorough of these studies are Okina and Shiratsuka (2004) and Baba et al. (2005b). However, Bernanke et al. (2004) argued that some of these studies did not adequately control how rates would have moved in the absence of the policies adopted. Using an 'event study' and 'macro/finance' model approach, they analyzed the effects of the Fed and the Bank of Japan statements on expected short-term interest rates, decomposing

Table 2.2 Effectiveness of commitment effect: empirical studies

	Methodology	Country	Yield curve	Credit spreads	Output	Inflation
Baba et al. (2005b)	Macro finance model with the use of augmented Taylor rule	Japan	Yes			
Baba et al. (2005a)	Time series/ cross sectional regression	Japan	Yes	Yes		
Bernanke et al. (2004)	Event study and macro/finance model with econometric model of yield curve	Japan, US	No Yes			
Braun and Waki (2006)	Macro model with Taylor rule	Japan			Yes	Yes
Fujiki et al. (2001)	Casual observation	Japan	Yes			
Fujiki & Shiratsuka (2002)	Econometric model of implied forward rates	Japan	Yes	Yes	Yes	Yes
Fujiwara et al. (2005)	Macro model with Taylor rule	Japan	Yes	Yes	Yes	Yes
Kuttner and Posen (2001)	Casual observation	Japan	No			
Oda and Ueda (2007)	Macro/finance model with econometric model of yield curve	Japan	Yes			
Okina and Shiratsuka (2004)	Instantaneous forward rate (IFR) econometric yield curve model	Japan	Yes			
Reifschneider and Williams (2000)	Macro model with Taylor rule	US			Yes	

Source: Author's compilation.

the impact into very short term, one year forward and five years forward. They found that in the case of Japan during the period of the ZIRP, effects were statistically significant, but of a much smaller magnitude than in the case of the US – only about one-third as large. Also, they tended to be concentrated at the shorter end of the yield curve; the impact on the long end of the curve was relatively modest. Notably, they found no impact of Bank of Japan statements on year-ahead expectations of short-term interest rates; a significant difference from the results for US Federal Reserve statements. This suggests that the Bank of Japan statements themselves may not have been framed carefully enough to have maximum impact on market expectations.

Oda and Ueda (2007) used a similar approach and found evidence that the commitment effect did tend to lower interest rates. However, the effect was most pronounced for rates of three years or less, and was much more pronounced after the economic recovery began. This suggests that the commitment effect is least effective when it is most needed, that is, when the economy is still in recession.

Fujiki and Shiratsuka (2002), Fujiwara et al. (2005) and Baba et al. (2005a) all found significant effects of the commitment effect in bringing down credit spreads as well. For example, Baba et al. (2005a) found that the switch to the ZIRP and then the adoption of definitions of ending deflation were correlated with a reduction in bank credit spreads.

Reifschneider and Williams (2000), using a macro model with a modified Taylor rule that took into account past deviations in output resulting from the zero bound, found that the commitment effect had a significant impact on output and inflation in the US. Fujiki and Shiratsuka (2002), Fujiwara et al. (2005) and Braun and Waki (2006) all found positive impacts on output and inflation in Japan using a similar approach. However, these results have to be treated with skepticism since, as mentioned above, they depend on the accuracy of the macro models used, which in most cases are highly simplified. The overall conclusion is that commitment effects do stabilize market expectations about the path of short-term interest rates and thereby tend to lower long-term rates. However, at least in the case of Japan, these effects were not large enough to affect expectations about the real economy and inflation sufficiently to produce effects on those variables.

The Fed reintroduced its commitment effect language in its statement on 16 December 2008 when it cut the target range for the Fed funds rate to 0–0.25 percent, noting that: 'the Committee anticipates that weak economic conditions are likely to warrant exceptionally low levels of the federal funds rate for some time' (US Federal Reserve Board 2008: 1). Figure 2.2 shows that longer-term and short-term interest rates all

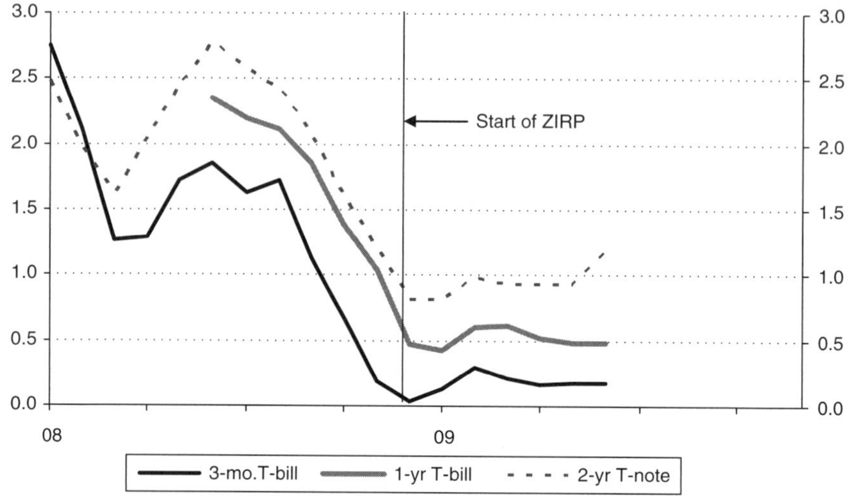

Note: ZIRP = zero-interest-rate policy.

Source: CEIC Data Co. Ltd Database (accessed 16 July 2009).

Figure 2.2 *US short-term government bond yields and zero-interest-rate policy*

fell sharply in December 2008. In particular, the one-year T-bill rate fell more than the three-month T-bill rate, and also considerably more than the two-year T-note rate. This suggests that the market expected that rates would stay 'very low' for up to one year, pointing to a significant commitment effect. Of course, it may simply have reflected the market's worsening assessment of the economic situation, but the differential performance between the one-year note and the two-year note suggests that the statement had some impact. Interestingly, no other central bank has adopted a formal commitment regarding its policy during the recent global downturn.

2.3.2 Quantitative Easing

The findings of the literature about the impacts of quantitative easing on interest rates and economic activity are generally positive, but more tentative than in the case of the commitment effect. The results of some major studies are summarized in Table 2.3.

Regarding the yield curve, Baba et al. (2005b) found that the level of CABs was significant in explaining the expectations theory component of

Table 2.3 Effectiveness of quantitative easing: empirical studies

	Methodology	Country	Yield curve	Credit spreads	Out-put	Price	Broad money	Cur-rency
Baba et al. (2005b)	Macro finance model with the use of augmented Taylor rule as monetary policy	Japan	Yes?					
Baba et al. (2005a)	Regression of credit spreads on ratings and time period	Japan		Yes				
Bernanke et al. (2004)	Event study and macro/ finance model with econometric model of yield curve	Japan, US	Yes?		Yes	Yes		
Hanes (2006)	Model of Treasury yields as function of reserve levels	US	Yes					
Honda et al. (2007)	VAR model	Japan			Yes	No		
Kuttner and Posen (2001)	VAR model to test impacts of shocks in M0	Japan					No	No
Meier (2009)	Casual observation	UK	Yes	Yes				
Okina and Shiratsuka (2004)	Instantaneous forward rate (IFR) econometric yield curve model	Japan	No					

Notes: M0 = monetary base; UK = United Kingdom; US = United States; VAR = vector autoregression.

Source: Author's compilation.

interest rates, that is, the market's expectations of future short-term interest rates, but not the risk premium. They suggested that the level of CABs could have functioned as a signaling mechanism to strengthen the commitment effect. However, they cautioned that this correlation could be spurious, and that statements by the Bank of Japan governors made at the same time as the CAB level announcements could have been the main factor instead. On the whole, they concluded that the Bank of Japan's monetary policy worked mainly through the commitment channel between 1999 and 2004. Bernanke et al. (2004) found evidence suggesting that Japanese bond yields were lower than otherwise would have been expected, but their model did not differentiate between the impacts of the commitment effect and the CAB level. Interestingly, Okina and Shiratsuka (2004: 94) concluded that the instantaneous forward rate curve:

> was hardly influenced by the increase in the target level of the current-account balance at the Bank of Japan from over 6 trillion yen to 10–15 trillion yen on 19 December 2001. This indicates that the strengthening of quantitative monetary easing was not perceived as sufficient stimulus to curb deflation, coupled with low economic growth.

This suggests that there was little independent contribution from quantitative easing beyond that of the commitment effect, which did seem to flatten the yield curve.

There is some evidence that the ample provision of liquidity did ease banks' funding constraints and shrink credit spreads. Baba et al. (2005a) found a positive effect of increasing CAB levels on reducing the dispersion of bank credit spreads in the interbank market. They noted that as the Bank of Japan had to fund successively higher CAB levels, it had to move further out along the yield curve to conduct its operations, which tended to flatten the yield curve. They concluded that both the commitment effect and quantitative easing probably tended to reduce credit spreads in the interbank market, although they were unable to quantify their relative contributions.

Figure 2.3 shows the relationship between the CAB level (inverted) and the ten year-JGB yield. The impact of the CAB levels on bond yields is not clear, as bond yields began falling in 2002 before CABs started to rise, and began rising again in mid-2003, even though the CABs continued to rise until late 2004. Moreover, bond yields began to rise sharply in late 2005, well before the fall of the CABs in mid-2006. CABs began to rise again in 2009, but there was little evident impact on bond yields.

The Bank of England (BoE) is the only major central bank to have adopted quantitative easing during the recent global financial crisis, as it set a target of £75 billion for reserve deposits on 5 March 2009 and

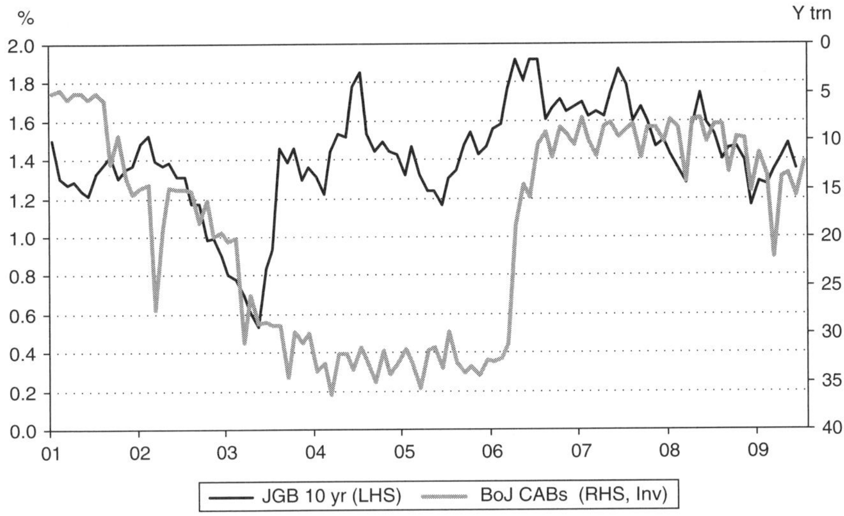

Notes: BoJ = Bank of Japan; CAB = current account balance; JGB = Japanese government bond; LHS = left-hand side; RHS = right-hand side.

Source: CEIC Data Co. Ltd Database (accessed 10 June 2009).

Figure 2.3 JGB yield and Bank of Japan current account balances

subsequently raised this to £125 billion on 7 May 2009 and again to £175 billion on 6 August 2009. The spread between the three-month sterling London Interbank Offered Rate (LIBOR) and the base rate narrowed rapidly after 20 March 2009, although it is not clear whether this was affected by other factors as well. This may provide some evidence of the effectiveness of quantitative easing in reducing credit spreads. The Bank of England's QE policy was actually a mix of both quantitative easing and qualitative easing; although it targeted the level of reserve deposits, it accomplished this primarily through purchases of UK government bonds (gilts) rather than short-term paper. Meier (2009) found these purchases to have been effective in lowering both gilt yields and interbank rate spreads.

Regarding impacts on output and inflation, Bernanke et al. (2004) ran simulations of QE policies on simple macro models of the US and Japan. They found that increases in CAB levels did have positive impacts on output and prices in both countries although, again, the impacts for Japan were much less than those for the US. Using a similar approach for Japan, Honda et al. (2007) found positive impacts on output but not on prices. They identified equity prices as the main channel by which the QE policy affected output, which implies that the portfolio-balance effect was the main transmission mechanism. However, the lack of impact on prices is puzzling, and does cast doubts on the validity of the model and the robustness of the conclusions.

On the whole, the evidence for a significant impact of the QE policy in addition to the commitment effect on interest rates, output and inflation looks limited. However, the evidence that the QE policy helps to ease tightness in credit markets appears to be stronger. As will be discussed next, qualitative easing targeted at specific asset markets is probably a more efficient way to lower credit spreads. Strikingly, the Bank of Japan did not return to quantitative easing during the latest downturn, despite the fact that growth had been far weaker than it was during the previous recession in 2001–2002. This suggests that the Bank of Japan does not appear to have had much confidence in its efficacy, aside from its role in easing stresses in the financial sector.

2.3.3 Qualitative Easing

Empirical research on the effects of qualitative easing is more limited (Table 2.4). Much of the analysis focuses on purchases of long-term government bonds, perhaps the logical first step toward unconventional purchasing operations. Shiller (1990) analyzed the attempts of the US Fed to influence the shape of the yield curve during the 1960s (operation twist), but was not able to find evidence that the effect of the policy was significant. However, this may be simply because the operation was not large enough. Bernanke et al. (2004) found that the announcement by the US Treasury in February 2000 that it would probably stop issuing 30-year bonds had a statistically significant impact in lowering yields on 20-year Treasury bond yields compared with Treasury bonds with shorter maturities. They also found evidence that purchases of US Treasury bills by the Japanese Ministry of Finance in 2003–2004 may have been consistent with a decline of bond yields of 50–100 basis points, but the evidence was not conclusive, as the contribution of other factors could not be ruled out, and the deviations could have been due to chance. They concluded on a positive note, however, stating that:

> If the Federal Reserve were willing to purchase an unlimited amount of a particular asset – say, a Treasury security – at a fixed price, there is little doubt that it could establish that asset's price. Presumably, this would be true even if the Federal Reserve's commitment to purchase the long-lived asset were promised for a future date. (Bernanke et al. 2004: 60)

Nonetheless, the Fed's recent experience with buying US Treasuries was not obviously successful. In the six months from the beginning of 2009,

Table 2.4 Effectiveness of qualitative easing: empirical studies

	Methodology	Country	Yield curve	Credit spreads	USD MM spread
Bernanke et al. (2004)	Event study and macro/finance model with econometric model of yield curve	US	Yes		
McAndrews (2009)	Econometric model of spread	US			Yes
Meier (2009)	Casual observation	UK	Yes		
Oda and Ueda (2007)	Macro/finance model with econometric model of yield curve	US	No		
Yuan and Zimmerman (1999)	DGE model	Canada		No	

Notes: DGE = dynamic general equilibrium model; MM = money market; UK = United Kingdom; US = United States.

Source: Author's compilation.

the Fed's outright holdings of US Treasury securities rose by US$172 billion (36 percent), but this did not stem a sharp rise in bond yields during that period, as the ten-year bond yield rose from 2.2 percent to 2.6 percent.

Of course, rates might have been even higher otherwise, but the Fed's goal of holding down mortgage loan rates was not achieved. Interestingly, the level of Fed holdings of treasuries declined substantially between late 2007 and mid-2008, but this does not seem to have put any upward pressure on bond yields. Baba et al. (2009) also noted that declines in bond yields in response to bond purchase announcements by both the Fed and the BoE were very short-lived. These results should not be surprising in light of the huge size and liquidity of the US Treasury market (total value

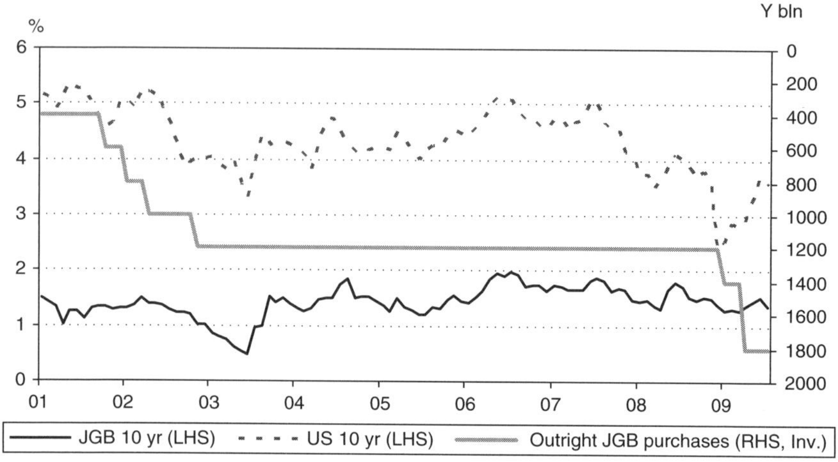

Notes: JGB = Japanese government bond; LHS = left-hand side; RHS = right-hand side; US = United States.

Source: CEIC Data Co. Ltd. Database (accessed 16 July 2009), Bank of Japan, various monetary policy announcements.

Figure 2.4 JGB yields and Bank of Japan outright bond purchases

of US$6.8 trillion in March 2009) relative to the Fed's purchasing operations, which were announced to total US$300 billion, or 4.4 percent of the total.

As noted above, the Bank of Japan also significantly increased its outright purchases of JGBs during the period of the QE policy between August 2001 and October 2002. However, as was the case with quantitative easing, Oda and Ueda (2007) concluded that the Bank of Japan's increased purchases of JGBs did not lead to a significant portfolio-rebalancing effect. Figure 2.4 shows that the increase in the level of outright purchases during period did lead the decline in ten-year JGB yields. However, this decline could also be attributed to the decline in US bond yields during the same period. Notably, Japanese bond yields rose in line with the increase in US bond yields from mid-2003, presumably reflecting the global economic recovery, even though outright bond purchases remained high at ¥1.2 trillion per month. Even more suggestively, Japanese bond yields rose after December 2008, again in sympathy with US bond yields, even though the outright purchases were increased dramatically further to ¥1.8 trillion per month by February 2009. Therefore, the most one can say is that the purchases may have diminished the extent of the increase of bond yields, but it is difficult to determine the size of this impact. The large size and liquidity of the Japanese bond market suggests that operations of this kind would have to be large indeed to have a substantial and lasting effect.

The Bank of England embarked on a large-scale program of purchasing UK government bonds (gilts) beginning in March 2009 in order to fund its target for central bank reserve deposits described above. Its purchasing operations were comparatively aggressive, as the Bank of England accumulated about 17 percent of total tradable government bonds in about four months (*Financial Times* 2009). Nevertheless, bond yields still rose by about 30 basis points between March and July 2009, after the start of the bond purchase program, so the effect looks somewhat limited. Taking into account relative movements of US and European bond yields over the same period, Meier (2009) estimated that four months after the announcement of the Bank of England's QE policy, it had lowered gilt yields by a range of at least 35–60 basis points, a significant but not huge decrease.

Qualitative easing may be effective in reducing some credit-related financial stresses. For Canada, Yuan and Zimmerman (1999) used a dynamic general equilibrium model to analyze the effects of monetary easing and changes in required loan-to-deposit ratios on credit availability. They found that direct easing of loan standards was much more effective than conventional monetary easing in counteracting a credit crunch. McAndrews (2009) found that the Fed's TAF and central bank swap programs were effective in reducing spreads between the US (federal funds purchases and sales) and European (eurodollar deposit) interbank markets. The announcement by the Bank of England on 13 October 2008 that it would provide unlimited dollar liquidity to the banking sector appears to have been the key factor in easing funding pressures in the interbank market at that time.

The Fed's recent qualitative easing moves appear to have had a significant impact on easing credit spreads of various kinds. For example, the 'Ted' spread (the spread between the three-month LIBOR rate and the three-month Treasury bill rate) peaked at over four percentage points in November 2008, but began to fall rapidly thereafter. During this period the US monetary base roughly doubled in size to about US$1.7 trillion as a result of the combined impacts of purchases under the TAF, CPFF and other programs, plus the Fed swap arrangements with other central banks. It is difficult to identify the relative effects of these different programs, but the combined impact appears to have been substantial. Because banks were the major beneficiaries of these moves, it is reasonable to see this reflected in the Ted spread, which mainly indicates the market's assessment of risk in the banking sector.

Spreads in the US money market and CP market also eased dramatically after the implementation of various Fed liquidity programs described

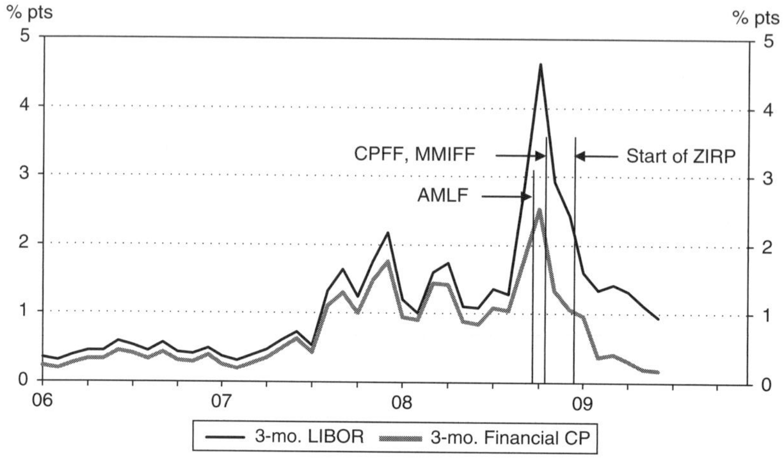

Notes: AMLF = Asset-Backed Commercial Paper Money Market Fund Liquidity Facility; CP = commercial paper; CPFF = Commercial Paper Funding Facility; MMIFF = Money Market Investor Funding Facility; US = United States; ZIRP = zero-interest-rate policy.

Source: CEIC Data Co. Ltd Database (accessed 16 July 2009).

Figure 2.5 US money market and CP spreads and Fed credit easing measures (% pts)

above, including the AMLF in September 2008 and the MMIFF and CPFF in October 2008. (Capital injections into nine major US banks, announced on 14 October 2008, probably contributed to this easing effect as well.) Figure 2.5 shows that spreads of both LIBOR and financial commercial paper over T-bill rates declined sharply beginning in November 2008, and then largely normalized. The start of the ZIRP and the commitment effect in December 2008 probably had a further downward impact on spreads, although this is more difficult to confirm in terms of timing.

In contrast, spreads of corporate bond yields over those of US Treasury bonds did not peak until 16 December 2008. This is precisely the day that the Fed announced the shift to the zero-interest-rate policy and the commitment to maintain it for 'some time', which is very strong evidence that this was the key factor, rather than the Fed's balance sheet activity. This suggests that rate expectations were more important for the non-financial corporate sector, rather than the direct effects of toxic items on the balance sheet. (The spread for AAA bonds did briefly spike higher in March 2009, but the spread for BAA bonds clearly peaked in mid-December 2009.)

The Bank of Japan also undertook a number of credit-easing measures,

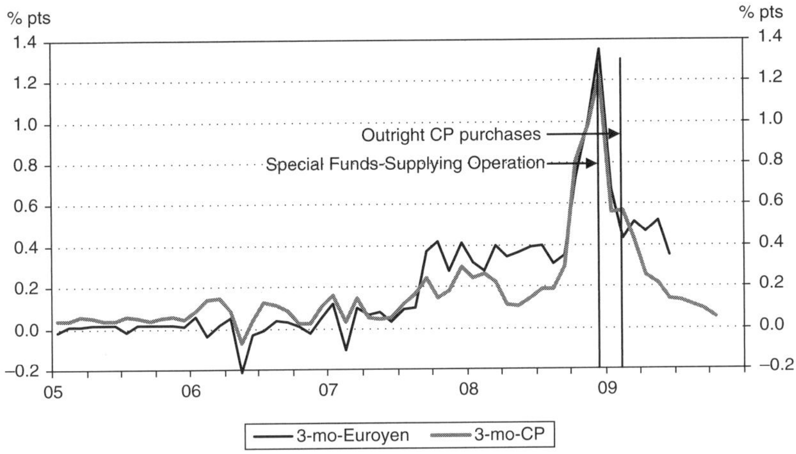

Note: CP = commercial paper.

Source: Bank of Japan Times Series Data Search, http://www.stat-search.boj.or.jp/ssi/cgi-bin/famecgi2?cgi=$nme_a010_en&obj_name=ST (accessed 10 August 2009).

Figure 2.6 Japanese euroyen deposit and CP spreads

including Special Funds-Supplying Operations to Facilitate Corporate Financing (19 December 2008), outright purchases of commercial paper (22 January 2009) and outright purchases of corporate bonds (19 February 2009). Figure 2.6 shows that the spreads of euroyen deposits and CP over financing bills declined markedly in the first three months of 2009. However, the spread for euroyen deposits remained considerably more elevated than that for CP, indicating residual concerns about the financial position of Japanese banks.

These results suggest that qualitative easing or credit easing measures are not very effective in affecting the level of government bond yields, but can be effective in reducing spreads of rates of other financial products over those of risk-free rates, especially short-term rates. This is particularly so when concerns about liquidity and solvency lead to a credit crunch that essentially prevents certain markets from functioning normally. In other words, the central bank can successfully unplug logjams arising from a scarcity of funds in a particular segment. However, there is little evidence that such measures can affect inflation expectations or the demand for credit at the macro level. Finally, these studies typically looked at individual countries in isolation, and hence may have missed spillover effects. For example, Fed policies implemented in US markets may have helped to relieve stress in overseas markets.

2.4 EXIT STRATEGY AND OTHER RISKS

Unconventional monetary policy measures that increase the size and/or riskiness of a central bank's balance sheet raise the possibility of large capital losses on those assets, potentially to the extent of making a central bank insolvent. A central bank can to some extent repair its losses by printing money. However, this is limited by its operational target of price stability, since printing too much money could cause inflation. Therefore, if its losses are large enough, presumably a government would have to recapitalize its central bank. This would require the issuance of new debt, which would tend to put further upward pressure on bond yields and possibly undermine the currency.

Another issue for unconventional monetary easing that is receiving increasing attention is that of the exit strategy, that is, how to unwind the unconventional policy measures once the economy is ready to go back onto a 'conventional' policy track. A central bank has to strike a delicate balance and reduce its balance sheet in a timely and non-disruptive way to avoid potential inflation risk on the one hand, and an overly abrupt monetary-tightening shock on the other. The key point is that the credit transmission mechanism does not function normally when the economy is in a liquidity trap, so that unconventional policies may lead to a very large expansion of a central bank's balance sheet without stimulating a commensurate increase in bank lending. However, once conditions in the financial sector normalize, the transmission belt could start up again, and bank lending could balloon rapidly, leading to unwelcome inflationary pressure. Also, if a central bank holds large amounts of government bonds, it could suffer large capital losses on those bond holdings, which would undermine a central bank's capital position. Large-scale sales of such bonds could exacerbate capital losses in this situation. Moreover, if a central bank holds large amounts of illiquid assets such as asset-backed securities as a result of qualitative easing measures, it might find it very hard to reduce these holdings in a timely manner. Finally, if interest rates rise too rapidly as a result of rapid sales of assets, this could undermine economic recovery.

A number of these issues are discussed in detail in Fujiki et al. (2001). One possible perverse effect would be that announcements by a central bank to buy government bonds would be perceived by the market as a loss of fiscal discipline, which could actually push up risk premiums and bond yields. They also argued that if bond yields rise and a central bank suffers losses on its holdings of government bonds, it would have to sell more government bonds than it bought in order to reduce base money by the same amount, thereby leading to further upward pressure on bond yields and capital losses.

Bernanke (2009b) argued that it will be relatively easy for the Fed to wind down its balance sheet when the time comes, because: (i) many lending programs extend credit primarily on a short-term basis at above-normal market rates, so demand for them by banks and other institutions will dwindle once the economy recovers and credit market conditions normalize; (ii) the Fed can conduct reverse repurchase agreements against its long-term securities holdings to drain bank reserves; (iii) some reserves can be absorbed by the Treasury's Supplementary Financing Program; and (iv) the Fed's ability to pay interest on reserve balances will encourage depository institutions to hold reserves with the Fed, rather than lending them into the federal funds market at a rate below the rate paid on reserves.

Of course, a central bank could always raise the reserve ratio if it found other means to decrease the level of reserves to be too disruptive. There are other possibilities as well. Bini Smaghi (2009) suggested that a fiscal authority could issue debt securities and deposit the proceeds with a central bank. This would effectively transfer the liquidity previously created from the private to the public sector. Where allowed, a central bank could also issue such certificates, with essentially the same effect.

The Bank of Japan's experience of winding down the QE policy in 2006 was uneventful, which should provide some confidence on this subject. It managed to shrink its balance sheet dramatically by ¥39 trillion (25 percent) between February and May 2006 without any obvious disruption of the markets. Roughly three-quarters of the reduction was accomplished by cuts of bills purchased, while the remainder came from sales of JGBs. JGB yields rose by about 35 basis points over that period, a measurable increase, but well within normal market fluctuations. Also, the Fed was successful in shrinking some of its lending programs fairly rapidly, including the foreign currency swap arrangements. However, the real test will come when it has to sell down its outright holdings of US Treasuries and other less liquid securities.

2.5 ISSUES FOR IMPLEMENTATION IN DEVELOPING AND EMERGING ECONOMIES

Analysis of the effectiveness of unconventional monetary policy so far has been conducted almost entirely on the US and Japanese economies, which are relatively closed, have large and well-developed domestic financial markets, independent central banks and floating exchange rates. The question arises as to how relevant the experiences of these economies might be for developing and emerging economies in Asia and elsewhere.

Unfortunately, there is almost no research on this subject. One recent report that touches on this area is Ghosh et al. (2009).

Factors that could constrain the implementation of unconventional monetary policy measures in developing and emerging economies include:

1. an insufficiently developed government bond market that limits a central bank's ability to buy such bonds;
2. an insufficiently developed corporate bond market, which limits its capacity to be a source of corporate funding even if it is functioning normally;
3. legal restrictions on central bank purchases of government assets and other securities;
4. a high degree of 'dollarization' of domestic liabilities that limits the lender-of-last-resort function of the central bank;
5. an exchange rate peg that limits monetary policy flexibility;
6. insufficient credibility on inflation fighting that might cause adoption of unconventional policy measures to be perceived by the market as a loss of inflation discipline; and
7. related to (6) above, vulnerability of the currency to capital outflows.

Calvo (2007) noted that the central bank of an emerging market economy may need to switch policy modes during periods of 'sudden stops', that is, foreign currency-based capital outflows. Specifically, he recommended that a central bank should switch to exchange rate targeting rather than using the policy interest rate as a target. However, he did not discuss exchange rate policy in conjunction with other unconventional policy measures. As noted above, a policy of deliberate currency depreciation could be an effective macroeconomic stabilization tool.

In countries with large stocks of foreign short-term capital inflows, currencies could react very sensitively to changes of market perception about monetary policy and inflation risk, thereby complicating the task of the monetary authorities. Of course, if an economy is experiencing deflation, some currency depreciation could be beneficial, but the risk of overshooting is serious. This risk points to the need for high levels of foreign exchange reserves as an insurance policy, both for foreign exchange intervention and for supplying foreign currency liquidity. Ghosh et al. (2009) advocated provision of foreign currency liquidity in situations where a sharp depreciation of the currency could be damaging because of large domestic liabilities denominated in foreign currencies. For example, if domestic banks cannot roll over existing sources of foreign currency credit, the central bank could step in to provide such credit to maintain domestic credit lines and draw out the adjustment process. This has been an important measure in countries such as the Republic of Korea, as discussed below.

Regarding quantitative easing policy (and presumably credit easing measures as well), Ghosh et al. (2009: 17) argued that: 'QE should only be attempted by countries with a history of low inflation and macroeconomic stability, with central bank independence and credibility'. Again, an exchange rate peg or concerns about exchange rate instability would limit policy options in this area.

A more general issue is that the dichotomy of 'standard' and 'unconventional' monetary policies does not necessarily apply to emerging markets, where markets are typically less developed and the monetary policy transmission mechanism works less smoothly. Another issue is whether policies have impacts on creating winners and losers. It is desirable to have neutrality in this dimension in order to avoid undesirable political implications of central bank policies.

In Asian emerging economies, unconventional measures have been adopted by the Bank of Korea, the Monetary Authority of Singapore, the Reserve Bank of India and the Central Bank of Taipei,China. Perhaps the most significant unconventional policy measures in the region outside Japan have been those involving provision of foreign currency liquidity via the Fed swap arrangements with other central banks in order to offset the shortage of US dollars arising from capital outflows. For example, the Fed and the Bank of Korea announced the implementation of a US$30 billion swap agreement on 29 October 2008. This appears to have been effective in easing the shortage of dollar funds in the Korean market. Figure 2.7 shows that the spread between the Korean one-year interbank rate and the one-year Treasury bill rate spiked upward from mid-2008 at the same time that foreign securities holdings (presumably mainly US Treasuries) of the Bank of Korea dropped sharply. However, once the holdings of foreign securities began to rise again in December, presumably as a result of the loan by the Fed, the spread shrank rapidly again. It appears that the Bank of Korea made full use of the Fed's swap line, since total foreign securities holdings rose by W40.8 trillion (about US$29 billion) during that period. The Bank of Korea also significantly expanded its won–yen swap agreement with the Bank of Japan from US$3 billion equivalent to US$20 billion equivalent, and established a won–yuan swap with the People's Bank of China of up to CNY180 billion, although it did not make use of these.

The Bank of Korea took a number of other unconventional actions, including broadening the list of eligible counterparties and collateral for repurchase operations, providing funding support to those financial institutions contributing to the Bond Market Stabilization Fund, and

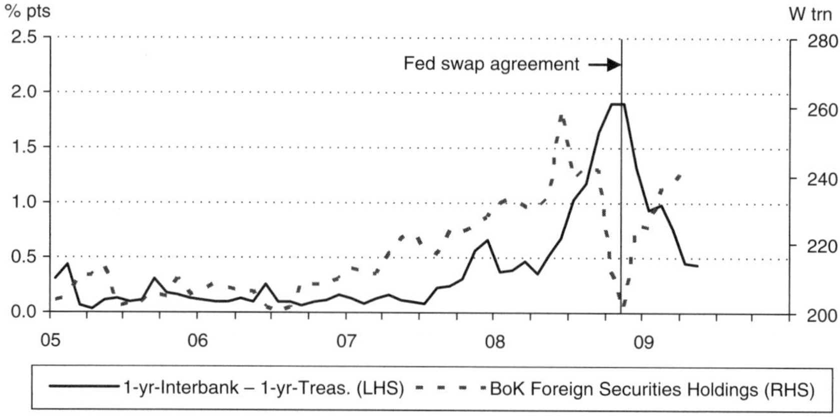

Notes: BoK = Bank of Korea; LHS = left-hand side; RHS = right-hand side.

Source: CEIC Data Co. Ltd Database (accessed 16 July 2009).

Figure 2.7 Korean money market spreads and Bank of Korea (BoK) foreign reserve holdings

providing funding support to the Bank Recapitalization Fund in order to facilitate banks' expansion of their equity capital (Bank of Korea 2009a). It also contributed funds to the Korea Credit Guarantee Fund to enable it to offer payment guarantees for the principal and interest of the loans (up to 10 trillion won) provided to the Fund through the Korea Development Bank, and expanded the range of firms qualified for foreign currency loans secured by export bills from small and medium-sized enterprises to all enterprises in order to encourage foreign domestic banks in the Republic of Korea to finance export trade (Bank of Korea 2009b).

The Monetary Authority of Singapore was the only other central bank in the region aside from the Bank of Japan, the Bank of Korea and the Reserve Bank of Australia to establish such a swap line with the Fed. However, it did not use the Fed's line of credit.

The Reserve Bank of India adopted a number of unconventional measures aimed at increasing the availability of both rupee and foreign currency liquidity. Unconventional measures aimed at expanding rupee liquidity included a special repo window under the liquidity adjustment facility for banks for lending to mutual funds, non-bank financial companies and housing finance companies, and a special refinance facility that banks can access without any collateral. The Reserve Bank of India also set up a special-purpose vehicle to provide liquidity support to non-banking financial companies (Reserve Bank of India 2009). However, the degree of unconventionality of these measures was modest.

The Central Bank of Taipei,China also adopted a number of unconventional measures in September and October 2008, including: expanding the eligible counterparties for its repo operations; extending the term of such operations from 30 days to 180 days; expanding eligible collateral to include certificates of deposit; and linking the interest rates on central bank reserve deposits to market rates (Central Bank of Taipei,China 2008a, 2008b). These operations seem to have been effective in reducing interbank spreads relative to policy rates by about 30–40 basis points during that period.

2.6 CONCLUSION

Once interbank rates fall to zero, a central bank must rely on other unconventional means to impart further easing stimulus to the economy. Moreover, even if interbank rates are still positive, the existence of a credit crunch may impair the normal transmission mechanism of monetary policy, calling for unconventional measures to break the logjam. Unconventional monetary policy measures encompass three broad categories: (i) commitment effect: that is, commitments by the central bank to maintain very low interest rates for a certain period, either conditionally or unconditionally; (ii) quantitative easing: that is, targeting the level of current account balances of the central bank; and (iii) qualitative or credit easing: which involves purchases of targeted assets to lower rates and/or increase liquidity in the target market.

The empirical literature examining the effectiveness of unconventional monetary policy is still limited. Moreover, a number of studies are based on simulations using macro models, so their conclusions are only as reliable as the models themselves. Nonetheless, some broad lessons can be drawn. First, most studies of the commitment effect (or duration effect) suggest that statements by a central bank regarding the duration of a policy of very low or zero interest rates do provide new information to the market and tend to pull down longer-term interest rates. However, the inevitable uncertainty regarding the future course of the economy and monetary policy means that the impact of such measures tends to be seen mainly in shorter-term interest rates of one- to two-year maturity, while the impact on longer-term rates is less clear.

The literature on the effects of quantitative easing monetary policy is less conclusive, especially when one accounts for other announcements by the central bank. The most definitive studies – for example Baba et al.

(2005b) and Bernanke et al. (2004) – do not rule out some influence, but find it to be secondary to that of the commitment effect. Some studies using VAR models have found a transmission effect to the real economy via the portfolio-balancing effect, for example on equities (Honda et al. 2007), but the results are not convincing. However, there is evidence that quantitative easing reduced spreads in the interbank market.

Formal investigations of qualitative easing (credit easing) policy are limited, since the examples of this kind of policy are few, at least until recently. The longest-running example is the Bank of Japan's deliberate use of outright purchases of Japanese government bonds as a policy tool, which began in 2001 and was expanded in late 2008 and early 2009. The basic conclusion of the literature is that the impact on longer-term bond yields of such purchases was limited. This is not surprising, in view of the large size of the government bond market in comparison with the size of the operations of the central bank and the impacts of many other factors, especially longer-term perceptions of the outlook for the economy and inflation. Although there is no theoretical limit to the ability of a central bank to purchase assets, practical considerations – mainly those related to the need to sell those assets later on as part of the exit strategy from unconventional policy – seem to limit the flexibility of a central bank in this area. It seems that the size of the market has to be smaller relative to the size of the operations for such operations to have an impact. Other kinds of asset purchase operations have been more successful. These include the foreign exchange swap operations conducted by the US Federal Reserve and other central banks (notably the Bank of Korea) and outright purchases of corporate paper. This suggests that central banks can use such policies successfully to deal with blockages and credit crunches in specific markets. However, precisely because of their effectiveness, intervention in smaller markets may also entail greater risks for the exit strategy.

Recent developments seem to support these general conclusions. The Fed's announcement of the zero-interest-rate policy and its commitment to maintain it for an extended period does seem to have been successful in lowering short-time rates and even corporate credit spreads. However, attempts by the Fed, the Bank of England and the Bank of Japan to keep government bond yields from rising significantly look unsuccessful. Conversely, a number of central banks have been successful in lowering spreads in interbank, commercial paper and corporate bond markets.

Some of the main concerns regarding unconventional policy center on what to do when it has achieved its purpose and the need for such policy ends, that is, the exit strategy. Too rapid a tightening of policy could stifle an economic recovery, but inflation risks could arise if the monetary base is not reduced in a timely fashion. Large-scale sales of government bonds could push up bond yields in an undesirable way. The greatest concerns center on large-scale purchases of illiquid assets, such as asset-backed securities, which would be difficult to unwind in a short period of time. The risk of losses on a central bank's balance sheet also needs to be taken into account. However, central banks have a number of tools at their disposal to limit such risks. The Bank of Japan managed to exit from quantitative easing in 2006 without any great difficulty.

What is the relevance of unconventional monetary policy for Asian economies aside from Japan? Although three other economies saw interbank rates fall to nearly zero – Hong Kong, China; Singapore; and Taipei,China – only Taipei,China adopted unconventional measures, and these were modest, mainly easing of collateral standards. This may reflect a judgment by these countries that it was easier simply to wait for a rebound of exports. However, if growth of US consumption slows structurally, this may force Asian economies to put greater reliance on unconventional monetary policy measures during future downturns.

The need to deal with credit crunches of various kinds even when interbank rates are still positive is probably more relevant for Asian economies. During the recent global financial crisis, Asian economies have mostly avoided a severe credit crunch of the kind afflicting the US and European economies, since financial sector losses have been much less. However, the Korean banking sector was unusually exposed, due to its high loan-to-deposit ratio and dependence on foreign currency wholesale funding. As a result, the Bank of Korea was most active in adopting unconventional measures, and its use of the swap line from the Fed seems to have been successful in easing the dollar shortage and bringing down interbank rates. The Bank of India also successfully implemented a number of policies to ease liquidity shortages.

REFERENCES

Auerbach, A.J. and M. Obstfeld (2005), 'The case for open-market purchases in a liquidity trap', *American Economic Review*, **95**, 110–37.

Baba, N., C. Ho and P. Hordahl (2009), 'Overview: risk appetite rebounds on stabilisation hopes', *BIS Quarterly Review*, June, available at http://www.bis.org/publ/qtrpdf/r_qt0906a.pdf (accessed 18 June 2009).

Baba, N., M. Nakashima, Y. Shigemi and K. Ueda (2005a), 'The Bank of Japan's monetary policy and bank risk premiums in the money market', CARF Working Paper CARF-F-034.

Baba, N., S. Nishioka, N. Oda, M. Shirakawa, K. Ueda and H. Ugai (2005b), 'Japan's deflation, problems in the financial system, and monetary policy', BIS Working Papers 188, Basel: Bank for International Settlements.

Bank for International Settlements (2009), *BIS Quarterly Review*, June.
Bank of Japan (2001), 'New procedures for money market operations and monetary easing', 19 March, available at http://www.boj.or.jp/en/type/release/zuiji/kako02/k010319a.htm (accessed 11 June 2009).
Bank of Japan (2003), 'Enhancement of monetary policy transparency', 10 October, available at http://www.boj.or.jp/en/type/release/zuiji/kako03/k031010b.htm (accessed 11 June 2009).
Bank of Japan (2009), 'Statement on monetary policy', 19 February, available at http://www.boj.or.jp/en/announcements/release_2009/k090219.pdf (accessed 10 June 2009).
Bank of Korea (2009a), *Financial Stability Report*, No. 13, 28 April.
Bank of Korea (2009b), Press Release, 'The BOK to expand range of those qualified for loans secured by export bills purchased', 2 January.
Benhabib, J., S. Schmitt-Grohe and M. Uribe (2002), 'Avoiding liquidity traps', *Journal of Political Economy*, **110** (3), 535–63.
Bernanke, B. (2009a), 'Federal Reserve policies to ease credit and their implications for the Fed's balance sheet', speech to the National Press Club, Washington, DC, 18 February, available at http://www.federalreserve.gov/newsevents/speech/bernanke20090218a.htm (accessed 11 June 2009).
Bernanke, B. (2009b), 'The Federal Reserve's balance sheet', speech at the Federal Reserve Bank of Richmond 2009 Credit Markets Symposium, Charlotte, NC, 3 April, available at http://www.federalreserve.gov/newsevents/speech/bernanke20090403a.htm (accessed 11 June 2009).
Bernanke, B. and V.R. Reinhart (2004), 'Conducting monetary policy at very low short-term interest rates', *American Economic Review*, **94** (2), 85–90.
Bernanke, B., V.R. Reinhart and B.P. Sack (2004), 'Monetary policy at the zero bound: an empirical assessment', *Brookings Papers on Economic Activity*, **2** (2004), 2–100.
Bini Smaghi, L. (2009), 'Conventional and unconventional monetary policy', Keynote Lecture at the International Center for Monetary and Banking Studies, Geneva, 28 April, available at http://www.ecb.int/press/key/date/2009/html/sp090428.en.html (accessed 18 June 2009).
Braun, R.A. and Y. Waki (2006), 'Monetary policy during Japan's lost decade', *Japanese Economic Review*, **57**, 324–44.
Calvo, G. (2007), 'Monetary policy challenges in emerging markets: sudden stop, liability dollarization, and lender of last resort', National Bureau of Economic Research Working Paper 12788, New York: NBER.
Central Bank of Taipei,China (2008a), 'Monetary policy decisions of the Executive Directors Meeting', 25 September, available at http://www.cbc.gov.tw/ct.asp?xItem=32637&ctNode=448&mp=2 (accessed 18 August 2009).
Central Bank of Taipei,China (2008b), 'Monetary policy decisions of the Executive Directors Meeting', 30 October, available at http://www.cbc.gov.tw/ct.asp?xItem=33012&ctNode=448&mp=2 (accessed 18 August 2009).
Eggertsson, G.B. and M. Woodford (2003), 'The zero bound on interest rates and optimal monetary policy', *Brookings Papers on Economic Activity*, **1** (2003), 139–233.
Financial Times (2009), 'Doubts grow over quantitative easing', 7 July.
Fujiki, H., K. Okina and S. Shiratsuka (2001), 'Monetary policy under zero interest rate: viewpoints of central bank economists', *Bank of Japan Monetary and Economic Studies*, February, 89–130.

Fujiki, H. and S. Shiratsuka (2002), 'Policy duration effect under the zero interest rate policy in 1999–2000: evidence from Japan's money market data', *Bank of Japan Monetary and Economic Studies*, **20** (1), 1–31.

Fujiwara, I., N. Hara, N. Hirakata, S. Watanabe and K. Yoshimura (2005), 'Monetary policy in a liquidity trap: what have we learned, and to what end?', *International Finance*, **8**, 471–508.

Ghosh, A., M. Chamon, C. Crowe, J.I. Kim and J. Ostry (2009), 'Coping with the crisis: policy options for emerging market countries', International Monetary Fund Position Note, 23 April, available at http://www.imf.org/external/pubs/ft/spn/2009/spn0908.pdf (accessed 18 June 2009).

Goodfriend, M. (2000), 'Overcoming the zero bound on interest rate policy', *Journal of Money, Credit and Banking*, **32,** 1007–35.

Hanes, C. (2006), 'The liquidity trap and US interest rates in the 1930s', *Journal of Money, Credit and Banking*, **38**, 163–94.

Her Majesty's Treasury (2009), 'Statement on financial intervention to support lending in the economy', January 19, available at http://www.hm-treasury.gov.uk/press_05_09.htm (accessed 7 July 2009).

Honda, Y., Y. Kuroki and M. Tachibana (2007), 'An injection of base money at zero interest rates: empirical evidence from the Japanese experience 2001–2006', Graduate School of Economics and Osaka School of International Public Policy Discussion Paper 07-08, Osaka, Japan: Osaka University.

Krugman, P.R., K.M. Dominquez and K. Rogoff (1998), 'It's Baaack: Japan's slump and the return of the liquidity trap', *Brookings Papers on Economic Activity*, **2**, (1998), 137–205.

Kuttner, K.N. and A.S. Posen (2001), 'The great recession: lessons for macroeconomic policy from Japan', *Brookings Papers on Economic Activity*, **2**, (2001), 93–186.

McAndrews, J. (2009), *Segmentation in the US Dollar Money Markets During the Financial Crisis*, New York: Federal Reserve Bank of New York.

Meier, A. (2009), 'Panacea, curse, or nonevent? Unconventional monetary policy in the United Kingdom', International Monetary Fund Working Paper No. WP/09/163, Washington, DC: International Monetary Fund.

Oda, N. and K. Ueda (2007), 'The effects of the Bank of Japan's zero interest rate commitment and quantitative monetary easing on the yield curve: a macro-finance approach', *Japanese Economic Review*, **58**, 303–28.

Okina, K. and S. Shiratsuka (2004), 'Policy commitment and expectation formation: Japan's experience under zero interest rates', *North American Journal of Economics and Finance*, **15** (1), 75–100.

Reifschneider, D. and J.C. Williams (2000), 'Three lessons for monetary policy in a low-inflation era', *Journal of Money, Credit and Banking*, **32** (4), 936–66.

Reserve Bank of India (2009), 'Third quarter review of RBI monetary policy 2008–09', Press Statement by Dr D. Subbarao, Governor, 27 January, available at http://www.banknetindia.com/banking/3qreview09_press.htm (accessed 7 July 2009).

Shiller, R. (1990), 'The term structure of interest rates', in B.M. Friedman and F.H. Hahn (eds), *Handbook of Monetary Economics 1*, Amsterdam: Elsevier Science Publishers, pp. 627–722.

Svensson, L.E.O. (2001), 'The zero bound in an open economy: a foolproof way of escaping from a liquidity trap', *Monetary and Economic Studies*, **19** (S-1), 277–312.

Taylor, J. (1993), 'Discretion versus policy rules in practice', *Carnegie-Rochester Conference Series on Public Policy*, **39**, 195–214.

US Federal Reserve Board (2003), Press Release, 12 August, available at http://www.federalreserve.gov/boarddocs/press/monetary/2003/20030812/default.htm (accessed 11 June 2009).

US Federal Reserve Board (2008), Press Release, 16 December, available at http://www.federalreserve.gov/newsevents/press/monetary/20081216a.htm (accessed 11 June 2009).

US Federal Reserve Board (2009), Press Release, 18 March, available at http://www.federalreserve.gov/newsevents/press/monetary/20090318a.htm (accessed 11 June 2009).

Wolman, A. (2005), 'Real implications of the zero bound on nominal interest rates', *Journal of Money, Credit, and Banking*, **37** (2), 273–96.

Yuan, M.W. and C. Zimmerman (1999), 'Credit crunch, bank lending and monetary policy: a model of financial intermediation with heterogeneous projects', Center for Research on Economic Fluctuations and Employment Working Paper 89, Montreal: Université du Quebec.

APPENDIX

Table 2A.1 Major monetary policy announcements

Central Bank	Date announced	Policy announced
US Federal Reserve	12 Dec. 2007	Term Auction Facility (TAF)
	12 Dec. 2007	Reciprocal currency arrangements with European Central Bank and Swiss National Bank (swap lines)
	11 Mar. 2008	Term Securities Lending Facility (TSLF)
	16 Mar. 2008	Primary Dealer Credit Facility (PDCF)
	18 Sep. 2008	Reciprocal currency arrangements with the European Central Bank, Bank of England, Swiss National Bank, Bank of Canada and Bank of Japan (swap lines)
	19 Sep. 2008	Asset-Backed Commercial Paper Money Market Fund Liquidity Facility (AMLF)
	7 Oct. 2008	Commercial Paper Funding Facility (CPFF)
	21 Oct. 2008	Money Market Investor Funding Facility (MMIFF)
	29 Oct. 2008	Reciprocal currency arrangements with Banco Central do Brasil, Bank of Korea, Monetary Authority of Singapore, and Banco de Mexico (swap lines)
	25 Nov. 2008	Term Asset-Backed Securities Loan Facility (TALF)
	16 Dec. 2008	Zero-interest-rate policy and commitment to maintain it for a considerable period
	29 Jan. 2009	Creation of excess balance accounts to allow payment of interest on excess balances
	10 Feb. 2009	Public–private Investment Fund on an initial scale of up to US$500 billion
	18 Mar. 2009	Increased purchases of mortgage-backed securities, agency bonds, and Treasuries
	25 Jun. 2009	TSLF operations backed by Schedule 1 collateral ended as of 30 June
Bank of Japan	31 Oct. 2008	Pay interest on excess reserve balances
	19 Dec. 2008	Increase outright bond purchases from ¥1.2 trillion per month to ¥1.4 trillion per month
	19 Dec. 2008	Introduction of Special Funds-Supplying Operations to Facilitate Corporate Financing

Table 2A.1 (continued)

Central Bank	Date announced	Policy announced
	19 Dec. 2008	Outright purchases of commercial paper
	19 Feb. 2009	Outright purchases of corporate bonds
	18 Mar. 2009	Increase outright bond purchases from ¥1.4 trillion per month to ¥1.8 trillion per month
Bank of England	21 Apr. 2008	Special Liquidity Facility (swap mortgage-backed securities for T-bills)
	18 Sep. 2008	Reciprocal currency arrangement with Fed (swap line)
	13 Oct. 2008	Unlimited lending of US liquidity to banking system
	19 Jan. 2009	Asset Purchase Facility of £50 billion
	5 Mar. 2009	Quantitative easing target of £75 billion for bank reserves
	7 May 2009	Quantitative easing target of £125 billion for bank reserves
European Central Bank	6 Sep. 2007	Fixed-rate auction with full allotment
	20 Jan. 2009	Acceptance of asset-backed securities as collateral for operations
	7 May 2009	Outright purchases of covered bonds
	24 Jun. 2009	Fixed-rate auction with full allotment of one-year loans (€442 billion)
Bank of Korea	17 Oct. 2008	Introduction of a competitive auction swap facility for foreign exchange
	29 Oct. 2008	Broadening of eligible collateral for repurchase operations
	30 Oct. 2008	Reciprocal currency arrangement with US Federal Reserve (swap lines)
	12 Dec. 2008	Expansion of yen–won swap agreement with Bank of Japan from US$3 billion to US$20 billion
	12 Dec. 2008	Establishment of yuan–won swap agreement with People's Bank of China of up to CNY180 billion
	30 Mar. 2009	Contribution of funds to the Korean Development Bank and Korea Credit Guarantee Fund
Monetary Authority of Singapore	30 Oct. 2008	Reciprocal currency arrangement with US Federal Reserve (swap lines)

Table 2A.1 (continued)

Central Bank	Date announced	Policy announced
Reserve Bank of India	16 Sep. 2008	Increasing of borrowing limit for banks of 1% of net domestic liabilities
	6 Dec. 2008	Institution of a rupee–dollar swap facility for banks with overseas branches
	6 Dec. 2008	Reduction of risk weights on lending to certain sectors

3. Monetary policy strategies in the Asia and Pacific region: which way forward?

Andrew Filardo and Hans Genberg

3.1 INTRODUCTION

The global financial crisis that started in the United States (US) in mid-2007 shook the financial systems in the US and Europe and brought about a worldwide economic recession. What have we learned about monetary policymaking and, more importantly, what might be the way forward?

While the proximate cause of the crisis can be traced to the subprime mortgage market in the US, the underlying sources went deeper than that and involved issues such as incentives in the structured finance market, overreliance on the ratings of financial products by rating agencies, and the regulatory treatment of structured investment vehicles.[1] Further removed, it has also been suggested that the conduct of monetary policy was a contributing factor – specifically that policy interest rates in the US and elsewhere were held too low for too long early in the decade after the burst of the 1995–2000 internet bubble. In this regard, the excess of liquidity helped to fuel the speculative bubble in the US housing market and, through various macroeconomic and financial channels, contributed to excessive risk-taking in financial markets more generally (Taylor 2009). Moreover, some scholars have argued that too narrow a focus by central banks on price stability may have unwittingly contributed to this precipitous boom–bust cycle and, therefore, conventional monetary policy frameworks may need to do a better job of incorporating concerns about financial stability (White 2006).

The macroeconomic consequences of the crisis also brought about innovations by several central banks in the conduct of monetary policy that a few years ago might have been considered highly improbable. As policy rates were lowered aggressively they hit the lower bound of zero in a number of jurisdictions, prompting central banks to engage in 'unconventional' monetary policies involving a massive expansion of central bank balance sheets. The growth of central bank balance sheets included purchases by central banks of private sector liabilities carrying significant credit risk.

Although most central banks in the Asia and Pacific region have not found it necessary to engage in the kind of unconventional policies practiced by their colleagues in the US, the eurozone and the United Kingdom (UK), it is useful to ask whether lessons can be drawn from the crisis for the conduct of monetary policy in the region. This chapter attempts to address this question.

Section 3.2 sets the stage by reviewing the nature of monetary policy regimes in the region prior to the crisis. Section 3.3 evaluates their performance before section 3.4 discusses three aspects of monetary policy that have received renewed attention in light of the crisis: unconventional monetary policies, the role of asset prices and financial imbalances in the conduct of monetary policy, and financial stability as an additional monetary policy objective. Section 3.5 summarizes the main conclusions of the analysis and what it implies for policy strategies going forward.

3.2 MONETARY POLICY OBJECTIVES AND INSTITUTIONAL ARRANGEMENTS IN THE ASIA AND PACIFIC REGION[2]

3.2.1 Objectives and Strategies

Along with an increasing number of monetary policy institutions elsewhere in the world, central banks in the Asia and Pacific region have chosen to pursue price stability as the principal objective of monetary policy. Based on information contained on their websites, of the 12 monetary authorities[3] studied in this chapter, six[4] aim for price stability as an overarching objective (Table 3.1).

For the others, three central banks – the People's Bank of China, Bank Indonesia and Bank Negara Malaysia – state the goal as maintaining the stability of the value of the currency, which could mean either the internal value in terms of goods and services (that is, the price level) or the external value (namely, the exchange rate), or some combination of the two. Bank Indonesia, for example, makes it explicit that the term refers to both aspects. Two central banks – the Reserve Bank of India and Bank Negara Malaysia – state that an adequate supply of credit to the economy is also an explicit goal. The remaining institution, the Hong Kong Monetary Authority, puts exclusive emphasis on exchange rate stability (vis-à-vis the US dollar) and pursues this goal by means of a currency board arrangement.

Table 3.1 Central bank policy objectives

Jurisdiction	Central bank	Policy objective	Description as stated on the official websites of each central bank
Australia	Reserve Bank of Australia	Price stability	To focus on price (currency) stability while taking account of the implications of monetary policy for activity and, therefore, employment in the short term.
People's Republic of China	The People's Bank of China	Value of the currency	The objective of the monetary policy is to maintain the stability of the value of the currency and thereby promote economic growth.
Hong Kong, China	Hong Kong Monetary Authority	Exchange rate stability	The primary monetary policy objective of the Hong Kong Monetary Authority is to maintain exchange rate stability.
India	Reserve Bank of India	Price stability and adequate credit supply	Maintaining price stability and ensuring adequate flow of credit to productive sectors.
Indonesia	Bank Indonesia	Price stability and exchange rate stability	Bank Indonesia has one single objective of achieving and maintaining stability of the rupiah value. The stability of the value of the rupiah comprises two aspects, one is stability of rupiah value against goods and services and the other is the stability of the exchange rate of the rupiah against other currencies.
Japan	Bank of Japan	Price stability	The Bank of Japan Law states that the Bank's monetary policy should be 'aimed at, through the pursuit of price stability, contributing to the sound development of the national economy'.

Korea	The Bank of Korea	Price stability	Like other central banks, the Bank of Korea takes price stability as the most important objective of its monetary policy. The Bank of Korea Act, which came into effect in April 1998 following its revision at the end of 1997, stipulates price stability as the purpose of the Bank of Korea.
Malaysia	Bank Negara Malaysia	Price stability and exchange rate stability	To issue currency and keep reserves safeguarding the value of the currency; To promote monetary stability and a sound financial structure; To influence the credit situation to the advantage of the country.
New Zealand	Reserve Bank of New Zealand	Price stability	The Reserve Bank of New Zealand Act 1989 specifies that the primary function of the Reserve Bank shall be to deliver 'stability in the general level of prices'.
Philippines	Bangko Sentral Ng Pilipinas (BSP)	Price stability	The primary objective of BSP's monetary policy is to promote a low and stable inflation conducive to a balanced and sustainable economic growth.
Singapore	Monetary Authority of Singapore	Price stability	The primary objective of monetary policy in Singapore is to promote price stability as a sound basis for sustainable economic growth.
Thailand	Bank of Thailand	Price stability	Setting the monetary policy direction which is consistent with the nation's economic conditions, with the ultimate objective of maintaining price stability and sustainable economic growth.

Source: Adapted from Genberg and He (2009).

Strategies adopted to achieve the objectives are quite diverse. Six central banks are self-proclaimed inflation targeters: the Reserve Bank of Australia, Bank Indonesia, Bank of Korea, the Reserve Bank of New Zealand, Bangko Sentral ng Pilipinas and Bank of Thailand. While Australia's and New Zealand's reserve banks are experienced at inflation targeting, having started in 1993 and 1990, respectively, the other four central banks are relative newcomers with the Republic of Korea (hereafter Korea) starting in 1999, Indonesia and Thailand in 2000, and the Philippines in 2002.

While not a formal inflation targeter, the Monetary Authority of Singapore has been described by outside observers as one, albeit following a fairly unique strategy in pursuing price stability by announcing the level as well as the rate of change of a target band for the nominal effective exchange rate of the Singapore dollar. The other central banks employ a range of diverse strategies reflecting a set of policy trade-offs, not least being those associated with targeting inflation, sustainable growth and exchange rate stability. The case of the 'two perspectives' framework of the Bank of Japan is particularly noteworthy. This framework seeks to avoid excessive weight being placed on short-term inflation pressures in policy decisions. The first perspective emphasizes developments affecting output and inflation at the one- to two-year horizon; the second perspective takes account of the longer-term risks, such as those arising from asset price bubbles and long-term resource misallocations that might be associated with interest rates being held too low for too long. Practically, this framework anticipates the possibility that the Bank of Japan may need to raise policy interest rates even though inflation forecasts at conventional horizons appear well behaved.

With respect to policy instruments, the majority of the institutions carry out their policies by means of targeting short-term interest rates (Table 3.2). The principal exceptions are: the Monetary Authority of Singapore, which, as already noted, uses the nominal effective exchange rate as an intermediate target; the Hong Kong Monetary Authority, which intervenes in the foreign exchange market to keep the exchange rate vis-à-vis the US dollar within a prespecified constant target zone; and the People's Bank of China (PBC). The PBC has adopted growth rates of monetary aggregates as intermediate targets and typically employs several instruments in the implementation of its monetary policy: exchange rate, required reserve ratio, interest rates and open market operations. Existing controls on the domestic financial system and on international capital flows arguably makes it possible for the PBC to use several instruments somewhat independently of each other, an option less feasible in jurisdictions with more liberalized and efficient domestic financial markets and with more open capital accounts.

Table 3.2 Institutional frameworks for monetary policy

	Inflation targeting?	Targeting arrangement	Formal policy rate	Formal operating target
Australia	Yes, 1993	Target for headline CPI consumer price inflation of 2–3% per annum on average over the business cycle	Target cash rate (=O/N rate target)	O/N cash rate
People's Republic of China	No	Reference to money growth targets	1-year deposit and loan reference rates	Excess reserves
Hong Kong, China	No	Currency board: target range centered on HKD7.8 = US$1		USD/HKD spot rate
India	No	Multiple objectives: price stability understanding – containing the perception of inflation in the range of 4.0%–4.5% so that an inflation rate of 3.0% becomes the medium term objective	1-day repo and reverse repo rates	No formal target
Indonesia	Yes, 2000	Inflation targeting: inflation target for 2008, 2009, and 2010 is 5±1%, 4.5±1% and 4±1% for year-on-year CPI inflation	BI rate (= target rate for 1-month SBI)	1-month SBI rate
Japan	No	Medium- to long-term price stability expressed in terms of year on year rate of change in the CPI (approximately between 0 and 2%)	Uncollateralized O/N call rate target	O/N call rate
Korea	Yes, 1999	Inflation targeting: target range of 3±0.5% in terms of 3-year average of annual CPI inflation	O/N call rate target	O/N call rate

Table 3.2 (continued)

	Inflation targeting?	Targeting arrangement	Formal policy rate	Formal operating target
Malaysia	No		O/N policy rate	Average O/N interbank rate
New Zealand	Yes, 1990	Inflation targeting: target range of 1% to 3% on average, over the medium-term, defined in terms of the All Groups Consumers Price Index (CPI)	Official cash rate (=O/N rate target)	O/N cash rate
Philippines	Yes, 2002	Inflation targeting: target range of 3.5±1% (2009), 4.5±1% (2010) for the average year-on-year change in the CPI over the calendar year	O/N repo and reverse repo rates	No formal target
Singapore	No	As of mid-2009, zero percent appreciation of the undisclosed Singapore dollar NEER policy band	Policy band for Singapore dollar NEER	Singapore dollar NEER
Thailand	Yes, 2000	Inflation targeting: target range of 0–3.5% for quarterly average of core inflation	1-day repo rate	1-day repo rate

Notes: BI = Bank Indonesia; CPI = consumer price index; HKD = Hong Kong, China dollar; NEER = nominal effective exchange rate; O/N = overnight; SBI = Bank Indonesia promissory notes.

Source: BIS Markets Committee (June 2008), 'Monetary policy frameworks and central bank market operations', available at http://www.bis.org/publ/mktc02.pdf (accessed June 2009); national central banks.

3.2.2 Central Bank Governance and Independence

The ability of a central bank to achieve its objective depends partly on the institutional environment in which it operates. A large amount of literature has investigated the link between measures of economic performance – usually inflation – and various indicators of central bank governance and independence (CBGI). A general conclusion is that central bank independence tends to be associated with better inflation performance, although there is some evidence that this result predominantly applies to developed economies (Cuikerman et al. 1992).

A recent paper on this topic focuses on Asia and the Pacific.[5] Ahsan et al. (2008) studied 36 economies in the region including 11 of the economies in our sample.[6] The authors constructed indices (hereafter referred to as the ASW indices) of CBGI using 27 variables meant to capture different aspects of governance and independence. Apart from an overall index, they tabulated indicators of: (i) legal independence ('Legal' in the figures that follow); (ii) political independence ('Political'); (iii) independence to pursue price stability as the main and sole objective ('Price stability'); (iv) independence to pursue exchange rate policy ('Forex policy'); (v) independence in the control of monetary policy instruments and non-obligation to finance government deficits ('Deficit finance'); and (vi) accountability and transparency ('Accountability and transparency'). A higher value of the index is designed to reflect a greater degree of independence. Using these indicators in regression analysis, the authors found that each of these is negatively associated with the inflation rate of the corresponding economy.

Rather than pursuing the link between CBGI in the region and macroeconomic performance, in this section we examine the evolution in the ASW indices with the view to detect any trends over time and to see whether there is any appreciable difference between those inflation targeting central banks and the other monetary authorities. We also examine whether the crisis in the region in 1997–1998 acted as a wake-up call for the authorities in the most affected economies in the sense that they altered the governance structure of their respective central banks after the crisis.

Figure 3.1 shows the overall value of the CBGI index for 1996 and 2005.[7] For each economy or group of economies, the first bar represents the situation before the 1997–1998 Asian crisis and the second is the latest available value in the ASW data set. With the exception of India and New Zealand for which there were no changes, all economies showed some improvement over time. This is consistent with the notion that policy-makers have accepted the view that greater central bank independence is desirable. The sets of bars on the right side of the graph show averages of

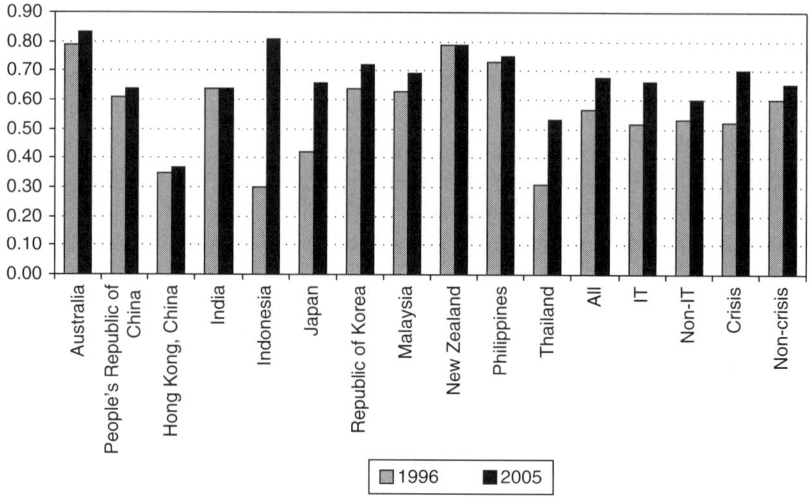

Notes: All = average for all economies; IT = average for inflation-targeting economies; Non-IT = average for non-inflation-targeting economies; Crisis = average for Indonesia, Korea, Malaysia, the Philippines and Thailand; Non-crisis = average for Australia; People's Republic of China; Hong Kong, China; India; Japan; and New Zealand.
No data available for Singapore.

Source: Ahsan et al. (2008).

Figure 3.1 Overall index of central bank governance and independence

five groups of jurisdictions: all jurisdictions in the sample, the inflation-targeting economies, central banks that are not inflation targeters, the economies most affected by the Asian crisis (Indonesia, Korea, Malaysia, the Philippines and Thailand), and finally the 'non-crisis' economies (Australia; PRC; Hong Kong, China; India; Japan; and New Zealand). These bars reveal that both inflation-targeting and crisis-hit economies have experienced larger changes in the overall index than their respective counterparts. Figures 3.2–3.5 explore these differences at a more disaggregated level.

Figure 3.2 illustrates the extent of the improvements of the CBGI in each of the seven dimensions, with the notable exception of the ability to pursue price stability in the non-inflation targeting central banks. Particularly large improvements are seen in: (i) political independence in the crisis economies; (ii) the ability to pursue price stability in inflation targeting and crisis economies (note that there is a large overlap in these groups as the inflation-targeting classification is based on the situation in 2005); and (iii) the ability to determine exchange rate policy independently.

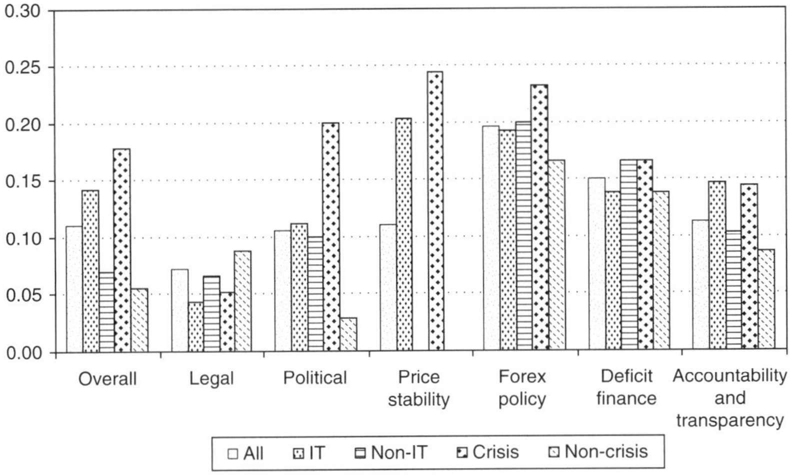

Notes: All = average for all economies; IT = inflation-targeting economies; Non-IT = non-inflation-targeting economies; Crisis = Indonesia, Korea, Malaysia, the Philippines and Thailand; Non-crisis = Australia; People's Republic of China; Hong Kong, China; India; Japan; and New Zealand.

Source: Ahsan et al. (2008).

Figure 3.2 Differences in the ASW index between 2005 and 1996

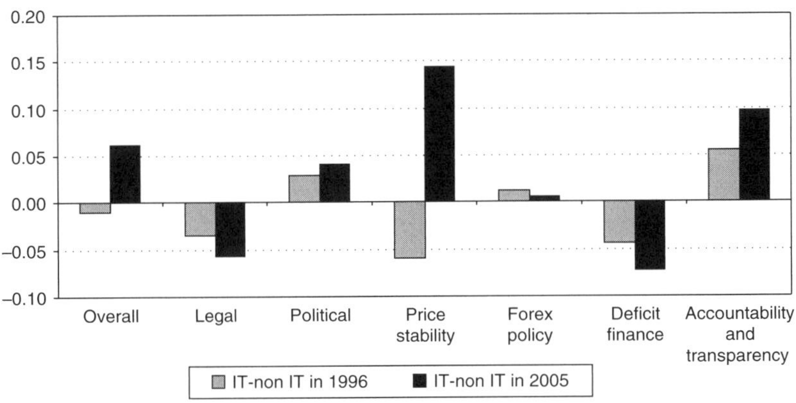

Notes: CBGI = central bank governance and independence; IT = inflation-targeting economies; Non-IT = non-inflation-targeting economies.

Source: Ahsan et al. (2008).

Figure 3.3 CBGI: Differences across economy groupings (IT-non IT)

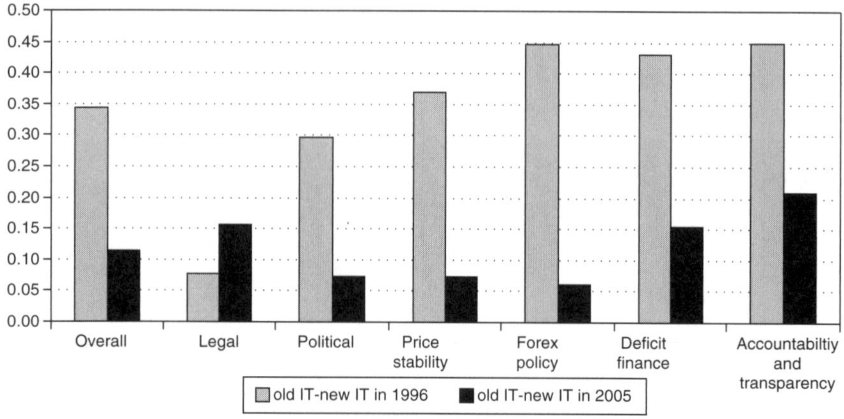

Notes: CBGI = central bank governance and independence; IT = inflation targeting.

Source: Ahsan et al. (2008).

Figure 3.4 CBGI: Differences across economy groupings (old IT-new IT)

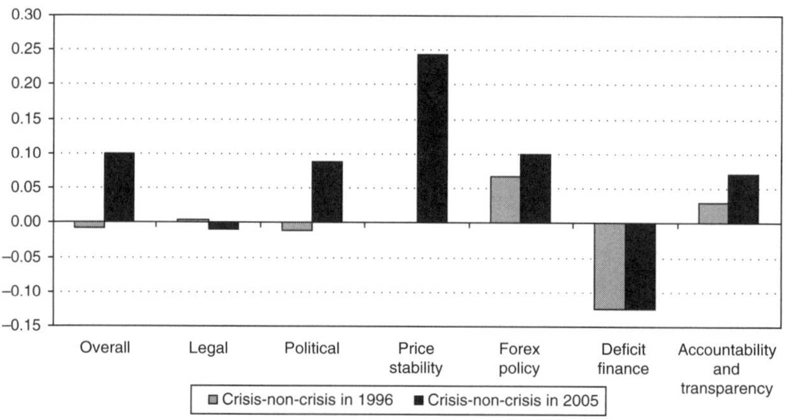

Notes: CBGI = central bank governance and independence.

Source: Ahsan et al. (2008).

Figure 3.5 CBGI: Differences across economy groupings (crisis-non-crisis)

Figures 3.3 to 3.5 present a more detailed evolution of differences across economy groupings. Figure 3.3 shows, not surprisingly, that compared to their non-inflation-targeting counterparts, central banks that are inflation targeters have been given more independence to pursue price stability as the sole objective of monetary policy. It also shows that the inflation-targeting central banks have become more accountable and transparent relative to their non-inflation-targeting colleagues. The latter finding is consistent with the notion that while greater accountability and transparency is desirable for all central banks (Figure 3.2) they have been given particular emphasis in the context of inflation-targeting monetary policy strategies. The graph also indicates that with respect to legal independence and the ability to set monetary policy independently from fiscal policy (the deficit finance columns) the greatest changes have actually occurred for non-inflation-targeting central banks, somewhat contrary to the idea that the lack of fiscal dominance is particularly important for inflation targeting strategies.[8]

Figure 3.4 reveals that the differences in the CBGI subindices for older inflation-targeting economies in the region (that is, Australia and New Zealand) and the newcomers were very large before the crisis and have fallen substantially since then.[9] This confirms that the introduction of inflation targeting coincided with a more general overhaul of the central banks' governance structure.

Finally, comparing the crisis-affected economies with the non-crisis economies (Figure 3.5) provides evidence that the Asian crisis led to significant reforms in the areas of political independence and in the ability to set price stability objectives; however, drawing conclusive inferences about the latter is difficult owing to the broad overlap in the sample between the crisis economies' grouping and inflation-targeting economies' grouping.

3.2.3 Transparency

Dincer and Eichengreen (2007) focused on the determinants and effects of central bank transparency in a sample of 100 central banks from developed and developing economies. Their regression results imply that greater transparency reduces inflation volatility and persistence. As their analysis also covered the central banks that we focus on, it is of interest to compare the indices of transparency they construct with those of Ahsan et al. (2008) described above in order assess the robustness of the results with respect to the data coding approach of different researchers.

Comparisons contained in Table 3.3 support the following conclusions. The ranking of the central banks in terms of the level of the transparency

Table 3.3 Central bank transparency: changes over time

	DE 2004	ASW 2005	DE 2004–1998	ASW 2005–1996
Jurisdictions				
Australia	9.0	0.86	1.0	0.0
People's Republic of China	4.5	0.61	3.5	0.0
Hong Kong, China	7.0	0.58	2.0	0.16
India	2.0	0.58	0.0	0.0
Indonesia	8.0	0.70	5.0	0.39
Japan	9.5	0.78	1.5	0.36
Korea	8.5	0.95	2.0	0.0
Malaysia	5.0	0.58	1.0	0.0
New Zealand	13.5	0.86	3.0	0.0
Philippines	10.0	0.83	6.5	0.08
Singapore	6.5		4.0	
Thailand	8.0	0.42	6.0	0.25
Averages				
All	7.6	0.7	3.0	0.1
Old Inflation Targeting	11.2	0.9	2.0	0.0
New Inflation Targeting	8.6	0.7	4.9	0.2
Non-inflation Targeting	5.8	0.6	2.0	0.1

Notes: DE and ASW refer to the results for the years indicated in Dincer and Eichengreen (2007) and Ahsan et al. (2008), respectively.

Source: Dincer and Eichengreen (2007); Ahsan et al. (2008).

index is relatively similar across the two indices with a correlation coefficient of 0.64. The consistency across the indices is less satisfactory with respect to the change over time, as the correlation coefficient falls to 0.46. Both indices show that the early inflation-targeting central banks are the most transparent and that the new inflation-targeting central banks have improved the most during the period covered by the indices. This seems to suggest that central banks that introduced inflation targeting either felt the need or took the opportunity also to increase transparency of their policy frameworks. Of course, it could also arise spuriously from the coding approach of Dincer and Eichengreen (2007), to the extent that inflation-targeting central banks were given higher marks for transparency (for example, for clearly articulating the policy objective) by simply announcing the adoption of formal inflation targeting.

Filardo and Guinigundo (forthcoming) offer a more recent assessment of the transparency and communication strategies of the central banks in a sample based on a survey of the central banks themselves. The responses to the survey give a snapshot of current practices in the region and indicate that central banks use 'a fairly sophisticated set of communication strategies . . . [reflecting] . . . the greater conscious effort within the policymaking circle to clearly communicate policy relevant information to financial markets, the media and the public at large' (Filardo and Guinigundo, forthcoming). Although it does not contain an explicit comparison with past communication practices, the message of the Filardo–Guinigundo study is consistent with the statistics reported above which show a general increase over time in the transparency and accountability of central banks in the Asia and Pacific region.

Corroborating this view, Garcia-Herrero and Remolona (forthcoming) find evidence that central banks in Asia and the Pacific have learned to conduct policy so as to take advantage of the expectations channel of monetary policy – that is, to become more transparent as to their future policy intentions. The authors' conclusion is based partly on examining the content of central banks' policy statements and partly by presenting evidence showing that yield curves reflect expectations of future policy interest rates. Yet they also note that: 'policy statements still appear to contain a larger element of surprise than do macroeconomic news, suggesting that there is still scope for central banks in the region to communicate more effectively the way they interpret economic data and the strategies that guide their decisions' (Garcia-Herrero and Remolona, forthcoming).

3.2.4 Summary

Whether formal inflation targeters or those merely targeting inflation, most central banks in the Asia and Pacific region have experienced gains in the degree of legal and/or political independence since the late 1990s. These banks have also seen improvements in other aspects of governance usually associated with the enhanced ability to control inflation.

While there are differences in the evolution of central bank independence and governance between inflation-targeting central banks and the other central banks in our sample, it is an open question whether these differences have resulted in differences in macroeconomic performance, in particular inflation performance, between the corresponding economies. The next section reviews evidence bearing on this question as well as the more specific issue of whether the adoption of inflation targeting confers some additional benefits.

3.3 INFLATION PERFORMANCE IN THE ASIA AND PACIFIC REGION: SOME EMPIRICAL EVIDENCE

Judged by the average inflation rate in the post-Asian crisis period, central banks in the Asia and Pacific region have performed very well both on an absolute level and relative to a comparison group consisting of economies whose inflation performance is regarded as exemplary (Table 3.4). The region's central banks' average inflation rate of slightly over 3 per cent per year from 1999 to 2008 compares favorably with Chile, an inflation-targeting emerging market that is often used as a success story as far as monetary policy is concerned. The average inflation rate among central banks in Asia and the Pacific is only slightly higher than that in the US, and while it is above the inflation rates of Canada, Switzerland and the eurozone, it is within striking distance of what is commonly thought of as price stability.[10]

Inflation rates in the region were generally higher before the Asian financial crisis,[11] suggesting that policy frameworks have improved over time, an observation consistent with the evolution of the indices of central bank governance and transparency presented in the previous section. An interesting question in this respect concerns the role of formal inflation targeting in this process. Filardo and Genberg (2009) reviewed empirical evidence on this issue. The authors presented three types of empirical results: one relating to the time series properties of the inflation processes themselves; another relating to the nature of private sector inflation forecasts; and a third to the impact of commodity price cycles on headline inflation rates.

Models of inflation typically suggest that if inflationary expectations are firmly anchored, the inflation process will exhibit less persistence.

Table 3.4 Average inflation rates

	1990–1997	1999–2008
Asia and Pacific region	5.83	3.03
Eurozone	–	2.20
Industrialized economies	3.28	2.17
Canada	2.41	2.26
Chile	13.64	3.67
Switzerland	2.82	1.08
United States	3.29	2.82

Source: Authors' calculations based on International Monetary Fund data.

The reason is that a purely temporary shock will not initiate a price–wage spiral that would lead to a drawn-out adjustment process. By estimating separate time series models for inflation in inflation-targeting and non-inflation-targeting central banks, Filardo and Genberg (2009) found evidence consistent with this hypothesis, although it is not entirely clear cut.

The properties of private sector inflation forecasts offer another way to investigate the importance of formal inflation-targeting. The hypothesis investigated is that the distribution of inflation forecasts across individual forecasters should be more concentrated in inflation-targeting economies than in non-inflation targeting economies, especially if the inflation target is credible. Panel regression analysis shows that a greater focus on inflation as a policy objective does indeed lead to less dispersion of inflation forecasts, but it does not appear that formal inflation targeting per se is the driving mechanism. Inflation forecasts for economies where central banks use more eclectic approaches have also become more concentrated over time.

The Filardo–Genberg (2009) study investigated the impact of the recent commodity price cycle on consumer price inflation rates in the region. They found that on the whole Asian economies weathered the cycle fairly well. While headline inflation rates showed considerable fluctuations as food and energy prices surged and collapsed, movements in measures of core inflation were much more muted. In other words, there was little evidence to suggest that second-round effects on inflation expectations took hold. Searching for evidence of differences between formal inflation-targeting economies and the others, they concluded that there is little in the data to suggest less sensitivity of underlying inflation to commodity prices (that is, relative price shocks) in formal inflation targeters. In other words, inflation rates in the region remained remarkably well anchored for both inflation targeters and non-inflation targeters.

In conclusion, current monetary policy frameworks in the Asia and Pacific region have delivered good performance, indicating that it is important for central banks to focus firmly on inflation as the primary policy objective. Specific details of how to achieve this objective appear less crucial. That said, the recent crisis led to new thinking about monetary policy strategies and whether they can be adapted so as to reduce the likelihood of a crisis happening again in the future. The next section looks at whether there are any lessons for monetary policy management in the Asia and Pacific region.

3.4 CHALLENGES FOR MONETARY POLICY IN LIGHT OF THE GLOBAL FINANCIAL CRISIS

The global financial crisis brought to the fore a number of issues related to the conduct of monetary policy. The most immediate issue relates to the policy response to the crisis itself. Central banks around the globe resorted to what have been called unconventional monetary policies. Many central banks found themselves needing to purchase private sector financial instruments, partly as a means to clear out impediments to the orderly operation of the monetary transmission mechanism. For some central banks, they had little choice but to vary the policy stance with quantitative measures as the interest rate channels of the monetary policy transmission mechanisms broke down when policy rates reached the zero lower bound. These policies also go under names such as balance sheet policies, quantitative easing and credit easing. Section 3.4.1 discusses the main issues related to these unconventional policies (see also Chapter 2 in this volume).

The crisis also revived the debate about the role of monetary policy in the presence of asset price misalignments and the build-up of financial imbalances. Until recently, the conventional wisdom had been that central banks should not lean against possible financial imbalances as they build up, but aggressively respond to the collapse. In part, the key arguments supporting this view rest on the assumptions that such systemically significant imbalances are nearly impossible to assess with confidence in real time, and that the costs of the clean-up are generally expected to be low and manageable.[12] There are other views that call for a more proactive approach. Cecchetti et al. (2000); Cecchetti et al. (2002); Borio and White (2004) and White (2009), among others, have questioned the conventional wisdom by suggesting that central banks should react to asset price misalignments and financial imbalances over and above what their effects on inflation during the usual policy horizon would call for. The crisis has reopened the debate regarding 'leaning versus cleaning' (White 2009).[13] Section 3.4.2 reviews the main issues.

Finally, the crisis has brought up the more extensive issue of whether the remit of central banks should be extended beyond securing low and stable rates of inflation (with some regard for fluctuations in output) to include the responsibility for ensuring financial stability. This raises a number of questions, starting with an operational definition of 'financial stability' and extending to the search for appropriate policy instruments for dealing with this additional objective and to the implications of an expanded mandate for the governance of the central bank, its independence from the fiscal authorities, and its communication strategy. These issues are taken up in section 3.4.3.

3.4.1 The Crisis, the Zero Lower Bound and Unconventional Monetary Policies[14]

The severe recession brought about by the global financial crisis elicited a strong response from central banks in the form of sharply lower policy interest rates. In some institutions – for example, the US Federal Reserve Board, the Bank of England and the Bank of Japan – the nominal target interest rates were brought very close to the lower bound of zero. Further monetary easing therefore cannot be achieved using traditional channels. In response, some central banks embarked on what have come to be known as unconventional monetary policies. These unconventional policies involve changes in the size and composition of a central bank's balance sheet rather than relying on changes in the cost of borrowing from or lending to the central bank.

Central banks may also resort to unconventional policies if the transmission mechanism linking the short-term policy interest rate to longer-term deposit and lending rates is impaired. As spending and investment decisions by households and firms depend primarily on longer-term rates, severing the link between the policy interest rate and these longer-term rates would limit the effectiveness of conventional monetary policy measures. The relationship between short-term policy rates and longer-term lending rates depends not only on expected future short rates as is the case with the standard expectations theory of the yield curve, but also on liquidity and risk premia. The importance of the latter was particularly strong during the recent global financial crisis.

In order to assess whether there is a case for unconventional monetary policies to be used independently from the interest rate, it is useful to review the full range of policy instruments available to central banks.[15] As noted, unconventional monetary policy instruments refer to those that affect either the size or the composition of a central bank's balance sheet. Stylized balance sheets of central banks and the commercial banking sector (Table 3.5) can be used to illustrate the main differences between the different types of instruments.

Quantitative easing (QE) refers to policies that aim to increase free reserves of the banking system with the intention to boost banks' incentives to expand lending to the non-banking sector of the economy. The two main methods are: (i) an open market purchase[16] of low risk short-dated government paper (TB in Table 3.5) from the banking sector in exchange for reserves (R); and (ii) to purchase foreign assets (F) in exchange for reserves.[17] Both balance sheet options can increase the size of a central bank's balance sheet, hence the term quantitative easing.

The principal difference between the two options has to do with the

Table 3.5 Stylized balance sheets of central banks and commercial banks

Central Bank				Commercial Bank			
Assets		Liabilities		Assets		Liabilities	
International reserves	F	Reserves of commercial banks	R	Reserves with central bank	R	Deposits	D
Domestic government bills	TB			Domestic government bills	TB	Capital	
Domestic government bonds	B			Domestic government bonds	B		
Other assets	OA			Foreign assets	F		
				Other assets	OA		

Source: Authors' construction.

impact on domestic short-term interest rates relative to the exchange rate. The open market purchase of domestic assets would naturally have a stronger effect on the interest rate, whereas the intervention in the foreign exchange market would impact relatively more on the exchange rate. The lower the degree of substitutability between domestic and foreign assets, the larger will be the differential impact.

It is important to note that in the ideal situation where financial markets are liquid and deep, a central bank following an interest rate policy setting rule allows the size of the balance sheet to be determined endogenously. During normal times in such an economy, the impact of balance sheet adjustments has, at best, a transitory impact on the stance of monetary policy. In other words, a decision to buy or sell a government security on the asset side of the ledger would require a similarly sized adjustment to offset the effect on total reserves in the banking system to ensure consistency with the policy rate target.

These arguments imply that the term 'unconventional' to describe policies that influence the size and composition of a central bank's balance sheet is suitable mostly when discussing central banks in advanced economies. In economies where financial systems are less developed, such policies are arguably more effective than the short-term interest rate in influencing lending conditions of the banking system. In these circumstances balance sheet policies become more conventional ways to conduct monetary policy.

Similarly, on the international side, the policy of intervening in the foreign exchange market against bank reserves results in normal times in the central bank sterilizing the effect of the intervention by selling an equivalent amount of domestic government bills. This is equivalent to exchanging international reserves (F) for government bills. It is therefore not a policy of quantitative easing and it is intended to influence the exchange rate rather than the overall liquidity in the banking system. In addition, unless it is done as a repurchase agreement at a predetermined exchange rate, it will also lead to a change in foreign exchange risk taken on by a central bank.

Credit easing (CE) describes policies aimed at affecting the composition of a central bank's balance sheet leaving the size unchanged. In terms of the stylized balance sheets in Table 3.5, the policy could take two forms: one involving an exchange of government bills for government bonds, and the other a purchase of other assets (OA) from commercial banks against government bills.[18] The former policy could be more accurately described as a yield curve policy as its intention is to alter conditions in long-term debt markets relative to those in shorter maturities and, by so doing, influence conditions in longer-term private credit markets.[19]

Purchasing claims on the non-financial private sector from commercial banks in exchange for risk-free government bills is intended to ease credit conditions for the non-banking sector. It implies that a central bank takes credit risk onto its balance sheet. Like the yield curve policy, its effectiveness depends on a certain degree of imperfect substitutability between the assets on the two sides of the transaction. While this is a plausible assumption when considering central bank purchases of mortgage backed securities or commercial paper against government bills in periods of market stress, it is more debatable in the case of exchanging short-term for long-term government securities, at least during normal market conditions. In economies where fixed-income markets are highly liquid it is believed that the relative supplies of short-term versus long-term government debt do not have a significant influence on the slope of the yield curve.[20] During the recent crisis, however, market conditions were not normal, and efforts by central banks to reduce term premia by purchasing long-term government debt appear to have had some success (BIS 2009a). One aspect of this success that deserves greater study is the differential roles of the signaling channel and of the actual purchases in boosting market confidence and in promoting a return to normalcy.

Looking beyond the recent crisis, an important issue for central banks is whether QE and CE policies should become part of the standard monetary policy toolkit to be available and used also during more normal conditions. With respect to quantitative easing the answer depends essentially on two essential conditions: (i) whether a central bank can influence both a short-term interest rate and the quantity of reserves in the banking system; and (ii) whether the impact of monetary policy is different when it is carried out by setting a short-term interest rate as opposed to the quantity of reserves.

When the interest rate is not at or close to the zero lower bound, and if the short-term interbank money market is highly efficient, the answer is, to a first approximation, that a central bank can influence either the interest rate or the quantity of reserves in the system, but not both. This suggests that as economies recover, those central banks using policy rate targets would find QE-type policies ineffective.[21]

Whether pure credit-easing policies should remain in a central bank's toolbox raises several additional issues. The most fundamental issue is that such policies involve a central bank directly in the financial intermediation process, arguably something that is best left to the private sector.[22] In addition, by taking on credit risk, a central bank runs the risk of having to ask its government for additional capital in case a significant portion of its credit portfolio underperforms. This in turn could compromise its political independence and lead to a deterioration of its ability to carry out its mandate.

A final issue is whether central bank policy should take more explicit account of variations in the spread between the overnight policy interest rate and the longer-term interest rate that enters into consumption and investment decisions. To the extent that this spread is variable and determined by some factors other than expected future policy rates, the answer is straightforward: the policy rate should be adjusted as a function of the spread in order that monetary conditions relevant for private sector intertemporal spending are consistent with the price stability objective of a central bank.[23] Extending the argument, it might be asked where in the term structure a central bank should intervene. If the majority of macroeconomic decisions are based on the n-month interest rate, should a central bank then not specify its target in terms of this interest rate and intervene directly in that segment of the market? The conventional objection to this idea is that it would make short-term interest rates more variable and could hinder the development of the overnight interbank market that is central for banks' liquidity management. The fact that the Swiss National Bank sets its policy target rate in terms of a three-month interest rate and not an overnight rate, and has been quite successful judged by its record of delivering price stability, casts some doubt on this objection. At a minimum, the issue deserves further study.

3.4.2 Financial Imbalances and Monetary Policy

Having observed that inflation-targeting economies were not spared from the fallout of the crisis, some observers have concluded that this monetary policy framework is no longer appropriate and needs to be replaced.[24] This assessment seems to be based on the view that by focusing too resolutely on the rate of inflation in setting policy interest rates, central banks failed to take into account the build-up of financial imbalances and asset price bubbles that ultimately precipitated the financial crisis.

We take the view that paying attention to financial imbalances and asset price misalignments is not incompatible with vigorously targeting inflation as the objective of central bank policy. On the contrary, we have previously argued that they are complementary (Cecchetti et al. 2002; Filardo 2004). For example, the report *Asset Prices and Central Bank Policy* contained the following statement:

> a central bank concerned with stabilizing inflation about a specific target level is likely to achieve superior performance by adjusting its policy instruments not only in response to its forecasts of future inflation and the output gap, but also to asset prices. (Cecchetti et al. 2000: xix)

At the time, this was a distinct minority view, but as noted above, while it is now less controversial, a consensus has not yet emerged. So what is the argument about? One way to frame this question more specifically is to pose the issue as follows: when formulating its policy, should a central bank consider the movements in asset prices over and above their influence on the inflation gap and the output gap?

In order to make some headway and to avoid misinterpretation, it is important to have a common understanding of what are the assumed objectives of monetary policy. In this section, we stick to the conventional case where a central bank attempts to minimize some combination of fluctuations in inflation around a target value and fluctuations of output around its natural level (the output gap, for short). In view of the lags with which monetary policy operates on the economy, it is clear that a central bank must be forward-looking and set its policy in response to deviations of future expected inflation and output levels from their respective targets. From this it follows that if a central bank takes into account the expected levels of inflation and output at all future horizons, weighted by the appropriate discount factor, then all relevant information is already factored in and there is no reason to include additional variables such as asset prices – or, for that matter, monetary aggregates – in the decision-making process. So to make the issue interesting, we must consider the case in which a central bank focuses on some particular horizon, two years say, as this is commonly used by central banks.

In Cecchetti et al. (2000), the issue was addressed by simulating a theoretical macroeconomic model that included a process that could generate asset price misalignments under different assumptions about the form of the monetary policy rule. The conclusion based on these simulations was that giving a small weight to asset price developments improved the performance of the economy as judged by an ad hoc welfare function that depended on the present discounted value of inflation and output deviations.

It is possible to construct counter examples where adjusting a policy interest rate in response to asset price misalignments would be counterproductive. The paper by Gruen et al. (2005) is such an example. However, it is also not robust to modification in the assumed stochastic process for asset prices (Haugh 2008). So the conclusions we draw appear to be model dependent. But this does not mean that we should ignore potentially relevant information, only that we cannot react to it mechanically without reflection.

A number of additional arguments have been raised purporting to show that reaction to asset price developments would be a mistake. Some of these are based on a different notion than ours of what reacting to asset prices means.

One objection argues that stabilizing asset prices would require such large adjustments in the policy interest rate that it would be destabilizing for inflation, output and employment. While this may be the case, it is not relevant for the issue as we see it. When we advocate taking asset price developments into account, we make it clear that it is for the purpose of stabilizing inflation and output, not for stabilizing asset prices themselves. For this reason the reaction to asset prices is likely to be relatively muted – that is, it would be to lean against the wind of asset price developments not to attempt to target some particular value.

A second objection claims that targeting an asset price is dangerous because we do not know what its equilibrium value is. As with the previous point, this argument is based on the idea that the central bank should try to achieve some particular value of the asset price – that is, that it should target asset prices. This is not what proponents have in mind. As with the output gap, a central bank does need to base its actions on an estimate of the difference between the actual and the equilibrium value of the variable it monitors. When there is uncertainty about the equilibrium value, it would be important to allow for some margin of error within which no action is taken as suggested by Haugh (2008). In other words, the policy reaction would be subject to some threshold effect. In addition, it may be useful to combine asset price information with information about credit or money growth in the economy to gauge whether there is a case for policy adjustment (Borio and Lowe 2002; Borio and Drehmann 2009). The implication is that theoretical and empirical modeling efforts must incorporate non-linearities explicitly in order to be informative (Filardo 2006).

According to a third objection, articulated notably by the former chairman of the US Federal Reserve, Alan Greenspan, monetary policy should not worry about the build-up of asset price bubbles, but should react swiftly and forcefully to the bursting of the bubble. This argument for an asymmetric response is based on the idea that it is difficult to identify the emergence of a bubble because the build-up is incremental in nature, whereas it is obvious when a bubble bursts. In addition, the sharp decline in the asset price associated with the bursting of the bubble can be very costly. This argument seems to stand William McChesney Martin's dictum on its head, namely: 'that we should keep the party bowl well filled because we do not really know the capacity of each partygoer to hold his liquor'.[25] Instead we should just be ready to treat the hangover. This asymmetry seems to be a recipe for moral hazard, because by promising to clean up after a collapse in asset prices we may make investors less likely to exercise appropriate caution on the way up. We are not arguing that a central bank should stand idly on the sidelines if financial instability and recession are brought about by a sharp asset price decline. We are arguing, however, that tightening policy somewhat in response to emerging asset price overvaluations would lead to a better outcome.

In an open economy context, the issue of reacting to financial imbalances or asset price movements naturally translates into a debate about whether a central bank should pay attention to exchange rate movements in deciding on monetary policy. Of course, to the extent that exchange rate movements have an impact on a central bank's inflation forecast at the policy horizon, they will already be factored in. Hence the question is again whether an additional policy adjustment is justifiable. In the context of emerging markets the issue is particularly important in periods of sudden capital inflows or outflows. Temporary surges of capital flows can have large impacts on the exchange rate, often pushing it well beyond a value reasonably implied by a conventional medium-term equilibrium analysis – that is, based on relative inflation rates and differential growth rates of productivity. The resulting misalignments can have undesirable real effects on the economy not unlike those associated with the 'Dutch disease', and a case can be made that a central bank should adjust its monetary policy to lean against the build-up of the misalignment.[26]

There are difficulties associated with the assessment of the nature of capital flows and the measurement of the equilibrium value of the exchange rate, but these are not unlike those a central bank faces in analyzing shocks to output or inflation, or in measuring the output gap. Therefore, in principle, these difficulties cannot justify inaction.

The reaction to exchange rate misalignments may take the form of direct interventions in the foreign exchange market. Indeed this may be the most efficient policy response in the case where domestic and foreign assets are not perfect substitutes. Do such interventions constitute 'beggar-thy-neighbor' behavior harmful to trading partners? We argue that they do not when they are undertaken to lean against misalignments in the exchange rate, because in this case they prevent rather than promote distorted relative price movements.

3.4.3 Financial Stability as an Additional Objective

The near collapse of the financial system during the height of the crisis triggered a more fundamental questioning of the role of central banks; namely whether the objective of their policy formulation should be extended to ensure financial stability in addition to monetary stability. While many central banks already undertake assessments of the stability of their financial systems, and publish financial stability reports in addition to inflation reports or monetary stability reports, these assessments do not typically form the basis for specific policy recommendations the way inflation reports do.

Adding financial stability to the objectives raises a number of difficult issues, including: is a central bank able to deliver financial stability using policy tools at its disposal? Could there be trade-offs between measures to deliver financial stability and monetary stability, and if so how should they to be resolved? What are the implications for the governance structure of a central bank if it is charged with delivering financial stability in addition to monetary stability? This subsection reviews the evolving debate regarding these questions.

In pursuing monetary stability, or more precisely price stability, a central bank can rely on: (i) a relatively clear and precise definition of its objective; (ii) a body of theory and empirical evidence relating to the determinants of price stability as well as the relationship between the policy instrument(s) and the ultimate objective; and (iii) readily available and relatively comprehensive data on the variables relevant for carrying out the mandate.

With respect to financial stability the situation is almost completely the reverse. There is no generally agreed definition of what constitutes a state of financial stability, let alone a single numerical indicator that could serve as a measure of success or failure. In fact, financial stability is typically defined by its negative, the absence of financial instability. But even here it has not as yet been possible to define a set of numerical indicators that could form the basis for a clear policy strategy. The problem is that financial instability can take many forms. It can be reflected in the banking sector or non-banking financial intermediaries, in short-term interbank money markets or in equity markets, in international financial flows or in exchange rate movements, among others.

Because financial instability can take many forms, there is no general model that can be relied on to account for all of its manifestations, and to link these to appropriate policy instruments. Partial equilibrium models of individual markets do exist, and while they can provide valuable insights about certain sources of financial instability, they are as yet not always well suited to provide recommendations with respect to specific policy actions.

As a matter of principle, for a policymaker to achieve a certain number of policy objectives it is necessary to be able to control an equal number of independent policy instruments. A central bank that is trying to achieve an inflation target while at the same time minimizing variability of output should ideally have two instruments, and adding a third objective related to financial stability would require yet an additional instrument. We may need to look beyond the traditional tools of a central bank for this.

In the area of traditional macroeconomic stabilization, automatic stabilizers in the fiscal system have proven to be useful complements for monetary policy. Other institutional arrangements relating, for example, to the functioning of the labor market or the tax code may also be relied on to make the economy more flexible and improve the ability of the economy to adjust to exogenous shocks.

Similar arrangements should be encouraged for the purpose of securing financial stability. The system put in place by the Spanish authorities comes to mind. This system involves requiring financial institutions to make capital provisions that are based on the state of the business cycle in a way that make them countercyclical (for example, see Fernández de Lis et al. 2001).

In response to the procyclical nature of a market-based financial system, the authors of the July 2009 Geneva Report on the World Economy propose to make countercyclical capital charges a feature of a new regulatory regime (Brunnermeier et al. 2009). They have in mind a scheme where the basic capital adequacy ratio (CAR) under Basel II would be multiplied by a factor that would be a function of, among other variables, credit expansion and asset price increases, as these are believed to be positively related to the build-up of systemic risk. They envisage that the scheme be governed by a regulator that has been granted independence from political and lobbying pressures.

But the strictures implied by the Tinbergen rule (the number of policy instruments needs to be at least as great as the number of policy targets) and the related assignment problem should not be overstated.[27] There are two basic reasons for not applying them too rigidly. First, goals related to financial, foreign exchange and capital flow volatility are not truly independent of the goal of price stability. Achieving price stability is a much more difficult task if stresses associated with these other factors are present in the economy. For example, if a strict focus on inflation control over a certain time horizon is associated with the build-up of imbalances in the economy that leads to inflation (or deflation) pressures further in the future, then it may be argued that monetary policy faces a trade-off between near- and longer-term inflation stability. Second, some central banks in the Asia and Pacific region have been able to achieve price stability while at the same time placing emphasis on exchange rate volatility, capital flows, and financial stability concerns (for example, in the People's Republic of China (PRC), India and Indonesia).[28]

This is not to say that central banks have an absolute or, in most cases, a comparative advantage in taking on these particular goals. But the experience in the region points out that one need not abandon inflation control when taking some actions to address these alternative, albeit subordinate, goals.

Even if additional policy instruments are available to deal with additional objectives, this does not imply that interest rate policy should be conducted completely independently of those other policy instruments. Coordinated actions involving all instruments are surely more efficient as some occurrences of financial instability may be related to general financial conditions rather than circumstances particular to a specific sector. In addition, there may be situations where there are conflicts between the achievement of price stability and financial stability. For example, concerns about illiquidity in the banking system may call for some form of easing of regulatory standards even if this may compromise the inflation objective in the future. If the policy interest rate is raised as a pre-emptive measure, the original illiquidity problem may become more acute, potentially eliciting a further regulatory response leading to an unstable interaction between the two policy instruments. In this case a coordinated policy response, in which the regulatory response and the interest rate policy are set cooperatively, is likely to produce a superior outcome.

Another situation where the interest rate instrument may have to be used in part to deal with a latent financial instability problem could arise if the agency charged with financial stability policy does not act for some reason. In this case it may be that a central bank has a comparative advantage (in the short term) to use the policy interest rate as a second-best solution trading off inflation and financial stability concerns.

The possible need for coordination between policies to deal with inflation on the one hand, and financial stability on the other, raises the question whether both policy instruments should be vested with a central bank. The benefits from coordination speak for combining both instruments in the same agency. Against such an arrangement it has been argued that assigning too many possibly conflicting goals to a central bank may negatively affect its credibility in carrying out its original objective of price stability. To guard against this, it may be desirable to separate clearly the duties by creating a financial stability committee that would be responsible for the analysis and policy recommendations with respect to financial stability policy. This committee would operate separately from the monetary policy committee, the primary responsibility of which would be to pursue price stability by setting the policy interest rate. Some organized form of coordination between the two committees would have to be designed, especially with respect to the effective sharing of information relevant to the two goals; in some cases, the ultimate responsibility may have to be accorded to the central bank governor. However the institutional arrangement is solved, the fact that there is a clear nexus between traditional interest rate policy and a newly created financial stability policy, and the potential for conflicts, points to considerable communication challenges for the policy authorities.

The issues discussed in this section are being considered by central banks and international bodies at the Bank for International Settlements (for example, the Basel Committee on Banking Supervision and the Financial Stability Board). Much theoretical and statistical work remains to be carried out in order for the pursuit of financial stability to be put on sound analytical and empirical foundations. Likewise, designing robust institutional arrangements, at both the national and international level, needs further analysis. In many ways, the work is still in its infancy; however, recent international efforts have instilled some confidence that much progress may be achieved in a relatively short period of time.

3.5 CONCLUSION

Monetary policy frameworks in the Asia and Pacific region have performed well since the late 1990s as judged by inflation outcomes. We argue that this is due to three principal factors: (i) central banks have focused on price stability as the primary objective of monetary policy;[29] (ii) the jurisdictions have put in place institutional set-ups that are supportive of central banks' ability to carry out their objectives; and (iii) economic policies have supported the pursuit of price stability, not least being the adoption of prudent fiscal policies that have reduced concerns of fiscal dominance.

The financial systems in the region have also held up well in face of the recent crisis, notwithstanding more adverse liquidity conditions in several markets and pressures on certain exchange rates that spilled over from the US and Europe during the crisis. Lessons learned from the Asian crisis have no doubt contributed to this outcome. The private sector learned about the perils of currency mismatches on balance sheets and between revenues and costs, and central banks found out that quasi-fixed exchange rates can be interpreted as a government guarantee. Consequently, the region entered the recent crisis in much better shape than it did the crisis of the mid-1990s.[30]

It may nevertheless be useful to ask whether changes in monetary policy frameworks should be contemplated. This chapter has discussed three possible areas of change: (i) whether unconventional monetary policies such as quantitative and credit easing should be added to the toolkit of a central bank's policy measures; (ii) what the role of asset prices and financial imbalances should be in the conduct of monetary policy; and (iii) whether financial stability more generally should be added as an objective to be pursued by a central bank in addition to price stability. We conclude that:

1. There is little need for unconventional monetary policies in normal times and where financial markets are well developed, because in this environment policies designed to influence the slope of the yield curve are not likely to be effective, and policies where central bank substitutes for the private sector in the intermediation process are likely to reduce the efficiency of the financial market.
2. A good case can be made for elevating the role of the misalignment of asset prices (including exchange rates) and financial imbalances in the conduct of monetary policy.
3. Financial stability should be significantly elevated as an objective for public policy. Whether and how much of it should be assigned to the central bank is still an open question. Much theoretical and empirical work still needs to be carried out to have a firm basis for deciding.

NOTES

1. For an in-depth analysis of the global financial crisis, see Bank for International Settlements (2009a).

2. This section draws heavily on Filardo and Genberg (2009).
3. Australia; People's Republic of China; Hong Kong, China; India; Indonesia; Japan; Korea; Malaysia; New Zealand; the Philippines; Singapore; and Thailand.
4. Australia, Japan, Korea, New Zealand, the Philippines, Singapore and Thailand.
5. Fry (1996) is a forerunner in this respect.
6. Singapore is not included. Ahsan et al. (2008) also contains an exhaustive survey of the literature relating CBGI and economic performance.
7. The overall value is the simple average of the six subindices. Corresponding graphs for the subindices are available from the authors.
8. Graph A1e in Appendix 1 in Filardo and Genberg (2009) illustrates that this result is not the consequence of non-inflation-targeting central banks catching up. On the contrary, they have a higher index both in 1996 and in 2005.
9. The only exception is the legal independence subindex.
10. It may be thought that the excellent performance of the Asia and Pacific region is simply a reflection of the actual deflation experienced by Japan in the 1999–2008 period. The averages for the region excluding Japan (6.23 per cent during 1990–1997 and 3.32 per cent during 1999–2008) suggest that this is not the case.
11. Australia and New Zealand are notable exceptions to this statement. They had introduced inflation targeting in 1993 and 1990, respectively, and had successfully brought down inflation rates earlier than other economies in the region.
12. See Blinder and Reis (2005) for a spirited defense of 'mop-up after' strategy.
13. See White (2009). White uses the phrase 'leaning versus cleaning' to differentiate between the view that central banks should act proactively and 'lean' against the build-up of financial imbalances by raising policy interest rates, and the view that they should wait and adjust policy interest rates ('clean') only in the event that such financial imbalances lead to serious economic disruptions.
14. Unconventional monetary policies have been the focus of a number of recent papers. See, for example, Borio and Disyatat (2009), Shiratsuka (2009) and Stella (2009).
15. Even though they did not face the zero lower bound constraint and did not implement unconventional monetary policies as we define them, central banks in the region did take actions to counter disruptions in local money markets during the crisis. These actions included modifying collateral requirements for access to central bank discount windows and concluding swap arrangements with the US Federal Reserve Board and with others in the region (bilaterally and multilaterally) to be able to offer foreign currency, principally US dollar funds, to local financial institutions.
16. For simplicity's sake, we refer to 'purchases' of assets by the central bank. In reality, central banks mostly engage in repurchase agreements when they conduct open market operations involving either domestic assets or foreign assets.
17. The domestic asset used in the transaction does not necessarily have to be a liability of the government. The collateral used in the repurchase agreement typically varies across jurisdictions.
18. Other assets typically include private sector financial instruments such as mortgage-backed securities and commercial paper. In principle they could also include loans to non-financial enterprises.
19. Operation twist carried out by the US Federal Reserve in the US in the early 1960s is an example of such a policy. Under this policy the US Treasury retired long-term debt by issuing short-term debt. The intention was to ease conditions in mortgage markets which were thought to be competing with long-term government debt for funds while at the same time attracting (or at least offsetting) international short-term capital flows. The effectiveness of this policy has been called into question by numerous observers, among them former Chairman Volcker of the US Federal Reserve Board (Volcker 2002).
20. See note 19.
21. Again it is important to keep in mind that in economies with fragmented financial markets, QE policies can be more important than interest rate-based policies, because

the binding constraint on lending in such economies may be the availability rather than the cost of credit.
22. This leaves out the political economy question of whether the central bank or the government has a comparative advantage to do so.
23. See, for example, Genberg (2007) and Cúrdia and Woodford (2009).
24. Wolf (2009) has expressed this view.
25. William McChesney Martin, Jr, who served as Chairman of the United States Federal Reserve System from 1951 to 1970, is widely cited as having joked that the job of the Federal Reserve is 'to take away the punch bowl just as the party gets going'.
26. See Devereux and Engel (2007) and Engel (2009) for arguments with similar conclusions.
27. This and the next paragraph are adapted from Filardo and Genberg (2009).
28. For some evidence that capital controls have allowed the Reserve Bank of India and the People's Bank of China to manage both the exchange rate and domestic monetary conditions, see Ouyang and Rajan (2008) and Ouyang et al. (2007) respectively.
29. The Hong Kong Monetary Authority is a notable exception, but by linking its monetary policy to that of the US Federal Reserve, it has effectively 'imported' price stability as a policy objective.
30. For a detailed discussion, see Bank for International Settlements (2009b).

REFERENCES

Ahsan, W., M. Skully and J. Wickramanayake (2008), 'Does central bank independence and governance matter in Asia Pacific?', Paolo Baffi Centre Research Paper Series, 2008-27, available at http://papers.ssrn.com/sol3/papers.cfm?abstract_id=1263908 (accessed June 2009).

Bank for International Settlements (BIS) (2009a), *Annual Report*, June, Basel: BIS.

Bank for International Settlements (BIS) (2009b), 'The international financial crisis, impact and policy response in Asia and the Pacific', paper prepared for the Wrap-up Conference of the Asian Research Programme, BIS, Shanghai, 7 August.

Blinder, A. and R. Reis (2005), 'Understanding the Greenspan standard', conference proceedings of the Federal Reserve Bank of Kansas City Jackson Hole Symposium on The Greenspan Era: Lessons for the Future, 25–27 August.

Borio, C. and P. Disyatat (2009), 'Unconventional monetary policies: an appraisal', Mimeo, 17 September, Basel: BIS.

Borio, C. and M. Drehmann (2009), 'Assessing the risk of banking crises – revisited', *BIS Quarterly Review*, March, 29–46.

Borio, C. and P. Lowe (2002), 'Asset prices financial and monetary stability: exploring the nexus', BIS Working Papers 114, Basel: BIS.

Borio, C. and W. White (2004), 'Whither monetary and financial stability? The implications of evolving policy regimes', BIS Working Papers 147, Basel: BIS.

Brunnermeier, M., A. Crocket, C. Goodhart, A. Persaud and H. Shin (2009), *The Fundamental Principles of Financial Regulation*, Geneva Reports on the World Economy 11, Geneva: International Center for Monetary and Banking Studies.

Cecchetti, S., H. Genberg, J. Lipsky and S. Wadhwani (2000), *Asset Prices and Central Bank Policy*, Geneva Report on the World Economy 2, London: Centre for Economic Policy Research and International Center for Monetary and Banking Studies.

Cecchetti, S., H. Genberg and S. Wadhwani (2002), 'Asset prices in a flexible inflation

targeting framework', in W.C. Hunger, G.G. Kaufman and M. Pomerleano (eds), *Asset Price Bubbles: the Implications for Monetary, Regulatory, and International Policies*, Cambridge, MA: MIT Press, pp. 427–44.
Cuikerman, A., S.B. Webb and B. Nyapti (1992), 'Measuring the independence of central banks and its effect on policy outcomes', *World Bank Economic Review*, **6**, 353–98.
Cúrdia, V. and M. Woodford (2009), 'Credit spreads and monetary policy', NBER Working Papers, 15289, Cambridge, MA: National Bureau of Economic Research.
Devereux, M.B. and C. Engel (2007), 'Expectations and exchange rate policy', Working Papers 062007, Hong Kong, China: Hong Kong Institute for Monetary Research.
Dincer, N. and B. Eichengreen (2007), 'Central bank transparency: where, why and with what effect?', NBER Working Paper Series 13003, March, Cambridge, MA: National Bureau of Economic Research.
Engel, C. (2009), 'Exchange rate policies', paper prepared for the Wrap-up Conference of the Asian Research Programme, BIS, Shanghai, 7 August.
Fernández de Lis, S., J. Martínez and J. Saurina (2001), 'Credit growth, problem loans and credit risk provisioning in Spain', *BIS Papers*, **1** (March), 331–53.
Filardo, A. (2004), 'Monetary policy and asset price bubbles: calibrating the monetary policy trade-offs', BIS Working Papers 155, Basel: BIS.
Filardo, A. (2006), 'Asset price bubbles and monetary policy: a multivariate extension', mimeo.
Filardo, A. and H. Genberg (2009), 'Targeting inflation in Asia and the Pacific: lessons from the recent past', paper prepared for the Sixth Norges Bank Conference on Monetary Policy, Norges Bank, Oslo, 11–12 June.
Filardo, A. and D. Guinigundo (forthcoming), 'Transparency and communication in monetary policy: a survey of Asian central banks', BIS Papers, Basel: BIS.
Fry, M. (1996), 'Governance at the macro level: assessing central bank independence in Pacific Asia and other developing areas', Department of Economics Discussion Papers, Birmingham: University of Birmingham.
Garcia-Herrero, A. and E. Remolona (forthcoming), 'Managing expectations by words and deeds: monetary policy in Asia and the Pacific', BIS Papers, Basel: BIS.
Genberg, H. (2007), 'The changing nature of financial intermediation and its implications for monetary policy', in *Financial Market Developments and Their Implications for Monetary Policy*, proceedings of a conference organized by Bank Negara Malaysia and the Bank for International Settlements, Kuala Lumpur: Bank Negara Malaysia, pp. 127–47.
Genberg, H. and D. He (2009), 'Monetary and financial cooperation among central banks in East Asia and the Pacific', in R. Rajan, S. Thangavelu and R. Parinduri (eds), *Exchange Rate, Monetary and Financial Issues and Policies In Asia*, Singapore: World Scientific Publishing, pp. 247–70.
Gruen, D., M. Plumb and A. Stone (2005), 'How should monetary policy respond to asset price bubbles?', *International Journal of Central Banking*, **1** (3), 1–31.
Haugh, D. (2008), 'Monetary policy under uncertainty about the nature of asset price shocks', *International Journal of Central Banking*, **4** (4), 39–83.
Ouyang, A.Y. and R.S. Rajan (2008), 'Reserve stockpiling and managing its liquidity impact: the case of India', *Macroeconomics and Finance in Emerging Market Economies*, **1** (1), 75–91.

Ouyang, A.Y., R.S. Rajan and T.D. Willett (2007), 'China as a reserve sink: the evidence from offset and sterilization coefficients', Hong Kong Institute for Monetary Research Working Paper 10/200, Hong Kong, China: Hong Kong Institute for Monetary Research.

Shiratsuka, S. (2009), 'Size and composition of the central bank balance sheet: revisiting Japan's experience of the quantitative easing policy', *Monetary and Economic Studies*, **28** (November), 79–106.

Stella, P. (2009), 'The Federal Reserve system balance sheet – what happened and why it matters', IMF Working Paper WP/09/120, Washington, DC: International Monetary Fund.

Taylor, J. (2009), *Getting Off Track: How Government Action and Intervention Caused, Prolonged, and Worsened the Financial Crisis*, Stanford, CA: Hoover Press.

Volcker, P. (2002), 'Monetary policy transmission: past and future challenges', *Federal Reserve Bank of New York Economic Policy Review*, **8** (1), May, 7–11.

White, W. (2006), 'Is price stability enough?', BIS Working Paper No. 205, Basel: BIS.

White, W. (2009), 'Should monetary policy "lean or clean?"', Federal Reserve Bank of Dallas Globalization and Monetary Policy Institute Working Paper 34, Dallas, TX: Federal Reserve Bank of Dallas.

Wolf, M. (2009), 'Central banks must target more than just inflation', *Financial Times*, 5 May.

PART II

Exchange Rate Policy and Reserve Management Issues

4. International monetary transmission and exchange rate regimes: floaters vs non-floaters in East Asia

Soyoung Kim and Doo Yong Yang

4.1 INTRODUCTION

Changes in United States (US) interest rates have a strong impact on economic conditions in other countries. With the increasing globalization of most countries in the world, the influence of US monetary shocks has been a major concern in developed as well as developing countries. The mechanism of international monetary transmission has a long history of debate. The Mundell–Fleming framework for analyzing the impacts of monetary and fiscal policy in an open economy shows that monetary expansion raises domestic production and income, but the monetary expansion-induced boom at home is at the expense of the foreign country, through the expenditure-switching mechanism under perfect capital mobility and a floating exchange rate regime. However, empirical evidence shows that the effects of US monetary policy has positive spillover effects on the non-US Group of Seven[1] countries' output and demand (Kim 2001). In this regard, modern sticky price models can theoretically reproduce the positive spillover effects of US monetary expansion on foreign output (Obstfeld and Rogoff 1995; Betts and Devereux 2001).

However, different transmission channels can be formed in response to external monetary shocks under different exchange rate regimes. Di Giovanni and Shambaugh (2008) concluded that only in countries with currency pegs is real gross domestic product (GDP) growth affected by external monetary shocks. Countries with a free-floating rate regime show no relationship between real GDP growth and interest rates in the base country. They concluded that the main transmission channel is interest rates, in that pegged countries move their interest rates with the base-country interest rates while floaters do not. Frankel et al. (2004) also investigated the transmission of international interest rates to domestic rates depending on the exchange rate regime. They concluded that the full transmission of domestic interest rates occurred in the long term regardless of the exchange rate regime, but that short-term effects differed across different regimes. Moreover, they found that interest rates of countries with more flexible exchange rate regimes adjust more slowly to changes in international rates, implying some degree of monetary independence. On the other hand, Miniane and Rogers (2007) found no evidence that countries with more capital controls are less affected by foreign monetary shocks, implying that capital controls do not play a role in the international transmission mechanism.

Since the global financial crisis of 2007–2009, the question of how a country can mitigate effects from external shocks has been increasingly raised among emerging market economies. East Asian[2] economies suffered from the shocks that originated with the subprime crisis in the US. One interesting area to investigate is how US monetary policy affects East Asia. This is relevant for the choice of exchange rate regime in the region. East Asian economies have various exchange rate regimes, from hard peg to free floating. The question is whether the choice of a different exchange rate regime can result in different spillover effects from the US monetary shocks. If so, what should Asian economies use as a desirable exchange rate regime?

To address these questions, this chapter analyzes the effects of US monetary policy shocks on monetary and foreign exchange policy variables and exchange rates. The chapter examines whether interest rates of East Asian economies are unaffected by US interest rate changes, thereby showing monetary policy autonomy; and whether US interest rate changes affect the exchange rates of East Asian economies against the dollar, and the extent of foreign exchange reserves changes, which might reflect strong foreign exchange intervention, among other issues.

These are important questions in relation to the transmission of US monetary policy shocks, since different response mechanisms have different implications on the influence of US monetary policy shocks for East Asian economies. For example, appreciation of East Asian exchange rates following US monetary expansion can make East Asian economies suffer from a negative 'beggar-thy-neighbor' effect. A decrease in East Asian interest rates following US monetary expansion, however, could generate a positive spillover effect to East Asian economies.

In addition, monetary independence has played a central role in the debate over the choice of exchange rate regimes. The well-known trilemma theory states that a country cannot simultaneously enjoy a fixed exchange rate, independent monetary policy and free capital flows. With capital now being mobile internationally, this presumably limits the choice to either a stable exchange rate or monetary independence. Proponents of floating rates have argued that floater countries would be able to pursue their own independent monetary goals, while advocates of a hard peg have questioned the feasibility of such a strategy in a world of highly mobile international capital. On the other hand, even under a fixed exchange rate regime, theoretically monetary independence can be secured with the help of capital account restrictions.

To examine these issues, we employed a structural block-exogenous vector autoregression (VAR) model. The structural VAR model is useful to identify US monetary policy shocks, which are the focus of this chapter. In this model the US variables are treated exogenously to the variables of East Asian economies because most are small, open economies that have only a minor effect on the US or global economic conditions. The use of block-exogenous VAR modeling also helps to save degrees of freedom.

This chapter is organized as follows. Section 4.2 summarizes the institutional arrangements in East Asia including exchange rate regimes, monetary policy rules and capital controls. Section 4.3 presents an empirical framework. Section 4.4 discusses empirical results, and section 4.5 concludes.

4.2 EXCHANGE RATE REGIMES, MONETARY POLICY AND CAPITAL RESTRICTIONS IN ASIA

This section describes exchange rate regimes, monetary policy rules and capital controls or restrictions of selected Asian economies. These are important for understanding the monetary transmission mechanism and policy reactions because international monetary policy transmission and most policy options are endogenously determined by the institutional arrangements in each country.

4.2.1 Exchange Rate Regimes

Before the 1997–1998 Asian crisis, most East Asian currencies were pegged to the US dollar with different degrees of fixity. After the crisis, however, affected countries tended to move toward freer floating exchange rate regimes and to liberalize capital and foreign exchange markets. In addition, other emerging economies that had previously chosen relatively fixed exchange rate regimes also moved toward less fixed regimes.

Some scholars have argued that, when the crisis subsided, some countries moved back to less flexible exchange rate systems due to difficulties in maintaining a floating exchange rate regime. Indeed, there is growing recognition that the exchange rate regime a country declares often differs from its operational regime (Calvo and Reinhart 2002). Even though crisis-hit economies in East Asia including the Republic of Korea (hereafter Korea), Indonesia, Thailand, as well as non-crisis economies such as Taipei,China, officially describe themselves as having free-floating exchange rate regimes, most of them have substantially less flexible exchange rates than officially announced, due to 'fear of floating'.

The International Monetary Fund (IMF) exchange rate classification has a long history of comprehensive and frequent updating. The original IMF exchange rate regime classification categorized members' exchange rate regimes based on their official announcements. From 1975 to 1998, countries' exchange rate regimes were classified into three basic categories – pegs, limited flexibility (usually within a band or cooperative arrangement) and greater flexibility (managed or free floaters) – that were further divided into 15 subcategories. However, the IMF classification did not always reflect the true exchange rate regime of a specific country, as exchange rate regimes often differed from what the authorities officially declared them to be.

Recognizing this problem, we use four de facto classification schemes for exchange rate regimes. First, the IMF's de facto classification system, adopted in January 1999, combines available information on exchange rate and monetary policies and formal or informal policy intentions with data on actual exchange rate and reserves movements to reach a judgment on the actual exchange rate regime (IMF 1999). The new IMF system classifies exchange rate regimes into eight categories: a regime with no separate legal tender, currency boards, conventional fixed (pegged against a single currency or a basket of currencies), pegged exchange rates within horizontal bands, crawling pegs, crawling bands, managed floating with no predetermined path for the exchange rate and, finally, independent floating. Second, Levy-Yeyati and Sturzenegger (2002) constructed a de facto classification based on data on exchange rates and international reserves from all IMF-reporting countries from 1974 to 2000. They used three variables related to exchange rate behavior: exchange rate volatility, volatility of exchange rate changes and volatility of reserves. Third, Reinhart and Rogoff (2004) proposed a non-arbitrary de facto classification, a so-called natural classification. They employed extensive data on market-determined parallel exchange rates, and found that there was a gap between de facto and de jure exchange rate regimes. Finally, Ogawa and Yang (2008) investigated the degrees of exchange rate flexibility in Asia. In theory, fixed exchange rate regimes require volatility in reserves, but zero or near-zero volatility in exchange rates. Therefore, the index should be zero or near zero. On the other hand, free-floating regimes are characterized by substantial volatility in exchange rates with stable reserves. The index for free-floating regimes should be close to 1.

As indicated in Table 4.1, following the Asian crisis, East Asian exchange rate regimes have moved toward more flexible exchange rate arrangements in terms of both de jure and de facto classifications. However, various exchange arrangements coexisted in the region, ranging from a hard peg (currency board) in Hong Kong, China; fixed regimes in the People's Republic of China (PRC) and Malaysia; relatively flexible regimes in Korea, Thailand and Indonesia; to mostly free floating in Japan.

4.2.2 Monetary Policy Rules

Monetary policy is related to exchange rate regimes. As most emerging Asian economies have moved toward more flexible exchange rate regimes, most monetary policies in the region have changed to allow more monetary autonomy, with inflation-targeting policies as an example. According to Stone and Bhundia (2004), after the 1990s the number of East Asian economies using fixed exchange rate regimes decreased, while the number of economies using inflation-targeting monetary policy frameworks increased rapidly. This change contributed to the stability of prices in the region and the transition of emerging markets' exchange rate systems from fixed rate to elastic floating rate.

However, East Asian economies had a variety of monetary policy frameworks. According to Stone and Bhundia (2004), Indonesia, the Philippines, Thailand, Korea and Japan all used inflation-targeting frameworks, even though they differed somewhat in their exchange rate regime. More specifically, based on their IMF classification (IMF 1999), the Philippines, Korea and Japan had independently floating exchange rate regimes while Indonesia and Thailand had managed floating exchange rate regimes. Malaysia followed a fixed exchange rate arrangement and did not have an explicitly stated nominal anchor for its monetary policy, but rather monitored various indicators. The PRC targeted monetary aggregates and had a de facto conventional crawling peg exchange rate arrangement. Singapore managed its exchange rate as an intermediate target, a monetary policy framework that had been in place since the early 1980s. Singapore's high import rate and its role as a price-taker in international markets makes the country highly susceptible to imported inflation. Thus, Singapore considers the exchange rate to be a more effective tool than the interest rate for stabilizing inflation. This monetary policy framework, however, can be considered a variant of inflation targeting (Table 4.2). Despite having different monetary policy frameworks and exchange rate regimes, countries in the region have generally been able to keep inflation under control since 1995.

Table 4.1 Exchange rate regime classifications in Asia

Economy	Classification	1995	1996	1997	1998	1999	2000	2001	2002	2003	2004	2005
People's Republic of China	IMF	3	3	3	3	3	3	3	3	3	3	3
	Levy-Yeyati	NA	NA	NA	NA	NA	NA	NA	NA	NA	NA	NA
	Reinhart and Rogoff	4	4	4	4	4	4	4	NA	NA	NA	NA
	Ogawa-Yang	NA	NA	NA	NA	0.0	0.0	0.0	0.0	0.0	NA	NA
Indonesia	IMF	7	7	8	8	8	8	7	7	7	7	7
	Levy-Yeyati	Interm*	Interm*	Interm*	Interm	Interm*	Interm*	NA	NA	NA	NA	NA
	Reinhart and Rogoff	7	7	14/13	14/13	13	13	13	NA	NA	NA	NA
	Ogawa-Yang	0.015	0.053	0.311	0.652	0.309	0.301	0.593	0.395	0.183	NA	NA
Japan	IMF	8	8	8	8	8	8	8	8	8	8	8
	Levy-Yeyati	Float	Float	Float	Float	Float	Float	NA	NA	NA	NA	NA
	Reinhart and Rogoff	13	13	13	13	13	13	13	NA	NA	NA	NA
	Ogawa-Yang	0.552	0.283	0.381	0.562	0.363	0.309	0.381	0.272	0.339	NA	NA
Republic of Korea	IMF	7	7	8	8	8	8	8	8	8	8	8
	Levy-Yeyati	Interm*2	Fix	Interm*	Interm*	Fix	Fix	NA	NA	NA	NA	NA
	Reinhart and Rogoff	7	7	14	13	13	13	13	NA	NA	NA	NA
	Ogawa-Yang	0.101	0.065	0.408	0.219	0.147	0.107	0.163	0.140	0.100	NA	NA

Malaysia	IMF	7	7	7	3	3	3	3	3	3	3	3
	Levy-Yeyati	Float2	Interm*2	Float	Interm*	Fix+	Fix+	NA	NA	NA	NA	NA
	Reinhart and Rogoff	8	8	13	4	4	4	4	NA	NA	NA	NA
	Ogawa-Yang	0.193	0.201	0.385	0.351	0.0	0.0	0.0	0.0	0.0	NA	NA
Philippines	IMF	8	8	8	8	8	8	8	8	8	8	8
	Levy-Yeyati	Float2	Fix2	Float	Float	Float2	Float	NA	NA	NA	NA	NA
	Reinhart and Rogoff	4	4	14/13	12	12	12	12	NA	NA	NA	NA
	Ogawa-Yang	0.323	0.018	0.493	0.591	0.301	0.338	0.288	0.126	0.187	NA	NA
Singapore	IMF	7	7	7	7	7	7	7	7	7	7	7
	Levy-Yeyati	Fix3	Fix3	Interm*	Float	Float2	Float	NA	NA	NA	NA	NA
	Reinhart and Rogoff	11	11	11	12	12	12	12	NA	NA	NA	NA
	Ogawa-Yang	0.104	0.045	0.268	0.194	0.091	0.078	0.148	0.074	0.086	NA	NA
Thailand	IMF	3	3	8	8	8	7	7	7	7	7	7
	Levy-Yeyati	Interm*2	Fix+	Interm*	Interm*	Float	Float	NA	-NA	NA	NA	NA
	Reinhart and Rogoff	4	4	14/13	12	12	12	12	NA	-NA	NA	NA
	Ogawa-Yang	0.101	0.083	0.278	0.472	0.391	0.371	0.364	0.258	0.272	NA	NA

Table 4.1 (continued)

Economy	Classification	1995	1996	1997	1998	1999	2000	2001	2002	2003	2004	2005
Taipei,China	IMF	NA	NA	NA	NA	NA	NA	NA	NA	NA	NA	NA
	Levy-Yeyati	NA	NA	NA	NA	NA	NA	NA	NA	NA	NA	NA
	Reinhart and Rogoff	NA	NA	NA	NA	NA	NA	NA	NA	NA	NA	NA
	Ogawa-Yang	0.284	0.136	0.480	0.517	0.244	0.258	0.243	0.139	0.116	NA	NA
United States (FI)		0.559	0.617	0.246	0.393	0.445	0.490	0.755	0.739	0.840	NA	NA

Notes: IMF classification (Annual Report on Exchange Arrangements and Exchange Restrictions): Exchange arrangement with no separate legal tender = 1; Currency board arrangement = 2; Conventional pegged arrangement = 3; Pegged exchange rate within horizontal bands = 4; Crawling peg = 5; Crawling band = 6; Managed floating with no pre-announced path = 7; Independently floating = 8.

Levy-Yeyati (Levy-Yeyati and Sturzenegger (2002): NA = not available; Fix+ = inconclusive; Fix* = uncontroversial; Interm = dirty; Interm* = dirty/crawling peg; 2 = classified in 2nd round; 3 = outliers.

Reinhart and Rogoff (2004): No separate legal tender = 1; Pre-announced peg or currency board arrangement = 2; Pre-announced horizontal band that is narrower than or equal to +/− 2% = 3; De facto peg = 4; Pre-announced crawling peg = 5; Pre-announced crawling band that is narrower than or equal to +/ − 2% = 6; De facto crawling peg = 7; De facto crawling peg that is narrower than or equal to +/− 2% = 8; Pre-announced crawling ban that is wider than or equal to +/− 2% = 9; De facto crawling peg that is narrower than or equal to +/− 5% = 10; Moving band that is narrower than or equal to +/− 2% = 11; Managed floating = 12; Free floating = 13; Freely falling = 14.

Flexibility Index (FI): Ogawa and Yang (2008).

Table 4.2 Monetary rule classifications in Asia

	1995	1996	1997	1998	1999	2000	2001	2002	2003	As of 2003 (de jure)
People's Republic of China	XRP	XRP	XRP	XRP	XRP	XRP	XRP	XRP	XRP	Monetary aggregate target
Indonesia	ITL	ITL	ITL	ITL	ITL	ITL	ITL	ITL	ITL	Inflation targeting (2003)
Japan	IIT	IIT	IIT	IIT	IIT	IIT	IIT	IIT	IIT	Inflation targeting (price stability)
Republic of Korea	MoA	MoA	ITL	ITL	ITL	ITL	FFIT	FFIT	FFIT	Inflation targeting (2002; CPI)
Malaysia	ITL	ITL	ITL	XRP	XRP	XRP	XRP	XRP	XRP	No explicit nominal anchor
Philippines	XRP	XRP	ITL	ITL	ITL	ITL	ITL	FFIT	FFIT	Inflation targeting (2001; CPI)
Singapore	IIT	IIT	IIT	IIT	IIT	IIT	IIT	IIT	IIT	Exchange rate-centered
Thailand	XRP	XRP	ITL	ITL	ITL	FFIT	FFIT	FFIT	FFIT	Inflation targeting (2000; core CPI)

Notes: XRP = exchange rate peg; MoA = monetary aggregate anchor; ITL= inflation-targeting lite; FFIT = fully fledged inflation targeting; IIT = implicit price stability anchor; CPI = consumer price index.

Source: Stone and Bhundia (2004).

4.2.3 Capital Restrictions

Capital controls for limiting capital flows are common tools to mitigate the adverse effects of external shocks in emerging market economies. While capital controls can take a variety of forms, for countries that have substantially liberalized the capital account, more market-based controls – such as the Chilean unremunerated reserve requirement imposed on capital inflows – have been the predominant option in recent years. Thailand adopted this measure in December 2006, but encountered a severe side-effect of rapidly falling stock prices, suggesting that designing and implementing capital inflow control is not an easy task. For those economies that have already substantially liberalized capital flows, returning to the days of draconian capital controls or recreating a system of extensive administrative controls is no longer an option.

Evidence on the effectiveness of capital inflow controls is mixed. Country experiences suggest that the best market-based controls can lengthen the maturity of inflows; such controls can have little impact on overall volume. The effectiveness of capital control measures tends to weaken over time as agents in the markets find ways to circumvent them. At the same time, capital controls can produce adverse effects: they tend to increase domestic financing costs, reduce market discipline, lead to inefficient allocations of financial capital, distort decision-making at the firm level, and can be difficult and costly to enforce. To the extent that capital controls are effective only for a relatively short time, such measures might be used at the time of surges of inflows rather than as a permanent measure. But again, effective implementation is not an easy task. Administering capital controls requires highly competent country regulatory authorities as they must constantly look out for unwanted flows – often disguised – entering through other channels.

Countries with significant capital controls have tried easing restrictions on capital outflows in a limited manner to reduce net capital inflows. Easing restrictions on capital outflows can generate some capital outflows, reduce the size of net capital inflows, and hence mitigate the upward pressure on exchange rates. This policy was pursued by many emerging market economies in Asia during the period of capital surges of the early 2000s. As these measures are expanded, it must be noted that a more liberal capital outflow policy could invite more capital inflows as well. Thus, to be effective, these measures need to be combined with other measures, such as strengthening financial sector supervision.

Asia has shown a varying degree of capital account openness as the Chinn–Ito index for selected economies illustrates for 1995 to 2007 (Table 4.3). A similar diversity is shown by Kaminsky and Schmukler (2003), who constructed a graded index of financial reforms. This index has three components: domestic financial sector liberalization, especially of interest rate and credit controls; capital account liberalization; and the openness of the equity market to foreign investment. Table 4.4 displays the Kaminsky and Schmukler index for selected economies.

As indicated by both indexes, since the 1990s most Asian economies have gradually liberalized their capital account transactions. One interesting exception is Malaysia, which imposed tight capital controls in the aftermath of the Asian crisis in order to mitigate the adverse effects of capital outflows. Singapore and Japan were the most liberalized economies

Table 4.3 Chinn–Ito index in Asia

	1995	1996	1997	1998	1999	2000	2001	2002	2003	2004	2005	2006	2007
People's Republic of China	−1.13	−1.13	−1.13	−1.13	−1.13	−1.13	−1.13	−1.13	−1.13	−1.13	−1.13	−1.13	−1.13
Indonesia	2.54	2.27	2.00	1.05	1.46	1.18	1.18	1.18	1.18	1.18	1.18	1.18	1.18
Japan	2.27	2.27	2.27	2.27	2.27	2.54	2.54	2.54	2.54	2.54	2.27	2.00	1.73
Republic of Korea	−0.09	−1.13	−1.13	−1.13	−1.13	−0.09	−0.09	−0.09	−0.09	−0.09	−0.09	−0.09	−0.09
Malaysia	1.27	1.00	0.73	0.46	0.19	−0.09	−0.09	−0.09	−0.09	−0.09	−0.09	−0.09	−0.09
Philippines	1.18	0.14	0.14	0.14	0.14	0.14	0.14	0.14	0.14	0.14	0.14	0.14	0.14
Singapore	2.54	2.54	1.50	1.50	2.54	2.54	2.54	2.54	2.54	2.54	2.54	2.54	2.54
Taipei,China	NA	NA	NA	NA	NA	NA	NA	NA	NA	NA	NA	NA	NA
Thailand	−0.09	−0.09	−0.09	−0.09	−0.09	−0.09	−0.09	−0.09	−0.09	−0.09	−0.09	−0.09	−1.13
United States	2.54	2.54	2.54	2.54	2.54	2.54	2.54	2.54	2.54	2.54	2.54	2.54	2.54

Notes: Chinn–Ito index measures degree of openness of capital account; NA = data not available.

Source: Econbrowser (http://www.econbrowser.com/archives/2008/05/updated_chinnit.html).

Table 4.4 Kaminsky and Schmukler index in Asia

	1995			1999			2000			2001			2005		
	DFS	KA	SM	DFS	KA	SM	DFS	KA	SM	DFS	KA	SM	DFS	KA	SM
Indonesia	1	3	1	1	3	1	1	3	1	1	3	1	1	3	1
Japan	1	1	1	1	1	1	1	1	1	1	1	1	1	1	1
Republic of Korea	1	2	2	1	1	1	1	1	1	1	1	1	1	1	1
Malaysia	2	1	1	2	3	2	2	3	2	2	3	1	1	2	1
Philippines	1	2	1	1	2	1	1	2	1	1	2	1	1	2	1
Taipei,China	1	2	2	1	1	1	1	1	1	1	1	1	1	1	1
Thailand	1	2	1	2	1	1	2	1	1	2	1	1	1	1	1

Notes: The value for each sector – domestic financial sector (DFS), capital account (KA), and stock market (SM) – is presented for each economy, 1 being the most liberalized and 3 the least liberalized.

Source: Indices of Financial Liberalization Data (http://home.gwu.edu/~graciela/HOME-PAGE/RESEARCH-WORK/MAIN-PAGE/working-papers.htm).

in terms of capital transactions. Indonesia, the Philippines, Thailand and Korea were in the middle; while the PRC was the most restrictive.

4.3 EMPIRICAL MODEL

We used the following empirical model to analyze the effects of changes in US monetary policy on East Asian economies. Because many East Asian economies can be treated as small, open economies, we assume a block-exogenous VAR model in which the US variables are treated as exogenous to the East Asian variables.[3] By constructing a block-exogenous VAR model, we can also save degrees of freedom (compared to considering all the interactions between the US and individual East Asian economies).

US monetary policy and East Asian economies endogenously respond to the US or world structural shocks. As a result, simple analysis of the relation between US monetary policy and East Asian economies can be misleading since the simple timing relation between US monetary policy and East Asian variables can originate from non-monetary structural shocks. Therefore, exogenous US monetary shocks are identified in the following model, by using the Christiano et al. (1999) method.

The empirical model assumes that the economy is described by the following structural equation system:

$$G(L)y(t) = e(t) \tag{4.1}$$

where $G(L)$ is a matrix polynomial in lag operator L, and $y(t)$ is an $m \times 1$ data vector with m the number of variables in the model. In addition, $\mathrm{var}(e(t)) = \Lambda$ where Λ is a diagonal matrix and the diagonal elements are variances of structural shocks.

We assumed that the equation system (4.1) can be expressed as:

$$y(t) = \begin{bmatrix} y_1(t) \\ y_2(t) \end{bmatrix}, \; G(L) = \begin{bmatrix} G_{11}(L) & 0 \\ G_{21}(L) & G_{22}(L) \end{bmatrix}, \; e(t) = \begin{bmatrix} e_1(t) \\ e_2(t) \end{bmatrix} \tag{4.2}$$

where $y_1(t)$ and $e_1(t)$ are $m_1 \times 1$ vectors, $y_2(t)$ and $e_2(t)$ are an $m_2 \times 1$ vectors, $G_{11}(L)$ is an $m_1 \times m_1$ matrix, $G_{21}(L)$ is an $m_2 \times m_1$ matrix, and $G_{22}(L)$ is an $m_2 \times m_2$ matrix.

We assumed that $G_{12}(L) = 0$. This assumption is the restriction of block-exogeneity, which implies that $y_1(t)$ is affected neither by current nor lagged $y_2(t)$. In the empirical model, $y_1(t)$ are the US variables and $y_2(t)$ are the variables of an East Asian economy. Therefore, the US variables are not affected by the variables of the small, open East Asian economy.

In the US block, the Christiano, Eichenbaum and Evans method was applied to identify US monetary policy shocks. $y_l(t)$ is [IP_US, CPI_US, CMP, FFR, NBR, M] where IP_US is industrial production, CPI_US is consumer price index, CMP is commodity price, FFR is the federal funds rate, NBR is non-borrowed reserves, and M is monetary aggregate. Following Christiano et al., we identified FFR shocks as monetary policy shocks by imposing restrictions on contemporaneous structural parameter $G_{11}(0)$ that IP, CPI, and CMP do not respond to FFR contemporaneously and FFR does not respond to NBR and M contemporaneously (for contemporaneous structural parameters).[4]

For the variables of the East Asian country ($y_2(t)$), CPI, industrial production (IP), the call rate (or interbank rate) (CR), and the exchange rate against the US dollar (ERA) are considered. CPI and IP are important economic variables indicating the price level and production level of the country. CR and ERA are included since those variables show monetary policy and foreign exchange policy for each country.[5] The basic model includes only these four variables since the sample period is relatively short. Then, the basic model is extended to include M1 and foreign exchange reserves (RES) additionally, one by one, in order to infer more detailed effects on the foreign exchange policy responses of the East Asian country.

Since the variables on the right-hand side are different in the reduced form block-exogenous VAR model, ordinary least square provides inconsistent estimates. We estimated the reduced form block-exogenous VAR model with seemingly unrelated regression and then transformed to structural VAR model.

Since the sample period is short, we used monthly data. The sample period is January 1999 to June 2007, which corresponds to the period after the Asian crisis but before the recent global financial crisis when the US adopted unconventional monetary policy measures (for example, quantitative easing). A constant and two lags are assumed in the VAR model.

4.4 EMPIRICAL RESULTS

Figure 4.1 shows the impulse responses of interest rates, exchange rates, and foreign exchange reserves to US monetary policy shocks over 24 months, with 90 percent probability bands. The economy names are noted at the top of each column while the names of responding variables are noted at the far left of each row. To compare the interest rate changes of each economy with those of the US, the interest rate response of the US is also reported at the last column in each figure. In addition, the scale of the graphs in each row is the same, in order to facilitate comparison across economies.[6]

The US interest rate rises by 0.15 percentage points on impact and rises up to 0.2 percentage points in approximately 5 months. Then, the US interest rate declines back to the initial level in about 20 months. Theoretically, such increases in the interest rate are likely to weaken East Asian currencies against the US dollar when exchange rate flexibility is allowed. However, the exchange rate depreciation is not significant (based on a 90 percent probability band) in almost all economies, except for Korea in the long term and Japan. Even in Korea, the exchange rate depreciation is not significant in the short and medium term although it is significant in the long term. In Japan, the short-term and medium-term depreciation is different from zero with more than 95 percent probability.

The exchange rate responses are quite interesting, given that many East Asian economies allowed some exchange rate flexibility during this period. These exchange rate responses are mostly explained by East Asian economies' interest rate and foreign exchange policy responses. The interest rates of most East Asian economies strongly respond to the US monetary policy shocks. In the Philippines; Thailand; and Taipei,China, the domestic interest rate tends to increase as much as the US interest rate, which can fully nullify the effects of US monetary policy shocks on the exchange rate. Also in Singapore and Korea, the interest rate increases are significant. In other countries, such as Malaysia and the PRC, the interest rate does not respond much, but a significant drop in foreign exchange reserves is observed, which can also contribute to exchange rate stability in response to the US interest rate increase. These two countries, in fact, adopted fixed exchange rate regimes. In addition, the capital account restrictions of these countries seem to help to stabilize the exchange rate while keeping the interest rate unchanged. On the other hand, the Japanese interest rate does not respond much to the US interest rate changes. Although foreign exchange reserves fall temporarily in the medium run, this does not seem to be enough to fully nullify the exchange rate depreciation. As a result, significant exchange rate depreciation is found in Japan.[7]

These results suggest that the conventional exchange rate channel does not seem to play much of a role in the transmission of the US monetary policy shocks to emerging East Asian economies, excluding Japan. For example, the conventional exchange rate switching effect that can generate the opposite real effects in East Asian economies does not appear to be important. On the other hand, many emerging Asian economies did increase their interest rates in response to a US interest rate increase. This suggests that US monetary policy changes – for example, monetary expansion – are likely to have a positive spillover effect to Asian real economies, and will help to synchronize US and Asian business cycles. However, in countries with capital account restrictions and a fixed exchange rate regime (for example, the PRC) neither channel appears to play a role in the transmission of US monetary policy shocks. Finally, in a genuine free floater like Japan, the exchange rate channel appears to be important.

Some scholars argue that after the Asian crisis, East Asian economies tended to adopt more flexible exchange rate arrangements with liberalized capital accounts. Theoretically, even with liberalized capital accounts, monetary autonomy can still be obtained by a country with a flexible exchange rate regime. Reflecting these theories, these East Asian economies tried to adopt monetary policy frameworks that would provide stronger monetary autonomy, for example, inflation targeting. However, our empirical results show that, at least conditional on US monetary policy shocks, these economies neither allowed the exchange rate to move freely nor conducted an independent interest rate policy. Fear of floating may have prevented these countries from securing monetary autonomy.

On the other hand, the trilemma also suggests that monetary autonomy can be achieved even under a fixed exchange rate regime by restricting capital mobility. Our empirical results show that the PRC and Malaysia with fixed exchange rate regimes and capital account restrictions appear to have been partially successful in keeping domestic monetary policy independent of US monetary policy.

These results are interesting because most past studies, such as di Giovanni and Shambaugh (2008) and Frankel et al. (2004), have suggested

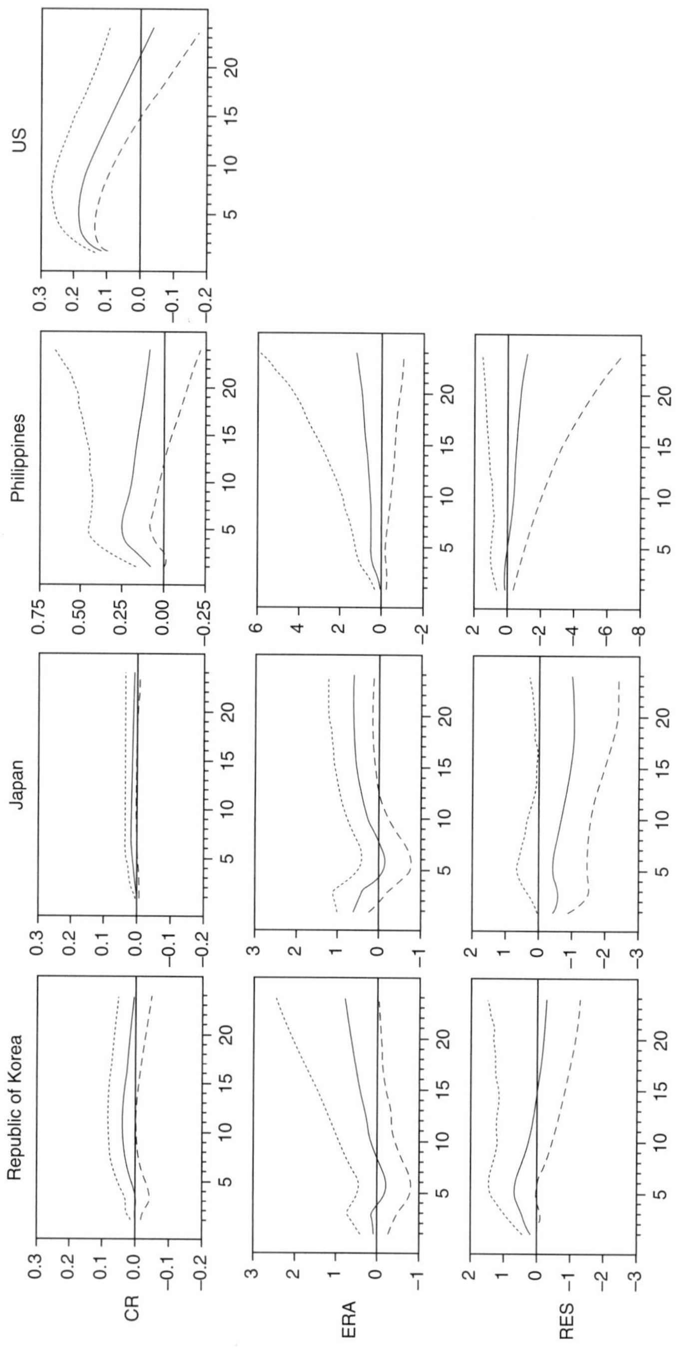
Republic of Korea
Japan
Philippines
US
CR
ERA
RES
0.3 0.2 0.1 0.0 −0.1 −0.2
0.75 0.50 0.25 0.00 −0.25
3 2 1 0 −1
6 4 2 0 −2
2 1 0 −1 −2 −3
2 0 −2 −4 −6 −8
5 10 15 20

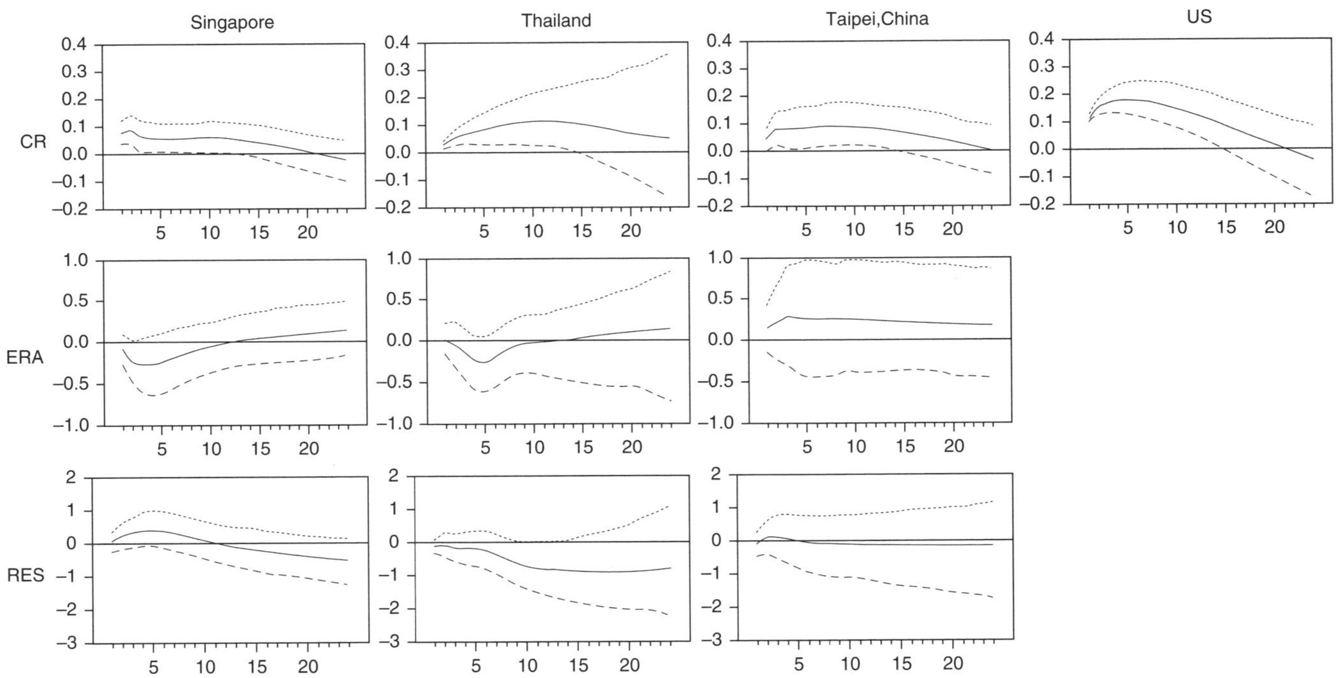

Note: CR = call rate; ERA = exchange rate against the US dollar; PRC = People's Republic of China; RES = foreign exchange reserves; US = United States.

Source: Authors' calculations.

Figure 4.1 Impulse responses of interest rates, exchange rates and foreign exchange reserves to US monetary policy shocks

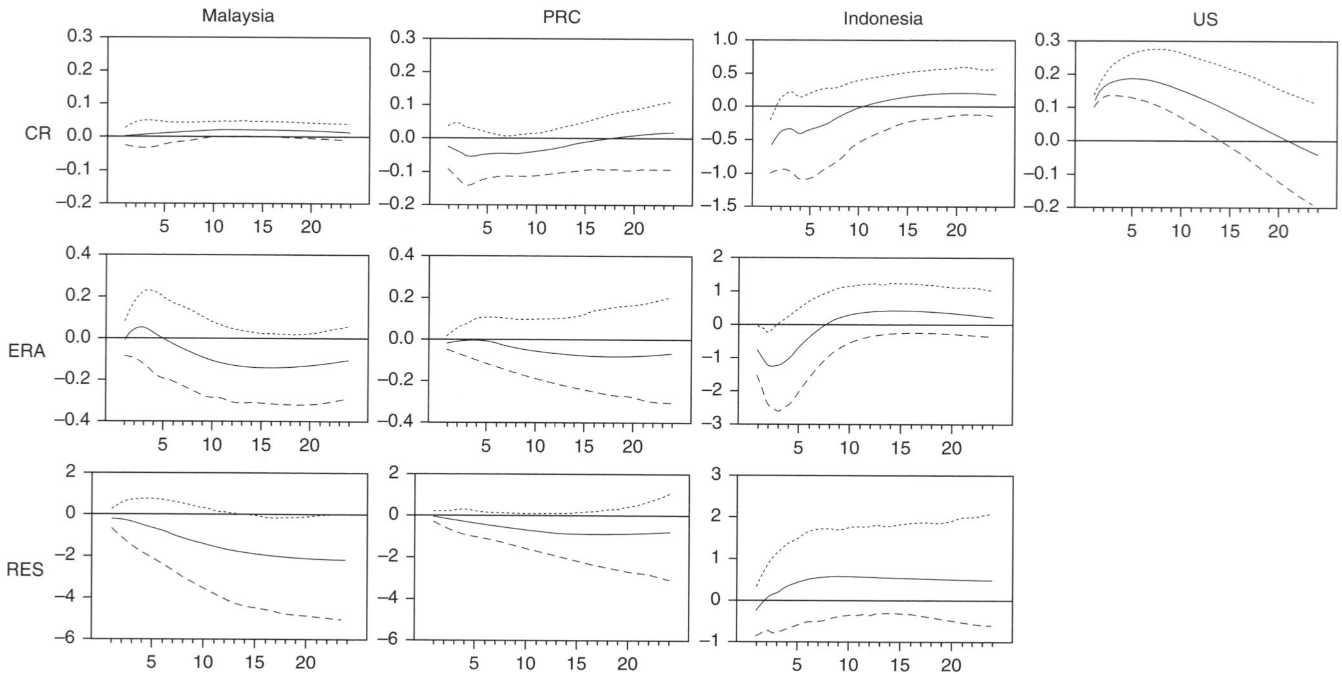

Figure 4.1 (continued)

that domestic interest rates respond more strongly in a fixed exchange rate regime. In our case, the fixed exchange rate regime countries imposed capital account restrictions, whereby contributing to their securing of monetary independence. On the other hand, in our sample at least some of the economies with a floating exchange rate were not genuine floaters, which may explain how their domestic interest rates responded strongly to US interest rate changes.

4.5 CONCLUSION

The impacts of the US monetary policy shocks on the exchange rates and domestic interest rates of individual East Asian economies differ depending on the exchange rate regime in place. The conventional wisdom suggests that in a floating exchange rate regime the expenditure-switching effect is the main channel, so that expansionary monetary policy in the US decreases real output in these countries while it increases output in the US. This effect occurs through the exchange rate channel. In contrast, the conventional wisdom suggests that in a fixed exchange rate regime, expansionary US monetary policy induces an increase in real output.

However, this conventional wisdom does not apply to Asia. This chapter has shown that the conventional exchange rate channel does not appear to play much role in the transmission of US monetary policy shocks to economies with floating exchange rates in East Asia, except for Japan, because they alter domestic interest rates strongly to offset a US interest rate change, and thereby give up monetary autonomy. This may be due to the fear of floating. On the other hand, in countries with capital account restrictions and fixed exchange rate regimes, such as the PRC and Malaysia, neither channel appears to play any role in the transmission of US monetary policy shocks. They enjoy independent monetary policy presumably as a result of capital account restrictions.

These findings are relevant not only for identifying the international monetary transmission mechanism framework in East Asia, but also for predicting the rebalancing process in the post-global financial crisis era. The expected prolonged expansionary monetary policy in the US will be helpful to Asia's floaters, as they will experience an increase in domestic demand and output without the corresponding expenditure-switching effects associated with US expansionary monetary policy shocks. The non-floaters may enjoy more room for maneuver in keeping domestic interest rates low. But such behavior may contain a seed of contradiction by prolonging the resolution of the global imbalances. If East Asian economies thereby continue to accumulate foreign reserves regardless of their choice of exchange rate regime, the global imbalances will remain, perpetuating the partial cause of the 2007–2009 global financial crisis.

NOTES

1. Canada, France, Germany, Italy, Japan and the United Kingdom.
2. East Asian economies here include the People's Republic of China; Hong Kong, China; Indonesia; Japan; Republic of Korea; Malaysia; the Philippines; Singapore; Taipei,China; and Thailand.
3. Although we used the same framework for all countries, it may be that the US is not fully exogenous to Japan and the PRC due to their large size. In this regard, the empirical results for Japan and the PRC should be interpreted with some caution. On the other hand, while an individual economy in East Asia is not likely to affect the US economy, Asia as a whole may affect the US economy (see Kim et al. 2009). We did not model such a possibility explicitly since such a modeling, together with analyzing the effects of US monetary policy shocks, is not easy, especially given our short sample period.
4. The US data are obtained from the database of the Federal Reserve Bank of St Louis. The intermediate material price index is used as the commodity price index. M1 is used as the monetary aggregate. We conducted experiments with various measures of commodity prices and monetary aggregates. Abnormal responses such as the price puzzle are relatively weaker when we use the intermediate material price and M1. Natural logarithms are used, multiplied by 100 for all variables except for the interest rate.
5. The data for East Asian economies are obtained from IMF International Financial Statistics and Census and Economic Information Center (CEIC). Natural logarithms are used, multiplied by 100 for all variables except for the interest rate.
6. The only exception is Indonesia.
7. Interpreting Indonesian responses is difficult in view of conventional theory.

REFERENCES

Betts, C. and M.B. Devereux (2001), 'The international effects of money and fiscal policy in a two-country model', in M. Obstfeld and G. Calvo (eds), *Essays in Honor of Robert A. Mundell*, Cambridge, MA: MIT Press, pp. 9–52.

Calvo, G. and C. Reinhart (2002), 'Fear of floating', *Quarterly Journal of Economics*, **117**, 379–408.

Christiano, L.J., M. Eichenbaum and C.L. Evans (1999), 'Monetary policy shocks: What have we learned and to what end?', in J. Taylor and M. Woodford (eds), *Handbook of Macroeconomics*, Amsterdam: Elsevier North-Holland, pp. 65–148.

di Giovanni, J. and J.C. Shambaugh (2008), 'The impact of foreign interest rates on the economy: the role of the exchange rate regime', *Journal of International Economics*, **74**, 341–61.

Frankel, J., S. Schmukler and L. Serven (2004), 'Global transmission of interest rates: monetary independence and currency regimes', *Journal of International Money and Finance*, **23**, 701–34.

IMF (1999), *Annual Report on Exchange Arrangements and Exchange Restrictions*, Washington, DC: IMF.

Kaminsky, G. and S.L. Schmukler (2003), 'Short-run pain, long-run gain: the

effects of financial liberalization', National Bureau of Economic Research (NBER) Working Paper Series 9787, Cambridge, MA: NBER.
Kim, S. (2001), 'International transmission of US monetary policy shocks: evidence from VARs', *Journal of Monetary Economics*, **48**, 339–72.
Kim, S., J. Lee and C.Y. Park (2009), 'Emerging Asia: decoupling or recoupling', ADB Working Paper Series on Regional Economic Integration No. 31, Manila: Asian Development Bank.
Levy Yeyati, E. and F. Sturzenegger (2002), 'Classifying exchange rate regimes: deed versus words', Univeridad Torcuato Di Tella, available at: http://profesores.utdt.edu/~fsturzen/DW2002.pdf (accessed 15 June 2009).
Miniane, J. and J.H. Rogers (2007), 'Capital controls and the international transmission of US money shocks', *Journal of Money, Credit, and Banking*, **39**, 1003–35.
Obstfeld, M. and K. Rogoff (1995), 'Exchange rate dynamics redux', *Journal of Political Economy*, **103**, 624–60.
Ogawa, E. and D.Y. Yang (2008), 'The dilemma of exchange rate arrangements in East Asia', *Japan and the World Economy*, **20**, 217–35.
Reinhart, C.M. and K.S. Rogoff (2004), 'The modern history of exchange rate arrangements: a reinterpretation', *Quarterly Journal of Economics*, **119**, 1–48.
Stone, M.R. and A.J. Bhundia (2004), 'A new taxonomy of monetary regimes', IMF Working Paper WP/04/191, Washington, DC: IMF.

5. Macroeconomic impacts of foreign exchange reserve accumulation: theory and international evidence

Shin-ichi Fukuda and Yoshifumi Kon

5.1 INTRODUCTION

Beginning in the late 1990s, a dramatic accumulation in foreign exchange reserves has been widely observed in emerging market and developing economies. As a result, by 2005 foreign exchange reserves of emerging market and developing economies, primarily in Asia and the Middle East, far exceeded those of industrial economies (Figure 5.1).

During the Asian crisis of 1997–98, emerging market and developing economies with smaller liquid foreign assets had difficulty averting panic

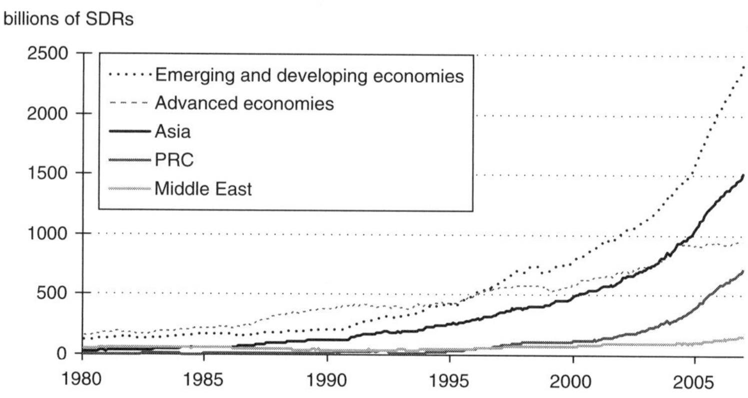

Notes: PRC = People's Republic of China; SDRs = Special Drawing Rights. Emerging market and developing economies include the PRC. Asia includes the PRC, but not Japan. Monthly, end of period.

Source: International Monetary Fund (2006).

Figure 5.1 Total reserves minus gold in emerging market and developing economies 1980–2005

in the financial markets and preventing sudden reversals in capital flows (see, for example, Corsetti et al. 1999; Sachs and Radelet 1998). Many emerging market and developing countries thus have recognized the importance of increased liquidity as a form of self-protection against crises. Replacing liquid, short-term debt with illiquid, long-term debt was a popular policy recommendation, at least initially. Ultimately, however, the course of action that most emerging market and developing economies took more seriously was raising foreign reserves. The acceleration in the accumulation of reserves was abetted by policymakers' desire to prevent currency appreciation and maintain the competitiveness of the tradable sector.

To the extent that a government's decision is exogenous, foreign exchange reserve accumulation will also influence and change the behavior of private agents. These changes in behavior may have various macroeconomic consequences that will be particularly important in the long term, when the temporary impacts of an accumulation in foreign exchange reserves disappear.

In this chapter, we explore the potential long-term impacts of foreign exchange reserve accumulation on macroeconomic variables in emerging market and developing countries. First, we analyze a simple open economy model where increased foreign reserves reduce the costs of liquidity risk. In the model, each representative agent maximizes the utility function from the consumption of tradable and non-tradable goods over time; the relative size of net foreign liquid debt to foreign exchange reserves reduces both the costs of liquidity risk and the liquidity premium. Given the amount of foreign exchange reserves, utility-maximizing representative agents decide consumption, capital stock and labor input, as well as the amounts of liquid and illiquid foreign debt. The equilibrium values of these macroeconomic variables thus depend on the amount of foreign exchange reserves.

An increase in foreign exchange reserves raises both liquid and total debt, while shortening debt maturity. To the extent that foreign exchange reserve interest rates are low, increased foreign reserves will cause a permanent decline in consumption, as well as move labor from the non-tradable to the tradable sector. However, if the tradable sector is capital intensive, increased foreign exchange reserves may enhance investment and economic growth.

The second part of the chapter provides empirical support for this theory using unbalanced panel data from the Penn World Table version 6.2 (Heston et al. 2006). The data cover 134 countries for 1980 to 2004. To allow a structural break after the Asian crisis, we included the post-crisis dummy in some regressions. The evidence on external debt shows that an increase in foreign reserves raises total external debt outstanding and shortens debt maturity. The evidence also reveals that increased foreign exchange reserves may cause a decline in consumption, but can also enhance investment and economic growth. These results are consistent with those predicted by theory, when the interest rates of foreign exchange reserves are low and the tradable sector is capital intensive. The positive impact on economic growth, however, disappears when we control the impact through investment.

It may be argued that an increase in foreign exchange reserves improves the current account, and consequently enhances aggregate output. In the short term, aggressive intervention could help maintain the competitiveness of the tradable sector, and manifest itself in a massive accumulation in foreign exchange reserves by the central bank. The argument may be particularly relevant in explaining reserve accumulation in the People's Republic of China (PRC), where the de facto dollar peg has been maintained. However, this is a Keynesian-type, demand-side outcome that will not be relevant in the long term. Even though the intervention may be effective in changing nominal exchange rates, the current account needs to be balanced in the long term, such that real exchange rates are fully adjusted to the equilibrium values. The results of our analysis are therefore instructive in determining the long-term, macroeconomic impacts of an exogenous accumulation in foreign exchange reserves.

In a previous study, Aizenman and Lee (2005) compared the relative importance of precautionary and mercantilist motives in explaining the hoarding of international reserves by emerging market and developing economies. Their empirical results suggest that precautionary motives have played a more prominent role in reserve accumulation. Meanwhile, a study by Rodrik (2006) revealed that reasonable spreads between the yield on reserve assets and the cost of foreign borrowing led to an income loss of nearly 1 percent of gross domestic product (GDP) in emerging market and developing economies that have rapidly increased foreign exchange reserves. In contrast, Levy Yeyati (2006) pointed out that the costs of foreign exchange reserves may have been considerably overstated in previous studies. He argued that to the extent that reserves lower the probability of a run-induced default, they reduce the spread paid on the stock of sovereign debt.

This chapter builds on these previous studies by investigating the macroeconomic effects of exogenous foreign exchange reserve accumulation, an issue that has not been well discussed in the literature. In particular, we distinguish liquid from illiquid debt and investigate how the maturity structure of external debt changes when foreign exchange reserves are accumulated. The model allows costs and benefits from foreign exchange reserve accumulation, as reported in the literature. It also incorporates both the tradable and non-tradable sectors, with different capital intensities. The different capital intensities are crucial in determining the long-term effects of foreign exchange reserve accumulation on capital accumulation and economic growth.

The rest of the chapter proceeds as follows. Section 5.2 sets up our small open economy model, while section 5.3 discusses the impacts of increased foreign exchange reserves. Section 5.4 provides supporting empirical evidence using panel data from the Penn World Table. Section 5.5 summarizes our main results and discusses their implications.

5.2 A SMALL OPEN ECONOMY

The main purpose of our theoretical model is to investigate the long-term impacts of accumulated foreign exchange reserves on macroeconomic variables in emerging market and developing economies. We consider a small open economy that produces two composite goods, tradables y_t^T and non-tradables y_t^N, relying on external debt. Each representative agent in the economy maximizes the following utility function:

$$\sum_{j=0}^{\infty} \beta^j U(c_{t+j}^T, c_{t+j}^N), \tag{5.1}$$

where c_t^T = consumption of the tradable good, and c_t^N = consumption of the non-tradable good. The parameter β is a discount factor, such that $0 < \beta < 1$. The subscript t denotes time period. The utility function $U(c_{t+j}^T, c_{t+j}^N)$ is increasing and strictly concave in c_{t+j}^T and c_{t+j}^N.

The representative agent is a net debtor in the international market. The budget constraint is:

$$b_{t+1}^A + b_{t+1}^B - k_{t+1} = (1 + r)\, b_t^A + (1 + r + \rho(b_t^A/R_t))\, b_t^B - k_t$$
$$- [y_t^T + p_t^N y_t^N - \phi(b_t^A/R_t) - c_t^T - p_t^N c_t^N - T_t]. \tag{5.2}$$

where b_t^A = net liquid debt outstanding; b_t^B = net illiquid debt outstanding; k_t = domestic capital stock; T_t = lump-sum tax; p_t^N = the price of the non-tradable good; r = real interest rate of liquid debt; and R_t = foreign exchange reserves. For simplicity, we assume that capital stock is tradable and that there is no capital depreciation. We also assume that $1 + r < 1/\beta$, to assure the existence of the steady state. Since the numeraire is the traded good, the real interest rate and the price of the non-tradable good are defined in terms of tradables.

Our model has two salient features that have not been commonly used in previous studies. One is a liquidity premium $\rho(b_t^A/R_t)$, which makes the real interest rate of illiquid debt higher than that of liquid debt. The other is an insurance premium $\phi(b_t^A/R_t)$, which increases as potential liquidity risk increases. In emerging market and developing economies, sudden reversals in capital flows are less likely when the borrower shifts its external debt from liquid to illiquid debt. The lender thus requires an interest rate premium when issuing illiquid debt. The liquidity premium $\rho(b_t^A/R_t)$ in the budget constraint reflects this premium. Unlike the liquidity premium $\rho(b_t^A/R_t)$, the insurance premium $\phi(b_t^A/R_t)$ is included as an independent cost in the budget constraint because it is a direct cost of holding liquid foreign debt. In our model, the net supply of domestic debt is always zero, such that b_t^A denotes net liquid foreign debt. As b_t^A becomes larger relative to R_t, the borrowing agent needs to pay larger costs to prevent a potential liquidity crisis. We assume that both of the premiums are increasing and convex in (b_t^A/R_t); that is, $\rho'(b_t^A/R_t) > 0$, $\rho''(b_t^A/R_t) > 0$, $\phi'(b_t^A/R_t) > 0$, and $\phi''(b_t^A/R_t) > 0$. This reflects the fact that a panic in the financial market is more likely when a country has higher (net) levels of liquid foreign debt, and less likely when it has higher levels of foreign exchange reserves. The relative size of net liquid foreign debt to foreign exchange reserve is thus a good proxy for the premiums.

In the following analysis, we assumed that each production function has constant returns to scale in capital stock and labor input. Denoting the labor input for tradable good by n_t and the total constant labor supply by N, our production functions are written as:

$$y_t^T = f(k_t^T/n_t)n_t \text{ and } y_t^N = g(k_t^N/(N - n_t))\,(N - n_t), \tag{5.3}$$

where $f' > 0$, $g' > 0$, $f'' < 0$, and $g'' < 0$. We defined capital stock held in the tradable and non-tradable sectors by k_t^T and k_t^N respectively. By definition, the total domestic capital stock is the sum of the two capital stocks, that is, $k_t = k_t^T + k_t^N$.

The amount of foreign exchange reserves R_t and the lump-sum tax T_t are exogenously given for the representative agent. The first-order conditions are thus derived by maximizing the following Lagrangian:

$$\begin{aligned} L = {} & \textstyle\sum_{j=0}^{\infty}\beta^j U(c_{t+j}^T, c_{t+j}^N) + \sum_{j=0}^{\infty}\beta^j\mu_{t+j}[b_{t+1+j}^A + b_{t+1+j}^B \\ & - (k_{t+1+j}^T + k_{t+1+j}^N) - (1 + r)b_{t+j}^A - (1 + r + \rho(b_{t+j}^A/R_{t+j}))b_{t+j}^B \\ & + (k_{t+j}^T + k_{t+j}^N) + f(k_{t+j}^T/n_{t+j})\,n_{t+j} + p_{t+j}^N g(k_t^N/(N - n_t))\,(N - n_{t+j}) \\ & - \phi(b_{t+j}^A/R_{t+j}) - c_{t+j}^T - p_{t+j}^N c_{t+j}^N - T_{i+j}]. \end{aligned} \tag{5.4}$$

Assuming interior solutions, the first-order conditions thus lead to:

$$U_2 \equiv \partial U(c_t^T, c_t^N)/\partial c = \mu_t p_t^N, \tag{5.5a}$$

$$U_1 \equiv \partial U(c_t^T, c_t^N)/\partial c_t^N = \mu_t, \tag{5.5b}$$

$$f(k_t^T/n_t) - f'(k_t^T/n_t)(k_t^T/n_t) = p_t^N[g(k_t^N/(N - n_t)) - g'(k_t^N/(N - n_t))\, k_t^N/(N - n_{t+j})], \tag{5.5c}$$

$$\mu_t = \beta\{(1 + r) + \rho'(b_{t+1}^A/R_{t+1})(b_{t+1}^B/R_{t+1}) + \phi'(b_{t+1}^A/R_{t+1})/R_{t+1}\}\, \mu_{t+1}, \tag{5.5d}$$

$$\mu_t = \beta\{(1 + r) + \rho(b_{t+1}^A/R_{t+1})\}\, \mu_{t+1}, \tag{5.5e}$$

$$\mu_t = \beta\{1 + f'(k_{t+1}^T/n_{t+1})\}\, \mu_{t+1}, \tag{5.5f}$$

$$\mu_t = \beta\{1 + p_{t+1}^N g'(k_t^N/(N - n_t))\}\, \mu_{t+1}. \tag{5.5g}$$

Under the assumption of perishable goods, it holds that $c_t^N = y_t^N$ in equilibrium. Since the numeraire is the traded good, the price of the non-tradable good p_t^N denotes the real exchange rate of this small open economy at time t, where a decline in p_t^N implies a depreciation of the real exchange rate. Equation (5.5a) implies that the real exchange rate is determined by U_2/U_1. Given the Lagrange multiplier, equation (5.5b) determines the amount of tradable good consumption. Equation (5.5e) shows that the amount of liquid foreign debt b_t^A is positively related to the amount of foreign exchange reserves R_t. This is because foreign reserves, which reduce liquidity risk, allow the representative agent to hold more liquid foreign debt.

At the steady state, the Lagrange multiplier μ_t is constant and equal to $\mu > 0$. This implies that all of the macro variables c_t^T, p_t^N, b_t^A, and $b_t^A + b_t^B$ are constant over time, in the absence of unanticipated external shocks. An unanticipated change in foreign exchange reserves affects the equilibrium values of these variables. However, at the steady state, it holds that $\mu_t = \mu_{t+1}$, so that equations (5.5d), (5.5e), (5.5f) and (5.5g) lead to:

$$\rho(b^A/R) = \rho'(b^A/R)(b^B/R) + \varphi'(b^A/R)/R = (1/\beta) - (1 + r), \tag{5.6}$$

$$f'(k^T/n) = p^N g'(k^N/(N - n)) = (1/\beta) - 1. \tag{5.7}$$

Equations (5.5c), (5.6), and (5.7) imply that b^A/R, k^T/n, $k^N/(N-n)$, and p^N remain unchanged at the steady state for alternative values of foreign exchange reserves.

5.3 THE IMPACTS OF INCREASED FOREIGN EXCHANGE RESERVES ON MACROECONOMIC VARIABLES

To determine the long-term impacts of increased foreign exchange reserves on macroeconomic variables, we explore the impacts of an unanticipated change in R_t on various macroeconomic variables at the steady state. A government has several alternatives for financing an increase in the amount of foreign exchange reserves. However, because of Ricardian equivalence (the assumption that households increase savings in response to expansionary fiscal policy), the method of finance will not affect resource allocation. We thus focus on the case where increases in foreign exchange reserves are solely financed by increases in the lump-sum tax T_t. In this case, the government budget constraint at period t is written as:

$$T_t = G^* + R_{t+1} - (1+r_R)\,R_t, \tag{5.8}$$

where G^* is exogenous government expenditure and r_R is the real interest rate of foreign exchange reserves. It is natural to assume that the rate of return from foreign exchange reserves is very low in the international capital market.

Assuming that there is an unanticipated increase in foreign reserves, we first consider the impacts of this increase on external debt and its components at the steady state. We denote the steady state value of variable x_t by x and its change by Δx. Since equation (5.6) holds at the steady state for any R_t, we obtain:

$$\Delta b^A/\Delta R = b^A/R > 0, \tag{5.9a}$$

$$\Delta b^B/\Delta R = \rho(b^A/R)/\rho'(b^A/R) > 0. \tag{5.9b}$$

Since there is no net supply of domestic debt, two types of debt b_t^A and b_t^B denote net liquid foreign debt and net illiquid foreign debt, respectively. Equations (5.9a) and (5.9b) imply that an unexpected rise in foreign exchange reserves increases not only liquid foreign debt but also the sum of liquid and illiquid foreign debt. Equations (5.9a) and (5.9b) also lead to:

$$\frac{\Delta(b^A - b^B)}{\Delta R} = \frac{b^A/R}{\rho'(b^A/R)}\left\{\rho'(b^A/R) - \frac{\rho(b^A/R)}{b^A/R}\right\}. \tag{5.10}$$

Equation (5.10) indicates that an unexpected rise in foreign exchange reserves always increases the share of liquid foreign debt to total foreign debt. This happens because foreign exchange reserves reduce liquidity risk, so that the value of holding illiquid debt declines. An unexpected rise in foreign exchange reserves not only has an income effect that increases total foreign debt; it also has a substitution effect that replaces illiquid foreign debt with liquid debt.

We next consider the impacts of increased foreign exchange reserves on macroeconomic variables. Recall that each of p^N, k^T/n, and $k^N/(N - n)$ relies solely on the rate of time preference, that is, $1/\beta$, and is independent of the amount of foreign exchange reserves at the steady state. This implies that an unanticipated increase in the foreign reserve has no impact on the real exchange rate or the capital–labor ratios of the two sectors, even in the long-term. However, the change in foreign reserves affects the steady state values of other macroeconomic variables such as consumption, capital stock, labor, and total output.

At the steady state, all the macroeconomic variables are constant over time. Since $y^T = f(k^T/n)n$, $T = G^* - r_R R$, and $c^N = y^N$, the budget constraint at the steady state implies that $rb^A + \{r + \rho(b^A/R)\}b^B = f(k^T/n)n - c^T - \varphi'(b^A/R) - G^* + r_R R$. Since b^A/R, k^T/n, and $k^N/(N - n)$ remain unchanged, we thus obtain:

$$r\Delta b^A + \{r+\rho(b^A/R)\}\Delta b^B = r_R \Delta R + f(k^T/n)\Delta n - \Delta c^T. \tag{5.11}$$

In addition, noting that $c^N = y^N = g(k^N/(N - n))(N - n)$, equations (5.5a), (5.5b), and (5.7) imply that:

$$\Delta c^T = B\,\Delta c^N, \tag{5.12a}$$

$$\Delta c^N = -\,g(k^N/(N - n)\,\Delta n, \tag{5.12b}$$

$$p^N = U_2/U_1 = f'(k^T/n)/g'(k^N/(N - n)), \tag{5.12c}$$

where $B \equiv \{(U_2/U_1)U_{12} - U_{22}\}/\{U_{12} - (U_2/U_1)U_{11}\}$. Since $B > 0$, equations (5.12a) and (5.12b) imply that consumption declines in both the tradable and non-tradable sectors when labor input increases in the tradable sector. Equation (5.12c) indicates that the real exchange rate is equal not only to the substitution rate of marginal utility, but also to the substitution rate of marginal transformation between the two sectors. The latter is the supply side determinant of the real exchange rate in our model.

Since $(1/\beta) - 1 = \rho(b^A/R) + r$, combining (5.12a) and (5.12b) with (5.9a), (5.9b) and (5.11) leads to:

$$\frac{\Delta(c^T + c^N)}{\Delta R} = -(1 + B)g(k^N/(N - n))]\frac{\Delta n}{\Delta R}, \tag{5.13a}$$

$$\frac{\Delta n}{\Delta R} = -\frac{\{(1/\beta) - 1\}\dfrac{\rho(b^A/R)}{\rho'(b^A/R)} + \{(b^A/R)r - r_R\}}{f(k^T/n) + Bg(k^N/(N - n))} \tag{5.13b}$$

Equations (5.13a) and (5.13b) determine the impacts of increased foreign reserves on total consumption and labor input in the tradable sector, respectively. In general, we cannot see whether the derivatives are positive or negative in these equations; while a low rate of return on foreign exchange reserves and increased total foreign debt reduce permanent income, a shift from illiquid to liquid debt may relieve the interest rate burden of foreign debt. However, we can show that $\Delta(c^T + c^N)/\Delta R < 0$ and $\Delta n/\Delta R > 0$, if and only if

$$r_R < [(1/\beta) - 1][\rho(b^A/R)/\rho'(b^A/R)] + (b^A/R)\, r. \tag{5.14}$$

The right-hand side of (5.14) is increasing in b^A/R. This implies that when b^A/R is large enough, an increase in foreign exchange reserves has a positive impact on consumption and shifts labor from the tradable to the non-tradable sector. This happens because increasing foreign exchange reserves reduces risk premiums when liquidity risk is sufficiently high. In contrast, the left-hand side of (5.14) is increasing in r_R. Therefore, when the interest rate of foreign exchange reserves r_R is sufficiently low, an unanticipated increase in foreign exchange reserves has a negative impact on consumption and shifts labor from the non-tradable to the tradable sector. When the interest rate of foreign exchange reserves is low, holding foreign reserves is costly and leads to a decline in permanent income in terms of tradable goods. Consequently, while the tradable sector expands to supplement this decline of permanent income, consumption declines in both sectors simultaneously.

Note that $\Delta k^T/\Delta R > 0$ and $\Delta\, k^N/\Delta R < 0$ when (5.14) holds, because capital–labor ratios k^T/n and $k^N/(N - n)$ are independent of the amount of foreign reserves at the steady state. Shifting labor from the non-tradable to the tradable sector increases capital stock in the tradable sector, but decreases the same in the non-tradable sector. We also obtain:

$$\frac{\Delta k}{\Delta R} = \frac{\Delta k^T}{\Delta R} + \frac{\Delta k^N}{\Delta R} = \left(\frac{k^T}{n} - \frac{k^N}{N-n}\right)\frac{\Delta n}{\Delta R'} \tag{5.15a}$$

$$\frac{\Delta y}{\Delta R} = \frac{\Delta y^T}{\Delta R} + p^N \frac{\Delta y^N}{\Delta R} \tag{5.15b}$$

$$= [f(k^T/n) - p^N g(k^N/(N-n))]\frac{\Delta n}{\Delta R'}$$

$$= f'(k^T/n)\,[\{f(k^T/n)/f'(k^T/n)\} - \{g(k^N/(N-n))/g'(k^N/(N-n))\}]\frac{\Delta n}{\Delta R}.$$

Equations (5.15a) and (5.15b) determine the impacts of increased foreign exchange reserves on total capital stock and total output, respectively. The impacts depend not only on the sign of $\Delta n/\Delta R$, but also on the relative capital intensity of each sector. When $\Delta n/\Delta R > 0$, increased foreign exchange reserves lead to an expansion in the tradable sector, but a contraction in the non-tradable sector. Consequently, when $\Delta n/\Delta R > 0$, total capital stock increases as foreign exchange reserves increase, if and only if the tradable sector is more capital intensive than the non-tradable sector; that is, $(k^T/n) > (k^N/(N-n))$. When $\Delta n/\Delta R > 0$, total output also increases as foreign exchange reserves increase, if and only if the tradable sector is more capital intensive than the non-tradable sector; that is, $f(k^T/n)/f'(k^T/n) > g(k^N/(N-n))/g'(k^N/(N-n))$. The relative capital intensities between the two sectors are crucial in determining the impacts of increased foreign reserves on aggregate capital stock and aggregate output.

5.4 INTERNATIONAL EVIDENCE

5.4.1 Impacts on External Debt

The main implication of our theoretical analysis is that an increase in foreign reserves has significant long-term impacts on several macroeconomic variables in emerging market and developing economies. The impacts, however, depend on the parameter values as well as on the interest rates. The purpose of this section is to test this theory using panel data on a large number of emerging market and developing countries. We first examine the relationship between foreign reserves and total external debt outstanding and their average maturity. In terms of liquidity, short-term debt is more liquid than long-term debt, because sudden reversals in capital flows are more likely when debt maturity is short. Shorter average foreign debt maturity can therefore proxy for the degree of vulnerability to foreign debt. Our theoretical analysis suggests that a rise in foreign exchange reserves not only increases foreign debt, but also causes a shift from illiquid to liquid debt. In the following estimation, we can therefore expect foreign exchange reserves to have a positive impact on total external debt outstanding and a negative impact on average maturity.

We estimated the following two equations:

$$\Delta(Debt_{j,t}/GNI_{j,t}) = a_1 \cdot \Delta(Foreign\ Reserve_{j,t}/GNI_{j,t}) + a_2 \cdot \log GNI_{j,t}, \tag{5.16}$$

$$Maturity_{j,t} = b_1 \cdot Foreign\ Reserve_{j,t}/GNI_{j,t} + b_2 \cdot \log GNI_{j,t}, \tag{5.17}$$

where *Debt* = total external debt outstanding; *Maturity* = average maturity of new commitments (years); *GNI* = gross national income; and *Foreign Reserve* = the amount of foreign exchange reserves. Subscript j denotes country j, while subscript t denotes year. The variable $\Delta x_{j,t}$ denotes the first difference of $x_{j,t}$. To avoid heteroskedasticity, foreign exchange reserve was divided by *GNI* in equation (5.17). To allow income differences and scale effects, we included *log GNI* as an explanatory variable in both equations. We also included auxiliary variables such as the import ratio, degree of openness, and an Asia dummy in equation (5.16).

Data on foreign exchange reserves was taken from the International Monetary Fund's *International Financial Statistics* (2006), while data on total external debt outstanding, average maturity of new commitments and *GNI* were derived from the World Bank's *Global Development Finance* (2006). The data is unbalanced panel data on 134 emerging market and developing countries, as classified by the World Bank (see Appendix Table 5A.1 for the list of countries). The sample period is from 1980 to 2004.

The method of estimation was ordinary least squares (OLS) with a constant term. To allow a structural break after the Asian crisis, we included a post-crisis dummy in some regressions. The post-crisis dummy is a time dummy that takes on a value of one from 1998 to 2004, and zero otherwise.

Tables 5.1 and 5.2 report the results of estimating equations (5.16) and (5.17), with and without the post-crisis dummy. Total external debt outstanding has a significantly positive correlation with foreign exchange reserves, and is negatively correlated with log *GNI*. The increase in foreign exchange reserves is financed by issuing new external debt when income differences are adjusted. The results are robust even if we include auxiliary variables. This supports the view that increased foreign exchange reserves increase external debt outstanding. In contrast, debt maturity is negatively correlated with foreign exchange reserves as well as with log *GNI*. This negative correlation implies that an increase in foreign exchange reserves shortens debt maturity.

Table 5.1 International evidence on the impacts on external debt (1)

$\Delta Debt_{j,t}$ = constant term + $a_1 \cdot \Delta Foreign\ Reserve_{j,t}$ + $a_2 \cdot \log GNI_{j,t}$,

Regression	1	2	3	4	5
Constant	7.0888**	7.6568**	7.0881**	7.0816*	6.9725
	(2.47)	(2.54)	(2.47)	(1.68)	(1.64)
Δ(*R/GNI*)	0.8547***	0.8525***	0.8580***	0.8542***	0.8552***
	(5.10)	(5.09)	(5.12)	(5.11)	(5.11)
log(GNI)	−0.6975**	−0.7755**	−0.6770**	−0.6225*	−0.6082
	(−2.18)	(−2.25)	(−2.09)	(−1.67)	(−1.59)
Asia-dummy		1.7918			
		(0.63)			
After98-dummy			−0.6220		0.1053**
			(−0.43)		(2.50)
Import/GNI				0.1049**	−0.0758***
				(2.49)	(−2.99)
Openness				−0.0763***	−0.2429
				(−3.03)	(−0.16)
adj. R squared	0.0153	0.0150	0.0149	0.0192	0.0187

Notes:

1. Number of observations = 1835 (134 countries, 1980–2004, unbalanced panel). The sample includes non-industrial countries only.
2. The method of estimation is pooled-OLS; t-statistics are in parentheses.
3. *Asia-dummy* takes on a value of 1 for five Asian countries (PRC, Indonesia, Malaysia, the Philippines and Thailand).
4. Openness is (Export+Import)/GDP (variable 'openk' of PWT 6.2).
5. Asterisks denote significance level of coefficient estimates: *** means at 1% level; ** means at 5% level; and * means at 10% level.

Source: Authors' compilation.

Our theoretical analysis implied that foreign exchange reserves reduce liquidity risk, so that their increase will cause a shift from illiquid to liquid debt. To the extent that short-term debt is more liquid than long-term debt, the empirical results support this implication. The negative correlation with log *GNI* implies that debt maturity is shorter in smaller countries.

5.4.2 Impacts on Macroeconomic Variables

Using the same panel data, we next examined the long-term impacts of foreign exchange reserves on consumption, capital investment, export share, and GDP growth rate. These are important variables to measure macroeconomic performance. Our theoretical model suggests that, when

Table 5.2 International evidence on the impacts on external debt (2)

$Maturity_{j,t}$ = constant term + $b_1 \cdot$ *Foreign* $Reserve_{j,t}/GNI_{j,t}$ + $b_2 \cdot \log GNI_{j,t}$				
Regression	1	2	3	4
Constant	44.6099***	44.8509***	44.7498***	45.1080***
	(41.25)	(39.60)	(41.46)	(39.86)
R/GNI	−0.0536***	−0.0549***	−0.0706***	−0.0729***
	(−2.90)	(−2.95)	(−3.72)	(−3.81)
Log(GNI)	−2.4161***	−2.4472***	−2.4807***	−2.5280***
	(−20.43)	(−19.42)	(−20.81)	(−19.84)
Asia-dummy		0.8480		1.2485
		(0.72)		(1.05)
After98-dummy			1.9947***	2.0435***
			(3.78)	(3.86)
adj. R squared	0.1390	0.1388	0.1434	0.1434

Notes:
1. Number of observations = 2411 (134 countries and 25 periods, unbalanced panel). The sample includes developing countries only.
2. The method of estimation is pooled-OLS; t-statistics are in parentheses.
3. *Asia-dummy* takes on a value of 1 for five Asian countries (PRC, Indonesia, Malaysia, the Philippines and Thailand).
4. Asterisks denote significance level of coefficient estimates: *** means at 1% level; ** means at 5% level; and * means at 10% level.

Source: Authors' compilation.

interest rates on foreign exchange reserves are low, an increase in foreign exchange reserves will have: (i) a negative impact on consumption; (ii) a positive impact on export share; and (iii) a positive impact on capital investment and output, if the tradable sector is more capital intensive than the non-tradable sector.

We estimated the following four equations:

$$Consumption_{j,t}/GDP_{j,t} = c_1\ (Foreign\ Reserve_{j,t}/GNI_{j,t}) + c_2 \cdot \log GNI_{j,t}, \tag{5.18}$$

$$Export_{j,t}/GNI_{j,t} = d_1\ (Foreign\ Reserve_{j,t}/GNI_{j,t}) + d_2 \cdot \log GNI_{j,t}, \tag{5.19}$$

$$Investment_{j,t}/GDP_{j,t} = e_1\ (Foreign\ Reserve_{j,t}/GNI_{j,t}) + e_2 \cdot \log GNI_{j,t}, \tag{5.20}$$

$$\Delta GDP_{j,t}/GDP_{j,t} = f_1\ (Foreign\ Reserve_{j,t}/GNI_{j,t}) + f_2 \cdot \log GNI_{j,t}, \tag{5.21}$$

where *Consumption* = domestic consumption; *GDP* = gross domestic product; *Export* = the amount of export; and *Investment* = domestic capital investment. Subscript j denotes country j, while subscript t denotes year. To avoid heteroskedasticity, foreign exchange reserves and exports were divided by *GNI*, while consumption and investment were divided by *GDP*.

Equations (5.18) and (5.19) explore the impacts of foreign exchange reserves on consumption and the export ratio respectively, while equations (5.20) and (5.21) investigate the impacts on capital stock and aggregate output. In equations (5.20) and (5.21), we used investment rate and GDP growth rate as dependent variables. If we strictly follow our theoretical discussions, we may use capital stock and the level of GDP as dependent variables in these equations. However, while consumption responds to a shock instantaneously, it usually takes a long time for capital stock to reach the steady state. In the estimations, we therefore explored whether investment and GDP growth are on the right transition path to the steady state, as predicted by our theory. To allow income differences and scale effects, we included *log GNI* in all equations. It may be of concern that the accumulation of foreign exchange reserves might be endogenous; however, the accumulation is a consequence of repeated changes in previous years. As such, reverse causality from the dependent variables to the level of foreign exchange reserves is less likely in our estimations.

The data on consumption, investment and GDP were taken from the Penn World Table Version 6.2 (Heston et al. 2006). The data is unbalanced panel data on 134 countries and the sample period is 1980–2004. The method of estimation is OLS with a constant term. To allow a structural break after the crisis, we included the post-crisis dummy in some regressions. The post-crisis dummy is a time dummy that takes on a value of one from 1998 to 2004 and zero otherwise.

Tables 5.3 to 5.6 report the results of our regressions with and without the post-crisis dummy. The coefficients of foreign exchange reserves are statistically significant in all cases. Foreign exchange reserve is negatively correlated with consumption in Table 5.3 and positively correlated with export ratio in Table 5.4. The results imply that an increase in foreign exchange reserves decreases consumption and expands the share of the tradable sector. To the extent that interest rate revenues from foreign exchange reserves are low, this is consistent with our theoretical results. Foreign exchange reserves are positively correlated with investment rate and GDP growth rate in Tables 5.5 and 5.6. This implies that the accumulation of foreign exchange reserves enhances capital accumulation and promotes sustainable growth in emerging market and developing countries. Our theory suggests that this happens when the tradable sector is more capital intensive than the non-tradable sector. Additional tests were

Table 5.3 Impacts of increased foreign exchange reserves on macroeconomic variables: international evidence (1)

$Consumption_{j,t}/GNI_{j,t}$ = constant term + c_1 $Foreign\ Reserve_{j,t}/GNI_{j,t}$ + c_2· $\log GNI_{j,t}$			
Regression	1	2	3
Constant	95.6620***	82.7353***	82.7034***
	(62.26)	(50.04)	(49.90)
R/GNI	−0.2537***	−0.1965***	−0.1948***
	(−9.05)	(−7.34)	(−7.09)
log(GNI)	−2.2701***	−1.2512***	−1.2425***
	(−13.64)	(−7.26)	(−7.10)
Asia-dummy		−9.0239***	−9.0628***
		(−5.88)	(−5.88)
Africa-dummy		10.1350***	10.1254***
		(14.90)	(14.87)
After98-dummy			−0.2070
			(−0.28)
adj. R squared	0.0985	0.1944	0.1941

Notes:
1. Number of observations = 2297 (134 countries, 1980–2004, unbalanced panel). The sample includes developing countries only.
2. The method of estimation is pooled-OLS; t-statistics are in parentheses.
3. *Asia-dummy* takes on a value of 1 for five Asian countries (PRC, Indonesia, Malaysia, the Philippines and Thailand).
4. *Africa-dummy* takes on a value of 1 for African countries listed in Appendix Table 5A.1.
5. Asterisks denote significance level of coefficient estimates: *** means at 1% level; ** means at 5% level; and * means at 10% level.

Source: Authors' compilation.

conducted for robustness, including the effects of changes in reserves and the current account, and using a neoclassical growth regression specification, which are described in Fukuda and Kon (2010). The results did not materially affect our conclusions.

5.5 CONCLUSION

The recent accumulation in foreign exchange reserves has reached record-breaking levels in many emerging market and developing countries. This chapter investigated the long-term macroeconomic impacts of this trend in emerging market and developing countries. First,

Table 5.4 Impacts of increased foreign exchange reserves on macroeconomic variables: international evidence (2)

$Export_{j,t}/GNI_{j,t} = d_1\ (Foreign\ Reserve_{j,t}/GNI_{j,t}) + d_2 \cdot \log GNI_{j,t},$

Regression	1	2	3	4
Constant	57.7109***	72.2412***	73.3367***	74.5535***
	(28.37)	(32.45)	(33.24)	(34.46)
R/GNI	0.6687***	0.6031***	0.5441***	0.4822***
	(18.02)	(16.72)	(14.89)	(13.28)
log(GNI)	−3.0394***	−4.2169***	−4.5163***	−4.5371***
	(−13.80)	(−18.17)	(−19.38)	(−19.89)
Asia-dummy		11.9238***	13.2619***	−17.0032***
		(5.77)	(6.47)	(−4.69)
Africa-dummy		−10.8637***	−10.5310***	−10.7252***
		(−11.86)	(−11.62)	(−12.08)
After98-dummy			7.1217***	6.3296***
			(7.33)	(6.63)
Asia(R/GNI)*				1.8677***
				(10.02)
adj. R squared	0.1928	0.2534	0.2702	0.3005

Notes:
1. Number of observations = 2297 (134 countries, 1980–2004, unbalanced panel). The sample includes developing countries only.
2. The method of estimation is pooled-OLS; t-statistics are in parentheses.
3. *Asia-dummy* takes on a value of 1 for five Asian countries (PRC, Indonesia, Malaysia, the Philippines and Thailand).
4. *Africa-dummy* takes on a value of 1 for African countries listed in Appendix Table 5A.1.
5. Asterisks denote significance level of coefficient estimates: *** means at 1% level; ** means at 5% level; and * means at 10% level.

Source: Authors' compilation.

we analyzed a simple open economy model where increased foreign exchange reserves reduce the costs of liquidity risk. An increase in foreign exchange reserves raises both liquid and total debt, while shortening debt maturity. It also leads to a decline in consumption, although investment and economic growth may improve when the tradable sector is capital intensive. Second, we attempted to provide empirical support for our theoretical analysis.

Since the late 1990s, financial globalization has been accompanied by frequent and painful financial crises. During these crises, countries with smaller liquid foreign assets had difficulty averting panic in financial

Table 5.5 Impacts of increased foreign exchange reserves on macroeconomic variables: international evidence (3)

$Investment_{j,t}/GDP_{j,t}$ = constant term + e_1 ($Foreign\ Reserve_{j,t}/\ GNI_{j,t}$) + $e_2 \cdot \log GNI_{j,t}$,

Regression	1	2	3	4
Constant	3.8187***	9.7789***	3.6617***	9.6381***
	(6.14)	(14.93)	(5.89)	(14.71)
R/GNI	0.1423***	0.1127***	0.1511***	0.1203***
	(12.55)	(10.63)	(13.04)	(11.09)
log(GNI)	0.7476***	0.2035***	0.7889***	0.2420***
	(11.11)	(2.98)	(11.57)	(3.50)
Asia-dummy		8.2814***		8.1094***
		(13.63)		(13.32)
Africa-dummy		−3.4497***		−3.4925***
		(−12.81)		(−12.97)
After98-dummy			−1.0852***	−0.9155***
			(−3.50)	(−3.17)
adj. R squared	0.1022	0.2307	0.1066	0.2337

Notes:
1. Number of observations = 2297 (134 countries, 1980–2004, unbalanced panel). The sample includes developing countries only.
2. The method of estimation is pooled-OLS; t-statistics are in parentheses.
3. *Asia-dummy* takes on a value of 1 for five Asian countries (PRC, Indonesia, Malaysia, the Philippines and Thailand).
4. *Africa-dummy* takes on a value of 1 for African countries listed in Appendix Table 5A.1.
5. Asterisks denote significance level of coefficient estimates: *** means at 1% level; ** means at 5% level; and * means at 10% level.

Source: Authors' compilation.

markets and preventing sudden reversals in capital flows. Many emerging market and developing countries thus came to recognize increased liquidity as an important form of self-protection against crises. Raising foreign exchange reserves was a popular strategy adopted by many emerging market and developing countries. However, the accumulation of foreign exchange reserves is accompanied by considerable social costs. It is therefore important to reconsider the optimal level of foreign exchange reserve accumulation in emerging market and developing countries.

Table 5.6 Impacts of increased foreign exchange reserves on macroeconomic variables: international evidence (4)

$\Delta GDP_{j,t}/GDP_{j,t}$ = constant term + f_1 (*Foreign Reserve*$_{j,t}$/*GNI*$_{j,t}$) + $f_2 \cdot$ *log GNI*$_{j,t}$,				
Regression	1	2	3	4
Constant	−0.8413	0.5695	−0.8428	0.5825
	(−1.41)	(0.84)	(−1.41)	(0.86)
R/GNI	0.0422***	0.0347***	0.0422***	0.0341***
	(3.83)	(3.13)	(3.76)	(3.01)
log(GNI)	0.1884***	0.0485	0.1888***	0.0455
	(2.91)	(0.68)	(2.87)	(0.63)
Asia-dummy	(0.00)	2.4535***		2.4632***
	(0.00)	(3.94)		(3.95)
Africa-dummy		−0.6193**		−0.6194**
		(−2.19)		(−2.19)
After98-dummy		(0.00)	−0.0118	0.0771
		(0.00)	(−0.04)	(0.24)
adj. R squared	0.0037	0.0057	0.0113	0.0132

Notes:

1. Number of observations = 2411 (134 countries and 25 periods, unbalanced panel). The sample includes developing countries only.
2. The method of estimation is pooled-OLS; t-statistics are in parentheses.
3. *Asia-dummy* takes on a value of 1 for five Asian countries (PRC, Indonesia, Malaysia, the Philippines and Thailand).
4. Asterisks denote significance level of coefficient estimates: *** means at 1% level; ** means at 5% level; and * means at 10% level.

Source: Authors' compilation.

REFERENCES

Aizenman, J. and J. Lee (2005), 'International reserves: precautionary versus mercantilist views, theory and evidence', National Bureau of Economic Research (NBER) Working Paper No. 11366, Cambridge, MA: NBER.

Corsetti, G., P. Pesenti and N. Roubini (1999), 'What caused the Asian currency and financial crisis?', *Japan and the World Economy*, **11**, 305–73.

Fukuda, S. and Y. Kon (2010), 'Macroeconomic impacts of foreign exchange reserve accumulation: theory and international evidence', ADBI Working Paper No. 197, Tokyo: Asian Development Bank Institute.

Heston, A., R. Summers and B. Aten (2006), *Penn World Table Version 6.2*, Center for International Comparisons of Production, Income and Prices at the University of Pennsylvania.

International Monetary Fund (2006), *International Financial Statistics*, Washington, DC: World Bank.

Levy Yeyati, E. (2006), 'The cost of reserves, 2006', World Bank Working Paper No. 585, Washington, DC: World Bank.
Rodrik, D. (2006), 'The social cost of foreign exchange reserves', *International Economic Journal*, **20**, 253–66.
Sachs, J. and S. Radelet (1998), 'The East Asian financial crisis: diagnosis, remedies, prospects', *Brookings Papers on Economic Activity*, Issue 1, 1–90.
World Bank (2006), *Global Development Finance*, Washington, DC: World Bank.

APPENDIX

Table 5A.1 List of sampled countries

Africa	Asia	Europe	Middle East	Western Hemisphere
Algeria	Bangladesh	Albania	Egypt	Argentina
Angola	Bhutan	Armenia	Iran	Barbados
Benin	Cambodia	Azerbaijan	Jordan	Belize
Botswana	Fiji Islands	Belarus	Lebanon	Bolivia
Burkina Faso	India	Bosnia and Herzegovina	Oman	Brazil
Burundi	Indonesia	Bulgaria	Syria	Chile
Cameroon	Lao PDR	Croatia	Yemen	Colombia
Cape Verde	Malaysia	Czech Republic		Costa Rica
Central African Republic	Maldives	Estonia		Dominica
Chad	Mongolia	Georgia		Dominican Republic
Comoros	Nepal	Hungary		Ecuador
Congo, Dem. Rep.	Pakistan	Kazakhstan		El Salvador
Congo, Republic of	Papua New Guinea	Kyrgyzstan		Grenada
Cote d'Ivoire	People's Republic of China (PRC)	Latvia		Guatemala
Djibouti	Philippines	Lithuania		Guyana
Equatorial Guinea	Samoa	Macedonia		Haiti
Eritrea	Solomon Islands	Moldova		Honduras
Ethiopia	Sri Lanka	Poland		Jamaica
Gabon	Thailand	Romania		Mexico
Gambia, The	Tonga	Russia		Nicaragua
Ghana	Vanuatu	Serbia and Montenegro		Panama
Guinea	Viet Nam	Slovak Republic		Paraguay
Guinea-Bissau		Tajikistan		Peru
Kenya		Turkey		St Kitts & Nevis
Lesotho		Ukraine		St Lucia
Liberia		Uzbekistan		St Vincent & Grenadines
Madagascar				Trinidad & Tobago
Malawi				Uruguay
Mali				Venezuela
Mauritania				
Mauritius				
Morocco				
Mozambique				
Niger				
Nigeria				
Rwanda				
Sao Tome and Principe				

Table 5A.1 (continued)

Africa	Asia	Europe	Middle East	Western Hemisphere
Senegal				
Seychelles				
Sierra Leone				
Somalia				
South Africa				
Sudan				
Swaziland				
Tanzania				
Togo				
Tunisia				
Uganda				
Zambia				
Zimbabwe				

Source: World Bank (2006).

PART III

Recommendations Related to the 'Impossible Trinity'

6. The financial crisis, rethinking of the global financial architecture and the trilemma

Joshua Aizenman, Menzie D. Chinn and Hiro Ito

6.1 INTRODUCTION

The global financial crisis that began in 2008 in the United States (US), but spread far and wide, had dire consequences for economic growth. While the extent of economic damage varied across countries, economists agree that the downturn was the worst since the Great Depression.

Just as the traumas of the Great Depression and World War II underpinned an initiative to set up a stable international financial architecture, the global financial crisis sparked a call for action. That action began with the November 2008 meeting of the Group of 20 (G20) that took place in the midst of the financial panic. As the G20 countries discussed the following year in Pittsburgh, it seemed that the time was ripe for a comprehensive re-evaluation of the international financial architecture – one that would probably be accompanied by changes in the macroeconomic policy combinations adopted by countries.

Whatever configuration of international financial architecture world leaders consider, they cannot avoid confronting the central policy trilemma in international finance, the existence of the 'impossible trinity'. The trilemma thesis states that a country simultaneously may choose any two, but not all, of the following three goals: monetary independence, exchange rate stability and financial integration.

A number of different international monetary and financial arrangements have been in place since the gold standard system. Each set of arrangements imposed different choices on countries. The Bretton Woods system sacrificed capital mobility for monetary autonomy and exchange rate stability. The euro system is built upon the fixed exchange rate arrangement and free capital mobility, but abandoned monetary autonomy of the member countries. Until recently, developing countries largely pursued monetary independence and exchange rate stability, at the expense of financial openness.

Although the trilemma has widespread adherence in both policy and academic circles, there has been almost no empirical work testing the concept. Our previous paper (Aizenman et al. 2008) is one of the few exceptions.[1] In that paper, we first developed the 'trilemma indexes' that quantify exchange rate stability, monetary independence and financial openness. Using these indexes, we have shown that the major crises since the 1970s – the collapse of the Bretton Woods system, the Latin American debt crisis of 1982 and the Asian crisis of 1997–1998 – caused structural breaks in the configuration of the trilemma indexes. We also tested whether the indexes are linearly related to each other and confirmed that a change in one of the trilemma variables induces a change with the opposite sign in the weighted average of the other two. This means that countries face a trade-off among the three policy choices. Armed with these results, we feel confident in predicting that the recent turbulence in the global financial markets will challenge the existing configuration of trilemma choices among countries.

In Aizenman et al. (2008) we also investigated the normative question of how the policy choices among the three trilemma policies affect macroeconomic performance such as output volatility, inflation volatility and the average rate of inflation. We found that countries with higher levels of monetary independence tend to experience lower output volatility. We also found that emerging market economies with higher levels of exchange rate fixity tend to experience higher output volatility, though this effect can be mitigated if they hold international reserves at a level higher than 19–22 percent of gross domestic product (GDP). This result is consistent with the observation of many emerging market countries holding massive foreign exchange reserves.

We also found that countries with greater monetary autonomy tend to experience higher inflation, while countries with higher exchange rate stability tend to experience lower inflation. Furthermore, financial openness helps a country to experience lower inflation, possibly indicating that globalization gives developing countries more discipline than monetary autonomy to a country's macroeconomic management.

While our previous paper shed important light on how the choices between trilemma policies can affect macroeconomic performance, we did not address other important questions relevant to the recent financial crisis. This chapter deals with those questions. We first identify the channels by which the trilemma policy choices affect output volatility. Second, we focus on the performance of the economies in crisis, and investigate how trilemma policy configurations affect the output loss experienced by these economies. Third, we look into how trilemma configurations have evolved in the aftermath of economic crises in the past, hoping to get some implications for the recent crisis.

Section 6.2 reviews the development of policy configurations based on the trilemma using our trilemma indexes (Aizenman et al. 2008). Section 6.3 revisits the statistical analysis of the effect of trilemma policy configurations on macroeconomic performance – namely, output volatility, inflation volatility, and the average rate of inflation – and focuses on the channels through which international macroeconomic policy configurations affect output volatility. Section 6.4 investigates the determinants of output loss when a country experiences an economic hardship, not necessarily currency or banking crises. Section 6.5 concludes.

6.2 DEVELOPMENT OF THE TRILEMMA DIMENSIONS

In Aizenman et al. (2008), we demonstrated that major crises since the 1970s – the collapse of the Bretton Woods system, the Latin American debt crisis of 1982 and the Asian crisis of 1997–1998 – caused structural breaks in the trilemma configurations. Here, we revisit the development of policy configurations pertaining to the trilemma and international reserves (IR) holding, using the updated trilemma indexes.

The trilemma indexes quantify the degree of achievement along the three dimensions for more than 170 countries from 1970 to 2007. The monetary independence index depends on the correlation of a country's interest rates with the base country's interest rate, the exchange rate stability index is measured by exchange rate volatility, and the degree of financial integration is measured with the Chinn–Ito (Chinn and Ito 2006, 2008) capital controls index. Additional details on the construction of the indexes can be found in the Appendix.

6.2.1 Development of the Trilemma Configurations

Comparing theses indexes provides some interesting insights into how the international financial architecture has evolved over time. Figure 6.1 shows the development paths of the trilemma indexes for different country groups.

For the industrialized countries (Figure 6.1a), financial openness increased in the 1980s, and surged in the early 1990s, while exchange rate stability rose at the end of the 1990s, reflecting the introduction of the euro in 1999. The extent of monetary independence trended downward, particularly after the early 1990s.[2]

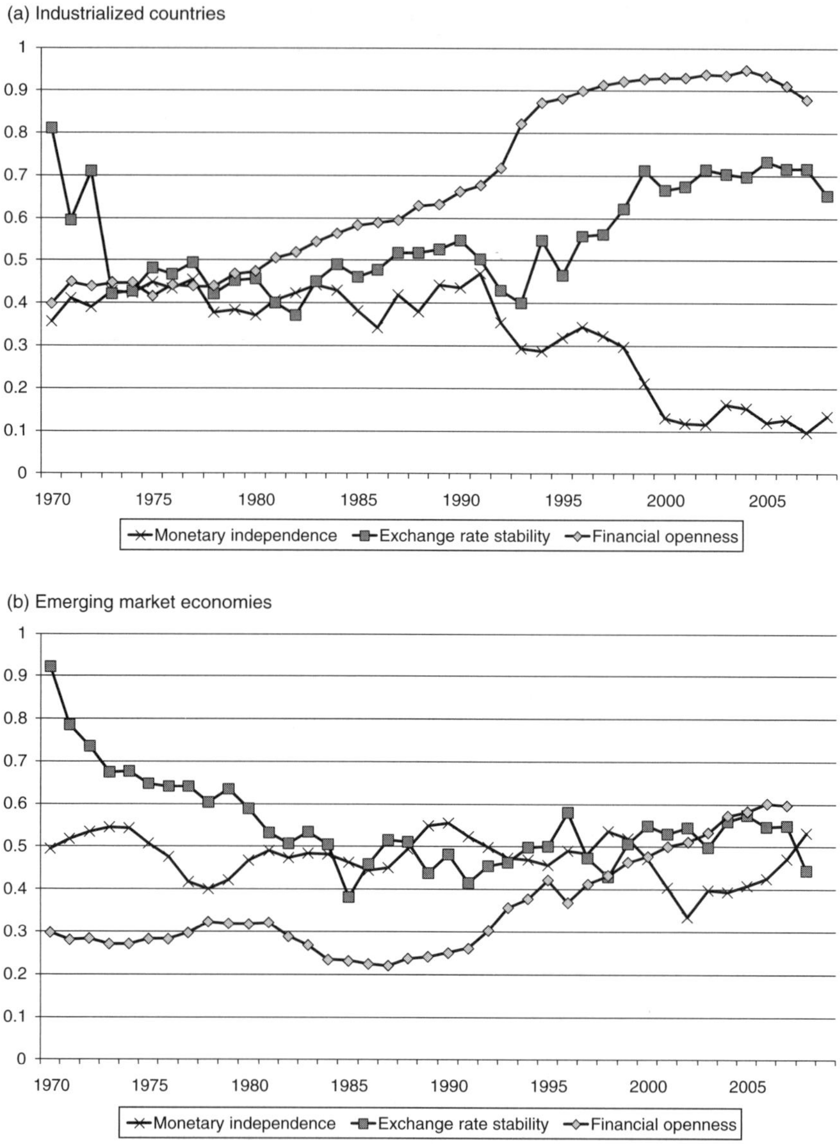

Source: Authors' calculations.

Figure 6.1 Development of the trilemma configurations over time: 1970–2007

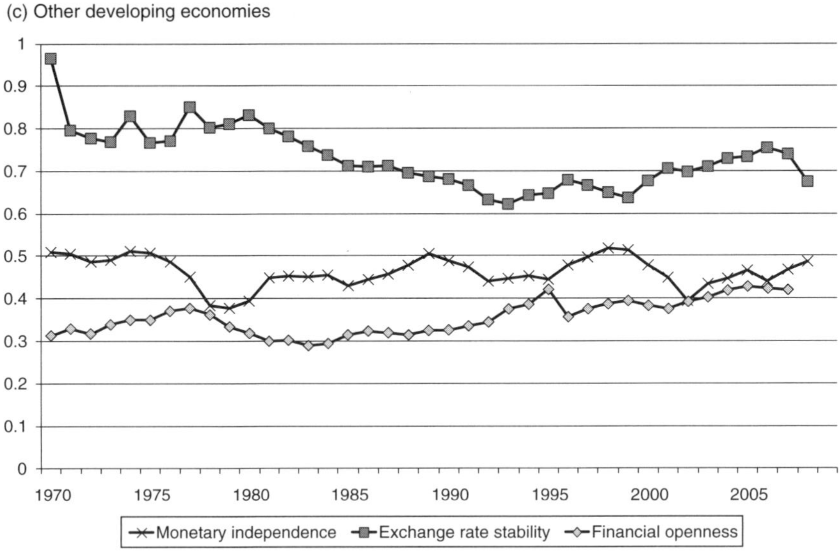

Figure 6.1 (continued)

Developing economies not only differ from industrialized ones in terms of not having a distinct divergence among the indexes, but also differ between emerging and non-emerging market ones.[3] For emerging market economies (Figure 6.1b), exchange rate stability declined rapidly from the 1970s to the mid-1980s. After some retrenchment after the early 1980s (in the wake of the debt crisis), financial openness started rising from 1990 onward. For the other developing countries, exchange rate stability declined less rapidly, and financial openness trended upward more slowly. In both cases, though, monetary independence remained more or less trendless.

Interestingly, for the emerging market economies our indexes suggest a convergence toward the middle ground. This pattern of results suggests that developing countries may have been trying to cling to moderate levels of both monetary independence and financial openness while maintaining higher levels of exchange rate stability – leaning against the trilemma, in other words – which interestingly coincides with the period when some of these economies started holding sizable international reserves, potentially as a buffer to the trade-off arising from the trilemma.[4]

None of these observations are applicable to non-emerging developing market countries (Figure 6.1c). For this group of countries, exchange rate stability has been the most aggressively pursued policy throughout the period. In contrast to the experience of the emerging market economies, financial liberalization is not proceeding rapidly for the non-emerging market developing economies.

The 'diamond charts' shown in Figures 6.2 and 6.3 are also useful for tracing the changing patterns of the trilemma configurations. Each of the charts shows the levels of the three policy goals as well as international reserves (as a ratio to GDP) with the origin normalized so as to represent zero monetary independence, pure float, zero international reserves and financial autarky. Figure 6.2 summarizes the trends for industrialized countries, those excluding the 12 eurozone countries but including Germany, emerging market economies and non-emerging market developing countries.[5]

These figures reveal that, while both industrialized countries and emerging market economies have moved towards deeper financial integration and declining monetary independence, non-emerging market developing countries have only inched toward financial integration. Emerging market economies, after giving up some exchange rate stability during the 1980s, have not changed their stance with respect to exchange rate stability, whereas non-emerging market developing countries seem to have remained, with some fluctuations, at a relatively high level of exchange rate stability. The pursuit of greater financial integration is much more pronounced among industrialized countries than developing countries, while emerging market economies increased financial openness. Interestingly, emerging market economies stand out from other groups by achieving a relatively balanced combination of the three macroeconomic goals by the 2000s, that is, middle-range levels of exchange rate stability and financial integration while retaining more monetary independence than industrialized countries did. The recent policy combination has been matched by a substantial increase in the IR–GDP ratio; such an occurrence is not observed in any other group.

Figure 6.3 compares developing countries across different geographical groups. Developing countries in both Asia and Latin America moved toward exchange rate flexibility, but Latin American countries rapidly increased financial openness while Asian counterparts have not. The emerging market subgroups of each regional group exhibited a much smaller difference, however.[6] Yet one key difference between the two groups is that the former held much greater international reserves than the latter. More importantly, Asian emerging market economies have opted for a more balanced combination of the three policy goals. We therefore suspect that the large international reserve accumulation may have allowed this group of countries to achieve such a trilemma configuration.

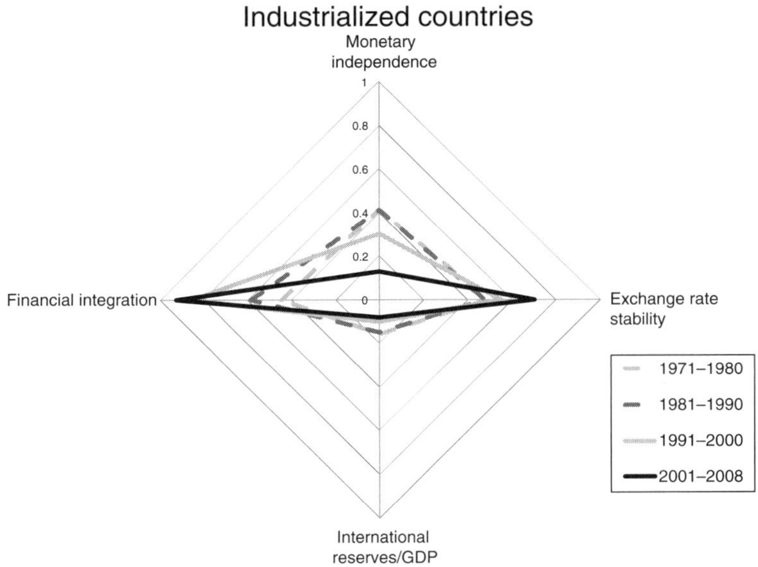

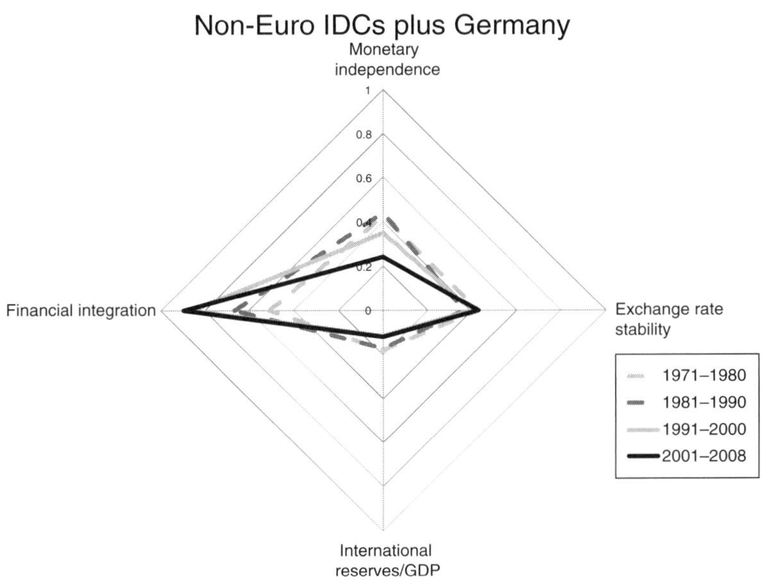

Source: Authors' calculations.

Figure 6.2 The Diamond charts: variation of the trilemma and IR configurations across different country groups

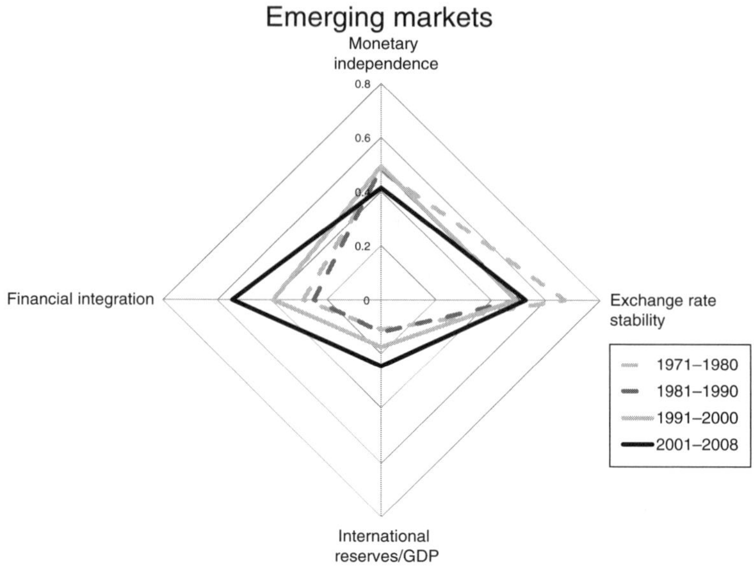

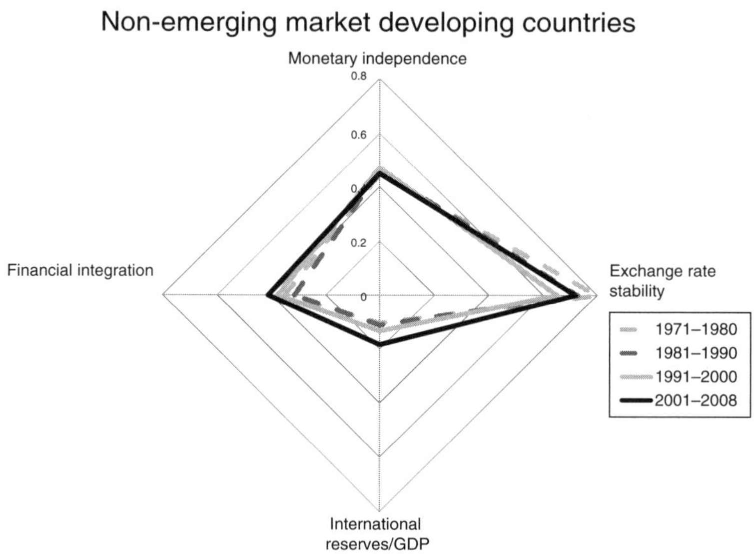

Figure 6.2 (continued)

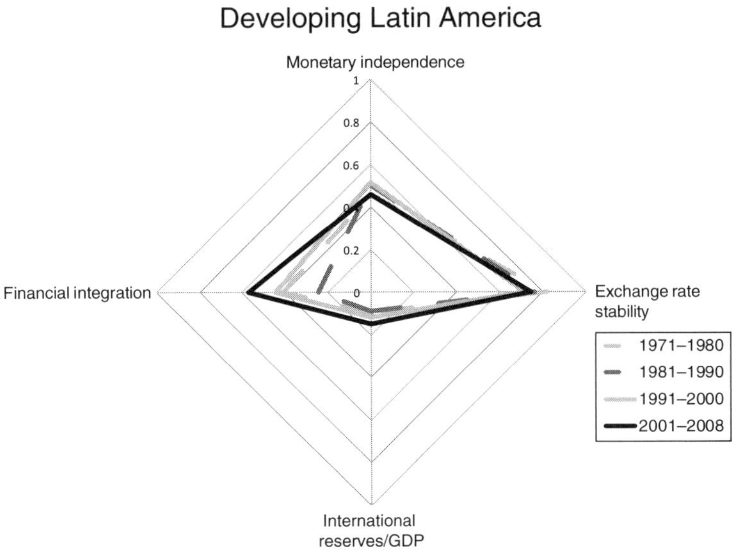

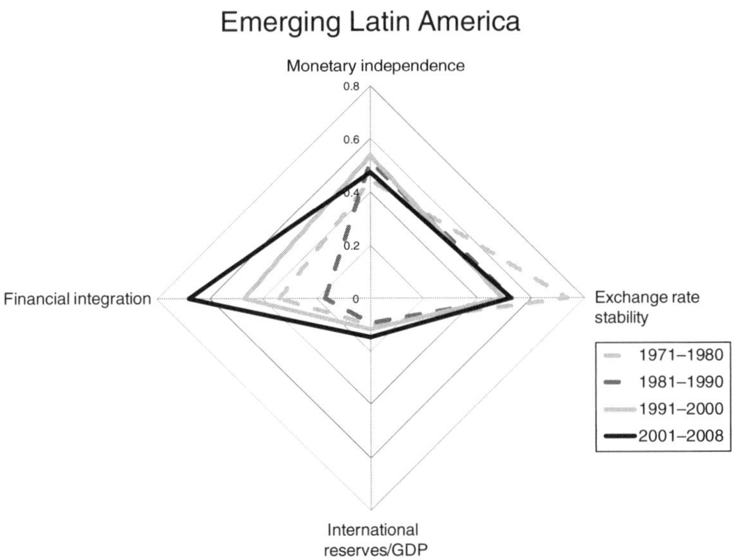

Notes: Emerging Asian economies include People's Republic of China (PRC); Hong Kong, China; Indonesia; Republic of Korea; Malaysia; the Philippines; Singapore; Taipei,China; and Thailand. Emerging Latin America includes Argentina, Brazil, Chile, Colombia, Ecuador, Jamaica, Mexico, Peru, Trinidad & Tobago and Venezuela.

Source: Authors' calculations.

Figure 6.3 Regional patterns of the trilemma and IR configurations

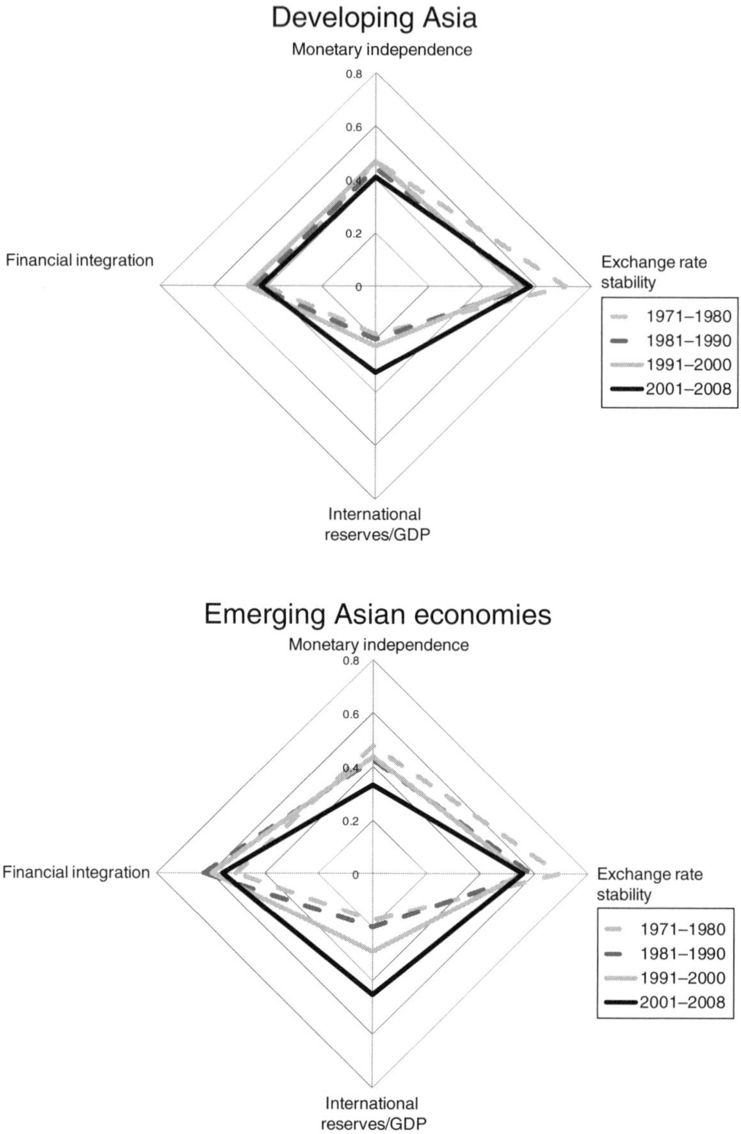

Figure 6.3 (continued)

6.3 REGRESSION ANALYSES

The above observations of the trilemma and IR configurations do not answer the question of what kind of goals policymakers would like to achieve by choosing a certain policy combination based on the trilemma. In Aizenman et al. (2008), we tested how the three policy choices individually or interactively could affect the macroeconomic outcomes such as output volatility, inflation volatility and medium-term inflation rates among developing countries.

Here, we replicate the model that examines the impact of the trilemma configurations and IR holding while controlling for the impact of external finance, which is most useful for examining the impact of the recent crisis, given the magnification effect attributable to the interlinked financial markets. The specification is given by:

$$y_{it} = \alpha_0 + \alpha_1 TLM_{it} + \alpha_2 IR_{it} + \alpha_3 (TLM_{it} \times IR_{it}) + ExtFin_{it}\mathrm{B} + X_{it}\Gamma + Z_t\Phi + D_i\Theta + \varepsilon_{it} \quad (6.1)$$

where y_{it} is the measure for macroeconomic policy performance for country i in year t. More specifically, y_{it} is either output volatility measured as the five-year standard deviations of the growth rate of per capita real output (using Penn World Table 6.2); inflation volatility as the five-year standard deviations of the monthly rate of inflation; or the five-year average of the monthly rate of inflation. TLM_{it} is a vector of any two of the three trilemma indexes, namely, monetary independence (*MI*), exchange rate stability (*ERS*), and financial openness/integration (*KAOPEN*).[7] IR_{it} is the level of international reserves (excluding gold) as a ratio to GDP, and $(TLM_{it} \times IR_{it})$ is an interaction term between the trilemma indexes and the level of international reserves, that may allow us to observe whether international reserves complement or substitute for other policy stances.

Financial liberalization has increased its pace since the 1990s. Nonetheless, the increasing volume of cross-border transactions of capital is increasingly blamed for economic instability. Motivated by this observation, we incorporate the effect of external financing in our specification by including in the vector $ExtFin_{it}$ variables that capture net foreign direct investment (FDI) inflows, net portfolio inflows, net 'other' inflows (which mostly include bank lending in *International Financial Statistics*, IFS), short-term debt and total debt service. For net capital flows, we use the IFS data and define them as external liabilities (= capital inflows with a positive sign) minus assets (= capital inflows with a negative sign) for each type of flow – negative values mean that a country experiences a net capital outflow of the relevant type. Short-term debt is included as the ratio of total external debt and total debt service as is that of gross national income (GNI). Both variables are retrieved from the World Development Indicators database.

X_{it} is a vector of macroeconomic control variables that include the variables most frequently used in the literature, namely, relative income (to the US based on Penn World Table per capita real income); its quadratic term; trade openness (=(*Export*+ *Import*)/*GDP*); the terms of trade (TOT) shock as defined as the five-year standard deviation of trade openness times TOT growth; fiscal procyclicality (as the correlations between Hodrick–Prescott (HP)-detrended government spending series and HP-detrended real GDP series); M2 (broad money) growth volatility (as five-year standard deviations of M2 growth); private credit creation as a ratio to GDP as a measure of financial development; the inflation rate; and inflation volatility. Z_t is a vector of global shocks that includes change in the US real interest rate, world output gap; and relative oil price shocks (measured as the log of the ratio of the oil price index to the world's consumer price index). D_i is a set of characteristic dummies that includes a dummy for oil exporting countries and regional dummies. We also include the dummy for currency crises.[8] Explanatory variables that persistently appear to be statistically insignificant are dropped from the estimation. ε_{it} is an *i.i.d.* error term.

The data set is organized into five-year panels of 1972–1976, 1977–1981, 1982–1986, 1987–1991, 1992–1996, 1997–2001, 2002–2006. All time-varying variables are included as five-year averages. The regression is conducted for the entire group of developing countries (DC) and a subgroup that only includes the emerging market economies (EMG).

We use the robust regression method because it reduces the weight of outliers that can arise in both the dependent variable and explanatory variables such as inflation volatility.[9] Furthermore, for comparison purposes, the same set of explanatory variables is used for the three subsamples, except for the regional dummies.

6.3.1 Estimation Results of the Basic Models

Output volatility

The regression results are reported in Tables 6.1 and 6.2 for developing countries and emerging market economies, respectively. The estimation results for output volatility are shown in columns 1 through 3. We refer to these as models (1), (2) and (3).

Overall, macroeconomic variables retain the characteristics that are consistent with what has been found in the literature. In the regressions for

Table 6.1 Impact of the trilemma configurations and external financing: developing countries

	Output volatility			Level of inflation		
	(1)	(2)	(3)	(4)	(5)	(6)
Relative income	–0.03	–0.13	–0.143	–0.163	–0.157	–0.182
	[0.035]	[0.036]***	[0.036]***	[0.087]*	[0.087]*	[0.084]**
Relative income, sq.	0.007	0.278	0.311	0.25	0.25	0.278
	[0.066]	[0.067]***	[0.067]***	[0.149]*	[0.150]*	[0.144]*
Change in US real interest rate	0.122	0.11	0.119			
	[0.049]**	[0.050]**	[0.050]**			
Volatility of (TOT*Trade openness)	0.026	0.03	0.027	0.021	0.019	0.018
	[0.009]***	[0.009]***	[0.009]***	[0.021]	[0.021]	[0.020]
Inflation volatility	0.023	0.02	0.023	0.299	0.284	0.297
	[0.006]***	[0.006]***	[0.006]***	[0.015]***	[0.015]***	[0.015]***
Fiscal procyclicality	0.002	0.004	0.004	–0.006	–0.005	–0.005
	[0.002]	[0.002]*	[0.002]*	[0.005]	[0.005]	[0.005]
Relative oil price shocks				0.014	0.007	0.012
				[0.006]**	[0.006]	[0.006]**
World output gap				0.323	0.159	0.276
				[0.304]	[0.308]	[0.294]
M2 growth				0.425	0.481	0.417
				[0.023]***	[0.023]***	[0.022]***
Currency crisis	0.005	0.005	0.005	0.031	0.032	0.029
	[0.003]*	[0.003]*	[0.003]*	[0.006]***	[0.007]***	[0.006]***

Table 6.1 (continued)

	Output volatility			Level of inflation		
	(1)	(2)	(3)	(4)	(5)	(6)
Private credit creation	–0.003	–0.008	–0.005	–0.018	–0.014	–0.019
	[0.006]	[0.006]	[0.007]	[0.017]	[0.017]	[0.016]
Total reserve	0.072	–0.055	0.065	–0.053	–0.182	–0.198
(as % of GDP)	[0.052]	[0.052]	[0.034]*	[0.122]	[0.123]	[0.076]***
Monetary independence	–0.019	–0.035		–0.002	–0.017	
(MI)	[0.014]	[0.014]**		[0.033]	[0.034]	
MI x reserves	0.005	0.112		–0.04	0.055	
	[0.085]	[0.089]		[0.199]	[0.208]	
Exchange rate stability	0.008		0.012	–0.04		–0.04
(ERS)	[0.007]		[0.006]*	[0.016]**		[0.015]***
ERS x reserves	–0.086		–0.095	0.074		0.071
	[0.044]*		[0.044]**	[0.104]		[0.098]
KA openness		–0.02	–0.014		–0.055	–0.055
		[0.008]**	[0.008]*		[0.019]***	[0.018]***

KAOPEN x reserves		0.086	0.048		0.261	0.254
		[0.045]*	[0.042]		[0.107]**	[0.097]***
Net FDI inflows/GDP	0.047	0.092	0.109	–0.477	–0.442	–0.441
	[0.068]	[0.071]	[0.070]	[0.177]***	[0.184]**	[0.173]**
Net portfolio inflows/GDP	0.241	0.289	0.286	0.064	0.297	0.228
	[0.122]**	[0.129]**	[0.127]**	[0.286]	[0.302]	[0.287]
Net 'other' inflows/GDP	0.069	0.063	0.071	0.037	0.09	0.045
	[0.029]**	[0.029]**	[0.029]**	[0.069]	[0.070]	[0.068]
Short-term debt (as % of	–0.009	–0.008	–0.007	–0.007	–0.003	0.012
total external debt)	[0.016]	[0.016]	[0.016]	[0.037]	[0.038]	[0.036]
Total debt service (as % of	0.063	0.081	0.078	0.176	0.184	0.154
GNI)	[0.035]*	[0.035]**	[0.035]**	[0.088]**	[0.088]**	[0.086]*
Observations	311	311	311	311	310	310
Adjusted R-squared	0.37	0.39	0.40	0.86	0.86	0.86

Notes: Robust regressions are implemented. * Significant at 10%; ** significant at 5%; *** significant at 1%. The dummy for sub-Saharan countries is included in the regressions for output and inflation volatility, so are the dummies for Latin America and Caribbean and East Europe and Central Asia in the regression for the level of inflation. Trade openness that is insignificant is omitted from presentation to conserve space.

Source: Authors' calculations.

Table 6.2 Impact of the trilemma configurations and external financing: emerging market economies

	Output volatility			Level of inflation		
	(1)	(2)	(3)	(4)	(5)	(6)
Relative income	–0.04	–0.028	–0.043	0.086	0.005	0.035
	[0.066]	[0.068]	[0.068]	[0.223]	[0.202]	[0.218]
Relative income, sq.	0.048	0.025	0.059	–0.398	–0.215	–0.281
	[0.145]	[0.151]	[0.150]	[0.458]	[0.421]	[0.449]
Change in US real interest rate	0.124	0.112	0.118			
	[0.056]**	[0.057]*	[0.056]**			
Volatility of (TOT*Trade Openness)	0.01	0.013	0.01	0.038	0.013	0.038
	[0.015]	[0.015]	[0.015]	[0.046]	[0.042]	[0.044]
Inflation volatility	0.037	0.034	0.036	0.325	0.381	0.322
	[0.007]***	[0.007]***	[0.007]***	[0.025]***	[0.023]***	[0.024]***
Fiscal procyclicality	0.002	0.003	0.003	–0.012	–0.011	–0.009
	[0.003]	[0.003]	[0.003]	[0.009]	[0.008]	[0.009]
Relative oil price shocks				–0.005	–0.008	–0.007
				[0.010]	[0.009]	[0.009]
World output gap				0.73	0.511	0.6
				[0.465]	[0.424]	[0.453]
M2 growth				0.449	0.417	0.436
				[0.034]***	[0.031]***	[0.033]***

Currency crisis	0.007	0.008	0.006	0.025	0.02	0.022
	[0.003]**	[0.003]**	[0.003]*	[0.009]***	[0.009]**	[0.009]**
Private credit creation	–0.001	–0.005	–0.001	–0.039	–0.032	–0.046
	[0.006]	[0.006]	[0.006]	[0.025]	[0.022]	[0.024]*
Total reserve (as % of GDP)	0.083	–0.04	0.078	–0.165	–0.185	–0.171
	[0.051]	[0.054]	[0.032]**	[0.156]	[0.151]	[0.095]*
Monetary independence (MI)	–0.018	–0.035		–0.032	–0.044	
	[0.016]	[0.017]**		[0.049]	[0.047]	
MI x reserves	0.009	0.089		0.048	0.095	
	[0.081]	[0.090]		[0.249]	[0.248]	
Exchange rate stability (ERS)	0.017		0.021	–0.053		–0.049
	[0.008]**		[0.008]***	[0.026]**		[0.025]**
ERS x reserves	–0.11		–0.12	0.243		0.233
	[0.048]**		[0.047]**	[0.145]*		[0.137]*
KA openness		–0.012	–0.005		–0.057	–0.042
		[0.009]	[0.008]		[0.024]**	[0.024]*

Table 6.2 (continued)

	Output volatility			Level of inflation		
	(1)	(2)	(3)	(4)	(5)	(6)
KAOPEN x reserves		0.066	0.035		0.203	0.099
		[0.045]	[0.039]		[0.125]	[0.119]
Net FDI inflows/GDP	–0.115	–0.082	–0.13	–0.823	–0.582	–0.667
	[0.098]	[0.107]	[0.104]	[0.330]**	[0.318]*	[0.335]**
Net portfolio inflows/GDP	–0.028	–0.02	0.026	–0.338	–0.119	–0.19
	[0.130]	[0.139]	[0.136]	[0.399]	[0.382]	[0.404]
Net 'other' inflows/GDP	0.031	0.03	0.028	0.037	0.08	0.032
	[0.034]	[0.035]	[0.034]	[0.115]	[0.106]	[0.112]
Short-term debt (as % of total	–0.007	–0.004	–0.005	0.051	0.05	0.073
external debt)	[0.017]	[0.018]	[0.018]	[0.055]	[0.051]	[0.054]
Total debt service (as % of GNI)	0.049	0.058	0.053	0.212	0.093	0.217
	[0.040]	[0.041]	[0.040]	[0.150]	[0.138]	[0.147]
Observations	159	159	159	159	159	159
Adjusted R-squared	0.32	0.29	0.31	0.88	0.90	0.88

Notes: Robust regressions are implemented. * Significant at 10%; ** significant at 5%; *** significant at 1%. The dummy for sub-Saharan countries is included in the regressions for output and inflation volatility, so are the dummies for Latin America and Caribbean and East Europe and Central Asia in the regression for the level of inflation.

Source: Authors' calculations.

output volatility, it is found that the higher the level of income is (relative to the US), the smaller the output volatility is, though the effect is non-linear. The larger the change in the US real interest rate, the higher the output volatility of developing countries becomes, indicating that the US real interest rate may represent the debt payment burden on these countries. The greater TOT shock there is, the higher the level of output volatility countries tend to experience. This finding is consistent with Rodrik (1998) and Easterly et al. (2001) who argued that volatility in world goods prices can raise output volatility through trade openness.[10] Countries with a procyclical fiscal policy tend to experience greater output volatility, while oil exporters also experience greater output volatility. Not surprisingly, currency crises increase the level of output volatility. The results hold qualitatively for the subsample of emerging market countries, though the statistical significance is weaker, reflecting the smaller variations of the variables for this group of economies.

Countries with more developed financial markets tend to experience lower output volatility, although the estimated effect is not statistically significant.[11] In Aizenman et al. (2008), we showed that financial development interacts with the exchange rate stability in a non-linear fashion for emerging market economies. Medium levels of financial development raise the volatility-enhancing impact of exchange rate stability. Highly developed financial markets boost the effect of financial openness on the reduction of output volatility while underdeveloped financial markets exacerbate output volatility. This last effect highlights the synergistic effects between financial development and financial opening.

Among the trilemma indexes, the monetary independence variable is found to have a significantly negative effect on output volatility: the greater monetary independence one embraces, the less output volatility the country tends to experience.[12] This finding is not surprising, considering that stabilization measures should reduce output volatility, with a higher degree of monetary independence.[13] Mishkin and Schmidt-Hebbel (2007) found that countries that adopt inflation targeting – one form of retaining monetary independence by having an automatic policy mechanism independent from external factors – reduce output volatility, and that the effect is bigger among emerging market countries.[14] This volatility-reducing effect of monetary independence may explain the reluctance of developing countries, especially non-emerging market ones, to reduce the extent of monetary independence over time.

More interestingly, the coefficient for exchange rate stability is found to be positive and significant for model (3) among developing countries (Table 6.1), and for both models (1) and (3) for emerging market economies (Table 6.2). This result implies a stabilizer effect of more flexible exchange rates, as in Edwards and Levy Yeyati (2005) and Haruka (2007). However, the interaction effect with IR holding is found to be statistically negative, suggesting that countries pursuing exchange rate stability can dampen output volatility enhancing effects by holding high levels of international reserves. The threshold level of international reserves holding is found to be 12.5 percent of GDP in model (3) for developing countries and 15.3–17.2 percent for emerging market economies. The volatility dampening effect can be large for some of the countries, as we discuss below.

Countries with a more open capital account tend to experience lower output volatility according to model (2) in Table 6.1. However, those with IR holding higher than 23 percent of GDP experience higher volatility by pursuing more financial openness – a somewhat counterintuitive finding.[15]

Among the external finance variables, the more 'other' capital inflows (that is, bank lending) or more net portfolio inflows a country receives, the more likely it is to experience higher output volatility, reflecting the fact that countries which experience macroeconomic turmoil often experienced an increase in inflows of bank lending or 'hot money', especially prior to the outbreak of the turmoil. Total debt service is found to be a positive contributor to output volatility while short-term debt does not seem to have an effect. This result contrasts with the conventional wisdom regarding short-term external debt.[16]

Inflation volatility

The regression models for inflation volatility do not turn out to be as robust as those for output volatility. We do not report the results in the table. The findings on the macroeconomic variables are generally consistent with the literature. Countries with higher relative incomes tend to experience lower inflation volatility, and those with higher rates of inflation and those which experience currency crises, are naturally expected to experience higher inflation volatility. A TOT shock increases inflation volatility, but only for emerging market economies.

The performance of the trilemma indexes appears to be the weakest for this group of estimations overall. However, once the interaction terms are removed from the models, the performance improves (results not reported), and monetary independence is found to be an inflation volatility-decreasing factor. FDI inflows appear to contribute to lowering inflation volatility. One possible explanation is that countries tend to stabilize inflation to attract FDI. Net portfolio inflows, on the other hand, positively contribute to inflation volatility.

Medium-run rate of inflation

The models for the medium-run rate of inflation fit as well as those for output volatility (shown in columns (4) to (6) in Tables 6.1 and 6.2). Countries with higher inflation volatility, higher M2 growth and oil price shocks tend to experience higher medium-run rates of inflation while currency crises lead to higher inflation, possibly reflecting the ending of fixed exchange rates during the crisis.

Among the trilemma variables, higher exchange rate stability is associated with lower inflation for both samples of developing and emerging market economies, a result consistent with the literature (such as Ghosh et al. 1997). This finding and the previously found positive association between exchange rate stability and output volatility are in line with the theoretical prediction that establishing stable exchange rates presents a trade-off for policymakers: it will help the country to achieve lower inflation by showing a higher level of credibility and commitment, but at the same time, the efforts of maintaining stable exchange rates will deprive the policymakers of an important adjustment mechanism through fluctuating exchange rates. This explains the negative coefficient on monetary independence in the output volatility regressions.

Financial openness contributes negatively to inflation in the medium term. The negative association between 'openness' and inflation has frequently been noted.[17] This finding may explain the reason why many countries, including developing countries, have experienced synchronized disinflation, with many of them having liberalized trade in goods and services as well as in financial assets. Furthermore, the interaction term between the financial openness variable and IR holding is found to be significantly positive for both samples of countries. For emerging market countries, the interaction term between exchange rate stability and IR holding is also found to be positive. These results may indicate that if the ratio of reserves holding to GDP is greater than some threshold – it ranges around 22–27 percent of GDP – the efforts of pursuing exchange rate stability or financial openness help to increase the rate of inflation. This means that countries with excess levels of reserve holdings will eventually face a limit on foreign exchange sterilization.[18]

6.3.2 Channels to Output Volatility

Given the current state of the world economy, one cannot help but focus on the estimation results for output volatility. One question that arises is: through what channels do these factors contribute to output volatility? To answer this question, we estimate similar models for output volatility but replace the dependent variable with real exchange rate stability, through which net exports can be affected, and the volatility of investment.

The first three columns in Tables 6.3 and 6.4 are the same as those in

Table 6.3 *Determinants of output volatility: developing countries*

	Output volatility			Real exchange rate volatility			Investment volatility		
	(1)	(2)	(3)	(4)	(5)	(6)	(7)	(8)	(9)
Relative income	–0.03	–0.13	–0.143	–0.016	0.027	–0.015	–0.098	–0.15	–0.125
	[0.035]	[0.036]***	[0.036]***	[0.020]	[0.031]	[0.020]	[0.143]	[0.142]	[0.139]
Relative income, sq.	0.007	0.278	0.311	0.017	–0.041	0.019	0.12	0.239	0.211
	[0.066]	[0.067]***	[0.067]***	[0.037]	[0.057]	[0.038]	[0.264]	[0.265]	[0.258]
Change in US real interest rate	0.122	0.11	0.119				0.388	0.306	0.259
	[0.049]**	[0.050]**	[0.050]**				[0.199]*	[0.198]	[0.194]
Volatility of TOT*OPN	0.026	0.03	0.027	0.007	0.011	0.008	0.095	0.121	0.103
	[0.009]***	[0.009]***	[0.009]***	[0.005]	[0.008]	[0.005]	[0.036]***	[0.036]***	[0.035]***
Inflation volatility (Infl. vol. differentials in (4)–(6))	0.023	0.02	0.023	0.038	0.031	0.038	0.135	0.133	0.131
	[0.006]***	[0.006]***	[0.006]***	[0.003]***	[0.005]***	[0.004]***	[0.025]***	[0.025]***	[0.025]***
Fiscal procyclicality	0.002	0.004	0.004				–0.001	0.003	0.004
	[0.002]	[0.002]*	[0.002]*				[0.009]	[0.009]	[0.009]
Trade openness				–0.005	–0.011	–0.005			
				[0.003]*	[0.004]***	[0.003]*			

Currency crisis	0.005	0.005	0.005	0.009	0.013	0.009	0.009	0.002	0.007
	[0.003]*	[0.003]*	[0.003]*	[0.002]***	[0.002]***	[0.002]***	[0.011]	[0.011]	[0.011]
Private credit creation	–0.003	–0.008	–0.005				–0.011	–0.012	–0.001
	[0.006]	[0.006]	[0.007]				[0.026]	[0.026]	[0.025]
Total reserve (as % of GDP)	0.072	–0.055	0.065	0.021	0.038	–0.013	–0.232	–0.393	0.158
	[0.052]	[0.052]	[0.034]*	[0.029]	[0.045]	[0.019]	[0.210]	[0.205]*	[0.132]
Monetary independence (MI)	–0.019	–0.035		0.004	0.025		–0.181	–0.159	
	[0.014]	[0.014]**		[0.008]	[0.012]**		[0.056]***	[0.057]***	
MI x reserves	0.005	0.112		–0.049	–0.086		1.2	0.785	
	[0.085]	[0.089]		[0.048]	[0.076]		[0.342]***	[0.351]**	
Exchange rate stability (ERS)	0.008		0.012	–0.037		–0.038	0.077		0.07
	[0.007]		[0.006]*	[0.004]***		[0.004]***	[0.026]***		[0.025]***
ERS x reserves	–0.086		–0.095	–0.007		0.001	–0.415		–0.254
	[0.044]*		[0.044]**	[0.025]		[0.024]	[0.179]**		[0.170]
KA Openness		–0.02	–0.014		–0.008	–0.004		–0.042	–0.012
		[0.008]**	[0.008]*		[0.007]	[0.004]		[0.032]	[0.030]
KAOPEN x reserves		0.086	0.048		0.029	0.019		0.223	0.051
		[0.045]*	[0.042]		[0.038]	[0.024]		[0.178]	[0.165]

Table 6.3 (continued)

	Output volatility			Real exchange rate volatility			Investment volatility		
	(1)	(2)	(3)	(4)	(5)	(6)	(7)	(8)	(9)
Net FDI	0.047	0.092	0.109	–0.04	–0.089	–0.033	0.325	0.347	0.25
inflows/GDP	[0.068]	[0.071]	[0.070]	[0.041]	[0.064]	[0.042]	[0.274]	[0.280]	[0.272]
Net portfolio	0.241	0.289	0.286	0.051	0.046	0.054	1.482	1.414	1.364
inflows/GDP	[0.122]**	[0.129]**	[0.127]**	[0.068]	[0.108]	[0.071]	[0.492]***	[0.508]***	[0.494]***
Net 'other'	0.069	0.063	0.071	–0.027	–0.014	–0.028	0.376	0.38	0.418
inflows/GDP	[0.029]**	[0.029]**	[0.029]**	[0.016]*	[0.025]	[0.016]*	[0.116]***	[0.116]***	[0.112]***
Short-term debt	–0.009	–0.008	–0.007	0.006	0.004	0.007	–0.042	–0.042	–0.042
(as % of total	[0.016]	[0.016]	[0.016]	[0.008]	[0.013]	[0.008]	[0.062]	[0.063]	[0.062]
external debt)									
Total debt service	0.063	0.081	0.078	0.02	0.081	0.02	0.262	0.232	0.213
(as % of GNI)	[0.035]*	[0.035]**	[0.035]**	[0.020]	[0.031]***	[0.021]	[0.140]*	[0.138]*	[0.136]
Observations	311	311	311	311	311	311	310	309	309
Adjusted R-squared	0.37	0.39	0.40	0.64	0.31	0.64	0.32	0.26	0.25

Notes: Robust regressions are implemented. * Significant at 10%; ** significant at 5%; *** significant at 1%. The dummy for sub-Saharan countries is included in the regressions for output and inflation volatility, so are the dummies for Latin America and Caribbean and East Europe and Central Asia in the regression for the level of inflation.

Source: Authors' calculations.

Table 6.4 Determinants of output volatility: emerging market countries

	Output volatility			Real exchange rate volatility			Investment volatility		
	(1)	(2)	(3)	(4)	(5)	(6)	(7)	(8)	(9)
Relative income	–0.04	–0.028	–0.043	–0.046	0.077	–0.071	0.298	0.097	0.168
	[0.066]	[0.068]	[0.068]	[0.053]	[0.073]	[0.051]	[0.255]	[0.256]	[0.265]
Relative income, sq.	0.048	0.025	0.059	0.096	–0.119	0.165	–0.767	–0.293	–0.41
	[0.145]	[0.151]	[0.150]	[0.118]	[0.165]	[0.113]	[0.561]	[0.570]	[0.585]
Change in US real interest rate	0.124	0.112	0.118				0.007	0.003	–0.083
	[0.056]**	[0.057]*	[0.056]**				[0.218]	[0.217]	[0.220]
Volatility of TOT*OPN	0.01	0.013	0.01	0.026	0.007	0.024	–0.074	0.005	–0.038
	[0.015]	[0.015]	[0.015]	[0.011]**	[0.016]	[0.011]**	[0.057]	[0.056]	[0.058]
Inflation volatility (Infl. vol. differentials in (4)–(6))	0.037	0.034	0.036	0.049	0.038	0.05	0.153	0.164	0.152
	[0.007]***	[0.007]***	[0.007]***	[0.006]***	[0.008]***	[0.005]***	[0.028]***	[0.028]***	[0.029]***
Fiscal procyclicality	0.002	0.003	0.003				0.013	0.012	0.015
	[0.003]	[0.003]	[0.003]				[0.010]	[0.011]	[0.011]
Trade openness				–0.004	–0.003	–0.005			
				[0.005]	[0.006]	[0.004]			
Currency crisis	0.007	0.008	0.006	0.01	0.013	0.009	0.033	0.029	0.026
	[0.003]**	[0.003]**	[0.003]*	[0.002]***	[0.003]***	[0.002]***	[0.012]***	[0.012]**	[0.012]**

Table 6.4 (continued)

	Output volatility			Real exchange rate volatility			Investment volatility		
	(1)	(2)	(3)	(4)	(5)	(6)	(7)	(8)	(9)
Private credit creation	–0.001	–0.005	–0.001				0.021	0.015	0.022
	[0.006]	[0.006]	[0.006]				[0.025]	[0.024]	[0.025]
Total reserve	0.083	–0.04	0.078	0.031	0.047	–0.002	–0.414	–0.268	0.147
(as % of GDP)	[0.051]	[0.054]	[0.032]**	[0.040]	[0.058]	[0.023]	[0.196]**	[0.201]	[0.126]
Monetary	–0.018	–0.035		0.027	0.041		–0.308	–0.182	
independence (MI)	[0.016]	[0.017]**		[0.013]**	[0.018]**		[0.061]***	[0.063]***	
MI x reserves	0.009	0.089		–0.066	–0.117		1.911	0.527	
	[0.081]	[0.090]		[0.065]	[0.097]		[0.314]***	[0.338]	
Exchange rate	0.017		0.021	–0.041		–0.04	0.113		0.065
stability (ERS)	[0.008]**		[0.008]***	[0.007]***		[0.006]***	[0.032]***		[0.031]**
ERS x reserves	–0.11		–0.12	–0.006		0	–0.751		–0.24
	[0.048]**		[0.047]**	[0.038]		[0.034]	[0.186]***		[0.183]
KA openness		–0.012	–0.005		–0.002	–0.009		–0.036	–0.003
		[0.009]	[0.008]		[0.009]	[0.006]		[0.032]	[0.031]
KAOPEN x reserves		0.066	0.035		–0.011	0.012		0.191	0.042
		[0.045]	[0.039]		[0.047]	[0.028]		[0.167]	[0.153]

Net FDI inflows/GDP	–0.115	–0.082	–0.13	–0.054	–0.125	0.022	–0.008	0.435	0.162
	[0.098]	[0.107]	[0.104]	[0.080]	[0.116]	[0.078]	[0.379]	[0.402]	[0.406]
Net portfolio	–0.028	–0.02	0.026	–0.046	–0.155	–0.017	0.875	1.29	1.036
inflows/GDP	[0.130]	[0.139]	[0.136]	[0.103]	[0.148]	[0.100]	[0.503]*	[0.523]**	[0.531]*
Net 'other' inflows/GDP	0.031	0.03	0.028	–0.085	–0.088	–0.067	0.57	0.664	0.595
	[0.034]	[0.035]	[0.034]	[0.027]***	[0.037]**	[0.025]***	[0.133]***	[0.132]***	[0.133]***
Short-term debt	–0.007	–0.004	–0.005	0.016	–0.003	0.013	–0.058	–0.053	–0.06
(as % of total external debt)	[0.017]	[0.018]	[0.018]	[0.012]	[0.017]	[0.011]	[0.067]	[0.067]	[0.068]
Total debt service	0.049	0.058	0.053	0.029	0.022	0.035	0.302	0.331	0.284
(as % of GNI)	[0.040]	[0.041]	[0.040]	[0.036]	[0.050]	[0.034]	[0.154]*	[0.154]**	[0.156]*
Observations	159	159	159	159	159	159	158	158	158
Adjusted R-squared	0.32	0.29	0.31	0.66	0.36	0.67	0.59	0.42	0.38

Notes: Robust regressions are implemented. * Significant at 10%; ** significant at 5%; *** significant at 1%. The dummy for sub-Saharan countries is included in the regressions for output and inflation volatility, so are the dummies for Latin America and Caribbean and East Europe and Central Asia in the regression for the level of inflation.

Source: Authors' calculations.

Tables 6.1 and 6.2, respectively. The results shown in columns (4) to (6) and those (7) to (9) correspond to the real exchange rate stability and investment volatility specifications, respectively. However, for the estimation of the real exchange rate stability, some of the explanatory variables are changed; the variables for the change in the US real interest rate, fiscal procyclicality and financial development (measured by private credit creation as a ratio to GDP) are dropped from the estimation, and replaced with inflation volatility, and differentials in inflation volatility between the home and base countries are included instead.[19]

By comparing the results of these different specifications with different dependent variables, we can make some interesting observations. First, the negative effect of monetary independence on output volatility is consistent with its negative effect on investment volatility. However, if the level of IR holding is above 15–23 percent of GDP, higher monetary independence leads to higher volatility in investment. This may be because higher levels of international reserves could lead to higher levels of liquidity, thus to more volatile movements in the cost of capital. Second, while a higher degree of exchange rate stability could (unsurprisingly) induce greater real exchange rate stability, it could also lead to more volatile investment. But as was the case with output volatility, if the level of IR holding exceeds a given threshold, greater exchange rate stability reduces investment volatility.[20] Third, financial openness has a negative impact on both real exchange rate stability and investment volatility. Hence, we can conclude that financial liberalization could help reduce output volatility by making both the real exchange rate and investment more stable. The investment volatility regressions show that net portfolio and banking inflows can be volatility-increasing, although banking inflows can reduce real exchange rate volatility.

The fact that the results from the investment volatility specification are more similar to those from the output volatility specification is not surprising. At the same time, the different dynamics between the trilemma configurations and real exchange rate stability that we have found suggests that the international macroeconomic policy configurations can depend upon how much weight policymakers place upon these two policy goals. For example, if policymakers put greater weight on real exchange rate stability, it is better to pursue greater exchange rate stability and greater financial openness (or lower levels of monetary independence), which could be volatility enhancing in terms of investment and output, depending on the level of IR holding. Specifically, the results from model (4) in Table 6.4 show that greater (weaker) monetary independence increases (decreases) real exchange rate volatility. The result from model (7) indicates that the threshold level of IR holding (as a ratio to GDP) for greater (weaker) monetary independence to have a positive (negative) effect on investment is 16 percent of GDP whereas that for greater (weaker) exchange rate stability to have a negative (positive) effect is 14 percent Hence, if an emerging market country holds a level of IR higher than 16 percent and tries to pursue a higher level of exchange rate stability and a lower level of monetary independence (that is, a combination of greater exchange rate stability and greater financial openness), it could achieve lower levels of not only real exchange rate stability but also investment.[21] This result may explain why many emerging market countries, especially those which are more open to international trade, tend to prefer exchange rate stability and holding a massive amount of IR while also pursuing financial liberalization.

6.4 PRELIMINARY ANALYSIS ON THE DETERMINANTS OF OUTPUT LOSSES DURING THE CRISIS

The preceding investigation focused on the general relationship between the variables such as the trilemma policy configurations, external finances and output volatility. However, the nature of the relationship may differ for the countries that are experiencing severe economic hardship such as currency crises, banking crises and other economic crises caused by socio-political events. This kind of relationship may be obscured in a panel data analysis such as recounted above, but it can still affect the decision making of policymakers even during 'tranquil' time periods. Furthermore, shedding light on such an extreme situation may provide some useful insights for the recent crisis. Hence, we will examine below how policy coordination based on the trilemma can affect the performance of an economy that is experiencing an extraordinary situation.

6.4.1 Measure of 'Excessive Underperformance'

Construction of the measure

The first effort we made was to create a measure that quantifies the output cost of an economic crisis. To construct our measure, we implemented the following procedure. First, we calculated the rolling standard deviations with five-year windows of the per capita output growth rate for 1955–2007 for the industrialized and developing country groupings. Second, if the actual growth rate is below the rolling one standard deviation band, the gap between the actual growth rate and the lower bound of the range is defined to be the measure of 'excessive underperformance' (severe recession).[22] Finally, if the state of excessive underperformance persists for more than one year, the gaps will be cumulated as long as the actual growth rate is below the lower band.[23] If recovery takes place for one year immediately after the period of excessive underperformance, but is followed by another excessive underperformance period in the following year, the one-year recovery period is still considered to be part of the state of excessive underperformance.[24] Thus, a single value of the measure of excessive underperformance is given to each episode of economic severity.

The state of excessive underperformance or simply 'crisis' does not necessarily mean either a currency crisis or banking crisis, but rather an unpredictable decline in per capita output growth. Therefore, the crisis in this exercise includes not only currency and financial crises, but also economic collapse induced by domestic political disorder, social unrests, or civil wars. One merit of this index is that it is strict in identifying a crisis economy when many economies are also experiencing a crisis: to be counted as a crisis economy it must experience an output loss whose magnitude is greater than a threshold that incorporates the variation of output growth on a global scale. Due to data limitations, the recent global financial crisis is not captured by this measure.

Summary statistics

With this measure of excessive underperformance, we found that between 1955 and 2007 there were 93 crisis episodes among industrialized countries and 411 among developing countries. Figure 6.4 presents summary statistics of the measure for both industrialized and developing countries.[25] In the figure, we observe that there is a significant difference in the size of crises between industrialized countries and developing countries. After peaking in the 1970s, both the size and the duration of a crisis had a declining trend for developing countries although such a trend was not observed for industrialized countries. In the 2000s (before the recent global financial crisis), developing countries had experienced the least number of crises with shorter durations on average. Figure 6.5 shows that the number of crises was on a declining trend from the mid-1980s.

6.4.2 Preliminary Regression Analysis on the Effect of the Trilemma Configurations on Output Underperformance

Using this measure of severe economic underperformance, we estimate the determinants of crises while focusing on the impact of the trilemma configurations. The estimation model is defined as:

$$SIZE\_CRISIS_{it} = \alpha_0 + \alpha_1 TLM_{it} + \alpha_2 IR_{it} + \alpha_3 (TLM_{it} \times IR_{it}) + X_{it}'B + \phi DUR\_CRISIS_{it} + D_i'\Theta + \varepsilon_{it} \quad (6.2)$$

The dependent variable $SIZE\_CRISIS_{it}$ is the measure of 'excessive underperformance' of country *i* in year *t*. Higher values mean more severe output losses. TLM_{it} and IR_{it} are vectors of two trilemma indexes and the ratio of IR holding to GDP, respectively. $(TLM_{it} \times IR_{it})$ is a vector of the interaction terms between TLM_{it} and IR_{it}. Control variables are included in the vector X_{it}, including relative per capita income level (to the US), its squares, GDP growth rate and fiscal procyclicality (correlations of detrended real government spending and real GDP series). These control variables are included as averages over three years prior to the first year of underperformance (or just 'crisis') – we use the time notation of $(t - 1)$ for brevity.[26] DUR_CRISIS_{it} is the number of years of underperformance.[27]

Additionally, the dummies for banking and currency crises as well as a dummy for civil wars were included, but they were not significant and were therefore removed. The currency crisis is based on the exchange rate market pressure (EMP) index as in the previous regressions, and the banking crisis dummy is based on Caprio and Klingebiel (2003). Another dummy for internal and external military conflict based on the Center for the Study of Civil Wars index on armed conflict was also included. However, this index turned out to be an insignificant factor, and therefore was removed from the estimation.[28]

As was the case with the previous exercise, we focus on the impacts of the trilemma indexes, namely, *MI*, *ERS* and *KAOPEN*, and IR holding as well as the interactions between IR and the trilemma indexes. These variables are included in two ways. In one set of models, they are included as averages over three years prior to the underperformance in an attempt to capture their impact as 'pre-crisis conditions' – we again use the time notation of (t − 1) for brevity. As another way of including these variables, we use their averages over the years of underperformance so as to examine the during-crisis conditions – we use the time notation of (t).

We use the sample of country-year episodes of excessive underperformance. In other words, the number of observations equals the number of crises among developing countries. We conduct two sets of ordinary least squares (OLS) regressions, one with precrisis conditions of the trilemma configurations, $MI_{(t-1)}$, $ERS_{(t-1)}$, $KAOPEN_{(t-1)}$, $IR_{(t-1)}$ and their interactions, and the other with $MI_{(t)}$, $ERS_{(t)}$, $KAOPEN_{(t)}$, $IR_{(t)}$ and their interactions.

The reason why we have these two separate models is as follows. The model with the pre-crisis conditions would control for endogeneity and

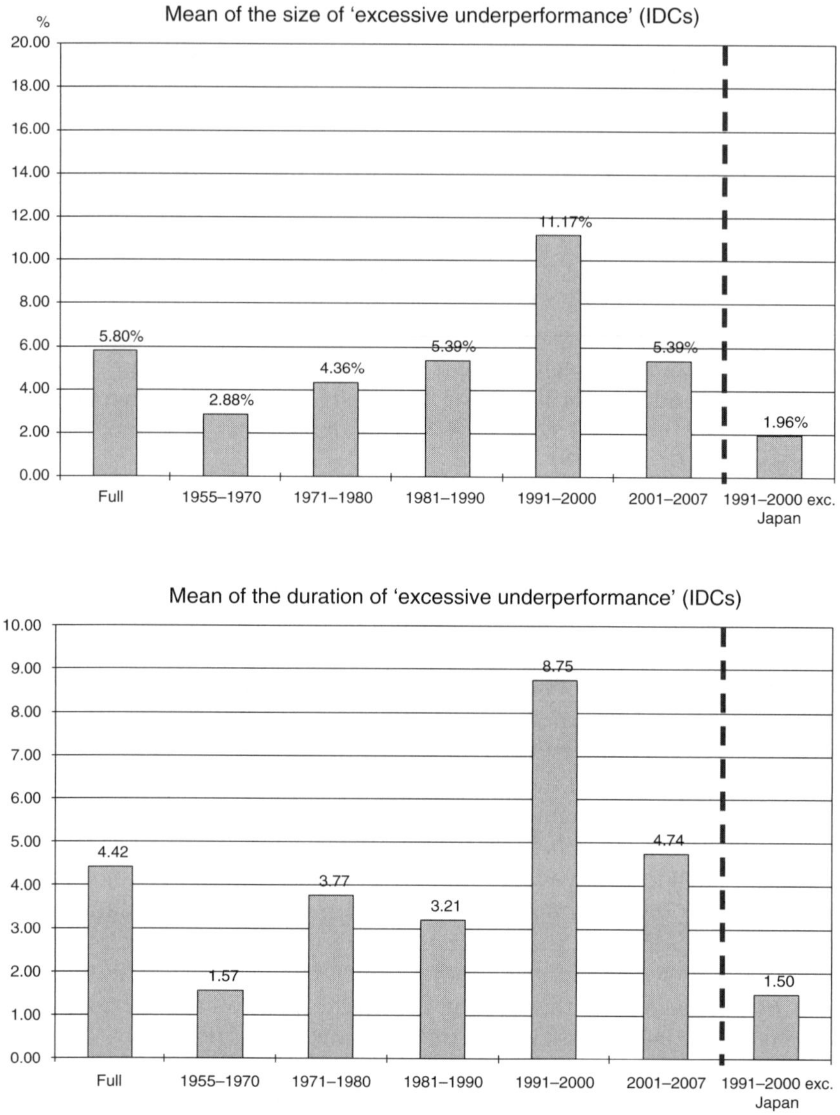

Notes: IDC = industrialized countries; LDC = less-developed countries.

Source: Authors' calculations.

Figure 6.4 Summary statistics of the measure of 'excessive underperformance'

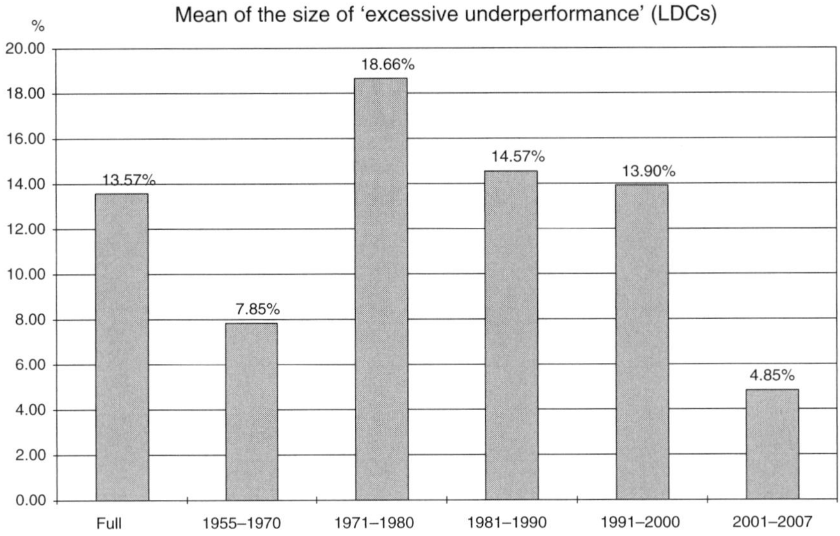

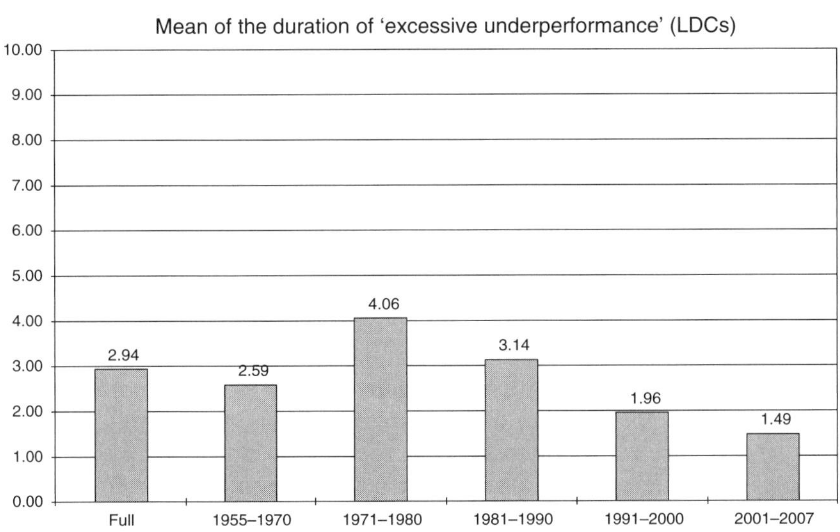

Figure 6.4 (continued)

may yield some results about how pre-crisis conditions affect the size of the crisis. The model with the during-crisis variables may entail the risk of endogeneity, but may provide some insights about how policy decisions made during the crisis can affect the size of the crisis.

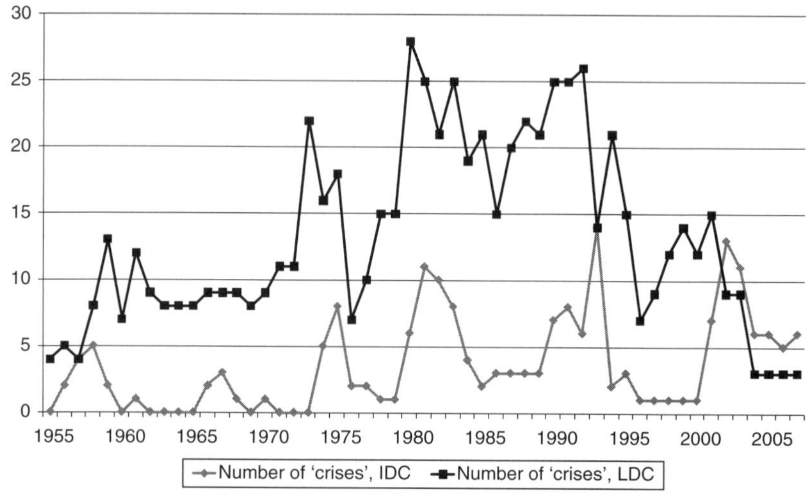

Notes: IDC = industrialized countries; LDC = less-developed countries.

Source: Authors' calculations.

Figure 6.5 Number of 'crises' among the sample countries

6.4.3 Estimation Results

Table 6.5 presents the regression results for the output cost of economic crises. The first six columns of the table show the results of the estimation models with pre-crisis trilemma configurations, whereas the next six columns report those of the estimation models with the trilemma conditions during the economic crisis. We implement the OLS estimation, and report heteroskedasticity-consistent standard errors.

The macroeconomic control variables behave as theory predicts. A country with a higher level of per capita income experiences a smaller output loss once it experiences a crisis, though its effect is non-linear. A country that enters a crisis after experiencing an economic boom tends to experience a larger output loss in a crisis. The tendency among developing countries to have procyclical fiscal policy is often noted as one of the weaknesses of these countries' macroeconomic management, and we found that procyclical fiscal policy does indeed lead to a greater output loss among crisis economies. The estimated coefficient on the duration of the crisis is found to be significantly positive, indicating that if a crisis lasts for one more year, the output loss will be larger by about three percentage points.

The estimated coefficient on financial development is persistently negative, though never statistically significant. An economy more open to international trade prior to the crisis tends to weather a crisis well. This result is consistent with the experience of the economies that were affected by the Asian crisis of 1997–1998.

Among the trilemma variables, in terms of the pre-crisis conditions, only the extent of exchange rate stability seems to matter for the size of output loss for crisis economies. An economy with a greater extent of exchange rate stability tends to experience a smaller output loss once it experiences an economic crisis. The level of IR holding prior to the crisis does not seem to matter as much. Financial openness seems to be an output loss reducer, but it is not statistically significant.

In the regressions incorporating the during-crisis conditions, the amount of IR holding does now matter. The greater the level of international reserves a crisis country retains even after a crisis breaks out, the smaller the resulting output loss will be. The variable for exchange rate stability does again enter positively in the estimation model but this time with greater statistical significance. It appears that a country that can sustain stability in its exchange rate movement can send a positive signal to both domestic and international investors, so that it does not lose access to the capital markets. Also, an economy with a stable exchange rate can avoid facing high volatility in the prices of goods and services.[29]

The effect of monetary independence in the midst of crises is also found to be significant, but this result is more difficult to interpret. Monetary independence is found to be a negative factor to the cost of economic crisis, but only up to the threshold in IR holding of 14–15 percent of GDP. Above this threshold, the impact of greater monetary independence becomes positive. The negative impact of greater monetary independence is easier to interpret, as we found in the regression for output volatility, because it reflects the stabilizing function of monetary independence. Using the results from model (8) in Table 6.5, we can conjecture that for the countries that hold IR greater than 14–15 percent of GDP to reduce the cost of output losses from experiencing an economic crisis, it is better to retain higher levels of exchange rate stability and lower levels of monetary independence.[30] Pursuing both weaker monetary independence and greater exchange rate stability means the country concerned must pursue a higher level of financial openness since these three policy goals need to be linearly related. Considering that the IR holding of 14–15 percent of GDP is well below the average ratio to GDP in 2008 (that is, about 21 percent), the countries with the level of IR holding above the threshold must be relatively more open economies. For those economies, it seems better to pursue greater financial openness rather than retaining greater monetary independence and exchange rate stability.

Table 6.5 Regressions on the output losses of economic crises

	(1)	(2)	(3)	(4)	(5)	(6)
Relative income ($t-1$)	–0.117 [0.065]*	–0.134 [0.068]**	–0.131 [0.068]*	–0.139 [0.068]**	–0.11 [0.064]*	–0.13 [0.066]**
Relative income, sq. ($t-1$)	0.262 [0.077]***	0.271 [0.081]***	0.271 [0.077]***	0.276 [0.080]***	0.258 [0.075]***	0.275 [0.080]***
GDP growth ($t-1$)	0.255 [0.108]**	0.26 [0.110]**	0.224 [0.111]**	0.227 [0.110]**	0.244 [0.107]**	0.24 [0.106]**
Fiscal pro-cyclical ($t-1$)	0.011 [0.008]	0.013 [0.009]	0.013 [0.008]	0.013 [0.009]	0.013 [0.008]	0.014 [0.009]
Duration of the crisis	0.03 [0.006]***	0.03 [0.006]***	0.03 [0.006]***	0.03 [0.006]***	0.03 [0.006]***	0.03 [0.006]***
Trade openness ($t-1$)	–0.028 [0.010]***	–0.03 [0.010]***	–0.028 [0.010]***	–0.028 [0.011]**	–0.025 [0.010]**	–0.022 [0.011]**
Private credit creation ($t-1$)	–0.014 [0.015]	–0.011 [0.015]	–0.009 [0.015]	–0.006 [0.016]	–0.013 [0.015]	–0.009 [0.016]
IR ($t-1$)	–0.011 [0.022]	–0.05 [0.093]	0.005 [0.022]	0.135 [0.103]	–0.008 [0.023]	–0.07 [0.091]
MI ($t-1$)	–0.017 [0.030]	–0.008 [0.035]	0.004 [0.029]	0.032 [0.034]		
MI x IR ($t-1$)		–0.082 [0.161]		–0.251 [0.179]		
ERS ($t-1$)	–0.031 [0.017]*	–0.045 [0.023]*			–0.028 [0.016]*	–0.045 [0.022]**
ERS x IR ($t-1$)		0.149 [0.108]				0.164 [0.120]
KAOPEN ($t-1$)			–0.022 [0.016]	–0.017 [0.022]	–0.02 [0.016]	–0.016 [0.024]
KAO x IR ($t-1$)				–0.038 [0.103]		–0.053 [0.107]
# of Obs.	139	139	139	139	139	139
Adjusted R2	0.35	0.35	0.34	0.34	0.36	0.36

Notes: Robust standard errors in brackets. * Significant at 10%; ** significant at 5%; *** significant at 1%. These control variables are included as the averages over three years prior to years of the first year of underperformance (or just 'crisis'). For the sake of brevity, we use the time notation of ($t-1$) for the variables that refer to the precrisis conditions and (t) for those that refer to the conditions during the crisis.

Source: Authors' calculations.

	(7)	(8)	(9)	(10)	(11)	(12)
Relative income (*t* – 1)	–0.14 [0.069]**	–0.129 [0.067]*	–0.138 [0.069]**	–0.117 [0.068]*	–0.136 [0.069]**	–0.146 [0.069]**
Relative income, sq. (*t* – 1)	0.278 [0.078]***	0.28 [0.075]***	0.276 [0.076]***	0.268 [0.076]***	0.278 [0.076]***	0.29 [0.077]***
GDP growth (*t* – 1)	0.24 [0.108]**	0.222 [0.110]**	0.228 [0.108]**	0.21 [0.109]*	0.232 [0.104]**	0.224 [0.104]**
Fiscal pro-cyclical (*t* – 1)	0.012 [0.008]	0.009 [0.008]	0.013 [0.008]	0.01 [0.009]	0.012 [0.008]	0.013 [0.008]
Duration of the crisis	0.03 [0.006]***	0.031 [0.006]***	0.029 [0.006]***	0.031 [0.006]***	0.03 [0.006]***	0.03 [0.006]***
Trade openness (*t* – 1)	–0.022 [0.010]**	–0.022 [0.010]**	–0.025 [0.010]**	–0.027 [0.010]***	–0.018 [0.011]*	–0.015 [0.011]
Private credit creation (*t* – 1)	–0.016 [0.015]	–0.02 [0.015]	–0.008 [0.015]	–0.015 [0.016]	–0.015 [0.015]	–0.013 [0.014]
IR (*t*)	–0.029 [0.019]	–0.315 [0.101]***	–0.011 [0.020]	–0.283 [0.097]***	–0.026 [0.020]	–0.006 [0.067]
MI (*t*)	–0.005 [0.026]	–0.081 [0.039]**	0 [0.025]	–0.077 [0.039]**		
MI x IR (*t*)		0.612 [0.222]***		0.609 [0.220]***		
ERS (*t*)	–0.026 [0.012]**	–0.034 [0.015]**			–0.026 [0.012]**	–0.03 [0.016]*
ERS x IR (*t*)		0.05 [0.057]				0.019 [0.067]
KAOPEN (*t*)			–0.019 [0.018]	–0.029 [0.023]	–0.017 [0.018]	–0.009 [0.021]
KAO x IR (*t*)				0.031 [0.068]		–0.064 [0.077]
# of Obs.	139	139	139	139	139	139
Adjusted R2	0.35	0.36	0.34	0.35	0.36	0.35

6.4.4 Policy Discussion

The preceding finding seems to contradict our previous finding that greater exchange rate stability leads to greater output volatility unless the economy concerned holds foreign exchange reserves. However, we must keep in mind that the preceding empirical analysis is conducted only for a sample of crisis economies; the two sets of regression analyses are therefore conducted on two different samples. We can reconcile these ostensibly conflicting results by resorting to the well-known 'fear of floating' thesis. That is, while greater exchange rate stability can be output volatility-enhancing in tranquil times, it can help countries once they experience economic crises. Therefore, countries can be discouraged from adopting more flexible exchange rates.

We have previously seen that the output volatility enhancing effect of greater exchange rate stability can be mitigated by holding levels of IR higher than certain thresholds. Furthermore, we have also seen that many countries do not attempt to adopt a policy combination of exchange rate stability and IR holding enough to lessen output volatility. However, Figure 6.2 shows that developing countries, especially non-emerging market developing countries, continue to maintain high levels of exchange rate stability, which can be evidence of the fear of floating.

The analogy to the peso problem – a situation where an extreme event that can occur with a very low probability dominates an economic agent's behavior or decision-making because of its significantly high cost – is clear. Even if economic crises are not very frequent, policymakers are motivated to prepare for costly crises, by maintaining exchange rate stability. Pursuing pure exchange rate stability can make countries prone to higher output volatility because the exchange rate cannot function as an automatic stabilizer. However, if a country holds a higher level of foreign reserves, it can mitigate the absence of the automatic stabilizing function of the exchange rate. In addition, we find that having a higher level of IR can allow a country to prepare for an economic crisis as well (Table 6.3). Hence, countries that hold high levels of IR can afford to adopt more flexible exchange rates. This may explain why emerging market countries, most of which are large IR holders, have adopted more flexible exchange rates than non-emerging market developing countries.

6.4.5 Does a Regime Change in the Aftermath of a Crisis?

As we write in 2011, the impact of the recent global crisis has not fully dissipated. Although there are signs of recovery in most parts of the world, it is uncertain whether the recovery will be sustained over the coming years.

While many industrialized and developing countries have faced a crisis situation, some countries have experienced a more severe economic situation than others.

As a final exercise, we will examine one natural question that can arise from the foregoing analysis: if we assume that countries are still experiencing a 'crisis' (in our sense), what kind of financial systems will they pursue in the aftermath of the crisis?

For this question, we can only present our plausible expectations from the above analyses. For this purpose, we conducted mean-equality tests of the trilemma indexes before and after the crisis which we identify using our measure of excessive underperformance. Specifically, we tested the equality of each of the indexes between three years before the first year of a crisis and three years after the last year of the crisis for the full sample and the subsamples of industrialized countries (IDC), developing countries (DC), and emerging market economies (EMG) from 1970 to 2007. Table 6.6 shows the test results for the different samples and different time periods. The table also shows the number of crisis episodes over which the trilemma index of interest rises or falls in a statistically significant sense as well as the percentage of the cases within each sample.[31]

Industrialized countries seem to have gone through a discernable path over the course of the sample period: the industrial crisis countries reduced the level of monetary independence and increased the levels of both exchange rate stability and financial openness throughout the time period, which dominantly reflects the path of the eurozone countries. This tendency would not change even if one compares the subsample periods.

Developing countries, on the other hand, increased the level of monetary independence, but reduced the level of exchange rate stability and financial openness in the aftermath of economic hardships. However, this tendency does not appear to be persistent. While increasing the levels of monetary independence and financial openness, and decreasing the level of exchange rate stability, was a more prevalent way of overcoming economic hardships before the 1990s, these countries tended to decrease the level of monetary independence and financial openness but to increase the degree of exchange rate stability. Among emerging market countries, the tendency to decrease the levels of monetary independence and financial openness in the post-crisis period was more evident.

This finding may reflect the greater vulnerability of developing countries, especially emerging market countries, to volatile financial flows as financial globalization became more widespread after the 1990s. Countries can be tempted to restrict cross-border capital flows and lose their monetary independence in the face of rapid and massive capital flows. Unlike in the period before the waves of financial globalization hit these economies,

Table 6.6 Results of the mean–equality tests with the trilemma indexes before and after the crises

1970–2007

	# of Obs.	Monetary independence (MI)				Exchange rate stability (ERS)				Financial openness (KAO)			
		Up	(%)	Down	(%)	Up	(%)	Down	(%)	Up	(%)	Down	(%)
FULL	230	53	0.230	62	**0.270**	34	**0.148**	29	0.126	39	**0.170**	32	0.139
IDC	49	8	0.163	20	**0.408**	12	**0.245**	4	0.082	15	**0.306**	5	0.102
LDC	151	36	**0.238**	34	0.225	18	0.119	21	**0.139**	20	0.132	23	**0.152**
EMG	49	13	**0.265**	12	0.245	6	0.122	13	**0.265**	11	**0.224**	9	0.184

1970s–1980s

	# of Obs.	Monetary independence (MI)				Exchange rate stability (ERS)				Financial openness (KAO)			
		Up	(%)	Down	(%)	Up	(%)	Down	(%)	Up	(%)	Down	(%)
FULL	123	32	**0.260**	30	0.244	21	0.171	21	0.171	21	**0.171**	13	0.106
IDC	25	6	0.240	10	**0.400**	9	**0.360**	3	0.120	6	**0.240**	1	0.040
LDC	73	18	**0.247**	14	0.192	9	0.123	14	**0.192**	13	**0.178**	8	0.110
EMG	27	9	**0.333**	4	0.148	2	0.074	9	**0.333**	7	**0.259**	4	0.148

1990s–2000s

	# of Obs.	Monetary independence (MI)				Exchange rate stability (ERS)				Financial openness (KAO)			
		Up	(%)	Down	(%)	Up	(%)	Down	(%)	Up	(%)	Down	(%)
FULL	107	21	0.196	32	**0.299**	13	**0.121**	8	0.075	18	0.168	19	**0.178**
IDC	24	2	0.083	10	**0.417**	3	**0.125**	1	0.042	9	**0.375**	4	0.167
LDC	78	18	0.231	20	**0.256**	9	**0.115**	7	0.090	7	0.090	15	**0.192**
EMG	22	4	0.182	8	**0.364**	4	0.182	4	0.182	4	0.182	5	**0.227**

Notes: IDC = industrialized countries; LDC = less developed countries; EMG = emerging market countries.

Source: Authors' calculations.

it may not be a good policy option to adopt a freely flexible exchange rate regime as a means to overcome an economic hardship.

If the reaction to the recent crisis is similar to the reaction observed since the 1990s, it is likely that developing countries will try to reduce the level of monetary independence and tighten capital controls policy in the coming years. However, it is premature to make such a prediction.

6.5 CONCLUSION

In the midst of the most severe and persistent crisis since the Great Depression, economists are re-evaluating international macroeconomic policies and rethinking architecture for international financial markets. For this effort, we need to know how the international financial architecture can affect the macroeconomic performance of individual economies. Theoretically, we know that any international architecture would be constrained by the impossible trinity or trilemma; namely, a country cannot achieve all three policy goals of monetary independence, exchange rate stability and financial openness. Despite its significance, this theory had not been widely tested empirically due to the lack of appropriate metrics to measure the extent of achievement in the three policy goals. Our previous work (Aizenman et al. 2008) attempted to fill the deficiency by developing the trilemma indexes and confirmed the validity of the theory. In this chapter, we extended our analysis and explored some of the questions that were not addressed in our previous work.

First, we examined through what channels the trilemma policy configurations affect output volatility. We found that the estimation on output volatility shares similar characteristics with the estimation on investment volatility, suggesting that trilemma policy configurations and external finances affect output volatility through investment. Specifically, as in the estimation on output volatility, greater monetary independence is found to help reduce investment volatility. However, if the level of IR holding rises above 15–23 percent of GDP, greater monetary independence would become volatility-enhancing for investment by providing too much liquidity and thereby making the cost of capital too volatile. While a higher degree of exchange rate stability could stabilize the real exchange rate, it could also make investment volatile, though the volatility-enhancing effect of exchange rate stability on investment can be offset by holding higher levels of IR. Greater financial openness is found to help reduce real exchange rate volatility. These results indicate that policymakers in a more open economy would prefer pursuing greater exchange rate stability and greater financial openness while holding a massive amount of IR because this policy combination would help them achieve stability in both investment and the real exchange rate. This finding might help to explain why small open economies in East Asia are holding massive amounts of IR.

Second, we investigated how trilemma policy configurations could affect the output performance of the economies that are experiencing severe circumstances. We found that crisis economies could exit a crisis situation with a smaller output loss if they entered a crisis with more stable exchange rates. Furthermore, a crisis country that maintains a higher level of IR and greater exchange rate stability during a crisis period could reduce the size of output loss.

Finally, we asked how trilemma configurations will evolve once the impact of the recent crisis has fully dissipated. Using data since the 1970s, we have shown that developing countries are more likely to decrease the level of monetary independence and financial openness but increase the level of exchange rate stability in the aftermath of an economic crisis. This has been the case since the 1990s. This finding indicates the vulnerability of developing countries, especially emerging market economies, to volatile capital flows.

NOTES

1. Of course, the notable exceptions include the papers by Obstfeld et al. (2005, 2008, 2009) and Shambaugh (2004).
2. If the eurozone countries are removed from the sample (not reported), financial openness evolves similarly to the industrial countries (IDC) group that includes the eurozone countries, but exchange rate stability hovers around the line for monetary independence, though at a bit higher levels, after the early 1990s. The difference between exchange rate stability and monetary independence slightly diverged after the end of the 1990s.
3. The emerging market countries are defined as the countries classified as either emerging or frontier during 1980–1997 by the International Financial Corporation, plus Hong Kong, China and Singapore.
4. Willett (2003) has called this compulsion by countries with a mediocre level of exchange rate fixity to hoard reserves the 'unstable middle' hypothesis (as opposed to the 'disappearing middle' view).
5. Germany is included as one of the 'non-euro industrialized countries' because, unlike the other euro member countries, Germany has retained monetary independence even after monetary integration started in Europe.
6. These are unweighted averages; if weighted by GDP, the differences would be larger.
7. Aizenman et al. (2008) have shown that these three measures of the trilemma are linearly related. Therefore, it is most reasonable to include two of the indexes concurrently, not just individually nor all three collectively.
8. The currency crisis dummy variable is derived from the conventional exchange rate market pressure (EMP) index pioneered by Eichengreen et al. (1996). The EMP index is defined as a weighted average of monthly changes in the nominal exchange rate, the percentage loss in international reserves and the nominal interest rate. The weights are inversely related to the pooled variance of changes in each component over the sample countries, and adjustment is made for the countries that experienced hyperinflation following Kaminsky and Reinhart (1999). For countries without data to compute

the EMP index, the currency crisis classifications in Glick and Hutchison (2001) and Kaminsky and Reinhart (1999) are used.

9. The robust regression procedure conducts iterative weighted least squares regressions while downweighting observations that have larger residuals until the coefficients converge. Also, we remove the observations if their values of inflation volatility are greater than a value of 30 or the rate of inflation (as an explanatory variable) is greater than 100 percent.
10. The effect of trade openness is found to have insignificant effects for all the samples and is therefore dropped from the estimations. This finding is insightful in view of the debate in the literature, in which both positive (that is, volatility-enhancing) and negative (that is, volatility-reducing) effects of trade openness have been reported. The volatility-enhancing effect in the sense of Easterly et al. (2001) and Rodrik (1998) is captured by the volatility of (*TOT*Trade Openness*). For the volatility-reducing effect of trade openness, refer to Calvo et al. (2004), Cavallo (2005, 2007) and Cavallo and Frankel (2008). The impact of trade openness on output volatility also depends on the type of trade, that is, whether it is interindustry trade (Krugman 1993) or intraindustry trade (Razin and Rose 1994).
11. For theoretical predictions on the effect of financial development, refer to Aghion et al. (1999) and Caballero and Krishnamurthy (2001). For empirical findings, see Blankenau et al. (2001) and Kose et al. (2003).
12. In model (1), once the interaction term between monetary independence and international reserves is removed from the model, the variable for monetary independence enters the model with a 5 percent significant negative coefficient. The same outcome is obtained for the EMG regression in model (1) of Table 6.2.
13. This finding can be surprising to some if the concept of monetary independence is taken synonymously to central bank independence because many authors, most typically Alesina and Summers (1993), have found that more independent central banks tend to have little, if any, impact on output variability. However, in this literature, the extent of central bank independence is usually measured by the legal definition of the central bankers or the turnover ratio of bank governors, which can bring about different inferences than our measure of monetary independence.
14. The link is not always predicted to be negative theoretically. When monetary authorities react to negative supply shocks, their action can amplify the shocks and exacerbate output volatility.
15. However, the result of model (2) in Table 6.1 is consistent with those of models (1) and (3). That is, model (2) predicts that if a country concurrently increases its level of monetary independence and financial openness, it could reduce output volatility. As long as the concept of the trilemma holds true, that is, the three policy goals are linearly related, which we empirically proved to be the case in Aizenman et al. (2008), the efforts of increasing both *MI* and *KAOPEN* is essentially the same as lowering the level of exchange rate stability. Models (1) and (3) predict that a smaller ERS leads to a smaller output volatility. But these models also predict that if the country holds IR more than the thresholds, it would have to face higher output volatility, which is found in model (2).
16. One might suspect that this result can be driven by multicollinearity between the short-term debt variable and the variables for the various net inflows. However, even when the three net inflow variables are removed from the models, total debt service remains a positive factor while the short-term debt variable continues to be insignificant.
17. Rogoff (2003) argues that globalization contributes to dwindling mark-ups, and thereby disinflation. Razin and Binyamini (2007) predicted that both trade and financial liberalization would flatten the Phillips curve, so that policymakers would become less responsive to output gaps and more aggressive in fighting inflation. Loungani et al. (2001) provides empirical evidence for the link.
18. Aizenman and Glick (2009) and Glick and Hutchison (2008) show that the PRC, whose ratio of reserves holding to GDP is estimated to be 50 percent, has started to face more inflationary pressure in 2007 as a result of intensive foreign exchange market intervention to sustain exchange rate stability.

19. Interest rate differentials are also tested but did not turn out to be significant. Therefore, they are not included in the estimation.
20. The threshold levels of IR holding are 18 percent and 28 percent of GDP in models (7) and (8) in Table 6.3, respectively. They are 14 percent and 26 percent in models (7) and (8) in Table 6.4, respectively.
21. This result can be obtained by assuming no interaction effects with IR in model (4) in Table 6.4.
22. If it is above the upper bound, then it can be considered to be 'excessive overperformance (boom)'. However, we do not look into the issue of excessive overperformance in this chapter.
23. For example, if the actual growth rate is below the band for country X in 1992 through 1996, the gaps for the five years will be added.
24. If the actual growth rate lies within the band in 1994 but below the band in 1992–1993 and 1995–1996, the 'crisis period' is considered to be from 1992 to 1996.
25. The episodes of excess underperformance are divided by the decade depending on their beginning year. For example, the size and the duration of the Japanese 1990s recession (that continued up to 2006) is included in the 1991–2000 period. As a matter of fact, the Japanese experience is an outlier in terms of both its size and duration. Therefore, the subsample average without Japan is also shown.
26. The variable for fiscal procyclicality is calculated as the correlation between the detrended series of real output and real fiscal expenditure over five years, since three years is not long enough to provide the general characteristics of fiscal policy.
27. Other control variables that persistently turned out to be insignificant and are therefore removed include: change in the US real interest rate, TOT shocks, trade openness, real exchange rate overvaluation, regional dummies, and the GDP growth rate of industrialized countries during the crisis.
28. The Center for the Study of Civil Wars index is not a perfect dummy for armed conflicts. It tends to be a little too inclusive. For example, the United Kingdom had been for many years until recently considered to be a country with 'internal armed conflicts' because of the Irish Republican Army's activities, although the country as a whole did not appear to have an 'internal conflict'. The Philippines has also been a country with internal conflicts due to occasional anti-government movements by Muslim insurgencies.
29. One reviewer pointed out that the finding that exchange rate stability and holding ample IR could help reduce the size of output loss sounds tautological, because crises usually lead to output loss through the balance sheet effect. It could be tautological if we were focusing on the currency crises. However, our definition of crisis includes not only currency or banking crises, but also dire economic situations caused by other, potentially non-economic factors. Hence, the criticism of tautology does not strictly apply.
30. From 1996, the average ratio of IR to GDP among developing economies was about 14 percent. As of 2008, it was about 21 percent after declining from the peak of 24 percent in 2007.
31. For example, there are 53 crisis episodes after which the level of monetary independence increased statistically significantly in the full sample, which accounts for 23 percent of total.

REFERENCES

Aghion, P., A. Banerjee and T. Piketty (1999), 'Dualism and macroeconomic volatility', *Quarterly Journal of Economics*, **114** (4), 359–97.

Aizenman, J., M.D. Chinn and H. Ito (2008), 'Assessing the emerging global financial architecture: measuring the trilemma's configurations over time', NBER Working Paper Series #14533 (December 2008; revised April 2009), Cambridge, MA: National Bureau of Economic Research (NBER).

Aizenman, J. and R. Glick (2009), 'Sterilization, monetary policy, and global financial integration', *Review of International Economics*, **17** (4), 777–801.
Alesina, A. and L. Summers (1993), 'Central bank independence and macroeconomic performance', *Journal of Money, Credit and Banking*, **25** (2), 151–62.
Blankenau, W., M.A. Kose and K. Yi (2001), 'Can world real interest rates explain business cycles in a small open economy?', *Journal of Economic Dynamics and Control*, **25** (6–7), 867–89.
Caballero, R.J. and A. Krishnamurthy (2001), 'International and domestic collateral constraints in a model of emerging market crises', *Journal of Monetary Economics*, **48** (3), 513–48.
Calvo, G.A., A. Izquierdo and L.F. Mejía (2004), 'On the empirics of sudden stops: the relevance of balance-sheet effects', Research Department Working Paper 509, Washington, DC: Inter-American Development Bank.
Caprio, G. and D. Klingebiel (2003), 'Episodes of systematic and borderline financial crises', manuscript, Washington, DC: World Bank.
Cavallo, E.A. (2005), 'Trade, gravity and sudden stops: on how commercial trade openness can increase the stability of capital flows', mimeo, Cambridge, MA: Harvard University.
Cavallo, E.A. (2007), 'Output volatility and openness to trade: a reassessment', Inter-American Development Bank Working Paper #604 (April), Washington, DC: Inter-American Development Bank.
Cavallo, E.A. and J. Frankel (2008), 'Does openness to trade make countries more vulnerable to sudden stops, or less? Using gravity to establish causality', *Journal of International Money and Finance*, **27** (8), 1430–52.
Chinn, M.D. and H. Ito (2006), 'What matters for financial development? Capital controls, institutions, and interactions', *Journal of Development Economics*, **81** (1), 163–92.
Chinn, M.D. and H. Ito (2008), 'A new measure of financial openness', *Journal of Comparative Policy Analysis*, **10** (3), 309–22.
Easterly, W., R. Islam and J. Stiglitz (2001), 'Shaken and stirred: explaining growth volatility', in B. Plesokovic and N. Stern (eds), *Annual World Bank Conference on Development Economics*, Washington, DC: World Bank, pp. 191–211.
Edison, H.J., M.W. Klein, L. Ricci and T. Sløk (2002), 'Capital account liberalization and economic performance: a review of the literature', IMF Working Paper 02/120, Washington, DC: IMF.
Edison, H.J. and F.E. Warnock (2001), 'A simple measure of the intensity of capital controls', International Finance Discussion Paper #708, Washington, DC: Board of Governors of the Federal Reserve System.
Edwards, S. (1999), 'How effective are capital controls?', *Journal of Economic Perspectives*, **13** (4), 65–84.
Edwards, S. (2001), 'Capital mobility and economic performance: are emerging economies different?', NBER Working Paper No. 8076, Cambridge, MA: NBER.
Edwards, S. and E. Levy Yeyati (2005), 'Flexible exchange rates as shock absorbers', *European Economic Review*, **49** (8), 2079–105.
Eichengreen, B., A.K. Rose and C. Wyplosz (1996), 'Contagious currency crises', NBER Working Paper No. 5681, Cambridge, MA: NBER.
Ghosh, A., A. Gulde and J. Ostry (1997), 'Does the nominal exchange rate regime matter?', NBER Working Paper No. 5874, Cambridge, MA: NBER.
Glick, R. and M. Hutchison (2001), 'Banking and currency crises: how common

are twins?' in R. Glick, R. Moreno and M. Spiegel (eds), *Financial Crises in Emerging Markets*, Cambridge: Cambridge University Press, pp. 35–69.
Glick, R. and M. Hutchison (2008), 'Are capital controls effective? Duration of capital controls and the survival of pegged exchange rate regimes with special reference to the People's Republic of China', mimeo, University of California, Santa Cruz.
Haruka, D.S. (2007), 'Output volatility and large output drops in emerging market and developing countries', IMF Working Paper WP/07/114, Washington, DC: IMF.
Kaminsky, G. and C. Reinhart (1999), 'The twin crises: the causes of banking and currency balance-of-payments problems', *American Economic Review*, **89** (3), 473–500.
Kose, M.A., E. Prasad, K. Rogoff and S.J. Wei (2006), 'Financial globalization: a reappraisal', IMF Working Paper WP/06/189, Washington, DC: IMF.
Kose, M.A., E. Prasad and M. Terrones (2003), 'Financial integration and macroeconomic volatility', IMF Working Paper WP/03/50, Washington, DC: IMF.
Krugman, P. (1993), 'Lessons of Massachusetts for EMU', in F. Giavazzi and F. Torres (eds), *The Transition to Economic and Monetary Union in Europe*, Cambridge: Cambridge University Press, pp. 241–66.
Lane, P.R. and G.M. Milesi-Ferretti (2006), 'The external wealth of nations mark II: Revised and extended estimates of foreign assets and liabilities, 1970–2004', IMF Working Paper 06/69, Washington, DC: IMF.
Loungani, P., A. Razin and C.W. Yuen (2001), 'Capital mobility and the output–inflation tradeoff', *Journal of Development Economics*, **64** (1), 255–74.
Mishkin, F.S. and K. Schmidt-Hebbel (2007), 'Does inflation targeting make a difference?', NBER Working Paper No.12876, Cambridge, MA: NBER.
Obstfeld, M., J.C. Shambaugh and A.M. Taylor (2005), 'The trilemma in history: tradeoffs among exchange rates, monetary policies, and capital mobility', *Review of Economics and Statistics*, **87** (August), 423–38.
Obstfeld, M., J.C. Shambaugh and A.M. Taylor (2008), 'Financial stability, the trilemma, and international reserves', NBER Working Paper No. 14217, Cambridge, MA: NBER.
Obstfeld, M., J.C. Shambaugh and A.M. Taylor (2009), 'Financial instability, reserves and central bank swap lines in the panic of 2008', NBER Working Paper No. 14826, Cambridge, MA: NBER.
Razin, A. and A. Binyamini (2007), 'Flattening the short-run trade-off between inflation and domestic activity: the analytics of the effects of globalization', Kiel Working Paper No. 1363 (June), Kiel: Kiel Institute for World Economics.
Razin, A. and A.K. Rose (1994), 'Business cycle volatility and openness: an exploratory cross-sectional analysis', in L. Leiderman and A. Razin (eds), *Capital Mobility: the Impact on Consumption, Investment, and Growth*, Cambridge: Cambridge University Press, pp. 48–75.
Rodrik, D. (1998), 'Why do more open economies have bigger governments?', *Journal of Political Economy*, **106** (5), 997–1032.
Rogoff, K. (2003), 'Globalization and global disinflation', *Federal Reserve Bank of Kansas City Economic Review* (4th quarter issue), 45–78.
Shambaugh, J.C. (2004), 'The effects of fixed exchange rates on monetary policy', *Quarterly Journal of Economics*, **119** (February), 301–52.
Willett, T. (2003), 'Fear of floating need not imply fixed exchange rates', *Open Economies Review*, **14** (January), 77–91.

APPENDIX: CONSTRUCTION OF THE TRILEMMA MEASURES

Monetary Independence

The extent of monetary independence (MI) is measured as the reciprocal of the annual correlation of the monthly interest rates between the home country and the base country. Money market rates are used.[1]

The index for the extent of monetary independence is defined as:

$$MI = 1 - \frac{corr(i_i, i_j) - (-1)}{1 - (-1)}$$

where *i* refers to home countries and *j* to the base country. By construction, the maximum and minimum values are 1 and 0, respectively. Higher values of the index mean more monetary policy independence.[2,3]

Here, the base country is defined as the country that a home country's monetary policy is most closely linked with as in Shambaugh (2004). The base countries are Australia, Belgium, France, Germany, India, Malaysia, South Africa, the United Kingdom and the US. For the countries and years for which Shambaugh's data are available, the base countries from his work are used, and for the others, the base countries are assigned based on IMF's *Annual Report on Exchange Arrangements and Exchange Restrictions)* and the *CIA Factbook.*

Exchange Rate Stability

To measure exchange rate stability (*ERS*), annual standard deviations (*stdev*) of the monthly exchange rate (*exch_rate*) between the home country and the base country are calculated. The following formula is used to normalize the index to fall between zero and one:

$$ERS = \frac{0.01}{0.01 + stdev(\Delta(\log(exch\_rate))}$$

Mechanically applying this formula can create a downward bias in the index, as it would overstate the 'flexibility' of the exchange rate especially when it moves within a narrow band but is realigned infrequently.[4] To avoid such downward bias, we apply a threshold to the exchange rate movement as has been done in the literature. That is, if the rate of monthly change in the exchange rate stayed within +/−0.33 percent bands, we consider the exchange rate is 'fixed' and assign the value of one for the ERS index. Furthermore, pegs that last only for one year are removed because they may not be the intended outcome of exchange rate regime choice.[5] Higher values of this index indicate more stable movement of the exchange rate against the currency of the base country.

Financial Openness/Integration

It is difficult to measure the extent of capital account controls.[6] Although many measures exist to describe the extent and intensity of capital account controls, it is generally agreed that such measures fail to capture fully the complexity of real-world capital controls. Nonetheless, as a measure of financial openness, we use the index of capital account openness, or KAOPEN, by Chinn and Ito (2006, 2008). KAOPEN is based on information in the IMF's *Annual Report on Exchange Arrangements and Exchange Restrictions*. Specifically, KAOPEN is the first standardized principal component of the variables that indicate the presence of multiple exchange rates, restrictions on current account transactions, those on capital account transactions, and surrender requirements for export proceeds.[7] Since KAOPEN is based upon reported restrictions, it is necessarily a de jure index of capital account openness (in contrast to de facto measures such as those in Lane and Milesi-Ferretti 2006). The choice of a de jure measure of capital account openness is driven by the motivation to look into policy intentions of the countries; de facto measures are more susceptible to other macroeconomic effects than policy decisions made solely with respect to capital controls.[8]

The Chinn–Ito index is normalized between zero and one. Higher values of this index indicate that a country is more open to cross-border capital transactions. The index is originally available for 181 countries from 1970 to 2007.[9] The data set we examine does not include the US.

Notes

1. The data are extracted from IMF's *International Financial Statistics* (IFS) (line 60B. . .ZF. . .). For the countries whose money market rates are unavailable or extremely limited, the money market data are supplemented by those from the Bloomberg terminal and also by the discount rates (line 60. . .ZF. . .) and the deposit rates (line 60L. . .ZF. . .) series from the *IFS*.
2. The index is smoothed out by applying the three-year moving average encompassing the preceding, concurrent and succeeding years ($t - 1, t, t + 1$) of observations.
3. We note one important caveat about this index. Among some countries and in some years, especially early in the sample, the interest rate used for the calculation of the MI index (see note 1) is often constant throughout a year, making the annual correlation of the interest rates between the home and base countries ($corr(i_i, i_j)$ in the formula) undefined. Since we treat the undefined *corr* the same as zero, it makes the MI index value 0.5. One may think that the policy interest rate being constant (regardless of the base

country's interest rate) is a sign of monetary independence. However, it can reflect one or more of the following possibilities: (i) the home country's monetary policy is independent from the base country's; (ii) the home country uses other tools to implement monetary policy than manipulating the interest rates, such as changing the required reserve ratios and providing window guidance (while leaving the policy interest rate unchanged); and (iii) the home country exercises a strong control over financial intermediaries, including through credit rationing, which as a result makes the policy interest rate appear constant. To make the matter more complicated, some countries have used the non-interest rate tools of monetary policy to exercise monetary independence, while others have used them while strictly following the base country's monetary policy. The bottom line is that it is impossible to incorporate these factors in the calculation of MI without over- or underestimating the degree of monetary independence. Therefore, assigning an MI value of 0.5 for such a case should be a reasonable compromise. However, it does not preclude the necessity of robustness checks on the index, which we plan to undertake.

4. In such a case, the average monthly change in the exchange rate would be so small that even a small change could make the standard deviation large and hence the ERS value small.
5. The choice of the +/−0.33 percent bands is based on the +/−2 percent band based on the annual rate, which is often used in the literature. Also, to prevent a break in the peg status due to one-time realignments, any exchange rate that had a percentage change of zero in 11 out of 12 months is considered fixed. When there are two exchange rate reassignments (whether devaluation or revaluation) in three months, they are considered to be one realignment event, and if the remaining ten months experience no exchange rate movement, the exchange rate is considered fixed for that year. This way of defining the threshold for the exchange rate is in line with the one adopted by Shambaugh (2004).
6. See Chinn and Ito (2008), Edison and Warnock (2001), Edwards (2001), Edison et al. (2002) and Kose et al. (2006) for discussions and comparisons of various measures on capital restrictions.
7. This index is described in greater detail in Chinn and Ito (2008).
8. De jure measures of financial openness also face their own limitations. As Edwards (1999) discusses, it is often the case that the private sector circumvents capital account restrictions, nullifying the expected effect of regulatory capital controls. Also, IMF-based variables are too aggregated to capture the subtleties of actual capital controls; that is, the direction of capital flows (that is, inflows or outflows) as well as the type of financial transactions targeted.
9. The original dataset covered 181 countries, but data availability is uneven among the three indexes. *MI* is available for 172 countries; *ERS* for 182; and *KAOPEN* for 178. Data for both *MI* and *ERS* start in 1960 whereas the *KAOPEN* data start in 1970. As a result, *MI* and *ERS* were updated to 2008 while *KAOPEN* was updated only to 2007, the last year for which IMF's *Annual Report on Exchange Arrangements and Exchange Restrictions* data were available.

7. Asia confronts the impossible trinity

Ila Patnaik and Ajay Shah

7.1 INTRODUCTION

A core idea in modern macroeconomics is that of the 'impossible trinity', the notion that a country can have only two of the following at any given time: an open capital account, a fixed exchange rate and an autonomous monetary policy. With the exception of the eurozone countries, most developed countries have an open capital account, a floating exchange rate and an autonomous monetary policy.[1]

In Asia, a few polar examples like Hong Kong, China have a fixed exchange rate, an open capital account and no monetary policy autonomy. In general, however, Asian economies tend to lack a well-defined monetary policy framework, with most having a combination of some capital controls and exchange rate inflexibility. This raises questions about the current state and possible evolution of monetary policy in Asia, and highlights the need for a consistent monetary policy framework.

In this chapter, we focus on 11 major economies in Asia: the People's Republic of China (PRC); Hong Kong, China; India; Indonesia; Republic of Korea (hereafter Korea); Malaysia; the Philippines; Singapore; Taipei,China; Thailand and Viet Nam. This is a highly heterogeneous group, ranging from city-states like Singapore to giants like the PRC, and poor economies like India to rich economies like Taipei,China and Korea. We refer to these economies as the Asia-11.

We examine where the Asia-11 stand with respect to the three corners of the impossible trinity: capital controls, the exchange rate regime and monetary policy autonomy. We obtained summary statistics for each of the 11 economies, and also focused on numerical values for the three largest economies: India, the PRC and Korea.

Since countries sometimes fail to do as they say, this chapter focuses on de facto rather than de jure capital controls, exchange rate regimes and monetary policy frameworks. More specifically, we focus on de facto conditions for capital account openness and exchange rate flexibility, and their implications for monetary policy as measured by the short-term real interest rate.

We find that while the Asia-11 have undergone some degree of de jure capital account liberalization, in most economies restrictions on capital flows are still in place. However, these restrictions have not impeded gradual capital account integration at the de facto level, assisted by a growing sophistication of the financial system.

Alongside this, Asia is characterized by substantial exchange rate inflexibility. Although exchange rate flexibility increased after 2000, it remains low by world standards. Even Korea's flexible exchange rate continues to lag the floating exchange rate.

Countercyclical monetary policy is one strategy which monetary authorities use to achieve the objective of stabilizing inflation and output. We focus on this objective in the context of inconsistencies arising from the impossible trinity. Today, most Asian economies are characterized by growing de facto capital account integration with substantial de facto exchange rate inflexibility. To the extent that capital flows are procyclical, currency trading by central banks will convert procyclical capital flows into procyclical monetary policy. The PRC and India are interesting test cases of this phenomenon, given the limited extent of de facto capital account opening in both countries and their relatively weak financial systems. Yet, even in these two countries we find that monetary policy has been fairly procyclical.

We argue that there are potential difficulties facing economies that have moved towards substantial de facto integration while continuing to have limited exchange rate flexibility. This is particularly a concern for Malaysia and Taipei,China, which combine: (i) sophisticated financial systems that erode the effectiveness of capital controls; (ii) substantial de facto openness; and (iii) rigidity in the exchange rate. Since pursuing countercyclical monetary policy becomes more difficult when economies with pegged exchange rates experience procyclical capital flows, this chapter makes a case for a consistent monetary policy framework.

This chapter is organized as follows: section 7.2 traces changes in de jure and de facto capital controls in the Asian-11 economies; section 7.3 discusses the de facto exchange rate regime in each of the 11 economies and for Asia as a whole; and section 7.4 draws the distinction between de jure and de facto openness and the extent to which monetary policy autonomy is ceded. Section 7.5 concludes.

7.2 CAPITAL CONTROLS

7.2.1 De Jure Controls: The Chinn–Ito Database

We start with a description of de jure capital controls in the Asian-11 economies, compared to the rest of the world. Using principal component analysis, Chinn and Ito (2008) have constructed a database of de jure capital controls based on information supplied by economies to the International Monetary Fund's (IMF) AREAER (Annual Report on Exchange Arrangements and Exchange Restrictions) database. The database yields an annual score for each economy, with values ranging from −1.81 for economies with completely closed capital accounts, to +2.53 for those with fully liberalized capital accounts.[2] Although the database is often used for analyzing de jure capital controls, it has limitations. First, it does not adequately capture the gradual easing of capital controls, since it continues to give the same score unless all restrictions are removed. Second, the index has declined significantly for most industrial countries in recent years, as they introduced prudential measures related to anti-money laundering and anti-terrorist financing, among others.

The Chinn–Ito database shows that, over the years, substantial capital account decontrol has taken place worldwide. Figure 7.1 shows the kernel density plot of the Chinn–Ito measure across all economies, for 1970 and

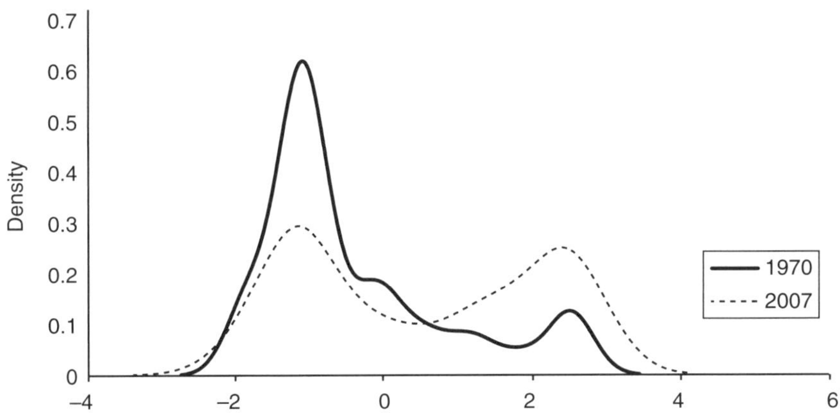

Source: Chinn and Ito (2008) and authors' calculations.

Figure 7.1 Density of the Chinn–Ito measure across all economies: 1970 and 2007

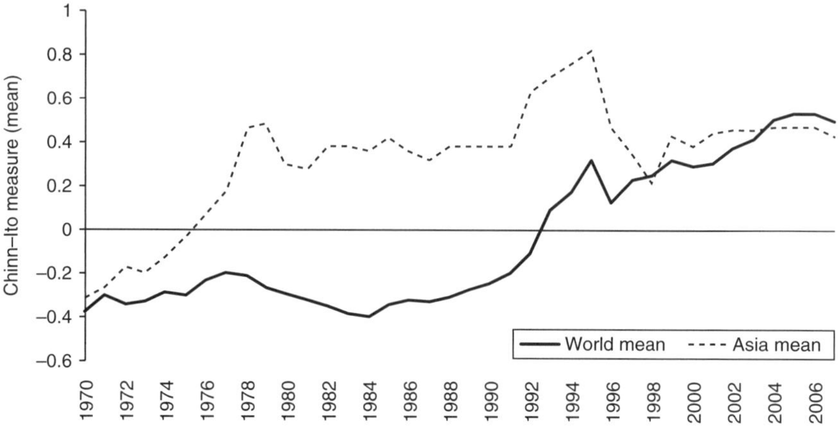

Note: Taipei,China is not available in the database published by Chinn and Ito. Consequently, Taipei,China has been excluded from aggregate calculations wherever de jure capital account openness is mentioned in this document.

Source: Chinn and Ito (2008) and authors'calculations.

Figure 7.2 Evolution of the average Chinn–Ito measure for the Asia-11

2007. In both years, the density is bimodal, with a cluster of economies with largely open capital accounts and a cluster of economies with largely closed capital accounts. This conveys a general shift away from being mostly closed to being mostly open. The distribution in 1970 had a sharp hump around a score of −1. This hump had come down sharply by 2007. Today, the distribution is more even, with roughly equal numbers of economies with high and low openness.

The Chinn–Ito database has information for all the Asia-11 economies except Taipei,China. Since Taipei,China's capital account is largely convertible, information about the Asia-11 drawn from this database is somewhat biased in the downward direction. Figure 7.2 shows trends in the average value of the Chinn–Ito measure for the Asia-11 (excluding Taipei,China) and the world from 1970 to 2007. At both the starting and end points, de jure controls in the Asia-11 were similar to the world average. However, there was an intermediate period when decontrol in the Asia-11 had advanced more rapidly than the world average. While the Asia-11 economies encouraged long-term capital flows like foreign direct investment, some imposed restrictions on short-term flows. One example is India, which imposed restrictions on short-term debt.

Table 7.1 shows the numerical values of the Chinn–Ito index for India, the PRC, Korea and the Asia-11 average (excluding Taipei,China). While the

Table 7.1 Evolution of the Chinn–Ito measure

Year	India	PRC	Korea	Asia-11 mean
1970	−1.13	−1.13	−1.13	−0.07
1975	−1.13	−1.13	−1.13	0.12
1980	−1.13	−1.13	−0.09	0.45
1985	−1.13	−1.13	−1.13	0.96
1990	−1.13	−1.81	−0.09	0.74
1995	−1.13	−1.13	−0.09	0.96
1996	−1.13	−1.13	−1.13	0.76
1997	−1.13	−1.13	−1.13	0.56
1998	−1.13	−1.13	−1.13	0.41
1999	−1.13	−1.13	−1.13	0.56
2000	−1.13	−1.13	−1.13	0.49
2001	−1.13	−1.13	−0.09	0.49
2002	−1.13	−1.13	−0.09	0.49
2003	−1.13	−1.13	−0.09	0.49
2004	−1.13	−1.13	−0.09	0.49
2005	−1.13	−1.13	−0.09	0.49
2006	−1.13	−1.13	−0.09	0.49
2007	−1.13	−1.13	0.18	0.36
Change 2000–2007	0	0	1.31	−0.13

Note: PRC = People's Republic of China.

Source: Chinn and Ito (2008) and authors' calculations.

index stayed the same for the PRC and India at −1.13, the trend in Korea was more erratic. Capital account liberalization prior to the 1997–1998 Asian crisis led to a rise in the index from −1.13 to −0.09 in 1995. In 1996, however, the index dropped back to −1.13, and there was no change until Korea went back to liberalizing the capital account in 2001. By 2007, Korea had attained a value of 0.18. This achievement notwithstanding, it lagged behind other Organisation for Economic Co-operation and Development (OECD) countries in terms of capital account openness.

The average openness of the Asia-11 rose sharply from −0.07 in 1970 to 0.96 in 1985.[3] After the Asian crisis, de jure controls resurfaced, and the average score dropped to 0.41 in 1998. The pre-crisis value of 0.96 has not been attained since. However, some of the recent progress made by Asian economies in de jure openness may not have been reflected in the Chinn–Ito measure due to a change in the measure's definition, as well as its inability to capture easing in controls that do not involve the complete removal of restrictions.

7.2.2 De Facto Capital Account Openness

Evidence from gross flows to gross domestic product (GDP)

The familiar trade–GDP ratio is defined as the sum of imports and exports, expressed as percentage of GDP. This measures trade openness. A simple extension of this idea is the ratio of gross cross-border financial flows in the balance of payments (BOP) to GDP. This measures financial integration.

The ability of a central bank to influence the exchange rate depends on the volume of cross-border flows occurring in foreign exchange markets. Even when transactions net out over a year, import payments, export earnings and financial flows influence the exchange rate on a daily basis. In addition, while gross flows comprise both current account and capital account transactions, bigger current account transactions can imply greater capital account openness, owing to cross-border capital transfers through possible trade misinvoicing. Patnaik et al. (2009) have shown that greater trade misinvoicing occurs when the current account is bigger, and acts as a mechanism to circumvent capital controls. Patnaik and Shah (2010) explored unexpected de facto capital account integration that arises once multinational corporations play a substantial role in the economy. Other related literature has emphasized the two-way links between openness on the current account and the capital account (Aizenman 2003; Aizenman and Noy 2004). We therefore look at gross flows on both the trade and capital accounts as a measure of globalization of an economy. This takes both trade and financial integration into account.

Table 7.2 shows how this measure of globalization evolved from 1998 to 2008 for Asia-11 (excluding Viet Nam, for which data were unavailable). The mean values rose from about 160 percent of GDP in 1998 to over 200 percent of GDP in 2008. The mean values were skewed upwards by the presence of small and highly open economies like Singapore and Hong Kong, China, but the underlying trend was upward as well. The pace of integration in both the PRC and India was relatively slow until 2000, after which there was a considerable increase in the rate of change. In India's case, there was a rise of 56 percentage points of GDP from 2000 to 2008. Similar trends were observed in the PRC (30 percentage points of GDP), Korea (69 percentage points of GDP) and the Asia-11 average (45 percentage points of GDP). These results suggest that while Asian economies might be reluctant liberalizers when it comes to de jure controls, in reality, they have been rapidly integrating into the world economy, de facto.

Table 7.2 Gross flows to GDP for India, the PRC and Korea (ratio)

Year	India	PRC	Korea	Mean for Asia-11
1998	0.44	0.48	0.85	1.52
1999	0.47	0.49	0.85	1.64
2000	0.56	0.58	1.00	1.79
2001	0.50	0.54	0.92	1.67
2002	0.53	0.56	0.76	1.63
2003	0.60	0.66	0.87	1.77
2004	0.68	0.75	0.89	1.94
2005	0.82	0.84	0.94	2.04
2006	1.00	0.89	1.01	2.16
2007	1.19	0.88	1.15	2.19
2008	1.12	0.88	1.69	2.24
Change 2000–2008	0.56	0.30	0.69	0.45

Note: PRC = People's Republic of China.

Source: Datastream.

Financial sector development

The extent to which capital controls are effective has a lot to do with domestic financial sector development. Increasing sophistication in the financial system tends to erode the effectiveness of capital controls over time. Increasing sophistication in the domestic market gives rise to a plethora of opportunities for re-creation of financial investments that are de jure unavailable to foreign investors. When discussing the effectiveness of de jure capital controls, therefore, it is important to look at the capability of the domestic financial system.

To do this, we turn to Dorrucci et al. (2009), who have developed a database with panel data on financial sector development in 26 emerging economies. This covers the Asia-11 economies, excluding Viet Nam. The values of this index range from 0 (undeveloped domestic financial system) to 1 (highly capable domestic financial system). We focus on their narrow measure of financial development as this measure is more frequently updated. Table 7.3 shows numerical values for this measure in India, the PRC, Korea and the average for the Asia-11 economies. The Asia-11 mean peaked at 0.55 in 1995. In the aftermath of the crisis, this dropped sharply to 0.45 in 2000. By 2001, however the Asia-11 economies were back on track, achieving an average value of 0.51 in 2006. This suggests that de jure controls are likely to have been more effective between 1998 and 2004, when the average score of financial system capability was low.

Table 7.3 Measure of financial system capability

Year	India	PRC	Korea	Asia-11
1991	0.28	–	0.65	0.50
1995	0.34	0.47	0.64	0.55
1996	0.34	0.45	0.65	0.54
1997	0.34	0.41	0.62	0.53
1998	0.33	0.42	0.57	0.46
1999	0.34	0.40	0.61	0.47
2000	0.34	0.38	0.57	0.45
2001	0.32	0.41	0.63	0.46
2002	0.32	0.42	0.62	0.48
2003	0.32	0.44	0.62	0.49
2004	0.35	0.43	0.58	0.49
2005	0.36	0.43	0.58	0.50
2006	0.39	0.43	0.60	0.51
Change 2000–2006	0.05	0.05	0.03	0.06

Note: PRC = People's Republic of China.

Source: Dorrucci et al. (2009) and authors' calculations.

Evidence from the Lane and Milesi-Ferretti database

The second methodology for measuring de facto integration into the world economy uses information from the Lane and Milesi-Ferretti database (Lane and Milesi-Ferretti 2007). This measures the stock of foreign assets and liabilities in the country, by summing up the flows on the BOP. This database measures the outcomes of capital controls as reflected in the BOP. However, it does not measure capital flows that take place through mechanisms such as trade misinvoicing, which involve evasion of capital controls and are not captured in the BOP.

This database reveals that from 1970 to 2007 substantial de facto capital account decontrol took place worldwide. Figure 7.3 shows the kernel density plot of the Lane and Milesi-Ferretti measure across all economies. Contrary to the results reported in Figure 7.1, this density plot is not bimodal: all economies moved from closed capital accounts to varied levels of open capital accounts. Furthermore, there is no congregation of economies at any one level of openness, suggesting that there is no broad consensus regarding the appropriate level of openness. Economies that had de facto liberalized continued to do so rapidly.

Table 7.4 shows a significant improvement in de facto integration by India, the PRC and Korea after 2000. The Asia-11 mean of 356 percent

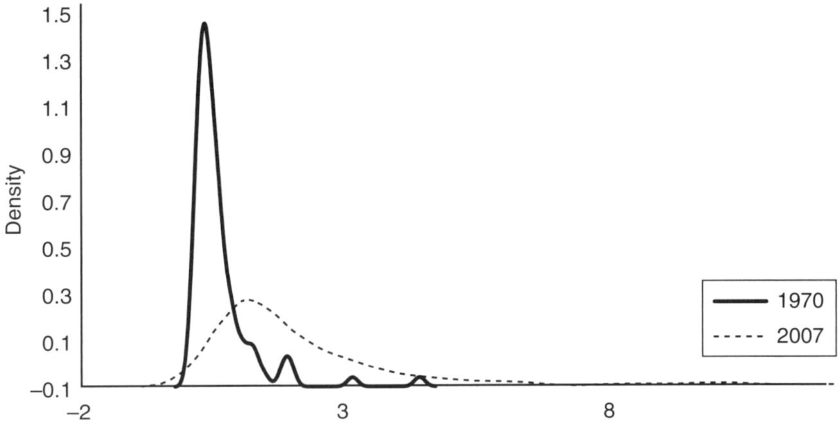

Source: Lane and Milesi-Ferretti (2007) and authors' calculations.

Figure 7.3 Density of the Lane and Milesi-Ferretti measure across all economies: 1970 vs 2007

Table 7.4 Lane and Milesi-Ferretti measure (ratio)

Year	India	PRC	Korea	Asia-11 mean
1995	0.40	0.59	0.51	2.46
1996	0.40	0.63	0.57	2.44
1997	0.39	0.72	0.61	2.43
1998	0.41	0.77	1.05	2.81
1999	0.41	0.82	0.94	3.12
2000	0.42	0.85	0.83	3.01
2001	0.44	0.88	0.91	3.04
2002	0.50	0.92	0.90	2.99
2003	0.56	0.99	1.01	3.35
2004	0.58	1.03	1.09	3.56
Change 2000–2004	0.16	0.18	0.26	0.55

Note: PRC = People's Republic of China.

Source: Lane and Milesi-Ferretti (2007) and authors' calculations.

of GDP in 2004 is partly due to the presence of small and highly open economies such as Hong Kong, China, and Singapore. In the case of India, the PRC and Korea, more modest values are reported at 58 percent, 103 percent, and 109 percent of GDP, respectively. Greater international economic integration led to significant increases between 2000 and 2004, with changes of 16 percent, 18 percent, 26 percent and 55 percent of GDP for India, the PRC, Korea and the Asia-11, respectively.

7.3 EXCHANGE RATE REGIMES

7.3.1 Methodology

Since 2000, the literature has revealed that, in many economies, the de jure exchange rate regimes announced by the central banks differ substantially from the de facto regimes in operation. This has motivated a small amount of literature on data-driven methods for classifying exchange rate regimes (Reinhart and Rogoff 2004; Levy Yeyati and Sturzenegger 2003; Calvo and Reinhart 2002). These studies have attempted to create datasets identifying de facto exchange rate regimes across all countries in recent decades, using a variety of alternative algorithms. While these databases are useful for many applications, they have limited usefulness in measuring the finer characteristics and structures of intermediate regimes. For instance, Reinhart and Rogoff (2004) classified the Indian rupee as a single exchange rate regime from 1993 onwards, but as this chapter shows, India switched to a different (intermediate) regime in 1993. This yields fresh insights into the drivers and consequences of the exchange rate regimes and monetary policy frameworks due to the impossible trinity.

A valuable tool for understanding the de facto exchange rate regime is a linear regression model based on cross-currency exchange rates (with respect to a suitable numeraire). Used at least since Haldane and Hall (1991), this model was popularized by Frankel and Wei (1994) (and is hence called the Frankel–Wei model). Recent applications of this estimation strategy include Bénassy-Quéré et al. (2006), Zeileis et al. (2005) and Frankel and Wei (2007). In this approach, an independent currency such as the Swiss franc (CHF) is chosen as an arbitrary 'numeraire'. If estimation using the Indian rupee (INR) is desired, the model estimated is:

$$d\log\left(\frac{INR}{CHF}\right) =$$

$$\beta_1 + \beta_2 d\log\left(\frac{USD}{CHF}\right) + \beta_3 d\log\left(\frac{JPY}{CHF}\right) + \beta_4 d\log\left(\frac{DEM}{CHF}\right) + \varepsilon$$

This regression picks up the extent to which the INR/CHF rate fluctuates in response to fluctuations in the US$/CHF rate. If there is pegging to the US dollar (US$), then fluctuations in the Japanese yen (JPY) and the Deutsche mark (DEM) will be zero. If there is no pegging, then all the three betas will be closer to zero. The R^2 of this regression is also of interest; values near 1 would suggest reduced exchange rate flexibility.

To understand the de facto exchange rate regime in a given country for a given time period, researchers and practitioners can easily fit this regression model to a given data window, or use rolling data windows. However, such a strategy lacks a formal inferential framework for determining changes in the regimes. This has motivated an extension of the econometrics of structural change, for the purpose of analyzing structural change in the Frankel–Wei model (Zeileis et al. 2010). This involves extending the familiar Perron–Bai methodology (Bai and Perron 2003) for identifying the dates of structural change in an ordinary least squares (OLS) regression. Through this, dates of structural change in the exchange rate regime are identified.

The methodology developed by Zeileis et al. (2010) was applied to identify dates of structural break in the exchange rate regression:

$$d\log\left(\frac{INR}{CHF}\right) =$$

$$\beta_1 + \beta_2 d\log\left(\frac{USD}{CHF}\right) + \beta_3 d\log\left(\frac{JPY}{CHF}\right) + \beta_4 d\log\left(\frac{DEM}{CHF}\right) + \varepsilon$$

For each country, a set of subperiods were identified. In each subperiod, the R^2 of the regression served as a summary statistic of exchange rate flexibility. Values near 1 convey tight pegs. Floating rates have values of between 0.4 and 0.5.

Using this classification scheme, we were able to do the following:

- Measure and quantify the fine structure of intermediate regimes using a real-value measure of exchange rate inflexibility (the regression R^2), which naturally suggests a real-value measure of exchange flexibility.
- Specify dates at which the exchange rate regime changed. We implemented these methods using weekly percentage changes in exchange rates, which yielded break dates to the resolution of the week. Through this, a time-series of exchange rate flexibility was obtained for each country, of the value of the R^2, which prevailed at a point in time.
- Determine the number of breaks and the placement of breaks based on sound inference procedures.

Table 7.5 India's de facto exchange rate regime

Period	USD	EUR	GBP	JPY	σe	R2
09 Jan 1976–21 Aug 1998	1.15	0	−0.15	−0.02	0.73	0.84
	−0.05	−0.03	−0.02	−0.02		
28 Sep 1998–19 Mar 2004	1.01	0	0	−0.01	0.26	0.97
	−0.01	−0.01	−0.02	−0.01		
26 Mar 2004–29 May 2009	1.24	−0.35	−0.15	−0.05	0.77	0.81
	−0.05	−0.08	−0.04	−0.03		

Notes: USD = United States dollar; EUR = euro; GBP = British pound; JPY = Japanese yen.

Source: Authors' calculations.

Table 7.6 The PRC's de facto exchange rate regime

Period	USD	EUR	GBP	JPY	σe	R2
09 Jan 1981–01 Nov 1985	0.76	0.33	−0.1	−0.06	0.72	0.89
	−0.13	−0.06	−0.04	−0.05		
08 Nov 1985–05 Apr 1991	1	0	0	0	0	1
12 Apr 1991–19 May 1995	0.97	0.04	0.02	−0.01	0.29	0.97
	−0.04	−0.02	−0.02	−0.02		
02 Jun 1995–15 Jul 2005	1	0	0	0	0	1
22 Jul 2005–29 May 2009	0.95	0.06	0	0	0.24	0.97
	−0.015	−0.025	−0.013	−0.012		

Notes: USD = United States dollar; EUR = euro; GBP = British pound; JPY = Japanese yen.

Source: Authors' calculations.

7.3.2 Evidence on Exchange Rate Flexibility of the Asia-11

We applied this methodology to examine the de facto exchange rate regimes of the Asia-11 economies. In this chapter, we focus on the period after 1976, and utilize weekly changes in exchange rates for these estimations. For each economy, a time-series of currency flexibility was obtained, providing summary statistics on exchange rate flexibility. We discuss the results for India, the PRC and Korea here, while the remaining results are in Appendix Table 7A.1. To capture the entire picture, we discuss the de facto average exchange rate regime in Asian-11 economies.

In India, the rupee began its life as a 'market-determined exchange rate'

Table 7.7 Korea's de facto exchange rate regime

Period	USD	EUR	GBP	JPY	σe	R2
24 Apr 1981–20 Jan 1995	0.97	0.03	0	0	0.25	0.98
	−0.02	−0.01	−0.01	−0.01		
27 Jan 1995–29 May 2009	1.25	−0.07	−0.17	−0.18	1.12	0.65
	−0.04	−0.03	−0.04	−0.03		

Notes: USD = United States dollar; EUR = euro; GBP = British pound; JPY = Japanese yen.

Source: Authors' calculations.

in March 1993. However, this date is not identified as a structural break in the data analysis as presented in Table 7.5. Instead, a subperiod for the exchange rate regime is found, from 1976 to 1998. During this period, the rupee was de facto pegged to the US dollar with a certain degree of exchange rate flexibility, with an R^2 of 0.84.

After the Asian crisis, India embarked on a tight rupee–US dollar peg. From 28 September 1998 to 19 March 2004, the US dollar coefficient reverted to 1.01. The other coefficients were not statistically significant. The R^2 rose to 0.97. During this period, the exchange rate regime in India was similar to the PRC's after July 2005.

Table 7.6 shows the results of this estimation strategy for the PRC yuan. It found that the first period ran from 9 January 1981 until 1 November 1985. This was a period with bigger currency flexibility by the PRC standards, with the R^2 at 0.89. Subsequently, the PRC moved to a tight US dollar peg. While there have been some minor changes in the exchange rate regime, it remained primarily a simple peg, with a US dollar coefficient of 1 and an R-squared ≈ 1.

In some respects, these results are consistent with official announcements and a simple examination of the exchange rate. The break date of 22 July 2005 that is derived from the regression is consistent with that announced by the authorities. The results for the PRC therefore suggest that the econometric analysis is on the right track.

At the same time, it is noteworthy that, after 22 July 2005, no further structural changes were evident from the econometric analysis. This contradicts a variety of official claims regarding the evolution of the exchange rate away from the US dollar peg towards a basket peg, and towards greater exchange rate flexibility.

The regression results suggest that remarkably little has changed in the actual prevailing exchange rate regime. The US dollar coefficient has

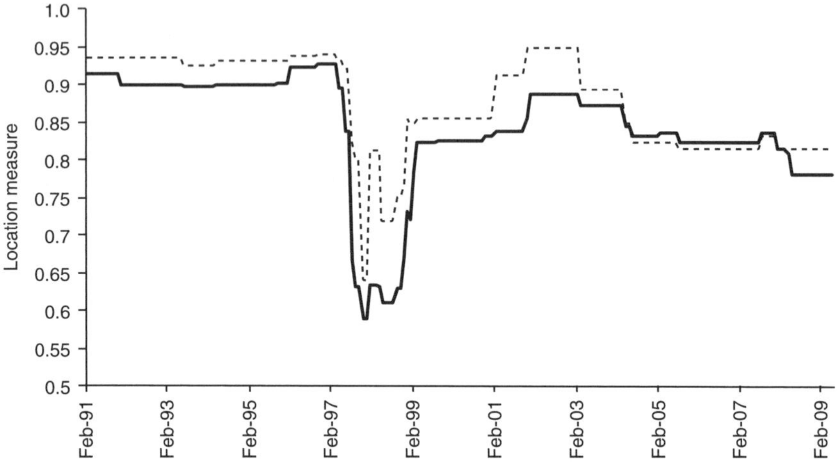

Source: Authors' calculations.

Figure 7.4 The evolution of exchange rate inflexibility in Asia

dropped to 0.95. A euro coefficient has emerged, with a small value of 0.06. The residual standard deviation has more than doubled to 0.24, but the R^2 has dropped only slightly to 0.97. While there was more exchange rate flexibility in this period, the change in the exchange rate regime was extremely small.

Finally, Table 7.7 shows the evolution of the exchange rate regime in Korea. From 1981 until early 1995, the country ran a de facto peg to the US dollar. In 1995, a big increase in currency flexibility came about and the R^2 dropped to 0.65. This is a regime with greater flexibility than India's.

For each of the Asia-11 economies, the dating methodology of Zeileis et al. (2010) was applied. This reveals the de facto exchange rate regime prevailing at different points in time. The R-squared values across all economies are summarized in Figure 7.4. Two location estimators, the mean and the median, are reported. This yields a summary statement of how exchange rate flexibility in Asia has evolved through time. The graph clearly reveals extreme exchange rate inflexibility in the decade preceding the Asian crisis, which is now understood to have been a key contributor to the crisis. In the immediate aftermath of the crisis, there was greater flexibility for a brief period, but then 'fear of floating' resurfaced, as pointed out by Calvo and Reinhart (2002). However, this graph suggests that exchange rate inflexibility in Asia did not go all the way back to pre-crisis levels. While Dooley et al. (2003) have emphasized the emergence of an Asian-led 'Bretton Woods II' regime, since 2000, exchange rate inflexibility in Asia has declined at a slow pace.

The average R^2 started out with a high value of 0.9. There was a small increase in flexibility in 1980 and 1981. Subsequently, however, there was a sustained period of exchange rate rigidity. From 1982 until 1997, the average R^2 was above 0.9. This exchange rate inflexibility, coupled with increasing de facto capital account openness, may have encouraged firms and banks to borrow in foreign currency based on expectations of exchange rate stability. The currency mismatch that resulted was an important aspect of the Asian crisis.

During the crisis, exchange rate flexibility increased. In 1998, the average R^2 dropped to 0.61. However, immediately afterwards, exchange rate rigidity rose again. This empirical fact was brought to prominence by Calvo and Reinhart (2002), who emphasized that after the crisis, little had changed with exchange rate regimes in Asia. This perspective was further amplified by the Bretton Woods II hypothesis, which tried to rationalize this exchange rate rigidity (Dooley et al. 2003).

Our evidence offers a somewhat different perspective in two respects. First, while exchange rate inflexibility in the Asia-11 economies rose after the crisis subsided, it reverted to lower values when compared to what prevailed before the crisis. The mean R^2 was 0.93 in 1997; post-crisis, this changed to 0.88 over the 2002–2004 period.

The second observation is that, from 2002, exchange rate flexibility in Asia-11 kept slowly rising. The mean R^2 dropped slightly from 0.886 in 2002–2004 to 0.85 in 2009. This suggests that while the Asia-11 economies maintained considerable exchange rate inflexibility, there was a gradual movement towards greater flexibility. With a mean R^2 of 0.85 in 2009, the environment became more flexible when compared with the mean of 0.93 in 1997.

7.4 POLICY ANALYSIS

Table 7.8 summarizes where Asia stands with regard to exchange rate regime choice and capital account openness. Two aspects are particularly important to our analysis: the distinction between de jure and de facto capital account restrictions, and the extent to which monetary policy autonomy is ceded.

Table 7.8 Asia and the impossible trinity (indexes)

Economy	Exchange rate	Capital account openness	
	Inflexibility (2009)	De jure (2007)	De facto (2007)
PRC	0.98	−1.13	1.13
Hong Kong, China	1.00	2.53	23.91
India	0.81	−1.13	0.71
Indonesia	0.68	1.18	0.87
Korea	0.65	0.18	1.35
Malaysia	0.92	−0.09	2.22
Philippines	0.78	0.14	1.32
Singapore	0.93	2.53	10.39
Taipei,China	0.90	N.A.	3.37
Thailand	0.83	−1.13	1.42
Viet Nam	0.87	−1.13	1.30
Mean	0.85	0.20	4.08
Median	0.87	0.03	1.58

Notes: Economies such as Taipei,China and Viet Nam are not included in the aggregate calculations. PRC = People's Republic of China.

Sources: Chinn and Ito (2008), Lane and Milesi–Ferretti (2007), and authors' calculations.

7.4.1 Asia and the Impossible Trinity

As mentioned earlier, the impossible trinity asserts that a country can only have two of three things: exchange rate flexibility, capital account openness and monetary policy autonomy.[4] In the typical Asian setting, increasing de facto openness has come about through de jure liberalization coupled with domestic financial sector development, and the evasion of capital controls that become possible with a large current account. Under these conditions, exchange rate inflexibility can lead to distortions in monetary policy. Even though a country might try to regain monetary policy autonomy through financial repression, imposition of capital controls or sterilization, the logic of the impossible trinity suggests that exchange rate pegging comes at the cost of autonomy in monetary policy.

In an emerging market setting, the procyclicality of capital flows is particularly important. When times are good and business cycle conditions are buoyant, capital tends to move into an economy. To prevent exchange rate appreciation, a central bank will buy US dollars, a move that will ultimately lower domestic interest rates. Conversely, when an economy is in a downturn, capital tends to leave the country. A central bank combats this by selling US dollars, which in turn raises domestic interest rates. Procyclical capital flows therefore interact with exchange rate pegging to induce procyclical monetary policy. This is the sense in which monetary policy is distorted in an emerging market setting. While sterilization of exchange market intervention could potentially decouple this impact, academic evidence on this question has been inconclusive.

Asia-11's response to the impossible trinity has been diverse: economies such as Singapore and Hong Kong, China have opted for high capital account openness and low or no exchange rate flexibility, while economies like India and the PRC have opted for low capital account openness and inflexible exchange rates. Between 2000 and 2008, Asia-11 economies, with the exception of Malaysia, the Philippines and Indonesia, moved towards greater de facto capital account openness. Meanwhile, exchange rate flexibility remained unchanged in most economies, except in Indonesia where it decreased, and Malaysia, India and the PRC where it increased.

In the impossible trinity framework, a country could have a fixed exchange rate and give up independent monetary policy. An open capital account with a fixed exchange rate leads to the loss of monetary policy autonomy, as has been experienced in Hong Kong, China. The currency board of Hong Kong, China has a consistent monetary policy framework, with domestic interest rates fluctuating as a result of the exchange rate peg.

A floating exchange rate with an open capital account is also consistent with the impossible trinity framework. Economies with floating exchange rates turn out to have an R^2 in the exchange rate regression of 0.4 to 0.5. These economies are able to achieve open capital accounts and monetary policy autonomy. The Asian country that is closest to this configuration is Korea. India, meanwhile, has made the biggest strides towards adopting the same configuration.

The interesting questions involve those economies with low capital account openness and inflexible exchange rates. If a country had an inflexible exchange rate and a de facto closed capital account – with gross flows on the BOP of well below 40 percent of GDP – then it could obtain monetary policy autonomy. For instance, in the late 1980s, India was able to have monetary policy autonomy since exchange rate inflexibility was combined with gross flows to GDP of roughly 25 percent.

The country that was closest to this configuration in 2008 was the PRC, which has been striving for very little exchange rate flexibility coupled with considerable capital account openness. This prompts us to ask whether the PRC has been able to preserve monetary policy autonomy.

In our analysis we treated issues such as the mechanisms for sterilization as intermediate factors that influence the outcome of monetary policy: the domestic short-term interest rate. We re-expressed the short-term interest rate in the PRC in real terms, and juxtaposed it against business cycle conditions. This allowed us to assess the extent to which interest rates were high in a business cycle expansion and vice versa, and examine whether monetary policy was countercyclical.

The PRC became procyclical in the recent business cycle expansion. From 2002 until early 2008, the real economy as measured by real GDP enjoyed a major boom, while the real interest rate dropped by an enormous 800 basis points. This suggests that monetary policy was expansionary during periods of growth. This view is consistent with the idea that exchange rate pegging converts procyclical capital flows into procyclical monetary policy. The use of loose monetary policy during an unprecedented business cycle expansion helped to accelerate inflation and induce an asset price boom.

The 800-basis point decline in the real interest rate during an unprecedented business cycle expansion suggests that the PRC was unable to avoid the impossible trinity, through sterilized intervention or other techniques based on either capital controls or financial repression. While a wide variety of these measures were attempted, they failed to prevent the outcome: the only way to obtain the pegged exchange rate was to have a very low interest rate in real terms.

A similar analysis was conducted for India, with similar results. Even though India had greater exchange rate flexibility than the PRC, monetary policy was ultimately forced to yield negative real rates in the expansion and switch around to positive real rates in the downturn.[5] In Asia, the PRC and India are in the best position to preserve monetary policy autonomy despite having exchange rate inflexibility, given relatively modest values of de facto openness and an underdeveloped domestic financial system. However, the evidence suggests that even in these two economies, exchange rate pegging resulted in procyclical monetary policy.

The constraints of the impossible trinity are likely to be even more acute in Malaysia, Taipei,China, and Thailand, which have more de facto openness and better developed financial systems than the PRC and India, but also less exchange rate flexibility than India.

Among the Asia-11 economies, Korea has made the most progress towards the mainstream configuration of industrial economies. Korea has high capital account openness, and the most flexible exchange rate in Asia. It has also made considerable progress in establishing the institutional capability of its central bank. However, the Korean exchange rate regime, with an R^2 of 0.65, lags the flexibility typically seen with floating rates, where the R^2 attains values of 0.4 to 0.5.

Financial sector development and de facto openness in the Philippines and Indonesia are low. In principle, these economies could have chosen exchange rate pegging with monetary policy autonomy. Among the Asia-11 economies, these are the two economies where the monetary policy distortions associated with exchange rate inflexibility would be the lowest. Despite this, these economies have chosen to have considerable exchange rate flexibility.

There are many reasons for choosing a tight peg over a more flexible exchange rate regime. For instance, a central bank may want to prevent depreciation in the context of high exchange rate pass-through, to keep inflation under control. Alternatively, if a large number of firms have large US dollar borrowings (the problem of the 'original sin'), a central bank may want to prevent large depreciations to protect the balance sheet of these companies. Under such conditions, a central bank may lean against the wind when there is downward pressure on the exchange rate, and prevent depreciation by selling foreign exchange reserves.

Conversely, central banks may want to prevent currency appreciation. Capital inflows to emerging economies since the early 2000s have put pressure on their exchange rates to appreciate. During this period, many emerging economies, including some in Asia, have been pursuing policies of export-led growth (Rodrik 2007). Allowing the exchange rate to appreciate can put export-led growth at risk; not surprisingly, the exchange rate regimes of most emerging markets in this period have been de jure managed floats, with central banks intervening in foreign exchange markets to prevent currency appreciation. Ramachandran and Srinivasan (2007) and Pontines and Rajan (2008) find evidence to support the hypothesis that Asian economies have intervened in the foreign exchange market to prevent currency appreciation. The rationale for doing so may lie in the large share of exports to GDP in many of these economies.

7.6 CONCLUSION

The main argument of this chapter is that it is more important to avoid an inconsistent monetary policy framework than it is to avoid capital account liberalization. While Asia has avoided de jure capital account liberalization, integration into the world economy has continued de facto.

Asia-11 economies have moved forward with domestic financial sector liberalization. The average value of the Dorrucci et al. (2009) measure of domestic financial system capability went from a low of 0.45 in 2000 up to 0.51 in 2006. The effectiveness of capital controls is diminished when the financial system is sophisticated, and growing current account integration gives economic agents the opportunity to engage in disguised transfers of capital. With the exception of Indonesia, the Philippines and Malaysia, the Asia-11 economies increased de facto capital account openness from 2000 to 2008.

Increasing de facto integration poses questions about the possible evolution of the exchange rate regime. On average, Asian exchange rate regimes have moved towards greater flexibility when compared with the 'fear of floating' that immediately succeeded the Asian crisis. At the same time, de facto arrangements showed considerable exchange rate pegging. None of the Asia-11 economies have a floating exchange rate – not even Korea, which has the most flexible exchange rate in Asia. From 2000 to 2008, Malaysia and India moved towards greater flexibility; the PRC likewise moved slightly towards more flexibility. Apart from this, the Asia-11 largely appears to be on a trajectory of increasing de facto openness, coupled with a lack of reform in the monetary policy regime.

Increasing de facto capital account openness while maintaining exchange rate rigidity has two consequences. First, central banks seeking exchange rate rigidity may have to distort the policy rate in order to achieve exchange rate targets. To the extent that capital flows are procyclical, exchange rate pegging would generate procyclical monetary policy. Of particular interest is the extent of procyclicality in the PRC and India, which have weaker financial systems and lower de facto openness than most of Asia. If these economies, despite their enviable position, are unable to avoid procyclical monetary policy in the presence of exchange rate inflexibility, then other Asian economies are likely to experience procyclicality to a far greater extent.

Second, systemic crises could also arise. Asian economies continue to experience clashes between speculators and central banks, problems with unhedged foreign currency borrowing by corporations, and other consequences of an inconsistent monetary policy regime. Bigger problems in the future cannot be ruled out, particularly in Malaysia and Taipei,China, where there is an awkward combination of: (i) considerable de facto openness; (ii) sophisticated domestic financial systems; and (iii) exchange rate inflexibility comparable to the PRC.

From the viewpoint of systemic crises, the key source of problems lies in households, banks and corporations that count on exchange rate rigidity. When it is felt that exchange rate fluctuations will not take place, substantial exchange rate exposures build up. This leads to difficulties when large exchange rate movements do take place. Hence, the first stages of reform should emphasize exchange rate flexibility and the development of currency derivatives markets. Exchange rate flexibility would give economic agents the incentive to undertake risk management, while currency derivatives markets would give them the ability to execute desired trades.

Asia is, by and large, disregarding this advice on sequencing, by moving forward with de facto capital account openness before bringing in currency flexibility.

NOTES

1. The euro is a flexible exchange rate with respect to other currencies. Eurozone countries have an open capital account and follow a eurozone autonomous monetary policy.
2. For instance France, which was one of the last industrial countries to open up, went from a value of −1.27 in 1970 to a value of 2.53 in 1995. In another example, Israel shifted from a value of −1.13 in 1997 to 2.53 in 2004.
3. The average openness for Asia-11 was higher in 1970 than that of the PRC and India in 2007.
4. Aizenman et al. (2008) find empirical support for the impossible trinity.
5. For a detailed analysis of the procyclicality of monetary policy in India, see Patnaik and Shah (2009), Bhattacharya et al. (2008) and Patnaik (2007).

REFERENCES

Aizenman, J. (2003), 'On the hidden links between financial and trade opening', Technical Report, National Bureau of Economic Research (NBER) Working Paper No. 9906, Cambridge, MA: NBER.

Aizenman, J., M. Chinn and H. Ito (2008), 'Assessing the emerging global financial architecture: measuring the trilemma's configurations over time', NBER Technical Report 14533, Cambridge, MA: NBER.

Aizenman, J. and I. Noy (2004), 'On the two way feedback between financial and trade openness', NBER Technical Report 10496, Cambridge, MA: NBER.

Bai, J. and P. Perron (2003), 'Computation and analysis of multiple structural change models', *Journal of Applied Econometrics*, **18**, 1–22.

Bénassy-Quéré, A., B. Coeuré and V. Mignon (2006), 'On the identification of de facto currency pegs', *Journal of the Japanese and International Economies*, **20** (1), 112–27.

Bhattacharya, R., I. Patnaik and A. Shah (2008), 'Early warnings of inflation in India', *Economic and Political Weekly*, **43**, 62–7.

Calvo, G.A. and C.M. Reinhart (2002), 'Fear of floating', *Quarterly Journal of Economics*, **117** (2), 379–408.

Chinn, M. and H. Ito (2008), 'A new measure of financial openness', *Journal of Comparative Policy Analysis: Research and Practice*, **10** (3), 309–22.

Dooley, M.P., D. Folkerts-Landau and P. Garber (2003), 'An essay on the revived Bretton Woods system', NBER Technical Report w9971, Cambridge, MA: NBER.

Dorrucci, E., A. Meyer-Cirkel and D. Santabarbara (2009), 'Domestic financial development in emerging economies: evidence and implications', European Central Bank Occasional Paper Series 102, Frankfurt: European Central Bank.

Frankel, J. and S.J. Wei (1994), 'Yen bloc or dollar bloc? Exchange rate policies of the East Asian countries', in T. Ito and A. Krueger (eds), *Macroeconomic*

Linkage: Savings, Exchange Rates and Capital Flows, Chicago, IL: University of Chicago Press, pp. 295–333.

Frankel, J. and S.J. Wei (2007), 'Assessing China's exchange rate regime', Technical Report, NBER Working Paper 13100, Cambridge, MA: NBER.

Haldane, A.G. and S.G. Hall (1991), 'Sterling's relationship with the dollar and the deutschemark: 1976–89', *Economic Journal*, **101**, 436–43.

Lane, P.R. and G.M. Milesi-Ferretti (2007), 'The external wealth of nations mark II: revised and extended estimates of foreign assets and liabilities, 1970–2004', *Journal of International Economics*, **73** (2), 223–50.

Levy Yeyati, E. and F. Sturzenegger (2003), 'To float or to fix: evidence on the impact of exchange rate regimes on growth', *American Economic Review*, **93** (4), 1173–93.

Patnaik, I. (2007), 'India's currency regime and its consequences', *Economic and Political Weekly*, **42**, 911–13.

Patnaik, I., A. Sengupta and A. Shah (2009), 'Trade misinvoicing: a channel for de facto capital account openness', Technical Report, National Institute of Public Finance and Policy, Department of Economic Affairs, India Ministry of Finance Research Program.

Patnaik, I. and A. Shah (2009), 'The difficulties of the Chinese and Indian exchange rate regimes', *European Journal of Comparative Economics*, **6** (1), 157–73.

Patnaik, I. and A. Shah (2010), 'Why India choked when Lehman broke', India Policy Forum, 6, available at http://www.ncaer.org/downloads/IPF2009/IPF09_Paper_PatnaikShah.pdf.

Pontines, V. and R. Rajan (2008), '"Fear of appreciation" not "fear of floating": foreign exchange rate market intervention in emerging Asia', paper presented at Fourth Annual APEA Conference, Beijing, PRC, 13–14 December, available at http://www.apeaweb.org/confer/bei08/papers/pontines-rajan.pdf.

Ramachandran, M. and N. Srinivasan (2007), 'Asymmetric exchange rate intervention and international reserve accumulation in India', *Economics Letters*, **94** (2), 259–65.

Reinhart, C.M. and K.S. Rogoff (2004), 'The modern history of exchange rate arrangements: a reinterpretation', *Quarterly Journal of Economics*, **117**, 1–48.

Rodrik, D. (2007), *The Real Exchange Rate and Economic Growth: Theory and Evidence*, Boston, MA: John F. Kennedy School of Government, Harvard University.

Zeileis A., A. Shah and I. Patnaik (2005), 'What is the new Chinese currency regime?', Report 23, Department of Statistics and Mathematics, Wirtschaftsuniversität Wien, Research Report Series, Vienna: Wirtschaftsuniversität Wien.

Zeileis A., A. Shah and I. Patnaik (2010), 'Testing, monitoring, and dating structural changes in exchange rate regimes', *Computational Statistics and Data Analysis*, **54** (6), 1696–706.

APPENDIX

In this chapter we have shown the results for India, the PRC, and Korea. This appendix shows results for six of the other economies.

Table 7A.1 Exchange rate regime analysis

Hong Kong, China: de facto exchange rate regime							
Start date	End date	R-squared	US$	EUR	GBP	JPY	Variance
11-01-1991	20-01-1995	1.00	1.02	−0.02	0.00	−0.01	0.01
			75.38	−2.38	0.39	−0.88	
27-01-1995	15-12-2000	1.00	1.00	0.00	0.00	0.00	0.00
			441.65	0.25	0.92	3.83	
22-12-2000	19-09-2003	1.00	1.00	0.00	0.00	−0.00	0.00
			1822.53	0.96	0.10	−0.10	
26-09-2003	29-05-2009	1.00	0.98	0.01	0.00	0.01	0.01
			218.94	1.33	0.01	2.54	

Indonesia: de facto exchange rate regime							
Start date	End date	R-squared	US$	EUR	GBP	JPY	Variance
15-11-1991	11-07-1997	0.98	1.03	0.00	−0.02	−0.01	0.05
			35.03	0.15	−1.65	−1.23	
18-07-1997	09-11-2001	0.16	1.10	−0.22	0.00	−0.13	12.68
			4.40	−2.12	0.01	−0.87	
16-11-2001	29-05-2009	0.68	1.35	−0.32	−0.14	−0.08	1.55
			22.72	−2.79	−2.33	−1.57	

The Philippines: de facto exchange rate regime							
Start date	End date	R-squared	US$	EUR	GBP	JPY	Variance
15-11-1991	12-29-1995	0.65	0.86	0.07	−0.02	−0.03	1.49
			4.64	0.73	−0.24	−0.49	
01-05-1996-	07-04-1997	1.00	1.01	0.01	−0.01	−0.01	0.00
			49.36	0.69	−1.82	−2.23	
07-11-1997	11-20-1998	0.30	−1.14	0.83	0.27	−0.45	4.63
			−1.94	2.67	0.91	−3.89	
11-27-1998	29-05-2009	0.78	1.12	−0.01	−0.08	−0.02	0.69
			33.29	−0.51	−2.40	−0.83	

Singapore: de facto exchange rate regime							
Start date	End date	R-squared	US$	EUR	GBP	JPY	Variance
11-01-1991	11-07-1997	0.94	0.98	−0.12	0.02	0.10	0.11
			23.26	−5.58	1.09	6.47	

Table 7A.1 (continued)

Singapore: de facto exchange rate regime							
Start date	End date	R-squared	US$	EUR	GBP	JPY	Variance
18-07-1997	08-01-1999	0.31	0.17	−0.04	0.44	0.21	1.52
			0.98	−1.15	2.33	3.07	
15-01-1999	29-05-2009	0.84	0.63	0.26	0.08	0.09	0.25
			31.39	6.80	3.83	5.92	

Thailand: de facto exchange rate regime							
Start date	End date	R-squared	US$	EUR	GBP	JPY	Variance
11-01-1991	16-05-1997	0.99	1.02	−0.09	0.01	0.07	0.02
			65.31	−11.39	1.18	12.36	
23-05-1997	25-09-1998	0.06	0.73	−0.42	−0.01	0.21	4.82
			0.98	−1.16	−0.03	1.06	
02-10-1998	29-05-2009	0.67	0.71	0.10	0.08	0.12	0.81
			20.53	3.87	2.31	4.75	

Taipei,China: de facto exchange rate regime							
Start date	End date	R-squared	US$	EUR	GBP	JPY	Variance
11-01-1991	25-07-1997	0.93	1.02	−0.07	0.03	0.05	0.17
			20.24	−2.82	1.49	2.52	
01-08-1997	30-10-1998	0.35	0.90	−0.26	0.20	0.23	1.32
			2.29	−1.38	1.21	3.68	
06-11-1998	29-05-2009	0.86	0.77	0.02	0.11	0.06	0.29
			35.75	1.09	5.40	3.55	

Notes: US$ = US dollar; EUR = euro; GBP = UK pound sterling; JPY = Japanese yen.

PART IV

Impacts on Asia of the Global Financial Crisis and Policy Responses

8. Asia's post-global financial crisis adjustment: a model-based dynamic analysis*

Masahiro Kawai and Fan Zhai

8.1 INTRODUCTION

Since the outbreak of the global financial crisis in the United States (US) in the third quarter of 2008, Asian economies have experienced substantial growth swings. In the initial stages of the crisis, as global aggregate demand dropped due to falling consumer and investor confidence, exports from all major East Asian economies declined sharply. Imports from these economies also plummeted at almost similar rates to those of export declines, reflecting the tightly knit regional production networks and supply chains in Asia. Given the high trade dependence in most Asian economies, the slump in trade significantly dragged down their economic growth in the fourth quarter of 2008 and the first quarter of 2009.

But the East Asian economies rebounded strongly beginning in the second quarter of 2009. The extraordinarily massive economic stimulus packages provided by governments and central banks in major advanced and emerging economies – including those in Asia – in response to the crisis helped to stabilize financial markets, improve the confidence of investors and consumers, and foster the recovery of economic activity.[1] As a result, the inventory cycle turned from depleting to rebuilding in most parts of the world and global trade rebounded. The improved external environment, together with stronger domestic demand spurred by these policy stimulus measures, led to a dramatic V-shaped recovery in Asian economies. By the end of 2009, most Asian economies had resumed their pre-crisis growth levels. Some of them have begun to moderate their macroeconomic stimulus policies in the face of the increasing risks of overheating, inflation and asset price bubbles.

The global recovery remains on track but faces considerable downside risks. The unfolding of the European sovereign debt crisis since November 2009 highlighted the risks arising from the rapid accumulation of public debt, suggesting that the positive effects of fiscal stimulus could be more than offset by the markets' concerns over long-term debt sustainability. With most advanced economies embracing fiscal consolidation in the coming years and inventory restocking gradually running its course, the future pace of global recovery will be largely contingent on the degree to which the sources of demand can shift from the public to the private sector. However, given that the reconstruction of the financial sector and the deleveraging of private balance sheets could take a long time to resolve, and that the unemployment rate remains high in major advanced economies, one would expect to observe slower global economic growth and consequently an extended shortfall in global aggregate demand in the years to come.

The slower growth of aggregate demand in the US and European economies will pose significant challenges for Asian economies. With an export-oriented development strategy, most emerging Asian economies have maintained not only high growth, but also large current account surpluses since the late 1990s, contributing to the global current account imbalance. As economic growth in advanced economies remains slow, Asian economies need to change the source of their growth from exports to extraregional markets to regional demand in order to sustain growth. The reorientation of growth toward Asia's internal demand can contribute to the orderly correction of the global imbalance. In fact, the recent crisis has induced a partial and disorderly correction of the global imbalance, with a large contraction of demand in the US, a sharp increase in US household savings and an improvement in its current account. This adjustment has not been accompanied by the collapse of the US dollar, however, as was feared by many experts and policymakers before the outbreak of the financial crisis; it has been accompanied by a global collapse of trade and output, and a rise in unemployment. The stance of monetary policy remains ultra-expansionary – including quantitative easing – and this could lead to a sharp US dollar depreciation, which may exert significant adjustment pressures on Asian economies.

This chapter aims to provide a model-based analysis of the adjustment of Asian economies in the wake of the global financial crisis. Specifically, it attempts to answer the following questions: what are the macroeconomic impacts of the global financial crisis on Asian economies? What are the effects of the global fiscal stimulus, and how will it contribute to mitigate the impacts of the crisis? What are the roles of emerging East Asia (EEA) in the rebalancing of global demand following the crisis? How much will EEA's efforts at currency appreciation and structural reforms for its own growth rebalancing contribute to sustained global economic growth? We use a multi-region, intertemporal dynamic general equilibrium model of the world economy to simulate different scenarios for the global financial crisis. Our quantitative simulations suggest that emerging East Asia is unlikely to be severely damaged permanently by the global financial crisis, and a worldwide fiscal stimulus could play an important role in stabilizing the global economy in crisis. East Asia's efforts at strengthening regional demand, in conjunction with adopting a more flexible exchange rate regime in the region, will promote more balanced regional growth and facilitate an orderly global rebalancing. However, despite the growing size of EEA in the global economy, Asia-led growth rebalancing has only had modest spillover effects on the rest of the world. Even though EEA can contribute to global growth, it alone cannot become the sole engine driving post-crisis growth in the world economy.

The chapter is organized as follows. Section 8.2 describes the model used in the analysis. Section 8.3 discusses the design of the simulation scenarios, reports their results and provides our interpretation. Finally section 8.4 offers conclusions.

8.2 THE MODEL

The model used in this study is a version of a multi-country dynamic general equilibrium model for the world economy inspired by the new open economy macroeconomics literature (Obstfeld and Rogoff 1995, 1996). It combines the long-term properties of neoclassical models with short-term dynamics arising from nominal rigidities à la new Keynesian macroeconomics. The structure of the model closely follows the global integrated monetary and fiscal model (GIMF) developed by the International Monetary Fund (IMF) (Kumhof and Laxton 2007; Laxton 2008).[2] Agents in the model are forward-looking, endowed with perfect foresight and subject to dynamic budget constraints. The model features overlapping generations agents with finite economic lifetime. This leads to the non-Ricardian aspect of the model – that is, private agents do not increase savings to offset fiscal easing – and makes it suitable for fiscal policy analysis. Countries and regions in the model are linked through trade and financial markets. Nominal price and wage stickiness, as well as real frictions in investment, are incorporated to generate more realistic adjustment dynamics. The presence of nominal price and wage rigidity allows monetary policy to play a key role. Different from the GIMF, our model is deterministic, excluding stochastic shocks or other uncertainties. The model is in annual frequency and calibrated to the Global Trade Analysis Project (GTAP) Version 7 global database with 2004 as the base year. This section outlines the basic structure of the model and discusses its parameters. The detailed specifications of the model are described in the Appendix.

8.2.1 Model Structure

The world economy in the model consists of four economic blocs: the US, Japan, EEA and the rest of the world (ROW). There are four types of agents in each region: households, labor unions, firms and government. Households have finite lives, facing a constant probability of survival, as in the perpetual youth model in line with Blanchard (1985) and Yaari (1965). Households consume a basket of goods and services and exhibit habit persistence in their consumption. The model distinguishes two types of households: forward-looking ones and liquidity-constrained ones. The former own the portfolio of domestic firms. They also hold two types of nominal bonds: domestic bonds issued by the domestic government denominated in domestic currency, and international bonds issued by the US and denominated in US dollars. International bonds are traded only bilaterally with the US and issued in zero net supply worldwide. The liquidity-constrained households do not have access to domestic or international capital markets. They finance their consumption exclusively with current disposable labor and transfer incomes. Firms' investment is subject to adjustment costs, which allow for the variation in Tobin's q (the ratio of the market value of a firm's assets to their replacement cost) and generate plausible investment dynamics.

The model assumes a continuum of labor unions in each economic bloc that purchase labor services from households and sell labor to firms.[3] Unions are monopolistic suppliers of differentiated labor inputs to domestic firms and face nominal rigidities in wage setting. They set nominal wages according to constant-elasticity downward-sloping demand schedules and quadratic costs of wage adjustment as in Rotemberg (1982).

The production activity is characterized by monopolistic competition. There is a continuum of firms in the production sector that produce differentiated varieties of products. They set the nominal prices of their products in domestic and exporting markets to maximize the present discounted value of profits. Similar to wage setting, price changes are subject to adjustment costs, which give rise to nominal price rigidities. When exporting, firms set prices in terms of the export-market currency; that is, traded goods are invoiced in the currencies of the importing economic bloc.

Production technology in each sector is modeled using nested constant elasticity of substitution (CES) and Cobb–Douglas functions. At the top level, the output is produced as a combination of public capital and an aggregate private input using Cobb–Douglas technology. At the second level, the aggregate private input is split into an intermediate input and aggregate primary factor. At the third level, the aggregate primary factor is further disaggregated into private capital and aggregate labor. Finally, at the bottom level, aggregate labor is decomposed into the differentiated labor input by each union. At each level of production, there is a unit cost function that is dual to the CES aggregator function and demand functions for corresponding inputs. The top-level unit cost function defines the marginal cost of sectoral output. The stock of public capital is identical for all firms and provided free of charge to them. As the production function exhibits decreasing returns to scale for private inputs, the return to public capital is distributed to firms as profits.

International trade is modeled using a nested Armington structure,[4] in which domestic absorption is allocated between domestic goods and aggregate imports, and then aggregate imports are allocated across sourcing countries, which determine bilateral trade flows. Demand for domestic and imported goods is expressed as a composite good defined by the Dixit–Stiglitz aggregator[5] over domestic and imported varieties, respectively. The Dixit–Stiglitz preference specification implies a constant elasticity of substitution between the varieties, and that consumers gain utility from an increase in choice of goods and services to consume.

Governments collect taxes and issue debts to finance their budget deficit. There are five types of tax in the model: labor income tax, capital income tax, sales tax, import tariff and lump sum tax on households. Government consumption and investment are exogenous and the lump sum tax on households is endogenously adjusted to achieve a target path for the desired government debt-to-gross domestic product (GDP) ratio. The monetary policy rule in the model follows a Henderson–McKibbin–Taylor rule[6] in which the nominal interest rate depends on the lagged nominal interest rate, the inflation gap and the output growth gap. For EEA, the monetary policy rule is augmented with the gap between actual and desired values of the bilateral nominal exchange rate against the US dollar, reflecting the dollar stabilization regimes in some EEA economies.

8.2.2 Model Calibration

The calibration of a dynamic model with the assumption of perfect foresight involves finding a set of data that covers all periods of the model and is consistent with the intra-period and intertemporal equilibria. This set of data needs to replicate the data of the base year and could serve as the dynamic benchmark equilibrium of the model. There could be two alternative calibration strategies here. The first, the so-called steady state calibration, would consider the base year as a steady state equilibrium and the dynamic benchmark equilibrium of the model as a steady state growth path. The second would assume that the economy in the base year is a temporal equilibrium along a dynamic adjustment path; that is, the dynamic benchmark equilibrium of the model is a transitional dynamic path to a final steady state (Knudsen et al. 1998; Wendner 1999). Here we follow the second approach and calibrate the model for a non-steady state situation.

The model is calibrated to the GTAP database with 2004 as the base year. The GTAP database contains a set of consistent input–output tables and bilateral trade data with detailed country and sector disaggregation. For most elasticity parameters and dynamic adjustment parameters, we draw on the GIMF and other dynamic general equilibrium models in determining their values.

In calibrating the household sector, we assume that in the US, Japan and ROW the share of liquidity-constrained consumers is 25 percent In EEA the share is higher at 40 percent, reflecting the underdeveloped nature of financial markets in this region. The households are assumed to have a finite planning horizon of 20 years, implying a constant yearly death rate of 5 percent. In addition, the labor productivity of each generation is assumed to decline throughout their lifetime at an annual rate of 5 percent. The value of the intertemporal elasticity of substitution is 0.33, slightly higher than those chosen in the GIMF model. The habit persistence parameter for consumption is set to 0.4 as in Kumhof and Laxton (2007). We set the weight parameters of leisure and consumption in a household's utility function in such a way that on aggregate 33 percent of available time endowment during work years is spent at work in the base year. The rate of time preference in each economic bloc is set to obtain a reasonable net foreign asset position in the steady state.

In the supply side, elasticity of substitution between capital and labor is set at 0.8. The elasticity of substitution between labor varieties, which determines the mark-up in the labor market, is assumed to be 7.3 in the US, Japan and EEA, and 6.0 in ROW. This assumption implies relatively competitive labor markets in the US, Japan and EEA. The depreciation rate of capital is assumed to be 8 percent per year. The data for capital stock in each economic bloc is taken from the GTAP database. The ratio of public capital to GDP is assumed to be 30 percent in the base year and the elasticity of GDP with respect to public capital is assumed to be 0.1.

Following the literature of business cycle models, the elasticity of substitution between imports and domestic goods – that is, the Armington elasticity – is set equal to 2.0.[7] The elasticity of substitution between imports across economic blocs is 2.5. Elasticity of substitution between varieties of goods ranges from 4.3 to 6.0, implying a markup of 20 percent to 30 percent. Japan and ROW have relatively high mark-ups while the mark-ups in the US and EEA are lower.

The parameters for nominal rigidity and real adjustment costs that govern the dynamics of the model are drawn from the GIMF and the Global Economy Model (GEM) of the IMF. In the monetary policy rule, the weights for the inflation gap and the output growth gap are both set at 0.5. For EEA, the weight on the changes in the exchange rate is set to 1. In the simulations for fiscal stimulus below in section 8.3, an alternative accommodative monetary policy rule is used with a zero weight for the output growth gap and the weight(s) on other gap(s) unchanged.

In the baseline scenario for model calibration, EEA is assumed to have a higher growth rate of productivity in initial periods. Its labor-augmented productivity grows at 10 percent in the base year and gradually declines to the global average growth trend of 3 percent after 25 years. In contrast, productivity growth in Japan is assumed to rise from 1.6 percent in the base year to 3 percent in the period after 25 years. The consumer price index (CPI) inflation target is set to 2 percent per annum for all regions. Time preference rates in the base year are endogenously determined in the baseline scenario to match the base year consumption in each economic bloc. These base-year time preference rates are assumed to converge gradually to their long-run values within 40 years. Similarly, a constant adjustment parameter for Tobin's q is added to the arbitrage equation for each sector's q to reproduce the baseline scenario investment level in the base year.[8]

8.3 SIMULATION SCENARIOS

To explore the implications of the global financial crisis for East Asia, we simulated five scenarios. These scenarios are simulated in a cumulative fashion, so that the second scenario includes the first as well as the second shocks; the third includes the first, second and third shocks; and so on.

The first scenario examined the effects of an economic crisis confined to the US alone. It assumes a US recession induced by a collapse of domestic investment and consumption. In this scenario, US households are assumed to be more concerned about their future; their desire to save increases and their consumption declines. In the model this is represented by lowering forward-looking households' time preference by two percentage points per annum permanently. In addition, we assume the risk premium of investors to rise by five percentage points for the next three years and gradually decline after that until it vanishes in another three years. This scenario simulates a temporary drop in domestic demand in the US triggered by the financial crisis.

The second scenario looked at a worldwide financial crisis that goes beyond the US recession. It assumes that, in addition to the US, all other regions also experience a fall in consumption and investment due to contagion through financial and confidence channels. The shocks in non-US regions are assumed to be half of that in the US, that is, a one percentage point reduction in households' time preference rate and a two and a half percentage point rise of the risk premium of investors.

The third scenario considered the impacts of globally concerted expansionary fiscal policies to deal with the global financial crisis. We assume a global fiscal stimulus package under which all countries increase government spending by 2 percent of GDP over a two year period. Such government spending is assumed to be distributed evenly between government consumption and investment. The fiscal stimulus is assumed to be temporary, as in the period following the expenditure expansion, lump sum taxes adjust to return the government debt-to-GDP ratio back to its baseline value over time. As monetary policy can play an important role in determining the effects of fiscal expansion, the simulations explore two types of monetary policy rule for the two years of fiscal stimulus: the standard interest rate rule in our benchmark model, and an accommodative interest rate rule. The standard interest rate rule has equal weights on the inflation gap and the output growth gap, while the accommodative interest rate rule has a zero weight on the output growth gap. Given that fiscal expansion tends to raise both output and inflation, the interest rate hikes are smaller in the latter policy rule, suggesting a more accommodative monetary policy in the face of fiscal stimulus.

The final two scenarios looked at the impact of other types of policy measures designed to rebalance growth in EEA. The fourth scenario examined the role of exchange rate policy. It assumes that EEA allows large currency movements against the US dollar by putting a zero weight on the exchange rate gap in its monetary policy reaction function. The fifth scenario postulated that, in addition to greater exchange rate flexibility, EEA boosts its domestic consumption and investment through structural reforms. Instead of specifying the exact nature for these structural reforms, we capture their effects using a permanent one percentage point increase in the time preference rate of EEA's forward-looking households and a one percentage point reduction of its investors' risk premium. These two scenarios simulate a partial global rebalancing initiative led by the adjustment in EEA.

8.3.1 US Recession

The macroeconomic effects of a US recession – the combined negative investment and consumption shocks – are reported in Figure 8.1. The US recession leads to a sharp output loss in the US, with real GDP falling by around 5 percent in the first two years compared with the baseline. The GDP reduction is tempered after that and output begins to expand after seven years, driven by stronger net external demand and the recovery in investment. Regarding the components of domestic demand, investment exhibits greater volatility than consumption. It contracts by around 15 percent in the initial years and then, along with the diminished investment risk premium, expands by nearly 20 percent after 12 to 15 years. In comparison with investment, the change in private consumption is more modest, but still significant. The consumption of US households declines by 9 percent in the first three years, but begins to increase after 15 years because of the expanded output and income.

As the shrinking domestic absorption significantly drags down imports, the US current account as a ratio to GDP improves by around five percentage points in the first five years. This improvement in the current account gradually diminishes to 3 percent of GDP in the medium term. The falling US demand depresses US domestic prices relative to foreign prices, leading to a real depreciation of the US dollar. The real effective exchange rate of the US dollar weakens by 10–12 percent initially relative to the baseline. The US dollar depreciation moderates to 3 percent in 15 years. The more rapid recovery of domestic demand relative to supply implies an excess demand in the medium term, thereby moderating the pace of US dollar depreciation.

The dynamics of prices are driven by supply and demand conditions, the degree of nominal rigidities, and monetary policy reactions. In tandem with the initial demand collapse, inflation falls by two percentage points initially. After five years, the drop in the inflation rate narrows to less than half of a percentage point. Lower inflation leads to a lower interest rate – through the Taylor rule-based monetary policy – causing larger interest differentials between the US and other economic blocs, which reinforces the initial US dollar depreciation. Nominal exchange rate changes are the major channel to achieve real exchange rate adjustment, reflecting the sluggish price responses, and the effects of inflation targeting and flexible exchange rates.

Reduced US import demand leads to trade spillover effects, with all other economic blocs experiencing falling external demand in comparison with the baseline. The extent of these spillovers in different economic

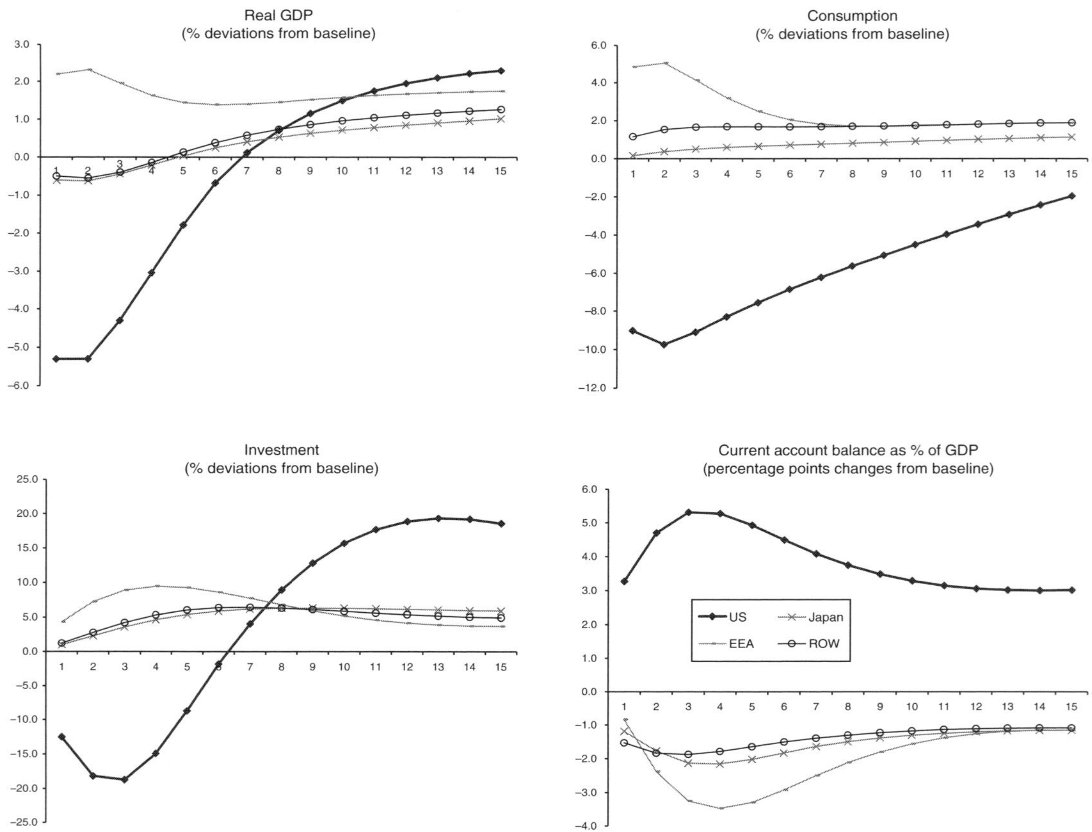
Real GDP
(% deviations from baseline)
Consumption
(% deviations from baseline)
Investment
(% deviations from baseline)
Current account balance as % of GDP
(percentage points changes from baseline)
US
Japan
EEA
ROW

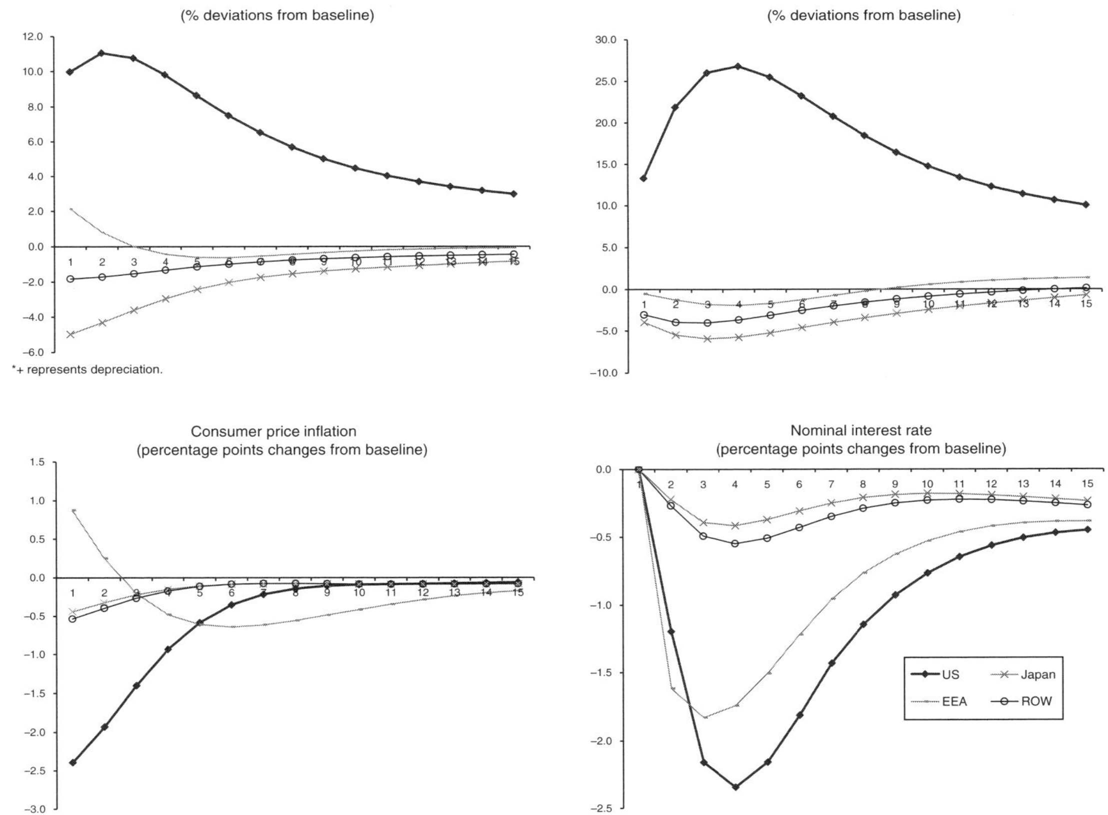

Notes: EEA = emerging East Asia; GDP = gross domestic product; ROW = rest of world; US = United States.

Source: Authors' model simulations.

Figure 8.1 Impacts of US recession

blocs depends on their respective trade dependence on the US. Generally, economies with larger export exposure to the US are more severely impacted than those less dependent on the US market. However, exchange rate policy also plays a significant role in determining the impact of trade spillovers of the US recession. This is evident from the divergent movements in real exchange rates in initial years between Japan (and ROW) and EEA. As Figure 8.1 shows, while both Japan and ROW experience large real appreciation initially, the real exchange rate of EEA depreciates in the first three years because of the non-zero weight on the gap of the nominal exchange rate against the US dollar in its monetary policy rule. Consequently, the export and current account balance of EEA decline only slightly in the initial two years, in contrast to those of Japan and ROW.

Beside the trade channel, international capital markets offer another channel through which the US recession impacts the world economy. The declining US import demand lowers the profitability of investment in the short term, leading to a tendency to reduce investment everywhere. However, investment may be boosted by the declines in real interest rates, made possible by monetary policy reactions in the short term and higher US savings in the longer term. The combined net effect is an investment rise in all the three non-US regions. In Japan and ROW, investment rises by 0.5–0.8 percent in the first year and 5–6 percent in the seventh year. In EEA where the exchange rate target in its monetary policy rule leads to a sharp drop in the nominal interest rate, investment expands by 5–10 percent in the initial six years in comparison with the baseline. Lower interest rates also stimulate consumption in EEA and ROW. In Japan, private consumption falls in the first year and rises only slightly from then on, mainly due to its relatively larger drops in employment and labor income. Given that Japan is a net holder of US dollar bonds, the negative revaluation effect arising from US dollar depreciation also contributes to its consumption weakness.

As trade and capital flow effects partly offset each other, the net effect of the US recession on output in other regions is relatively modest, standing around a 1 percent decline in the first four years in Japan and ROW. EEA's real GDP expands by 2–3 percent in the initial years, at the expense of higher inflation, due to its policy of partially stabilizing the exchange rate against the US dollar. Consistent with other studies such as McKibbin and Stoeckel (2009), our results suggest that a recession in the US alone would have small negative impacts on the world economy. A US recession can even raise economic growth in the short term in economies whose exchange rates are relatively stable against the US dollar through real effective currency depreciation. Of course given the pivotal role of the

US in the global financial market, the contagion effect leads to a worldwide demand slowdown.

8.3.2 Global Financial Crisis

The results of the scenario of the global financial crisis are reported in Figure 8.2. Given that the US has small external trade exposure relative to its GDP, the worldwide demand slowdown brings only modest additional impacts on the US economy in comparison with the scenario of US only recession. However, for other regions, the contagion-induced demand drops cause significant impacts on their domestic economy. Both consumption and investment fall in initial years in comparison with the baseline in Japan and ROW, leading to a sharp contraction in their real GDP. CPI inflation drops by as much as two percentage points initially in these two regions. In EEA, despite a larger drop in the nominal interest rate in response to lower inflation, consumption hardly expands in the first six years and investment increases only by 2 percent or so initially. As a result, EEA's real GDP shrinks by 1 percent in the first three years in comparison with the baseline.

Global trade is also negatively impacted by the declining demand in the wake of a global financial crisis. With a relatively sharper drop in domestic demand, the US dollar depreciates against other currencies and, consequently, US exports increase by around 10–15 percent relative to the baseline. However, all other regions experience declines in exports in the initial eight years, ranging from around 3 percent for EEA and around 7 percent for Japan. The relatively smaller export decline in EEA is mainly a result of its monetary policy, which partially stabilizes its currency to the US dollar. As shown in Figure 8.2, the real effective exchange rate of EEA economies depreciates in the first two years in the wake of the global financial crisis. Despite a relatively modest drop in exports, EEA's current account surplus shrinks by nearly 3 percent of its GDP, a larger relative decline than that in Japan and other regions of the world, due to the region's large volume of exports relative to GDP.

8.3.3 Global Fiscal Expansion with Alternative Monetary Policy Rules

The third scenario assumes that all economic blocs in the world increase government spending – by 2 percent of GDP – for two years, while following their respective monetary policy rules. Figure 8.3 presents the dynamic impacts of globally concerted fiscal stimulus packages under the benchmark monetary policy rule, which are plotted as changes from the second scenario; that is, the scenario of a global financial crisis. The

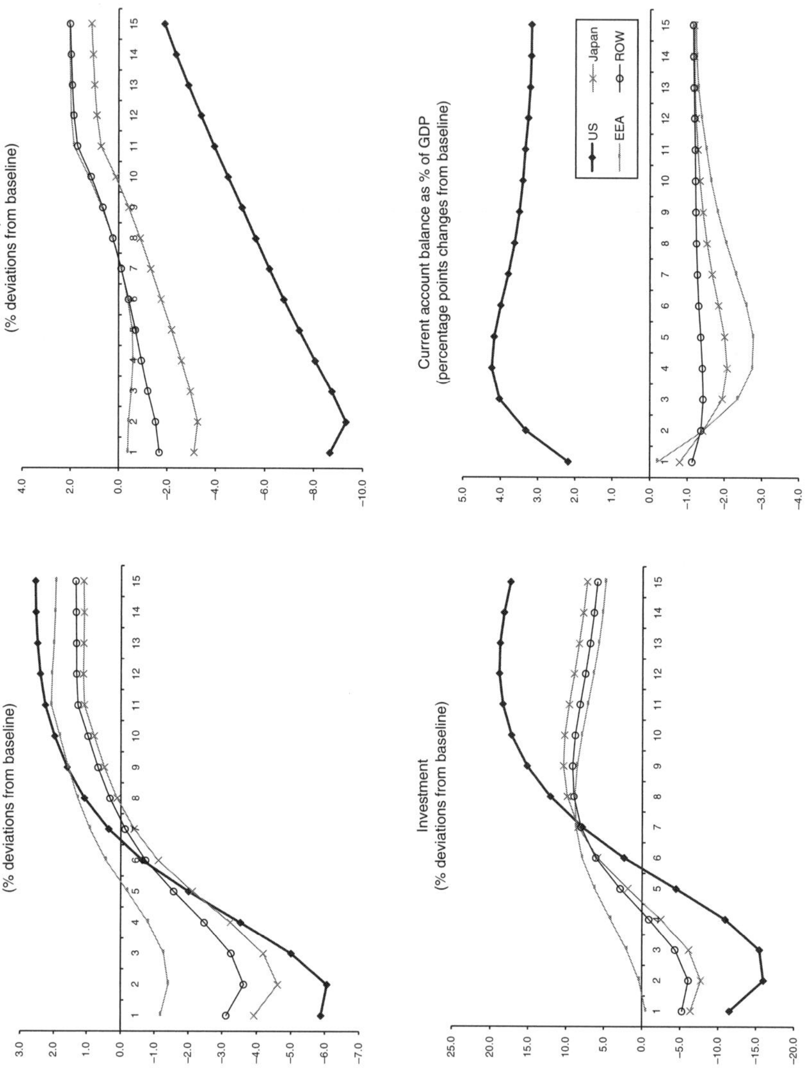
Real GDP
(% deviations from baseline)
Consumption
(% deviations from baseline)
Investment
(% deviations from baseline)
Current account balance as % of GDP
(percentage points changes from baseline)
US
Japan
EEA
ROW

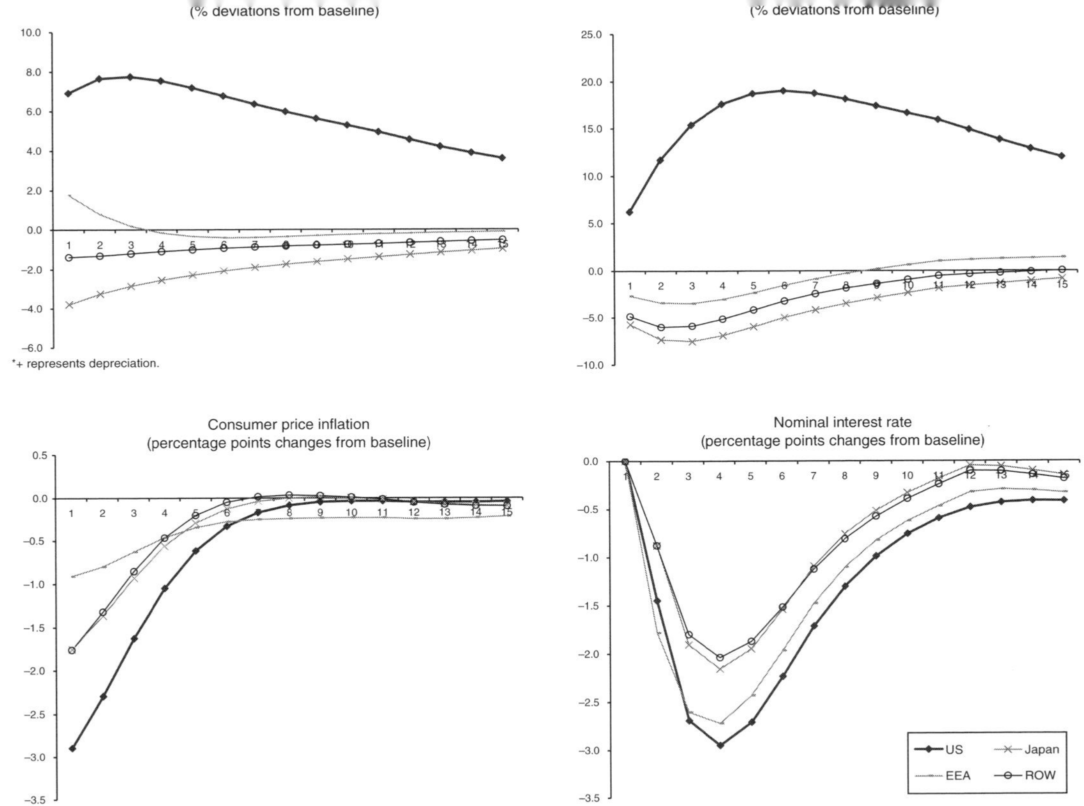

Notes: EEA = emerging East Asia; GDP = gross domestic product; ROW = rest of world; US = United States.

Source: Authors' model simulations.

Figure 8.2 Impacts of the global financial crisis

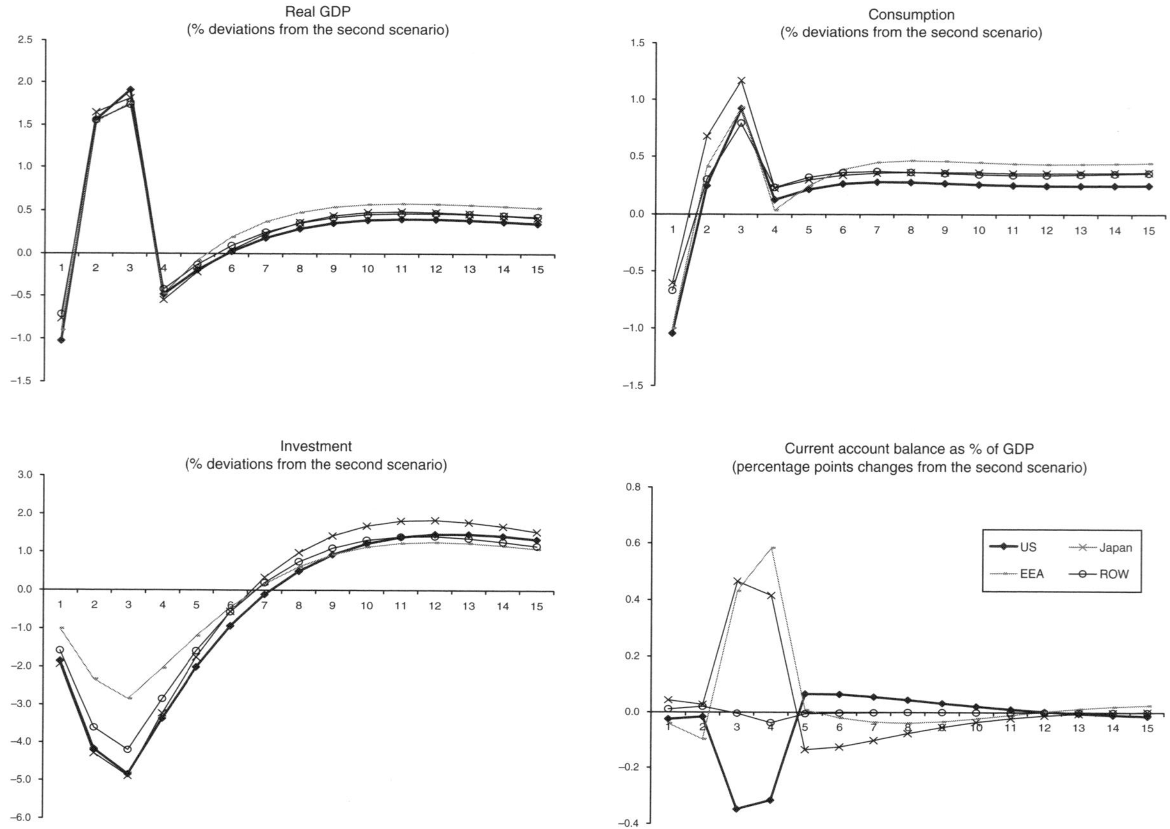
Real GDP
(% deviations from the second scenario)
Consumption
(% deviations from the second scenario)
Investment
(% deviations from the second scenario)
Current account balance as % of GDP
(percentage points changes from the second scenario)
US
Japan
EEA
ROW

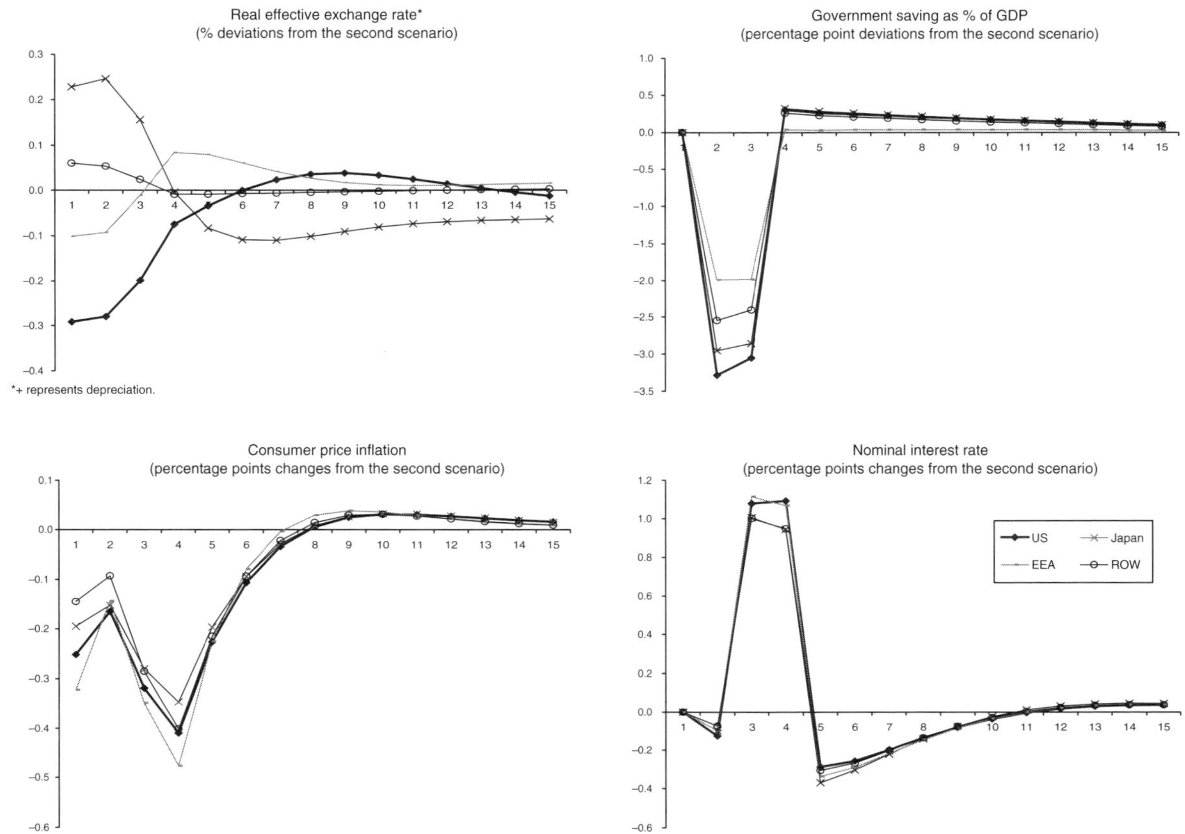

Notes: EEA = emerging East Asia; GDP = gross domestic product; ROW = rest of world; US = United States.

Source: Authors' model simulations.

Figure 8.3 Impacts of global fiscal expansion under the benchmark monetary policy rule benchmark monetary policy rule follows the standard Taylor rule, except in EEA where the interest rate responds positively to the exchange rate gap as well as the inflation and output growth gaps. With the temporary fiscal expansion all over the world, real GDP, consumption and investment all rise during the period of fiscal stimulus and beyond. The increase in real GDP during the two years of fiscal expansion is around 1.5 percent, suggesting fiscal multipliers of 0.75. Real GDP drops by around 0.2 percent after the completion of fiscal stimulus, but begins to expand by around 0.5 percent after six years, largely due to the larger stock of public capital. Increased fiscal expenditures lead to more employment and higher wages, boosting private consumption. EEA experiences the largest rise in private consumption during the period of fiscal expansion, reflecting its higher share of liquidity-constrained households. During the years of fiscal stimulus, private investment drops by around 4 percent in the US, Japan and ROW, and more than 2 percent in EEA reflecting the crowding-out effects through rises in interest rates. However, private investment enjoys larger gains in the medium and long term, thanks to the crowding-in effect of public investment.

Current account balances and real exchange rates are generally little impacted by the worldwide fiscal expansion. Fiscal deficits in the two expansion years widen by 1.7–1.8 percent of GDP, as government spending of 2 percent of GDP is offset by additional tax revenues due to faster economic growth. Consequently, the ratio of government debt to GDP rises only by two to three percentage points in the fourth year, then gradually fall to the baseline level with increases in household lump-sum tax.

Figure 8.4 presents the effects of global fiscal stimulus under the accommodative monetary policy rule, where the interest rate responds only to the inflation gap (and the exchange rate gap in EEA). With monetary accommodation, inflation is generally higher and the real interest rate is lower, which facilitates the expansion of consumption and investment. As a result, there is almost no crowding out of fiscal spending. This is in sharp contrast with the simulation results under the benchmark monetary policy rule, as shown in Figure 8.3, where private investment during the years of fiscal expansion is negatively affected, showing evidence of strong crowding-out effects of public expenditure.

To deepen our analysis of the impact of globally concerted fiscal stimulus, we have run separate simulations under which each economic bloc alone engages in fiscal stimulus. Table 8.1 summarizes the fiscal multipliers of individual regions' fiscal actions and of worldwide fiscal actions. Several interesting observations can be made. First, the fiscal multipliers rise significantly by moving from the benchmark to the accommodative monetary policy rule in every region of the world. Under the benchmark rule, the fiscal multipliers are in the range of 0.55 (Japan) to 0.80 (EEA), while under the accommodative rule they rise to the range of 1.01 (EEA) to 1.42 (US). This can be explained by the change in the interest rate rule from one that responds to the output growth gap (benchmark rule) to one that does not (accommodative rule). Under the benchmark rule, the interest rate rises in response to both the inflationary pressure and output expansion (and declines in response to exchange rate appreciation in EEA) arising from fiscal stimulus, while under the accommodative rule the interest rate rises less responding only to the inflationary pressure (and declines in response to exchange rate appreciation in EEA). In other words, the smaller interest rate increase makes the fiscal multipliers larger under the accommodative rule than under the benchmark monetary policy rule.

Second, the extent of the rise in fiscal multipliers, associated with a move from the benchmark to the accommodative policy rule, varies across regions in the world; fiscal multipliers rise the least in EEA (from 0.80 to 1.01) while those in other regions rise much more substantially (for example from 0.61 to 1.42 in the US). This can be explained by the specific interest rate rule chosen for EEA – that is, the inclusion of the exchange rate gap – as well as this region's large trade leakage from its imports. Under either monetary policy rule, EEA's interest rate would rise the least among the four regions in the world because the interest rate rise resulting from the positive inflationary gap (and the output growth gap under the benchmark rule) associated with fiscal expansion would be partly offset by the interest rate decline resulting from the real currency appreciation pressure. Under the benchmark monetary policy rule, EEA's own fiscal multiplier is 0.80, the largest among the four regions in the world. In this rule, even though the impact of fiscal expansion would leak out most substantially in EEA to other regions due to its having the highest ratio of imports to GDP, the favorable effect of the interest rate change dominates the unfavorable trade leakage effect, thereby making EEA's fiscal multiplier the largest in the world. Under the accommodative monetary policy rule, however, EEA's own fiscal multiplier is 1.01, the smallest among the four economic blocs. This is explained by the fact that the favorable interest rate effect is more than offset by the unfavorable trade leakage effect. That is, although EEA's interest rate rises in response to its own fiscal expansion the least among the four regions in the world, the large trade leakage effect dominates the interest rate effect, thereby making EEA's fiscal multiplier the smallest in the world.

Finally, under the accommodative monetary policy rule, nearly 30 percent of the impact of the global financial expansion on EEA's fiscal multiplier effect comes from the stimulus in other regions. This suggests that under an accommodative global monetary policy environment, a

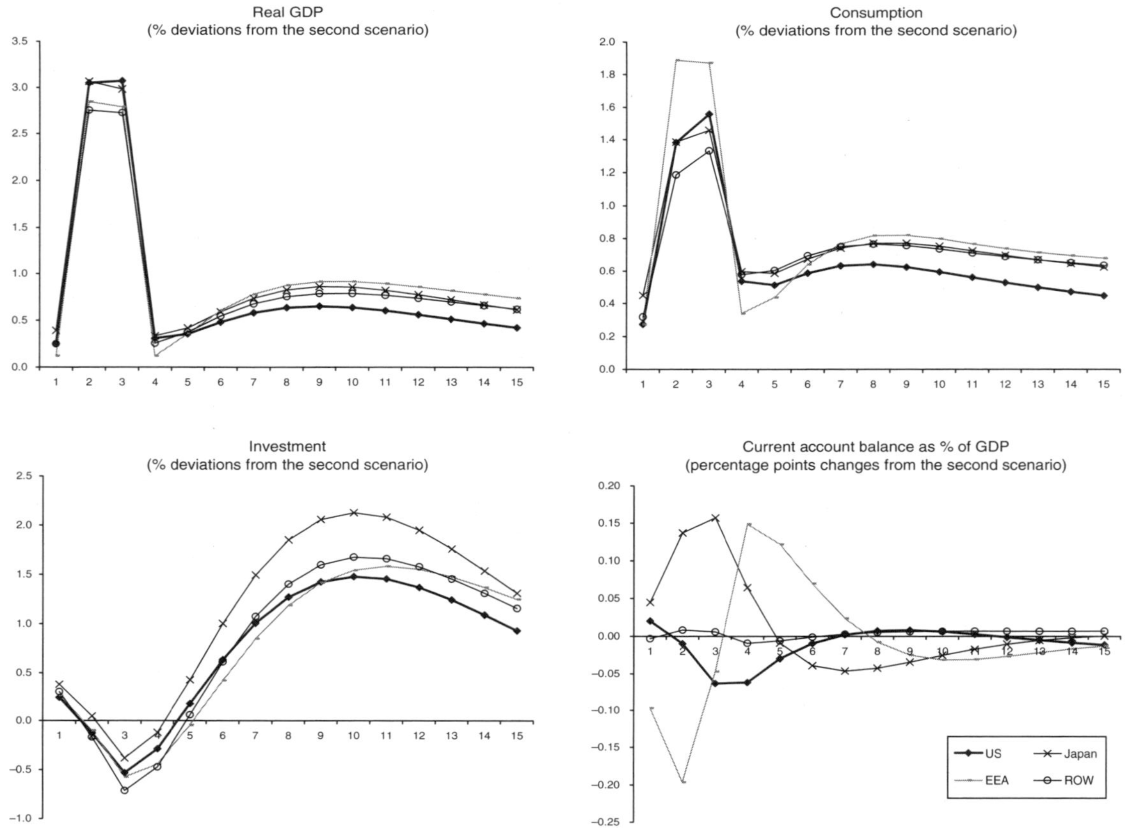

Real GDP
(% deviations from the second scenario)
Consumption
(% deviations from the second scenario)
Investment
(% deviations from the second scenario)
Current account balance as % of GDP
(percentage points changes from the second scenario)
US
Japan
EEA
ROW

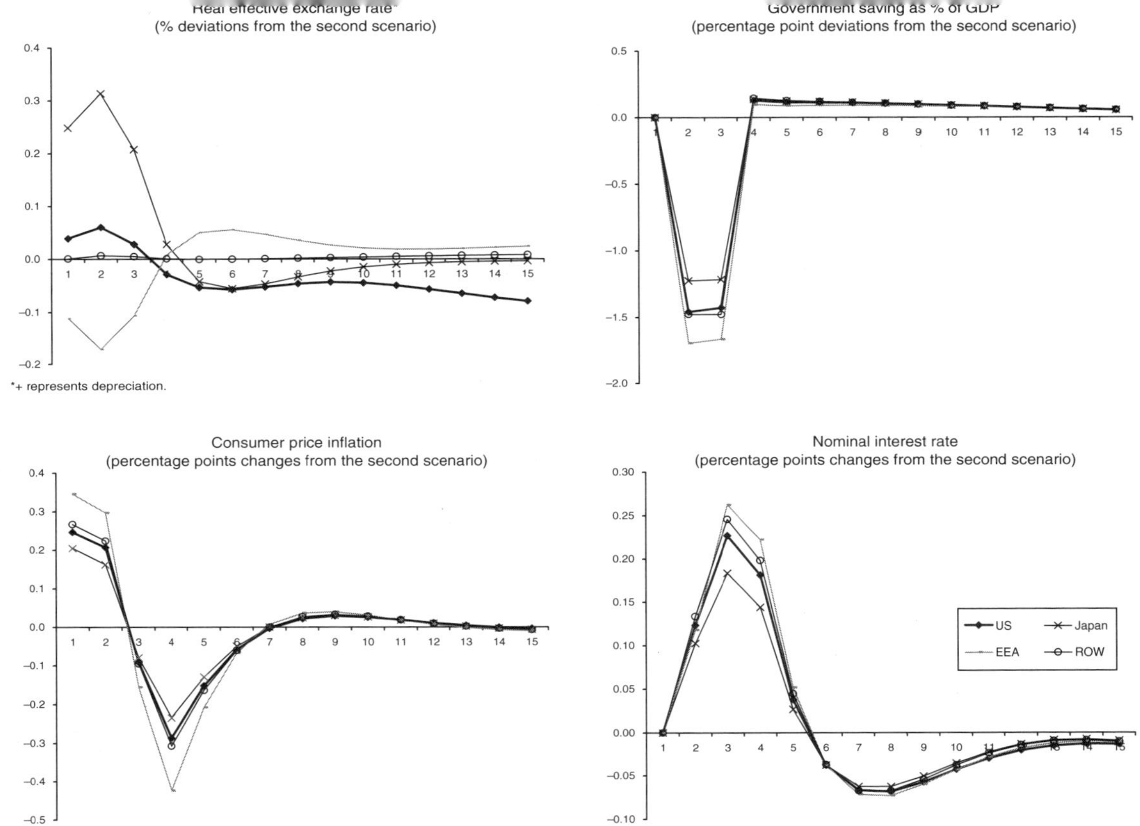

Notes: EEA = emerging East Asia; GDP = gross domestic product; ROW = rest of world; US = United States.

Source: Authors' model simulations.

Figure 8.4 Impacts of global fiscal expansion under the accommodative monetary policy rule

Table 8.1 *Comparison of fiscal multipliers by economic bloc*

	Stimulus in				
	US	Japan	EEA	ROW	World
Benchmark monetary policy rule					
US	0.61	0.02	0.03	0.15	0.81
Japan	0.08	0.55	0.06	0.12	0.81
EEA	−0.30	0.06	0.80	0.24	0.80
ROW	0.10	0.02	0.04	0.62	0.78
World	0.20	0.08	0.11	0.40	0.79
Accommodative monetary policy rule					
US	1.42	0.13	0.15	0.28	1.65
Japan	0.18	1.37	0.21	0.23	1.64
EEA	0.23	0.14	1.01	0.33	1.48
ROW	0.15	0.09	0.12	1.30	1.45
World	0.52	0.25	0.23	0.80	1.53

Note: Fiscal multiplier is defined as a percentage change in GDP induced by fiscal expansion of 1% of GDP. US = United States; EEA = emerging East Asia; ROW = rest of the world.

Source: Authors' model simulations.

globally coordinated fiscal stimulus action will be desirable for EEA (as well as for other economic blocs in the world).

8.3.4 Exchange Rate Flexibility in Emerging East Asia

The results of the fourth scenario – impacts of increasing exchange rate flexibility of the EEA currency vis-à-vis the US dollar – are presented in Figure 8.5. As a result of dropping the exchange rate target in its monetary policy rule, EEA's nominal exchange rate appreciates against the US dollar by 7.3 percent and 4.8 percent in the first and second years respectively. An appreciating exchange rate leads to falling exports and, consequently, shrinking aggregate demand. With excess supply over demand, CPI inflation falls by around three percentage points in the initial two years. Because of differential inflation rates between EEA and other regions in the world, EEA's real effective exchange rate appreciates 2.5 percent and 1.2 percent in the first and second years.

EEA's exports fall by 2 percent in the first two years after introducing full exchange rate flexibility, then gradually recover and begin to expand in the fifteenth year. It might be surprising that EEA's imports also decline at around the same pace as exports, despite currency appreciation inducing a substitution toward cheaper imports. Falling income associated with output contraction, as well as rising real interest rates due to lower inflation, lead to weaker domestic demand. As shown in Figure 8.5, EEA's investment and consumption fall by 3–4 percent in the initial two years, dampening demand for imports. As a result, EEA's current account surplus declines only by 0.8 percent of GDP in the first year. Reflecting the importance of export demand in EEA economies, this economic bloc experiences a large and sustained GDP contraction in the wake of its currency appreciation.

Despite the relatively large effect on its own economy, EEA's currency appreciation has only modest impacts on other regions, as indicated in the left panel of Figure 8.6. Given its strong economic linkage with EEA, Japan experiences the largest contraction in trade, with a 0.8 percent decline in exports and a 0.5 percent decline in imports in the initial two years. The US is less impacted and ROW is the least impacted, consistent with their limited respective export dependence on EEA. As both exports and imports shrink, the current account balances of the US, Japan and ROW change little following EEA's introduction of full exchange rate flexibility and currency appreciation. Consequently, the impacts on their real GDP range from 0.20 percent to 0.35 percent in the initial years and are less than 0.1 percent annually afterwards.

8.3.5 Expanding Regional Demand in Emerging East Asia

The results of our fifth scenario – EEA's domestic demand expansion in addition to its full exchange rate flexibility – are plotted in Figure 8.5 and the right panel of Figure 8.6. As Figure 8.5 shows, the rise in domestic consumption and investment partly offsets the negative impacts from currency appreciation on EEA's output, resulting in a smaller initial loss in GDP compared with the fourth scenario. As stronger domestic demand sucks more imports and discourages exports, the imports of EEA rise by 2–6 percent and its exports fall by around 6 percent initially. As a result, the current account surplus of EEA declines by 5 percent of GDP over a period of a decade. Reflecting the changes in relative prices induced by the demand expansion in EEA, the real effective exchange rate of the EEA currency appreciates much more – by around 4 percent initially – than in the fourth scenario.

The deterioration in EEA's current account balance is mirrored in the improvement in the current account balances in other regions of the world. As shown in the right panel of Figure 8.6, the current account balances of

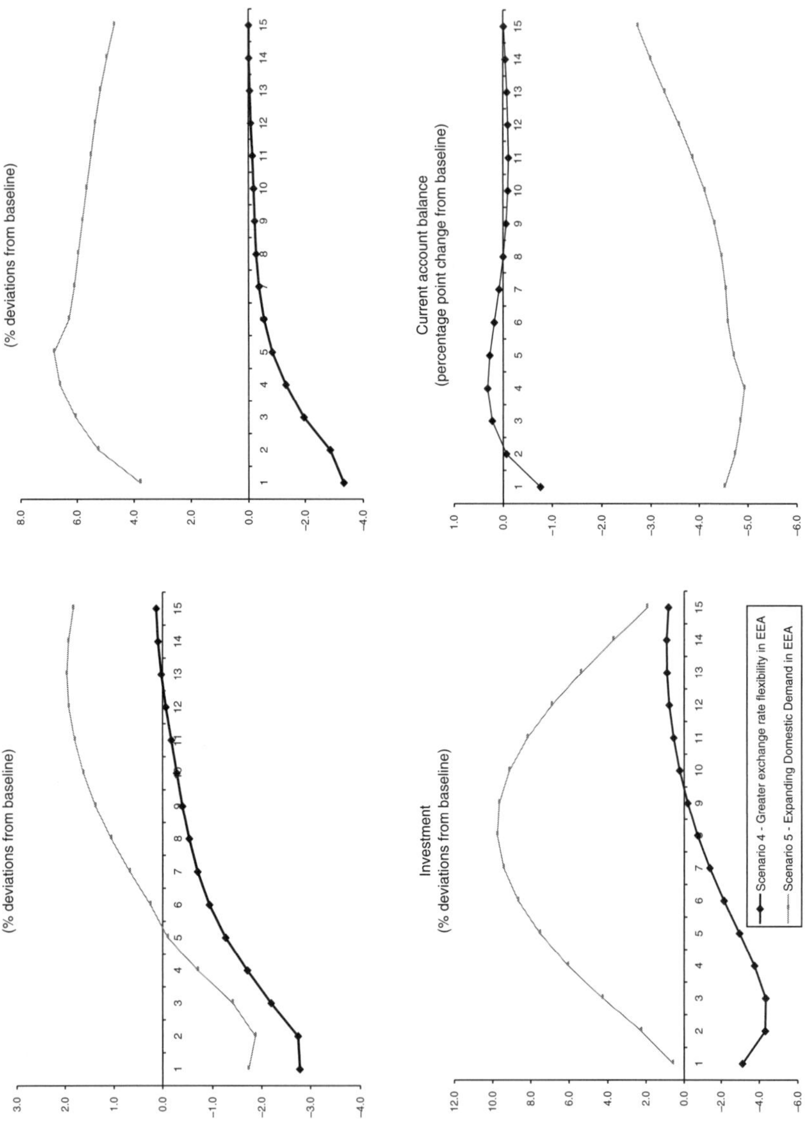

Consumption
(% deviations from baseline)
Current account balance
(percentage point change from baseline)
GDP
(% deviations from baseline)
Investment
(% deviations from baseline)
Scenario 4 - Greater exchange rate flexibility in EEA
Scenario 5 - Expanding Domestic Demand in EEA

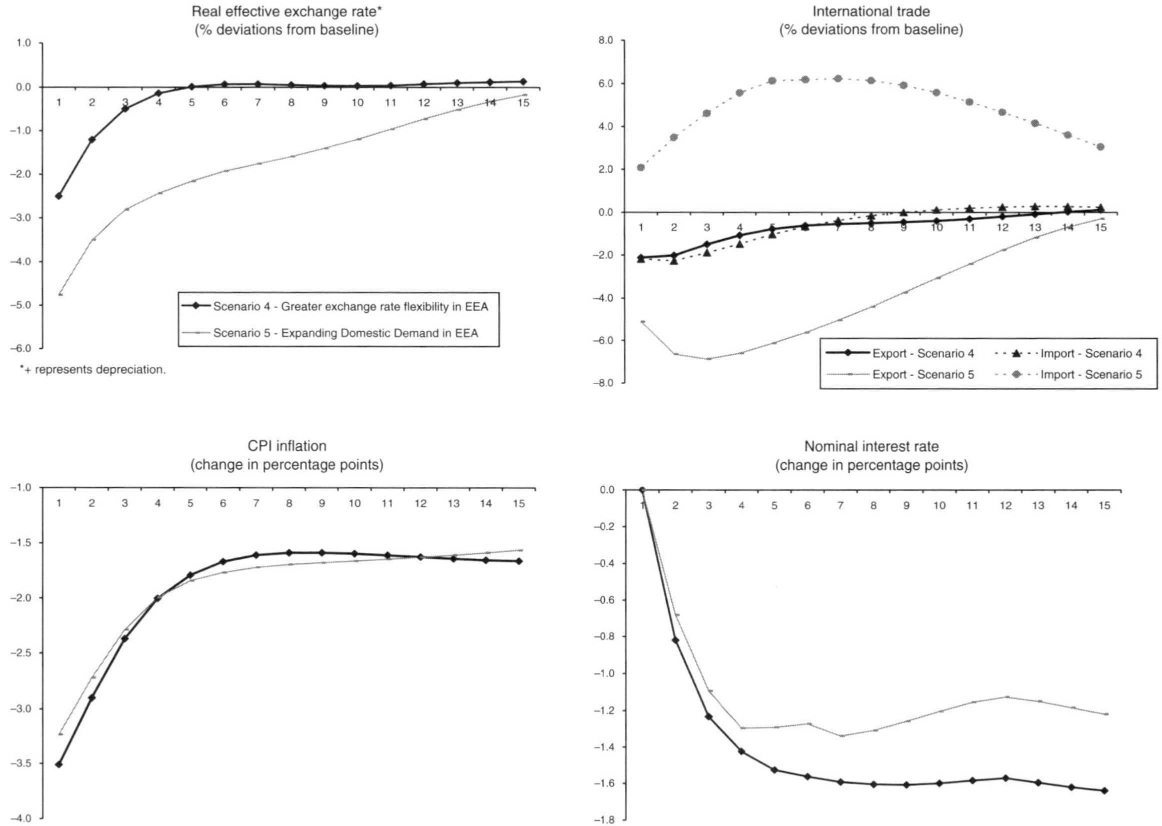

Notes: CPI = consumer price index; EEA = emerging East Asia; GDP = gross domestic product.

Source: Authors' model simulations.

Figure 8.5 Impacts of EEA's growth rebalancing policies on EEA

Real GDP – Scenario 4
(% deviations from the third scenario)

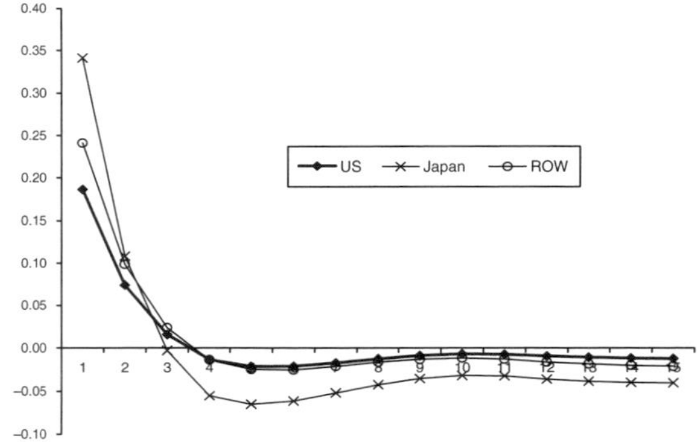

Real GDP – Scenario 5
(% deviations from the third scenario)

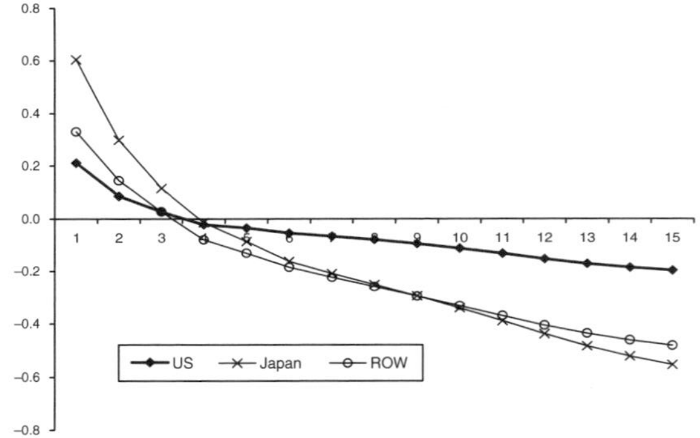

Current account balance as % of GDP – Scenario 4
(percentage points changes from the third scenario)

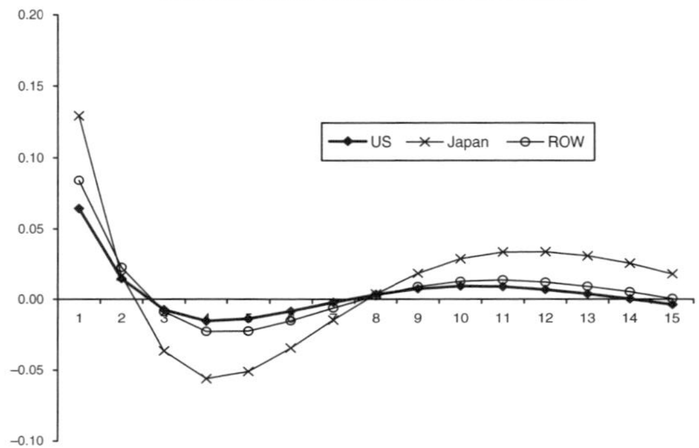

Current account balance as % of GDP – Scenario 5
(percentage points changes from the third scenario)

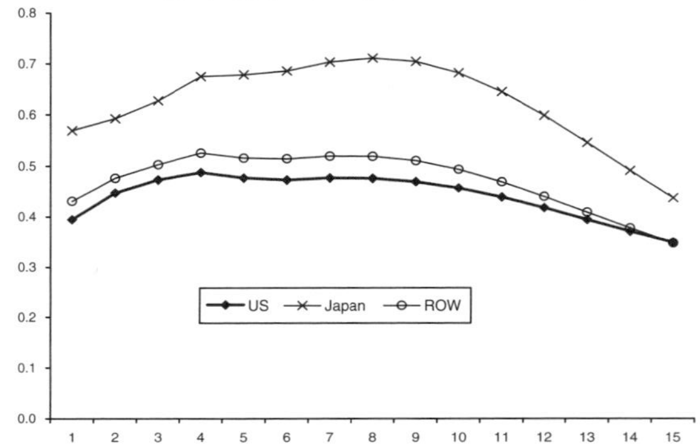

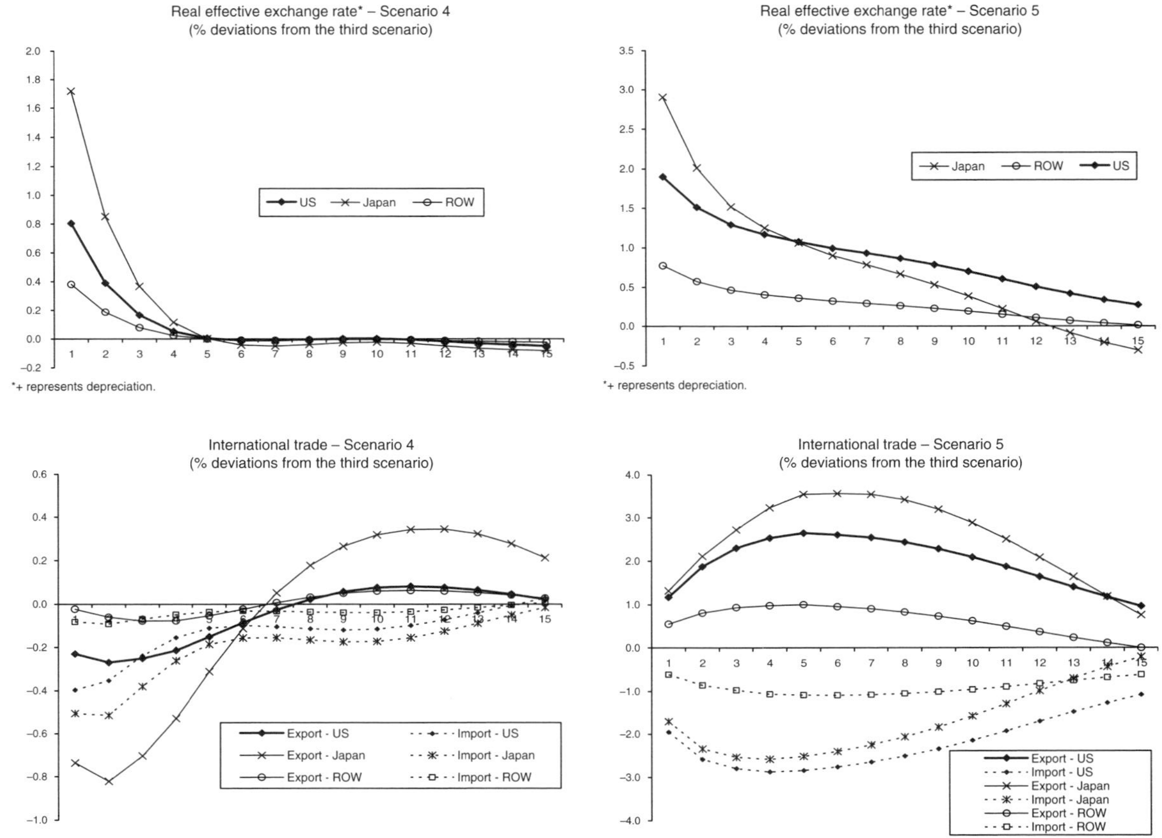

Notes: ROW = rest of world; US = United States.

Source: Authors' model simulations.

Figure 8.6 Impacts of EEA's growth rebalancing policies on other regions the US, Japan and ROW improve by 0.4–0.6 percent of their respective GDP. Although the US experiences larger export expansion in comparison to ROW, its gain in the current account balance is smaller due to its lower trade dependence. Rising net exports in non-EEA regions stimulate their GDP growth in the short term, but declining domestic demand soon dominates the improvement in net exports, resulting in GDP contraction from the fourth year onwards. The reason is that rising domestic demand in EEA reduces its trade surplus and, hence, net capital outflows, pushing up real interest rates globally. With the negative effect of higher real interest rates on investment and consumption dominating the improvement in net exports, real GDP contracts in the US, Japan and ROW over the medium term. This result highlights the importance of the general equilibrium impacts on international capital flows in analyzing the long-term implications of adjustment in global current account imbalances.

8.4 CONCLUSION

This chapter has examined the implications of the global financial crisis, emanating from the US, and of a global fiscal stimulus package as well as EEA's dynamic adjustment toward global rebalancing. Using a calibrated global dynamic general equilibrium model, we have simulated the scenarios of a US recession, a global recession, worldwide expansion in fiscal spending, and EEA's rebalancing policies – such as introducing full exchange rate flexibility and expansion in regional demand. Simulation results of the first two scenarios suggest that a financial crisis, if confined to the US alone, would have only small negative impacts on the world economy. A global financial crisis, which spreads demand contraction from the US to other regions in the world, would cause a slowdown in economic growth and trade all over the world. But the negative impacts are not evenly distributed across regions. Because of its exchange rate regime that stabilizes the currency against the US dollar, EEA is least impacted by a financial crisis, whether in the US alone or worldwide, in terms of output.

We have also investigated the effects of global fiscal stimulus packages in response to a crisis. With a global fiscal stimulus package of 2 percent of GDP for two years, world GDP is likely to be lifted by 2 percent and 3 percent during the period of fiscal expansion under the benchmark and accommodative monetary policy rules, respectively. This result suggests that fiscal stimulus combined with an appropriate monetary policy rule can serve as an important stabilizer for the world economy during a crisis. For EEA economies, given their high level of trade dependence, globally coordinated fiscal stimulus would be much more desirable than acting alone.

With its large current account surplus and increasing importance in the world economy, EEA's growth rebalancing policy is an important component of the global effort to unwind the global imbalance. The exchange rate inflexibility in EEA is widely regarded as a major impediment to global rebalancing. Our simulation results show that exchange rate flexibility alone in EEA would not contribute much to the correction of its current account imbalance. Given EEA's highly export-dependent growth pattern, its currency appreciation would lead to large output and income losses, depressing its appetite for imports and reducing its current account surplus by only 2 percent of GDP. Other policies – particularly structural reform in nature – to boost regional demand, supported by greater flexibility in the regional currency, would be needed to have a much larger and persistent impact on EEA's current account.

Indeed, an appreciation of 5 percent in EEA's real effective exchange rate, driven by its domestic demand expansion and nominal currency appreciation, is likely to reduce its own current account balance by 5 percent of GDP. However, without any adjustment in any other country, this change in EEA's current account will be largely evenly distributed among other regions of the world. The simulation results show that the US current account deficit narrows only by 0.5 percent of GDP under this scenario, hardly correcting the US and, hence, global imbalances. Although the global economic impact of EEA is growing, its rebalancing policy has limited impact globally, suggesting the need for policy actions on the part of the US in reducing its own current account deficit. Essentially, both the current account surplus and deficit economies should implement their respective policies in order to reduce the global imbalance and achieve sustained global economic growth.

Several important limitations of our modeling exercises should be mentioned. First, our model does not explicitly incorporate the linkages through global financial markets and the mechanisms of co-movements in asset prices. As they are important transmission channels through which the US recession may drag down the EEA and world economies, our results likely underestimate the impacts of the US and global financial crises on the Asian economies. Second, the global financial crisis and the need for global rebalancing would require EEA economies to shift demand from external to internal sources. Using a static multisectoral general equilibrium model, our previous work has shown that, given the different product composition in domestic and external demand, this would involve substantial structural shifts in their production activities (Kawai and Zhai 2009). Without sectoral disaggregation, our model does not fully capture the role of structural adjustment and the associated adjustment costs required for growth rebalancing. A dynamic general equilibrium model incorporating detailed sectoral disaggregation – including tradable and non-tradable sectors – and intersectoral labor adjustment frictions would better serve the detailed analysis of dynamic impacts of the global financial crisis. Finally, recent advances in trade theory have emphasized the importance of the extensive margin in trade adjustment. Incorporating firm heterogeneity and dynamics of firm entry and exit into the traditional framework of a new open economy macroeconomics model may somewhat alter the analytical results, and provide new insights about the implications of the global financial crisis and rebalancing.[9]

NOTES

* This chapter was originally published in the *Asian Development Review*, **27** (2), December, 122–51.

1. Immediately after the eruption of the global financial crisis, governments and central banks around the world responded swiftly to deal with liquidity and solvency problems of affected financial institutions through easing monetary policy and recapitalizing or restructuring troubled financial institutions. In addition to such measures, fiscal stimulus packages have been implemented around the world to boost demand. The IMF estimated that the total amount of fiscal stimulus in the Group of Twenty (G20) countries amounted to US$692 billion in 2009, about 1.4 percent of their combined GDP. The US, the PRC, Japan and Germany are the key contributors of global fiscal stimulus, with stimulus packages worth approximately 2 percent of their respective GDP.
2. See Zhang et al. (2010) for a recent application of the GIMF model to evaluating the impacts of the US credit crisis on Asia.
3. The introduction of labor unions is for model simplification, as aggregation across generations would be difficult if nominal rigidities were faced by households rather than unions.
4. See Armington (1969) for a description.
5. See, for example, Dixit and Stiglitz (1977).
6. See, for example, Henderson and McKibbin (1993).
7. The trade literature on empirical estimation of the Armington elasticity usually found a high value ranging from about 6 to 15, and these estimates are typically used in applied general equilibrium models for trade policy analysis (see, for example, Hertel et al. 2007). See Ruhl (2003) for a reconciliation of the low elasticity value found in aggregate high-frequency time series data with the high elasticity found in cross-section data.
8. This constant adjustment parameter can be interpreted as a risk premium. See McKibbin and Wilcoxen (1998) for a similar treatment in their multisectoral, intertemporal G-Cubed model.
9. See Bilbiie et al. (2007) and Kumhof et al. (2008) for the incorporation of firm dynamics into dynamic stochastic general equilibrium models. Corsetti et al. (2008) analyzed the exchange rate adjustment to correct the global imbalance in consideration of endogenous firm entry and new varieties of exports of goods and services, suggesting milder exchange rate adjustments for reducing US current account deficits.

REFERENCES

Armington, P. (1969), 'A theory of demand for products distinguished by place of production', *International Monetary Fund Staff Papers*, **16**, 159–76.

Bilbiie, F., F. Ghironi and M. Melitz (2007), 'Monetary policy and business cycles with endogenous entry and product variety', NBER Working Paper 13199, Cambridge, MA: National Bureau of Economic Research.

Blanchard, O.J. (1985), 'Debt, deficits, and finite horizons', *Journal of Political Economy*, **93** (2), 223–47.

Corsetti, G., P. Martin and P. Pesenti (2008), 'Varieties and the transfer problem: the extensive margin of current account adjustment', NBER Working Paper 1379, Cambridge, MA: National Bureau of Economic Research.

Dixit, A. and J. Stiglitz (1977), 'Monopolistic competition and optimum product diversity', *American Economic Review*, **67**, 297–308.

Henderson, D. and W. McKibbin (1993), 'A comparison of some basic monetary policy regimes for open economies: implications of different degrees of instrument adjustment and wage persistence', *Carnegie-Rochester Conference Series on Public Policy*, **39**, 221–318.

Hertel, T., D. Hummels, M. Ivanic and R. Keeney (2007), 'How confident can we be of CGE-based assessments of free trade agreements?', *Economic Modelling*, **24** (4), 611–35.

Kawai, M. and F. Zhai (2009), 'China–Japan–United States integration amid global rebalancing: a computable general equilibrium analysis', *Journal of Asian Economics*, **20** (6), 688–99.

Knudsen, M., L.H. Pedersen, T.W. Petersen, P. Stephensen and P. Trier (1998), 'Dynamic calibration of a CGE-model with a demographic application', mimeo, Copenhagen: Statistics Denmark.

Kumhof, M. and D. Laxton (2007), 'A party without a hangover? On the effects of US fiscal deficits', IMF Working Paper 07/202, Washington, DC: IMF.

Kumhof, M., D. Laxton and K. Naknoi (2008), 'Does the exchange rate belong in monetary policy rules: new answers from a DSGE model with endogenous tradability and trade frictions', proceedings from the ECB Conference on Globalization and the Macroeconomy, Frankfurt: European Central Bank.

Laxton, D. (2008), 'Getting to know the global economy model and its philosophy', *IMF Staff Papers*, **55** (2), 213–42.

McKibbin, W.J. and A. Stoeckel (2009), 'Modelling the global financial crisis', CAMA Working Paper Series 25/2009, Canberra: Centre for Applied Macroeconomic Analysis, Australian National University.

McKibbin, W.J. and P.J. Wilcoxen (1998), 'The theoretical and empirical structure of the G-Cubed model', *Economic Modelling*, **16** (1), 123–48.

Obstfeld, M. and K. Rogoff (1995), 'Exchange rate dynamics redux', *Journal of Political Economy*, **103** (3), 624–60.

Obstfeld, M. and K. Rogoff (1996), *Foundations of International Macroeconomics*, Cambridge, MA: MIT Press.

Rotemberg, J. (1982), 'Sticky Prices in the United States', *Journal of Political Economy*, **90** (6), 1187–211.

Ruhl, K. (2003), 'Solving the elasticity puzzle in international economics', mimeo, Austin, TX: University of Texas.

Wendner, R.A. (1999), 'Calibration procedure of dynamic CGE models for non-steady state situations using GEMPACK', *Computational Economics*, **13** (3), 265–87.
Yaari, M.E. (1965), 'Uncertain lifetime, life insurance, and the theory of the consumer', *Review of Economic Studies*, **32**, 137–50.
Zhang, W., Z. Zhang and G. Han (2010), 'How does the US credit crisis affect the Asia-Pacific economies? Analysis based on a general equilibrium model', *Journal of Asian Economics*, **21** (3), 280–92.

APPENDIX: MODEL SPECIFICATION

Basic Set-Up

The model economy consists of four regional blocs, which are indexed by r or s. Each region is populated by overlapping generations' households with finite planning horizons as in Blanchard (1985). Households are indexed by age a. In each region there are a continuum of firms and a continuum of labor unions, which are indexed by $n \in [0, 1]$ and $\mu \in [0, 1]$, respectively. The time index in the model is t.

The model assumes the presence of an exogenous trend in labor productivity growth (at rate $g - 1$). For a clear separation of an endogenous dynamic from an exogenous trend, we present all variables in detrended form through division by g. In each region the CPI is the numéraire of the economy and all national prices are expressed in terms of domestic consumption units.

In the model described below, subscripts denote region and/or time. The time index, t, is omitted when all variables in an equation are with the same time index. Regional subscript, r, is also omitted where doing so does not lead to confusion.

Demand and Trade

Domestic demand in each region comprises consumption and investment by households, firms and government. A composite good, XA, is used for final and intermediate demand. This composite good is a constant elasticity of substitution (CES) aggregation of domestic goods, XD, and aggregate imports, XM.

$$XA = ((\alpha^d)^{1/\sigma^m}(XD)^{(\sigma^m - 1)/\sigma^m} + (\alpha^m)^{1/\sigma^m}(XM)^{(\sigma^m - 1)/\sigma^m})^{\sigma^m/(\sigma^m - 1)} \quad (8.1)$$

where σ^m is the elasticity of substitution between imports and domestic goods. The Armington share parameters α^d and α^m reflect the preference of agents biased for home or imported products. The sales price for composite good, PA, is the tax-included dual price index defined over the prices of domestic and imported goods, PD and PM, respectively:

$$PA = (1 + \tau^s)(\alpha^d(PD)^{1-\sigma^m} + \alpha^m(PM)^{1-\sigma^m})^{1/(1-\sigma^m)} \quad (8.2)$$

where τ^s is the sales tax rate.

The demand functions generated from (8.1) and (8.2) are:

$$\frac{XD}{XA} = \alpha^{d}\left(\frac{PA}{(1 + \tau^{s})PD}\right)^{\sigma^{m}} \tag{8.3}$$

$$\frac{XM}{XA} = \alpha^{m}\left(\frac{PA}{(1 + \tau^{s})PM}\right)^{\sigma^{m}} \tag{8.4}$$

Aggregate import demand, *XM*, is a CES aggregation of imports from each region, that is:

$$XM_s = \left(\sum_{r\in R}(\alpha_{rs})^{1/\sigma_s^w}(XE_{rs})^{(\sigma_s^w - 1)/\sigma_s^w}\right)^{\sigma_s^w/(\sigma_s^w - 1)} \tag{8.5}$$

where α_{rs} is the preference of agents in region s biased for goods imported from region r; XE_{rs} represents the quantity of goods produced in region r and sold in (or exported to) the market of region s; and σ^w is the second-level Armington elasticity of substitution among imports from different regions. The dual price index of aggregate import, PM_s, is defined over the prices of each import supplier or export goods producer, PE_{rs}:

$$PM_s = \left(\sum_{r\in R}\alpha_{rs}\left(\frac{\varepsilon_s}{\varepsilon_r}(1 + \tau_{rs})PE_{rs}\right)^{1-\sigma_s^w}\right)^{1/(1-\sigma_s^w)} \tag{8.6}$$

where τ_{rs} is the tariff rate imposed on imports from region r and ε_r is the CPI-based real exchange rate of region r, expressed as the price of one unit of US consumption in terms of domestic consumption in region r.

The demand function generated from (8.5) and (8.6) is:

$$\frac{XE_{rs}}{XM_s} = \alpha_{rs}\left(\frac{\varepsilon_s}{\varepsilon_r}\frac{(1 + \tau_{rs})PE_{rs}}{PM_s}\right)^{\sigma_s^w} \tag{8.7}$$

Each firm is assumed to produce a differentiated product and each variety is an equally imperfect substitute for all others across all varieties. The goods produced are either domestically demanded or exported. The aggregate demand for domestic goods, *XD*, and aggregate exports, *XE*, are further decomposed into demand for variety provided by each firm, following the standard Dixit–Stiglitz framework:

$$\frac{xd_{n,s}^{n}}{XD_s} = \left(\frac{pd_{n,s}}{PD_s}\right)^{\sigma_s^f} \tag{8.8}$$

$$\frac{xe_{n,rs}^{n}}{XE_{rs}} = \left(\frac{pe_{n,rs}}{PE_{rs}}\right)^{\sigma_s^f} \tag{8.9}$$

where $xd^n_{n,s}$ represents the demand in region s for domestic good variety n produced in region s; $xe^n_{n,rs}$ represents the demand in region s for export variety n produced in region r; $pd_{n,s}$ is the price of domestic good variety n set by the firm in region s; $pe_{n,rs}$ is the price of export variety n in market s set by the firm located in region r; and σ^f is the substitution elasticity among varieties of each firm.

Firms

Production technology of firms is modeled using a nested CES function. At the top level, the output is produced as a combination of public capital and an aggregate private input using Cobb–Douglas technology. At the second level, the aggregate private input is split into an intermediate input and an aggregate primary factor. At the third level, the aggregate primary factor is further disaggregated into a bundle of private capital and aggregate labor. Finally, at the bottom level, aggregate labor is decomposed into the differentiated labor input by each union. The stock of public capital is identical for all firms and provided free of charge to them. As the production function exhibits decreasing returns to scale for private inputs, the return to public capital is distributed to firms as profits.

Each firm produces a different variety and sets the price of its product facing isoelastic demand functions in both domestic and foreign markets, as shown in (8.8) and (8.9). There is an adjustment cost for price setting, which, expressed as a proportion of total sales, is assumed to be given by the following functions:

$$\Gamma^{pd}_{n,r,t} = \frac{\phi^p_r}{2}\left(\pi_{r,t}\frac{pd_{n,r,t}/pd_{n,r,t-1}}{\bar{\pi}_{r,t}} - 1\right)^2 \quad (8.10)$$

$$\Gamma^{pe}_{n,r,s,t} = \frac{\phi^p_s}{2}\left(\pi_{r,t}\frac{\varepsilon_{t,s}}{\varepsilon_{t,r}}\frac{\varepsilon_{t-1,r}}{\varepsilon_{t-1,s}}\frac{pe_{n,r,s,t}/pe_{n,r,s,t-1}}{\bar{\pi}_{s,t}} - 1\right)^2 \quad (8.11)$$

where ϕ^p_r and ϕ^p_s are respectively adjustment cost coefficients in region r and region s; and $\pi_{r,t}$ is the inflation rate in region r at time t. These adjustment cost functions indicate that the cost is related to changes in nominal prices of products relative to the contemporaneous inflation target for the CPI, shown by $\bar{\pi}_{r,t}$. Equation (8.11) indicates that the export price is set in the currency of the destination market, that is, local-currency pricing.

A firm n is assumed to maximize the discounted value of current and future profits, denoted as div_n, which are distributed as dividends to shareholders:

$$\max \sum_{t=0}^{\infty} \left(\prod_{\tau=0}^{t} \frac{g_{\tau}\pi_{\tau,r}}{1 + i_{\tau,r}} \right) div_{n,r,t}$$

$$div_{n,r,t} = (1 - \tau_r^k) R_{r,t} K_{n,r,t} - I^n_{n,r,t}$$

$$+ R^g_{r,t} K^g_{n,r,t} + (pd_{n,r,t} - PX_{r,t}) xd_{n,r,t} (1 - \Gamma^{pd}_{n,r,t})$$

$$+ \sum_{s \in R} (pe_{n,r,s,t} - PX_{r,t}) xe^n_{n,r,s,t} (1 - \Gamma^{pe}_{n,r,s,t}) \tag{8.12}$$

subject to CES production technology, the demand functions of (8.8) and (8.9), and the adjustment costs in price setting of (8.10) and (8.11), and given the price of aggregate output, PX, and the law of motion of capital:

$$K_{n,t+1} g_{t+1} = (1 - \delta) K_{n,t} + \Gamma^I_{n,t} K_{n,t} \tag{8.13}$$

where $K_{n,r,t}$ and $I^n_{n,r,t}$ are respectively private capital stock and investment of firm n in region r at time t; $K^g_{n,r,t}$ is the stock of public capital; $R_{r,t}$ and $R^g_{r,t}$ are respectively the prices of private and public capital; δ is the depreciation rate of capital. Γ^I_n is the adjustment cost of investment, which is a function of the investment-to-capital ratio and takes on value zero in the steady state:

$$\Gamma^I_{n,t} = \frac{I^n_{n,t}}{K_{n,t}} - \frac{\phi^I}{2} \left(\frac{I^n_{n,t}}{K_{n,t}} - \frac{I_{t-1}}{K_{t-1}} \right)^2 \tag{8.14}$$

As shown in (8.12), the firm's profits (or dividends) include the after-tax return to its private capital, the return to public capital captured, and the gains the firm obtains from selling products in the domestic and foreign markets. The optimization problem of the firm is to set its levels of investment, the labor input, the intermediate input, and the nominal prices of its products in domestic and exporting markets in order to maximize the discounted present value of its profits (or dividends). The resulting first-order conditions with respect to I and K are:

$$\frac{1}{q_t} = 1 - \phi^I \left(\frac{I^n_{n,t}}{K_{n,t}} - \frac{I_{t-1}}{K_{t-1}} \right) \tag{8.15}$$

$$(1 - \tau_t^k) R_t + q_t (1 - \delta + \Gamma^I_{n,t}) - \frac{I_t}{K_t} - q_{t-1} \frac{1 + i_t}{\pi_t} = 0 \tag{8.16}$$

where q is the shadow price of private capital, that is, Tobin's q.

The resulting first-order conditions with respect to pd and pe are:

$$(1 - \Gamma^{pd}_{n,r,t})(pd_{n,r,t}(1 - \sigma^f_r) + PX_{r,t}\sigma^f_r) = (pd_{n,r,t} - PX_{r,t})\phi^p_r\left(\frac{\pi^{pd}_{n,r,t}}{\overline{\pi}_{r,t}} - 1\right)\frac{\pi^{pd}_{n,r,t}}{\overline{\pi}_{r,t}}$$

$$-\frac{g_{t+1}\pi_{t+1}}{1 + i_{t+1}}\frac{XD_{r,t+1}}{XD_{r,t}}(pd_{n,r,t+1} - PX_{r,t+1})\phi^p_r\left(\frac{\pi^{pd}_{n,r,t+1}}{\overline{\pi}_{r,t+1}} - 1\right)\frac{\pi^{pd}_{n,r,t+1}}{\overline{\pi}_{r,t+1}} \quad (8.17)$$

$$(1 - \Gamma^{pe}_{n,r,s,t})(pe_{n,r,s,t}(1 - \sigma^f_s) + PX_{r,t}\sigma^f_s) =$$

$$(pe_{n,r,s,t} - PX_{r,t})\phi^p_s\left(\frac{\pi^{pe}_{n,r,s,t}}{\overline{\pi}_{s,t}} - 1\right)\frac{\pi^{pe}_{n,r,s,t}}{\overline{\pi}_{s,t}}$$

$$-\frac{g_{t+1}\pi_{t+1}}{1 + i_{t+1}}\frac{XE_{r,s,t+1}}{XE_{r,s,t}}(pe_{n,r,s,t+1} - PX_{r,t+1})\phi^p_s\left(\frac{\pi^{pe}_{n,r,s.t+1}}{\overline{\pi}_{s,t+1}} - 1\right)\frac{\pi^{pe}_{n,r,s.t+1}}{\overline{\pi}_{s,t+1}} \quad (8.18)$$

where $\pi^{pd}_{n,r,t}$ is the inflation rate of variety n in domestic market and $\pi^{pe}_{n,r,s,t}$ is the inflation rate of variety n produced in country r and sold in region s.

The first-order conditions with respect to production inputs lead to the following demand functions and price indices of aggregate inputs:

$$XN = \alpha^n \cdot X \cdot PX/PN \quad (8.19)$$

$$K^g = (1 - \alpha^n) \cdot X \cdot PX/R^g \quad (8.20)$$

$$X = A \cdot (K^g)^{1-\alpha^n} XN^{\alpha^n} \quad (8.21)$$

$$VA = \alpha^v \cdot XN \quad (8.22)$$

$$XI = \alpha^n \cdot XN \quad (8.23)$$

$$PN = \alpha^v PV + \alpha^n PI \quad (8.24)$$

$$L = \alpha^l \left[\frac{PV}{W}\right]^{\sigma^v} VA \quad (8.25)$$

$$K = \alpha^k \left[\frac{PV}{R}\right]^{\sigma^v} VA \quad (8.26)$$

$$PV = [\alpha^l (W)^{1-\sigma^v} + \alpha^k (R)^{1-\sigma^v}]^{1/(1-\sigma^v)} \quad (8.27)$$

where α^n and α^v are respectively the share parameters for the aggregate primary factor and the intermediate input in the production function of aggregate private input; α^l and α^k are respectively the share parameters for the aggregate labor input and private capital in the production function of the aggregate primary factor; X, K^g, XN, VA, XI, L, K represent output, public capital, aggregate private input, aggregate primary factor, intermediate input, aggregate labor and private capital, respectively; and PX, R^g, PN, PV, PI, W and R are their corresponding price indices. σ^v is elasticity of substitution between labor and capital.

Firms have the CES aggregator of the differentiated labor varieties provided by labor unions. As firms are assumed to be identical, the aggregate labor demand, L, can be expressed as:

$$L = \left[\int_0^1 (l_\mu)^{\frac{\sigma^l - 1}{\sigma^l}} d\mu\right]^{\frac{\sigma^l}{\sigma^l - 1}} \quad (8.28)$$

where l_μ is the quantity of labor provided by union μ and σ^l is the elasticity of substitution across labor varieties. Cost minimization of firms implies that demand for labor μ is a function of the relative wage:

$$\frac{l_\mu}{L} = \left[\frac{w_\mu}{W}\right]^{-\sigma^l} \quad (8.29)$$

where w_μ is the wage paid to union μ and the region's wage, W, is defined as:

$$W = \left[\int_0^1 (w_\mu)^{1-\sigma^l} d\mu\right]^{\frac{1}{1-\sigma^l}} \quad (8.30)$$

Households

In each period, $m_r(1 - \theta)$ individuals are born in region r and they face a constant probability of death $(1 - \theta)$ after their birth. This implies that the total number of population is m_r in region r. We distinguish two types of households: forward-looking ones denoted by FL, and liquidity-constrained ones denoted by LC. For a representative household of age a, its period utility in time t, $u_{a,t}$, is a function of its (detrended) consumption c and labor effort l^h:

$$u_{a,t}(c_{a,t}, l^h_{a,t}) = \frac{1}{1 - \sigma}[(c_{a,t}/(\tilde{c}_{t-1})^v)^\eta(1 - l^h_{a,t})^{1-\eta}]^{1-\sigma} \quad (8.31)$$

where σ is the inverse elasticity of intertemporal substitution and η is the weight of consumption in the utility function. The term $\tilde{c}_{t-1}$ represents past per capita consumption of household h's peers, that is, FL

households or *LC* households. v parameterizes the degree of habit persistence. This exhibits the 'keeping up with the Joneses' type of external habit formation.

The lifetime utility of age a household at time t, $U_{a,t}$, is the sum of discounted period utility:

$$U_{a,t} = \sum_{\tau=0}^{\infty} (g^{1-\sigma}\beta\theta)^{\tau} u_{a+\tau,t+\tau} \tag{8.32}$$

where β is the subjective discount rate, possibly time-variable but converging to a steady state constant in the long run.

The decision problem of a forward-looking household is to maximize its lifetime utility (8.32) subject to the following sequences of period budget constraints:

$$\begin{aligned}\theta(B_{a+1,t+1}\pi_{t+1} + \varepsilon_t B^*_{a+1,t+1}\pi^*_{t+1} + V_{t+1}z_{a,t+1}\pi_{t+1})g_{t+1} &= (1+i_t)B_{a,t} \\ +(1+i^*_t)(1-\zeta_t)\varepsilon_t B^*_{a,t} + (V_{t+1}\pi_{t+1}g_{t+1}\theta + Div_t)z_{a,t} \\ +TR^{FL}_{at} + (1-\tau_l)w^h_t\phi_a l^h_{a,t} - c_{a,t} - TT_{a,t}\end{aligned} \tag{8.33}$$

In the above expression, B_a is the amount of domestic government bonds held by the representative household at age a, denominated in domestic currency; B^*_a is the amount of international bonds held by household a, denominated in the US dollar; V denotes the value of a claim to firm profits in current and all future periods; z_a is the share of firms owned by the represent household at age a; π and π^* are respectively domestic and US CPI inflation rates; i and i^* are respectively the domestic and US nominal interest rates; ζ is the risk premium on international bonds; *Div* is the total dividends paid by all firms to households; TR^{FL}_a represents revenue from unions' profits rebated to forward-looking household a in a lump-sum way; and TT_a is the lump-sum net tax for household a. Labor incomes $w^h\phi_a l^h_a$ are taxed at the rate τ^l. And ϕ_a is the labor productivity of age a household, given by:

$$\phi_a = \frac{1-\theta\chi}{1-\theta}\chi^a \tag{8.34}$$

where θ is the constant probability of survival in each period and χ (<1) determines the speed of decline of an individual household's labor productivity throughout his lifetime.

The first-order conditions of the forward-looking household's optimization problem with respect to B, B^*, c, l and z yield the following arbitrage equations:

$$\frac{\pi_{t+1}}{1+i_{t+1}} = \frac{\pi^*_{t+1}}{(1+i^*_{t+1})(1-\zeta)}\frac{\varepsilon_t}{\varepsilon_{t+1}} \tag{8.35}$$

$$J_{t+1} = \frac{g_{t+1}c_{a,t+1}}{c_{a,t}} = \left(\frac{(1+i_t)\beta_{t+1}}{\pi_{t+1}}\right)^{1/\gamma}\left(\frac{w^h_{t+1}}{w^h_t}\chi\right)^{(1-\eta)(1-1/\gamma)}\left(\frac{c_t}{c_{t-1}}g_{t+1}\right)^{v\eta(1-1/\gamma)} \tag{8.36}$$

$$\frac{c_{a,t}}{1-l^h_{a,t}} = \frac{\eta^{FL}}{1-\eta^{FL}}w^h_t\phi_a \tag{8.37}$$

$$V_t(1+i_t) = Div_t + V_{t+1}g_{t+1}\pi_{t+1} \tag{8.38}$$

With some algebraic derivations, the aggregate consumption of all forward-looking households can be expressed as a fraction of the sum of their financial wealth, FW, and human wealth, HW. Human wealth is composed of two parts: the expected present discounted value of future labor income, HWL; and the expected present discounted value of future transfer incomes, HWT:

$$C^{FL}_t\Theta_t = (1+i_t)(HW_t + FW_t) \tag{8.39}$$

$$FW_t = B_t + \varepsilon_{t-1}B^*_t + V_t \tag{8.40}$$

$$HW_t = HWL_t + HWT_t \tag{8.41}$$

$$HWL_t(1+i_t) = w^h_t L^{FL}_t + HWL_{t+1}g_{t+1}\pi_{t+1}\theta\chi \tag{8.42}$$

$$HWT_t(1+i_t) = TR^{FL}_t + HWT_{t+1}g_{t+1}\pi_{t+1}\theta \tag{8.43}$$

Θ^{-1} is the marginal propensity to consume out of total wealth. This inverse of the marginal propensity of consume evolves according to:

$$\Theta_t = \frac{1}{\eta^{Fl}} + \frac{\theta J_{t+1}\pi_{t+1}}{1+i_{t+1}}\Theta_{t+1} \tag{8.44}$$

where J is already defined in (8.36).

A liquidity-constrained household has no access to capital markets. Its decision problem is purely static, confined to the choices of labor supply. Its budget constraint is:

$$c_{a,t} = (1-\tau^l)w^h_t\phi_a l^h_{a,t} + TR^{LC}_{at} - TT_{a,t} \tag{8.45}$$

where TR_a^{LC} is the lump-sum revenue from union's profits rebated to the liquidity-constrained household a. The first-order conditions with respect to consumption and labor supply yield the following relationship between aggregate consumption and labor supply:

$$\frac{c_t^{LC}}{m \cdot s^{LC} - L_t^{LC}} = \frac{\eta^{LC}}{1 - \eta^{LC}} w_t^h \tag{8.46}$$

where s^{LC} is the share of liquidity-constrained agents in total households and L^{LC} is the effective aggregate labor supply of liquidity-constrained households.

Unions

In each region, there is a continuum of unions which buy labor from households and sell labor to firms. They are perfectly competitive in their input markets and monopolistically competitive in their output market. Each union has power to set the nominal wage of the labor they provide. Similarly to the price setting by firms, wage changes are subject to adjustment costs. The adjustment cost function of nominal wage change is assumed as follows:

$$\Gamma_{\mu,t}^{w} = \frac{\phi^w}{2}\left(\pi_t \frac{w_{\mu,t}/w_{\mu,t-1}}{\bar{\pi}_t} - 1\right)^2 \tag{8.47}$$

The decision problem of each union is to maximize the present discounted value of nominal wages paid by firms, w_u, minus nominal wages paid out to households, w^h, minus wage change adjustment cost, by setting the nominal wage:

$$\max \sum_{t=0}^{\infty}\left(\prod_{\tau=0}^{t}\frac{g_\tau \pi_{\tau,r}}{1 + i_{\tau,r}}\right)(w_{\mu,t}(1 - \Gamma_{\mu,t}^{w}) - w_t^h) l_{\mu,t} \tag{8.48}$$

subject to the demand function (8.29). The resulting wage setting equation is:

$$\frac{w_t^h \sigma^l}{(1 - \tau^w) w_{\mu,t}} = (\sigma^l - 1)(1 - \Gamma_{\mu,t}^{w}) + \phi^w\left(\frac{\pi_{\mu,t}^{w}}{\bar{\pi}_t} - 1\right)\frac{\pi_{\mu,t}^{w}}{\bar{\pi}_t}$$
$$- \frac{g_{t+1}\pi_{t+1}L_{t+1}}{1 + i_{t+1} L_t}\phi^w\left(\frac{\pi_{\mu,t+1}^{w}}{\bar{\pi}_{t+1}} - 1\right)\frac{(\pi_{\mu,t+1}^{w})^2}{\bar{\pi}_{t+1}} \tag{8.49}$$

where $\pi_{\mu,t}^{w} = \pi_t \cdot w_{\mu,t}/w_{\mu,t-1}$ is the wage inflation rate.

Government

Government in region s has the following budget constraint:

$$B_{s,t+1}g_{t+1}\pi_{t+1} = (1 + i_{s,t})B_{s,t} + G^C_{s,t} + G^I_{s,t} - \tau^k_s R_{s,t}K_{s,t} - \tau^l_s W_{s,t}L_{s,t} - TT_{s,t}m_s$$

$$- \tau^s_s PA_{s,t}XA_{s,t} - \sum_r (\tau_{rs}PE_{rs,t}XE_{rs,t}\varepsilon_{s,t}/\varepsilon_{r,t}) \qquad (8.50)$$

where G^C and G^I are government consumption and investment, respectively. The accumulation of public capital follows:

$$K^g_{t+1}g_{t+1} = (1 - \delta)K^g_t + G^I_t \qquad (8.51)$$

The central bank in each region is assumed to set the nominal interest rate by employing the following monetary policy rule:

$$i_t = i_{t-1} + \omega_\pi(\pi_{t-1} - \bar{\pi}_{t-1}) + \omega_y(\Delta GDP_{t-1} - \Delta\overline{GDP}_{t-1})$$

$$+ \omega_e(\Delta\varepsilon_{t-1} - \Delta\bar{\varepsilon}_{t-1}) \qquad (8.52)$$

where ω_π, ω_y and ω_e are the weights for the inflation gap, the output growth gap and the exchange rate gap, respectively. The variables with bars are target values of the respective variables. Note that $\omega_e > 0$ for the emerging East Asian central bank, while $\omega_e = 0$ for the central banks in other regions of the world.

Equilibrium

The equilibrium condition in the composite good market is that the supply of the composite good, XA, is equal to the sum of household consumption demand, government demand for consumption and investment, and private demand for intermediate inputs:

$$XA = C^{FL} + C^{LC} + G^C + G^I + I \qquad (8.53)$$

The equilibrium condition in the labor market in each region is:

$$L = L^{FL} + L^{LC} \qquad (8.54)$$

The international bond is in zero net supply internationally. The market clearing condition for international bonds requires:

$$0 = \sum_r B^*_r \qquad (8.55)$$

PART V

Regional Cooperation Issues

9. A proposal for exchange rate policy coordination in East Asia

Masahiro Kawai and Shinji Takagi

9.1 INTRODUCTION

This chapter considers issues of exchange rate policy coordination for East Asia, a region that is becoming increasingly integrated both regionally and globally. Following the Asian crisis of 1997–1998, the region has experienced deepening integration in the context of recovery and expansion. Within the broad East Asia region including the Association of Southeast Asian Nations (ASEAN) member countries; the People's Republic of China (PRC); Japan; Republic of Korea (henceforth Korea); Hong Kong, China; and Taipei,China, for example, the share of intraregional trade – measured by an average of export and import shares – rose from 37 percent from 1980 to 1990 to a peak of 53 percent in 2004 (though it declined to 50 percent in 2009). Closely related is intraregional foreign direct investment (FDI), which in 2000–2004 accounted for as much as half of the region's total FDI (Hattari and Rajan 2008). Direct investment in plants and equipment has created production networks in some industries that cut across national borders.

With increasing intraregional trade and the formation of production networks across borders, macroeconomic interdependence has strengthened, both within the region and with the rest of the world (ADB 2008). In our earlier work (Kawai and Takagi 2005a), we presented evidence to show that East Asia in the early 2000s was no less integrated than Western Europe in terms of the share of intraregional trade in total trade, the share of trade in total output, the degree of trade intensity between regional trading partners, and the similarity of trade structure (with a dominant share of manufactures on the export side). More recent evidence indicates that, as a result of further economic integration, price arbitrage has strengthened, output and price correlations have increased, and the output and price impacts of shocks originating within the region have risen, relative to the pre-Asian financial crisis period (see, for example, Takagi and Kozuru 2010).

Increasing economic interdependence means that the action of a policymaker in one economy to pursue its own interests could more frequently come into conflict with other economies in the region. Cognizant of the consequence of growing economic interdependence, policymakers among ASEAN+3 countries – comprising the ten ASEAN members plus the PRC, Japan and Korea – have begun to develop the region's own institutions for macroeconomic and financial policy management, most notably the Economic Review and Policy Dialogue (ERPD) process, the multilateralization of the Chiang Mai Initiative (CMI), and the Asian Bond Markets Initiative (ABMI). In May 2010, the finance ministers further agreed that an independent surveillance unit, called the ASEAN+3 Macroeconomic Research Office (AMRO), would be located in Singapore and begin operation in 2011. Although the precise role that the AMRO will play over the coming years has yet to be fully articulated, regional economic surveillance is expected to be one of its principal functions. Effective regional economic surveillance would require that the region's policymakers agree on the choice of objective indicators to monitor macroeconomic developments, the most critical of which is to measure exchange rate misalignment. Thus, the region's policymakers would have to address the need for some form of exchange rate policy coordination, however elementary it may be.

Despite the fact that exchange rates constitute a critical link among interdependent economies and should therefore be a focus of any serious attempt at policy coordination, exchange rate policy has so far been one of the least coordinated policy areas regionally in East Asia. Before the Asian crisis of 1997–1998, most emerging economies in the region had managed their currencies tightly in relation to the United States (US) dollar. In this de facto dollar peg or stabilization policy, the exchange rates of East Asian currencies had fluctuated sharply against the Japanese yen, then the most important regional currency, whenever the yen fluctuated against the dollar. Takagi (1999) showed that the Japanese yen figured prominently in the exchange rate management practices of these economies only when the yen sharply depreciated against the US dollar, reflecting the desire of Asian emerging economy authorities not to lose international price competitiveness against Japan in third markets.

When the Asian crisis led to a collapse of the de facto US dollar peg in the crisis-hit economies, these economies temporarily moved to a more flexible exchange rate regime. But as normalcy returned in the third quarter of 1998, they initially attempted to revert back to an informal dollar peg, though in a much softer way than before the crisis. Malaysia adopted a formal US dollar peg in September 1998,[1] while Hong Kong, China maintained its currency peg to the US dollar under a currency board arrangement. The PRC had a de jure managed float, which was in practice administered as a de facto peg to the US dollar. Japan was almost alone in maintaining an independent float, although it too intervened heavily in the foreign exchange market to ease any appreciation pressure against the US dollar, particularly from January 2003 to March 2004.[2]

Over time, policymakers in several economies have shifted the way of managing exchange rates, from lesser to greater flexibility against the US dollar. For example, the authorities in countries like Korea and Thailand began to adopt a de facto currency basket regime by assigning increasing weights on the Japanese yen while maintaining still high, but declining weights on the US dollar. The PRC decided, in July 2005, to revalue the yuan upward against the US dollar and at the same time to set its value with reference to a basket of currencies. The PRC's new exchange rate policy was temporarily halted during the global financial crisis but was restored in June 2010. Eventually Korea and, to a lesser extent, Indonesia, the Philippines and Thailand, switched from a managed exchange rate arrangement to a floating arrangement, albeit not free floating. In this way, several Asian currencies have become more flexible compared to the exchange rate behavior prior to the crisis.

However, one of the problems with East Asian exchange rate arrangements is that the two giant economies in the region – that is, Japan and the PRC – adopted very different exchange rate regimes: Japan a free-floating arrangement, and the PRC a stabilized or heavily managed arrangement with reference to the US dollar. Most other currencies maintain the middle ground. These developments mean that there is now greater diversity in exchange rate arrangements within the region, without any policy coordination (Table 9.1; see also Kawai 2008).

Does this suggest a polarization of exchange rate regimes in the region, either towards a hard peg or towards an independent float? Some scholars have argued that in a world of high capital mobility most countries have little alternative but to float their currencies, unless special circumstances make it feasible to lock them in through a currency board or a common currency arrangement (Eichengreen 1999). In one of the earliest statements of this view, Obstfeld and Rogoff (1995) argued that a conventional fixed exchange rate was costly if the government's promise not to devalue lacked credibility, and that it was becoming increasingly difficult to establish such credibility. Thus, unless the government concerned can assume the obligations of a rigid peg, the alternative is to let the currency float freely – the so-called two-corner solution or bipolar view (Fischer 2001). Until recently, this was also the dominant view within the International Monetary Fund (IMF) (see IEO 2007).[3]

The exchange rate policies of East Asian economies are too complex to

Table 9.1 Exchange rate arrangements and monetary policy frameworks in selected East Asian economies (end-April 2010)

Exchange rate arrangement	Monetary policy framework		
	Exchange rate anchor	Inflation targeting	Other
Currency board	Brunei Darussalam Hong Kong, China		
Stabilized arrangement	Cambodia People's Republic of China Viet Nam		Lao People's Democratic Republic
Other managed arrangement	Singapore		Malaysia Myanmar
Near free floating*		Indonesia Korea Philippines Thailand	
Free floating			Japan

Note: * IMF calls this arrangement simply 'floating'.

Source: International Monetary Fund (2010).

be explained by the simple bipolar view; neither does such a view appear to present a sensible policy prescription for East Asia. The objectives of exchange rate policy are multidimensional. While the bipolar view gives exclusive attention to the objective of crisis prevention, countries can pursue economic growth, trade expansion and other objectives through their use of exchange rate policy. Frankel (1999) argued that the optimal exchange rate regime depends on the circumstances of a particular country, and that there is no single regime that can fit all emerging market economies at all times. In the choice of an exchange rate regime for East Asia, the potential benefits of free floating as a crisis prevention device must be balanced against the potential costs. This chapter explores issues involved in that choice and considers scope for regional exchange rate coordination to pursue shared objectives.

The rest of the chapter is organized as follows. Section 9.2 discusses theoretical and empirical aspects of exchange rate policy, including alternative objectives and empirical evidence on the impact of exchange rate volatility. Section 9.3 considers practical aspects of exchange rate policy coordination in East Asia, including potential benefits and issues related to the management of cooperation. Section 9.4 outlines the steps involved in moving forward by discussing both institutional issues and how the use of an Asian currency unit could be intensified as policy coordination deepens. Section 9.5 concludes.

9.2 THEORETICAL AND EMPIRICAL ASPECTS OF EXCHANGE RATE POLICY

9.2.1 Objectives of Exchange Rate Policy

Crisis prevention and exchange rate flexibility

In recent discussions of exchange rate policy for emerging economies, crisis prevention has received almost exclusive attention, so that an independent float has been enshrined as the preferred exchange rate regime unless an institutional mechanism can be put in place to make an exchange rate peg credible. It is being increasingly recognized in the broader international policymaking community, however, that crisis prevention is only one of many possible objectives of exchange rate policy (IMF 2009), a position that has consistently been upheld by many policymakers in Asia. Countries should then balance the benefit of crisis prevention that could potentially come from a free float against the costs of foregoing the attainment of other possible goals, such as the promotion of trade, FDI and economic growth. In the absence of sound macroeconomic policy and prudential measures, moreover, a free float alone might not prevent a currency crisis from occurring in any case; conversely, even in the absence of a free float, crisis prevention could be feasible if supporting measures were put in place. Consideration of the optimal exchange rate regime must therefore be made in a broader context of competing policy objectives and the associated costs and benefits of each regime.

Macroeconomic stabilization

For most practical purposes, exchange rate policy for small open economies may broadly be considered to have two roles: a microeconomic or resource allocation role – for example, maintaining international price competitiveness or facilitating relative price adjustment – and a macroeconomic role including that of anchoring domestic prices or acting as a shock absorber. At times, these two roles could become conflicting, with one requiring exchange rate flexibility and the other exchange rate stability. In this context, our earlier work (Kawai and Takagi 2005a) showed within the framework of a structural vector autoregression (VAR) model that real gross domestic product (GDP) growth and price inflation of East Asian emerging economies were highly sensitive to changes in the real exchange rates against a basket of the US dollar, the euro and the Japanese yen.[4] Thus, from the standpoint of minimizing domestic output and price fluctuations, it is important that the East Asian emerging economies pay sufficient attention to maintaining real effective exchange rate stability. A peg to a single currency – be it the US dollar, the yen or the euro – cannot be a good option, given the region's geographically diversified trade pattern.

As emerging economies are subject to numerous types of shocks – such as sudden changes in terms of trade, foreign demand and global interest rates – exchange rate flexibility is useful as a buffer against these external shocks. Indeed, there is evidence to suggest that economies with greater exchange rate flexibility tend to experience smaller output volatility, possibly reflecting the ability of a flexible exchange rate to allow countercyclical use of monetary policy (Aizenman et al. 2008). Recent IMF research further shows that countries with flexible exchange rates have recovered more rapidly from the global financial crisis, possibly reflecting the useful role of exchange rate flexibility in responding to shocks (Tsangarides 2010). In small open economies, however, exchange rate instability due to free floating could become a source of additional shocks to output, prices and other macroeconomic variables and make macroeconomic policy management difficult. The potential benefits of floating as a shock absorber, therefore, must be weighed against the potential costs of greater difficulty in macroeconomic management associated with exchange rate instability.

The exchange rate as a nominal anchor with potential risks

Related to the question of macroeconomic stability is the nominal anchor role of the exchange rate. Both theoretically and empirically, there is a strong case for arguing that a pegged exchange rate delivers lower inflation than a flexible exchange rate. IMF (2009) reports that, in the case of emerging economies, pegged exchange rates outperformed inflation targeting (with flexible exchange rates) in terms of inflation performance for 2000–2007, although the association between pegged exchange rates and lower inflation was not observed in the case of advanced economies. The same study reports that the association was stronger for de jure pegs than for de facto pegs, suggesting the possible importance of the impact of formal commitment on private sector expectations. Nominal price stability, however, may not be compatible with nominal exchange rate stability if the real exchange rate is under pressure to change.

In this context, some authors have argued that the achievement of relative price stability in much of East Asia has not necessarily relied on the use of the exchange rate as a nominal anchor. Glick et al. (1999), for example, noted that in East Asia the economies whose currencies appreciated relatively less against the US dollar in nominal terms tended to experience higher inflation, and argued that the exchange rate pegging policies of the 1990s did not necessarily promote price stability but rather created inflationary pressure. According to their interpretation, the higher rate of inflation in East Asia in the 1990s could be explained by the fact that the policy of nominal exchange rate stability against the US dollar forced the needed real exchange rate appreciation to take place through price-level adjustment – rather than nominal exchange rate adjustment – given the presumed higher productivity growth relative to the US. Although nominal exchange rate stability contributes to overall price stability, inflationary pressure could still emerge if productivity growth is sufficiently high relative to that of the anchor currency country.

In the presence of persistent payments imbalances, nominal exchange rate stability can aggravate macroeconomic and financial sector conditions in an economy. For example, with continuous payments surpluses due to persistent current account surpluses or capital inflows, a fixed exchange rate regime requires continuous intervention in the foreign exchange market and accumulation of foreign exchange reserves. This is often matched by increases in domestic liquidity, leading to money supply increases – through loan expansion by banks – and the consequent inflationary pressure, economic overheating and asset market bubbles. These developments can make the financial sector potentially vulnerable, and be a source of financial crisis. Sterilization may prevent these from taking place, but it is difficult to use sterilized intervention as a permanent measure. Exchange rate flexibility is often an effective instrument to avoid these developments, by allowing the central bank to pursue independent monetary policy to contain inflation, overheating and asset price bubbles.

Price competitiveness and orderly resource allocation

In a broader context of emerging and developing economies in general, the microeconomic role of exchange rate policy is important because they are more likely to face balance-of-payments constraints or external shocks. Aghevli et al. (1991), for example, argued that exchange rate policy in developing countries should aim at protecting international price competitiveness by stabilizing the real effective exchange rate. In some cases, however, microeconomic considerations would call for relative price changes through greater exchange rate flexibility in order to reduce large current account imbalances (Dornbusch and Park 1999).

Exchange rate flexibility is not the same as a flexible exchange rate regime. While exchange rate flexibility can be a tool of relative price adjustment, a flexible exchange rate regime has often led to the emergence of large currency misalignment. Williamson (1999) argued that, in terms of limiting currency misalignment, a free float is the worst possible regime, with the most resilient arrangement being a crawling band, followed by a managed float, and a fixed rate system. He then explains the difference in economic performance between India (good) and New Zealand (bad) following economic liberalization by the fact that India managed the exchange rate with an objective of maintaining international price competitiveness, while New Zealand made no attempt to contain the upward float of the exchange rate. A flexible exchange rate regime does not always ensure the maintenance of international price competitiveness.

Over the medium term, achieving exchange rate stability can be a more sensible means of maintaining price competitiveness. Such considerations are particularly important for a highly integrated region such as East Asia, where the economies not only trade with each other but also compete against each other in third markets. In such an environment, an attempt by one economy to undercut another by depreciating its currency will result in a large reallocation of resources across the region, which may not be justified by long-run equilibrium considerations. Some mechanism of avoiding beggar-thy-neighbor exchange rate policies and promoting intraregional exchange rate stability may be useful, not least in minimizing wasteful exchange rate-induced resource reallocation.

9.2.2 Real Impact of Exchange Rate Volatility

Exchange rate volatility could also have impacts on trade and investment. Although the literature on the impact of exchange rate volatility on trade is inconclusive for advanced economies, exchange rate volatility seems to exert greater adverse effects on emerging and developing countries (see McKenzie 1999 for a survey; Calvo and Reinhart 2005; IMF 2009). For example, Kumar and Dhawan's (1991) work on Pakistan's exports to Germany, Japan and the US for 1974–1985 suggested that exports were significantly adversely affected by variability in nominal bilateral exchange rates. Looking at the effect of real exchange rate variability on the exports of the Philippines, Thailand, and four other emerging economies, Caballero and Corbo (1989) obtained clear evidence of significantly negative and substantial impact. Likewise, Arize et al. (2000) used quarterly data for 13 emerging economies (including Indonesia; Korea; Malaysia; the Philippines; Taipei,China; and Thailand) from 1973 to 1996 to confirm the significantly negative effect of real effective exchange rate volatility on exports. IMF (2009), based on data for some 150 countries from 1980 to 2007, confirmed the trade-enhancing effect of exchange rate stability, concluding that bilateral trade increases by a factor of 1.3 if two countries either are in a currency union or have a fixed exchange rate against each other.

Recent studies suggest that exchange rate volatility may affect trade in final goods and in intermediate goods differently. For example, Hayakawa and Kimura (2008) found that the negative impact of exchange rate volatility on intraregional trade was substantially greater for East Asia than for any other region during 1992–2005 and concluded that the predominance of the region's trade in intermediate goods was mainly responsible. Looking more closely at the impact of exchange rate volatility on trade in intermediate goods, Thorbecke (2008) found that one standard deviation increase in contemporaneous (one-year lagged) exchange rate volatility would reduce East Asia's electronic components exports by an average of US$200 million (US$300 million), and thus concluded that nominal exchange rate volatility (but not the real bilateral exchange rate) could discourage the region's production fragmentation activities.

Exchange rate volatility may also have negative impact on domestic investment, because its longer-term orientation can magnify the effect of uncertainty.[5] This may particularly be the case in East Asia where much of FDI is directed towards manufacturing exports as opposed to domestic sales.[6] Given the uncertainty, firms may find it optimal to wait rather than to commit to a decision. Waiting thus becomes an alternative to investing or not investing. By incorporating exchange rate uncertainty to the Dixit–Pindyck model,[7] Darby et al. (1999) have shown that there is a threshold level of exchange rate uncertainty beyond which investment is adversely affected.[8]

In terms of promoting economic growth, IMF (2009) reported that intermediate exchange rate regimes deliver an economic growth that is on average 0.5 percentage points per year higher than pegged or floating exchange rate regimes in the case of emerging economies. This finding for emerging economies is robust to alternative econometric specifications. The results likely reflect the observation that intermediate regimes avoid both the likely real exchange rate overvaluation of pegged regimes and the typically high real exchange rate volatility of floating regimes. The superior growth performance of intermediate regimes, however, is specific to emerging economies, and is not observed, at least as strongly, for advanced and developing countries.

9.3 PRACTICAL ASPECTS OF EXCHANGE RATE POLICY COORDINATION IN EAST ASIA

9.3.1 Benefits of Regional Exchange Rate Policy Coordination

The discussion above suggests that though some flexibility is desirable, a pure float is not a practical option for most East Asian emerging economies, given the potential for excessive volatility and misalignment, and the possibly adverse impact on trade and investment. The discussion also suggests that as the economies are competitors to each other, some intraregional exchange rate stability is desirable to prevent an unnecessary reallocation of resources that may be reversed within a short period (Dornbusch and Park 1999). What is needed for East Asia is a type of regional framework for exchange rate stabilization, which promotes intraregional exchange rate stability while retaining sufficient flexibility against external currencies.

Need for coordinated action

Several authors have noted that the de facto dollar peg policy of the 1990s helped to promote intraregional exchange rate stability, an important policy objective for a highly integrated region such as East Asia (Bayoumi et al. 2000; McKinnon 2000).[9] Against the benefit of intraregional exchange rate stability, Williamson (1999) characterized this de facto regional arrangement as a collective action problem, whereby each country was compelled to stay close to the US dollar because it feared that currency appreciation vis-à-vis the US dollar would weaken its competitiveness against its regional competitors.

This situation is a classic case of strategic interdependence that exists in the choice of exchange rate regimes for economies that produce similar goods, rival each other as host locations for FDI inflows, and compete for exports in common third markets. Honohan and Lane (1999) emphasized that exchange rate stabilization to a common anchor currency could be regarded as strategic complements; if a country stabilizes its exchange rate to an anchor currency, then other neighboring countries would also find it attractive to stabilize their exchange rates against the same anchor currency. In this sense, exchange rate stabilization vis-à-vis the US dollar in pre-crisis emerging East Asia was an alternative to costly beggar-thy-neighbor competitive depreciation strategies. This was obviously a Nash (non-cooperative) equilibrium and, hence, the question remains whether coordination could improve the outcome in a Pareto sense.[10]

Regional currency basket system

As a specific example of exchange rate policy coordination, Williamson (1999) suggested the adoption of a common basket peg, which ensures intraregional exchange rate stability while allowing some flexibility against the dollar, the yen and the euro (see also Bayoumi et al. 2000). The collective choice of a common basket for emerging East Asia would help to avoid the possibility that changes in advanced economy exchange rates would destabilize effective exchange rates, as would be the case when each currency was pegged to the US dollar. According to Williamson's (1999) simulation with a common basket – consisting of the US dollar, the yen and the euro – for nine East Asian emerging economies (People's Republic of China; Hong Kong, China; Indonesia; Korea; Malaysia; the Philippines; Singapore; Taipei,China; and Thailand), it would have produced a greater convergence of real effective exchange rates than was the case with the actual exchange rate policies taken, given the broadly similar geographical and industrial trade structures across these economies. A common basket would give results surprisingly close to those of individually tailored currency baskets in terms of stabilizing the real effective exchange rates for almost all economies.

9.3.2 Exchange Rate Management under a Common Currency Basket

Currency weights and composition

Joint management of exchange rates with reference to a common currency basket is a way of overcoming the collective action problem for an integrated region. But what is the basket around which exchange rates should be targeted? There is a large amount of theoretical literature on how to calculate the optimal currency weights of a basket (see Williamson 1982 for a survey of the literature). Not unexpectedly, the literature suggests that the optimal weights depend on the objective function of exchange rate policy. Thus, agreement on currency weights presupposes agreement on policy objectives (as well as the model to relate the exchange rate to those objectives), which is not easy to achieve in the real world. Under these circumstances, a broad qualitative approach may be justified. Fortunately, it is well known that exact weights make little difference in the overall performance of a currency basket because any weighted averaging tends to reduce the variance of the effective exchange rate. On this basis Williamson (1999) proposed for his basket the weights of 0.4 for the US dollar and 0.3 each for the yen and the euro, which corresponded broadly to the weighted average shares of East Asian emerging economies' trade with the US, Japan and Europe.

A more fundamental issue concerns whether the basket should include internal or external currencies. In early discussions of the currency basket approach to regional monetary cooperation in emerging East Asia, many authors – including Williamson (1999) and Ogawa and Ito (2002) – assumed that the basket would only include the three major external currencies, the US dollar, the euro, and the Japanese yen. If countries in the region decide to maintain the stability of their currencies against a basket of external currencies (with the weights broadly approximating the external trade shares), this will not only promote intraregional nominal exchange rate stability but also stabilize their effective exchange rates. In these early proposals, the Japanese yen was often considered as external to the region and, thus, Japan was treated asymmetrically to the other East Asian economies.

Implicitly, there were three reasons for treating the Japanese yen and Japan asymmetrically. First, Japan was unlike any other Asian economy, given its economic size, high stage of development, and its status as an important destination for the export of final goods from the rest of Asia. Second, the Japanese yen was virtually the only Asian currency that was flexible, free from control and widely traded in world foreign exchange markets, a feature necessary to make the currency truly an international one. Third, there was potential for the yen to become the region's key currency, so it was considered appropriate to treat the yen asymmetrically and as external to other currencies.

The economic landscape of East Asia, however, has changed drastically since these papers were written. It is now more compelling to include the region's own currencies in the currency basket, and to treat the yen and Japan more symmetrically in the region. First and foremost, with the significant elevation of income levels throughout the region – not to mention the emergence of the PRC as the region's largest economy – the Japanese economy no longer dominates the region as it once did. Second, much of the significant increase in intraregional trade since the late 1990s has involved trade in parts and components, and Japan is now a key part of the region-wide production network in a number of manufacturing sectors. There is little reason to treat Japan differently as a market for final goods, co-equal in importance to the US and Europe. Third, with no progress on the internationalization of the yen and no prospect for the yen to become the region's key currency, there is no convincing reason to treat the yen differently from the other currencies.

Modality of exchange rate policy coordination

At least initially, the operation of a regional exchange rate policy coordination mechanism in East Asia should be less formal and more flexible than the European Monetary System (EMS) of 1979–1998, given the current lack of commitment to full-fledged regional monetary union, the greater diversity in the level of economic and financial development across the region, and the dynamic nature of East Asian economies with rapid growth, evolving economic structures and possibly differing inflationary tendencies. These features make it likely that the East Asian economies face very different economic shocks and imbalances in certain circumstances, thus necessitating nominal exchange rate adjustment from time to time. There should be a presumption that the economies adjust the reference rates with respect to the basket differently over the medium term.

Given the need for flexibility, Williamson (1999) envisaged that each economy could choose its own exchange rate system with respect to the common basket. Hong Kong, China, for example, could continue to use a currency board arrangement, except that the dollar would be replaced by the basket. For most economies, however, the combination of a crawl and a band would be the norm. Dornbusch and Park (1999) call this arrangement 'BBC' – for 'band, basket and crawl' – which presumably offers the desirable possibility of flexibility of nominal rates without sacrificing the predictability of real exchange rates. In their view, however, the BBC proposal is only a learning mechanism and operating setting in transition to a more flexible regime. This is where they depart from the spirit of the Williamson (1999) proposal and our own view that the regional use of a common basket as a reference for exchange rate policy should ideally become a catalyst for greater nominal convergence and greater exchange rate stability within East Asia. Whatever the formal exchange rate arrangement may be – a free-floating regime or a managed rate regime – the important point is that each economy in the region should stabilize the real effective exchange rate at normal times by managing the nominal value of its currency with respect to a common currency basket.

At a time of a currency crisis, many economies would find it necessary to allow for large exchange rate depreciation. In such a situation, credibility for exchange rate stability can be maintained by establishing what McKinnon (2000) calls 'the restoration rule': the authorities are allowed to suspend the peg (or quasi-peg) temporarily when faced with a massive speculative attack, subject to the condition that the exchange rate will be restored back to the original parity as soon as practical. The restoration rule is a way of instilling regressivity into exchange rates even when a rare and extreme event calls for a temporary suspension of the peg. The restoration rule not only makes exchange rate expectations – hence the actual exchange rates – more regressive, but also may diminish the potential for speculative attack to begin with. If the shock is sufficiently large and permanent, the post-crisis rate may need to be set at a level consistent with the new equilibrium.

Compatibility with inflation targeting

In recent years, a number of emerging market economies including some in East Asia – such as Indonesia, Korea, the Philippines and Thailand – have adopted inflation targeting as a means of securing a nominal anchor under flexible exchange rate regimes. The policy of pre-announcing target ranges for inflation, moreover, is expected to serve as a way of imposing accountability on central banks, as they have assumed greater independence in these countries. Within the present context of East Asia, the policy of exchange rate flexibility combined with inflation targeting may well be a reasonable mechanism of securing price and exchange rate stability. The type of regional monetary arrangement we envision is compatible with the appropriately defined policy of inflation targeting, as long as the economies in the region share a broadly similar target for inflation (subject to country-specific factors), especially given the freedom for each economy to set its own exchange rate regime with respect to the common currency basket. It is important to keep in mind that the operation of the arrangement is more like a managed or a less than free-floating regime, especially against the currencies of outside countries, with the basket serving only as a reference within the system.

9.4 MOVING THE AGENDA AHEAD

9.4.1 Economic Policy Coordination

Types of policy coordination

Regional economic policy coordination may be classified into three types: information sharing, regime choice and policy optimization.[11] First, information sharing is the least formal of the three and only involves a mechanism of policy dialogue (and possibly surveillance), designed to improve each economy's understanding of the economic performance, macroeconomic and structural issues, policy objectives and policy choices of its peers. Second, regime choice is a joint exercise to agree on a set of rules of the game, within which individual economies can conduct their independent policymaking to pursue their own economic interests. This type of policy coordination includes agreements on regional payment settlements, regional liquidity support arrangements, regional exchange rate regimes and regional frameworks for concerted action at the time of a crisis. Finally, policy optimization is a joint maximization, by the economies concerned, of a weighted sum of their economic welfare. This is the highest form of policy coordination among policymakers.

A regional liquidity support arrangement

Initiatives to strengthen regional macroeconomic policy coordination in East Asia have now entered the second stage. With recent efforts at CMI multilateralization (CMIM), including the creation of the AMRO, the ASEAN+3 finance ministries and central banks are well on the way to establishing a regional liquidity support facility of their own. Regional policy coordination will further strengthen if the AMRO develops into an effective surveillance unit that is also capable of formulating conditionality in the event of crisis lending. Particularly significant in this respect is the May 2010 agreement on the member contributions to the CMIM, with 32 percent each for the PRC (including Hong Kong, China whose contribution is 3.5 percent) and Japan, 16 percent for Korea, and 20 percent for the ten ASEAN countries combined (Table 9.2).

The efficacy of the regional liquidity support facility is yet to be tested as a crisis management tool. In the meantime, the region's economies are continuing to pile up foreign exchange reserves. The accumulation of foreign exchange reserves is not only an insurance against a sudden reversal of capital inflows, but it may also allow these economies to achieve a degree of monetary independence and exchange rate stability while moving gradually toward greater capital account openness. Aizenman et al. (2010) showed that countries aiming at exchange rate stability could minimize the associated increase in output volatility by holding high levels (over 20 percent of GDP) of international reserves. Reserve accumulation may have thus served some useful purposes from the point of view of individual economies. From a more global standpoint, however, the outcome was costly. It allowed large US current account deficits to be financed at low cost and contributed to the global imbalance, which was considered by some as a cause of the build-up of financial risks that eventually led to the global financial crisis in 2007–2009. The policy of further accumulating foreign exchange reserves should not continue, not least because reserve holding represents a deadweight loss in terms of foregone income and consumption (Fukuda and Kon 2010).

Continued efforts to strengthen the regional liquidity support facility should be made by further raising the amount of funds available and also possibly by removing what may act as a deterrent: namely, the requirement that providing liquidity beyond 20 percent of the borrowing quota be linked to an IMF program. Once the member authorities agree on the transparent rules under which the resources can be used, the regional liquidity support mechanism should help reduce the cost of wasteful reserve accumulation. The provision of US dollar liquidity by the US Federal Reserve through swap arrangements with several emerging economies, including Korea and Singapore, during the global financial

Table 9.2 Financial contributions and voting power under the Chiang Mai Initiative Multilateralization (CMIM)

Members	Financial contributions		Voting power (in % of total)
	Billions of US dollars	% of total	
Plus Three Countries	96.00	80.00	71.59
People's Republic of China (includes Hong Kong, China)	38.40	32.00	28.41
People's Republic of China	34.20	28.50	25.43
Hong Kong, China	4.20	3.50	2.98
Japan	38.40	32.00	28.41
Republic of Korea	19.20	16.00	14.77
ASEAN	24.00	20.00	28.41
Brunei Darussalam	0.030	0.025	1.158
Cambodia	0.120	0.100	1.222
Indonesia	4.552	3.793	4.369
Lao People's Democratic Republic	0.030	0.025	1.158
Malaysia	4.552	3.793	4.369
Myanmar	0.060	0.050	1.179
Philippines	4.552	3.793	4.369
Singapore	4.552	3.793	4.369
Thailand	4.552	3.793	4.369
Viet Nam	1.000	0.833	1.847
ASEAN+3	120.00	100.00	100.00

Note: ASEAN = Association of Southeast Asian Nations.

Source: Joint Ministerial Statement of the 13th ASEAN+3 Finance Ministers' Meeting, Tashkent, 2 May 2010.

crisis has been credited with stabilizing the markets for short-term US dollar funds. Given the large balance of foreign exchange reserves held in the region, there is no reason why the Asian economies cannot provide liquidity support to each other when there is a need. In order to remove the IMF link, the AMRO must create an effective mechanism for regional economic surveillance to achieve the right balance between financing and adjustment, and thus remove the concern that the underlying problem is fundamental in nature, and any potential moral hazard that may be associated with easy financing.

Strengthening regional institutions

The multilateralization of the CMI and the establishment of the AMRO are only the beginning. The ERPD process, first introduced in 2000 by ASEAN+3 finance ministers to conduct policy dialogue for regional economic monitoring and surveillance, will involve central bank governors from 2012. The AMRO could play a secretariat role to manage the pooled resources and to negotiate a program of economic policies with a country seeking financial support in the event of a crisis, in addition to providing significant inputs to the ERPD process. It is not clear at this stage whether the AMRO will evolve into such a full-fledged secretariat for the CMIM and ERPD, but this is likely to happen.

From the standpoint of securing independence and credibility, it is important that the administrative expenses of the secretariat would be financed by the interest earnings on the management of the pooled reserves and from the lending operations. In a more advanced stage of exchange rate policy coordination (see subsection 9.4.2), the secretariat could evolve into an Asian monetary cooperation fund, charged with the responsibility for keeping accounts of financial transactions among the member economies and administering various facilities for intervention and other exchange rate management needs,[12] or even an Asian monetary fund with broader responsibilities for macroeconomic policy coordination. In the future, several other economies – such as India; Mongolia; and Taipei,China; and even Australia and New Zealand – may be invited to join.

9.4.2 Exchange Rate Policy Coordination through an Asian Currency Unit

An Asian currency unit for exchange rate surveillance

To give teeth to the process of policy dialogue and surveillance, policymakers must agree on the choice of analytical tools to use in monitoring economic developments and addressing policy spillovers across economies in the region. There has been much talk on the need to do so, but little concrete progress has yet been made. The most important indicator to agree on is an indicator of exchange rate misalignment. The least challenging way to devise such an indicator is to calculate a separate effective exchange rate index for each economy and monitor how the value of each currency is changing in effective terms. The purpose of such an indicator, at least initially, is not necessarily to explore policy corrections to maintain exchange rate stability, but more critically to help identify the reasons why the effective exchange rate index for a particular currency is moving in a particular direction.

Once there is agreement on the choice of weights, a currency basket – called the Asian currency unit (ACU) – could be used as a divergence indicator of the type used in the EMS (Takagi 1989).[13] The determination of the ACU weights could become political if the weights are related to the voting powers of the respective member economies in the decision-making process of regional institutions.[14] Fortunately, an agreement has been reached on the member contributions to, and voting shares in, the CMIM (Table 9.2). It would thus be conceivable to use the CMIM shares (in terms of either contributions or voting shares) as the currency weights in constructing the ACU. Alternatively, because precise weights matter little in the determination of the broad performance of the basket, simple weights could also be considered (Takagi 1988). Such weights should be parsimonious – as is the case with the Special Drawing Right (SDR) – and could be based broadly on GDP, trade and capital account openness, among others (Kawai 2009).

Informal coordination of exchange rate regimes

The first step for concrete exchange rate policy coordination is to introduce an informal process to achieve both greater exchange rate flexibility vis-à-vis the US dollar and some exchange rate stability within East Asia. This could be done using a common or a similar basket of SDR-plus currencies (the US dollar, the euro, the British pound, the yen and emerging East Asian currencies) as a loose reference. Under this scheme, those economies under US dollar pegs would increase exchange rate flexibility; all emerging East Asian economies would essentially adopt a managed float targeted at an SDR-plus currency basket – as is currently practiced by Singapore.[15]

Such exchange rate policy coordination – even of the most rudimentary form – would have been useful at the height of the global financial crisis in late 2008, when most economies in East Asia either allowed their currencies to depreciate against the US dollar or terminated the policy of gradual appreciation. On the other hand, the Japanese yen – virtually the only freely floating currency in the region – appreciated sharply against the US dollar in part because of the unwinding of the yen carry trade (Figure 9.1). While sharp currency depreciation was a significant disruption to some economies, notably Korea which experienced a mini currency crisis in the third quarter of 2008, it also helped in engineering a relatively early recovery. However, this came at the expense of Japan, which had to assume more than its share of the adjustment burden. Exchange rate policy coordination would have helped avoid large bilateral exchange rate volatility between the yen and the won and spread the burden of adjustment more evenly across the region.

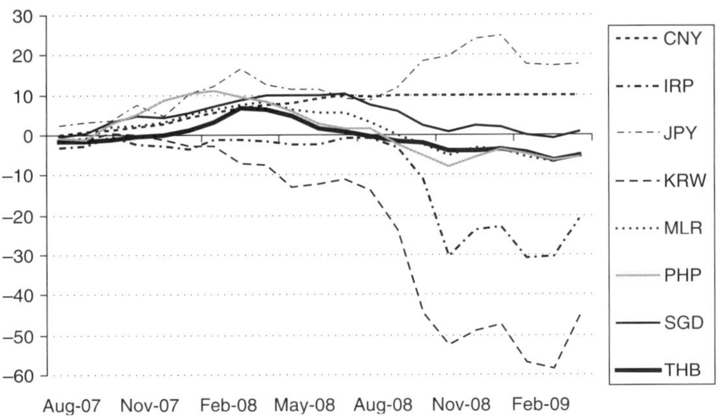

Notes: CNY = PRC yuan; IRP = Indonesian rupiah; JPY = Japanese yen; KRW = Korean won; MLR = Malaysian ringgit; PHP = Philippine peso; SGD = Singapore dollar; THB = Thai baht.

Source: IMF, International Financial Statistics, online database, available at http://www.imfstatistics.org/imf/.

Figure 9.1 Movements of selected Asian currencies vis-à-vis the US dollar during the global financial crisis, August 2007–April 2009

The currency weights in the proposed SDR-plus basket could vary across economies in the region, at least initially. How strictly each economy stabilizes its currency to this basket would depend on its own conditions and preferences. National monetary authorities could maintain most of their autonomous policymaking by combining an appropriately defined inflation-targeting policy and basket-based managed floating. At this stage, the ACU could also be introduced as a tool for measuring the degree of joint movements of East Asian currencies and the degree of divergence of the movement of each currency from the regional average (as determined by the ACU).

It should be stressed that, because there are no official central rates proposed under this informal policy coordination mechanism, use of the ACU basket as a divergence indicator differs from the European Currency Unit (ECU)-based divergence indicator previously used in Europe. The ACU-based indicator is only intended to promote dialogue and cooperation on exchange rates by providing a common measure of how individual currencies have moved from the regional average during a given period. How this works can be illustrated by using an ACU basket with the CMIM contribution weights (Figure 9.2). This shows that the Korean

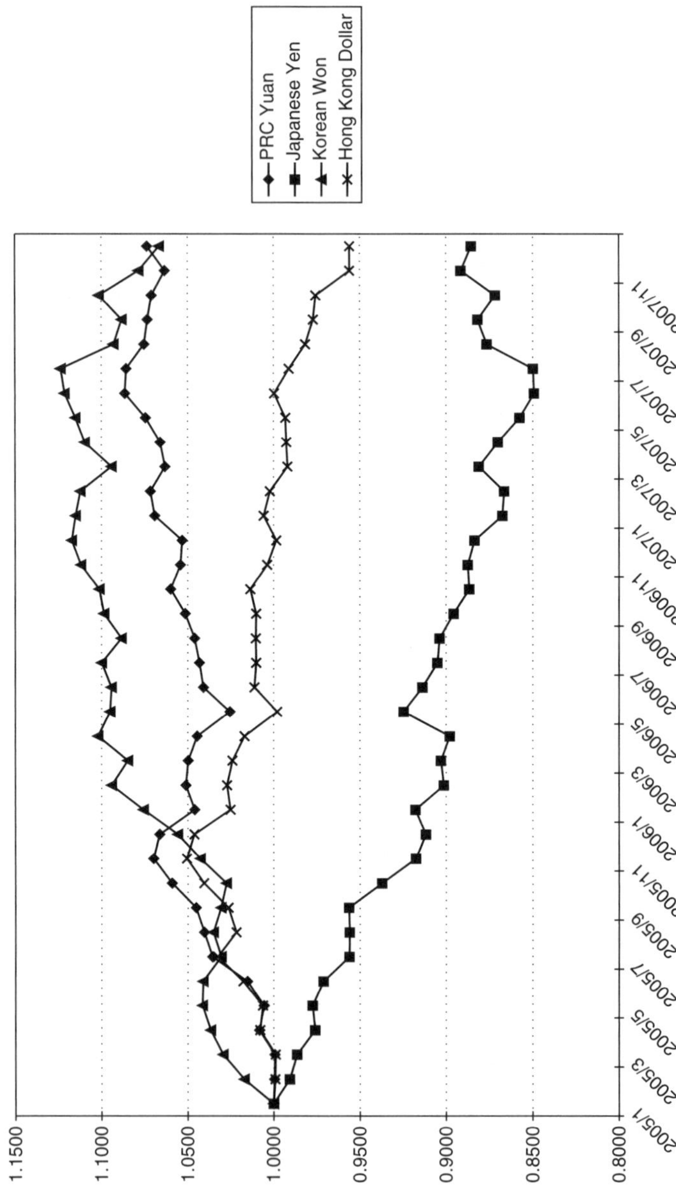
PRC Yuan
Japanese Yen
Korean Won
Hong Kong Dollar
1.1500
1.1000
1.0500
1.0000
0.9500
0.9000
0.8500
0.8000
2005/1
2005/3
2005/5
2005/7
2005/9
2005/11
2006/1
2006/3
2006/5
2006/7
2006/9
2006/11
2007/1
2007/3
2007/5
2007/7
2007/9
2007/11

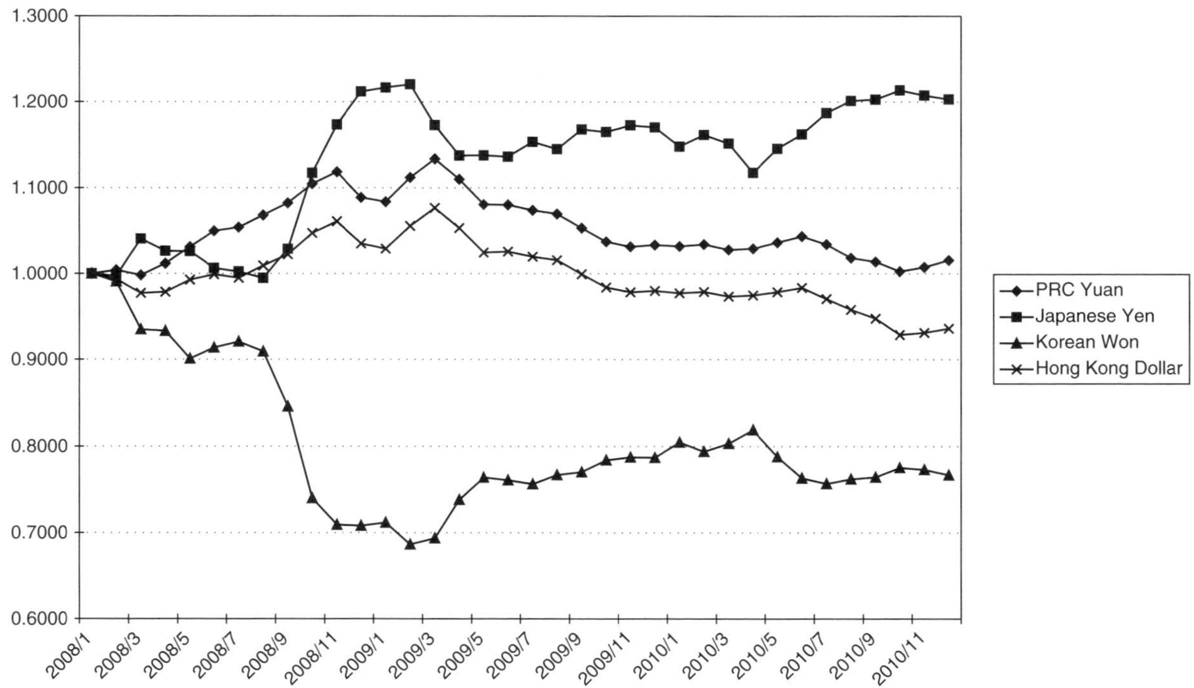

Source: Authors' construction, using CMIM contribution weights, from monthly average exchange rates in IMF, *International Financial Statistics*, online database, available at http://www.imfstatistics.org/imf/.

Figure 9.2 Deviations of selected East Asian currencies from the ACU rate, 2005–2007 and 2008–2010 won and the Japanese yen moved in divergent directions before and after the onset of the global financial crisis. In contrast, the Hong Kong dollar (which was pegged to the US dollar) and the yuan remained in the middle. Once the PRC moves to a more flexible exchange rate regime, ACU index movements and divergences of component currency movements can provide more meaningful information about the underlying macroeconomic policies and conditions in the region.

This type of informal exchange rate policy cooperation will become increasingly important in East Asia as global financial stability is restored over the coming years. As many East Asian economies recover from the crisis and begin to tighten monetary policy, large capital inflows may resume. Without collective action, a recipient of capital flows might be reluctant to allow its currency to appreciate out of fear that it might lose price competitiveness vis-à-vis its competitors in the region. If loss of competitiveness is the reason for the reluctance to allow a currency to appreciate, joint action to appreciate the currencies against third currencies would be an obvious solution.[16]

Formal, loose exchange rate policy coordination

The second step for concrete exchange rate policy coordination is jointly to adopt a formal policy of stabilizing intraregional exchange rates using a common basket of SDR-plus currencies (that is, the US dollar, the euro, the pound and the ACU) as a reference. The basket stabilization policy will have to be well defined with respect to how the central rates should be defended. Initially, the band around the central rate could be made relatively wide (say ±10 percent), with relatively frequent adjustment of both the central rate and the band – along the lines proposed by Williamson (2001). The authorities would allow greater exchange rate flexibility vis-à-vis the US dollar while enjoying a lesser degree of national monetary policy autonomy. The ACU index should continue to serve as an important indicator in measuring the joint movements and divergences of East Asian currencies, and its use in the financial markets should be encouraged.

The AMRO – or any full-fledged CMIM–ERPD secretariat that may succeed it – could then be transformed into a more structured Asian monetary cooperation fund (AMCF). Unlike its European counterpart – the European Monetary Cooperation Fund (EMCF), its role should go beyond simply administering the pooled resources. The secretariat should also conduct more intensive ERPD, with advanced peer review and due diligence elements, and draft lending conditionality when a member economy needs to draw CMIM resources without requiring an IMF program. A credible regional liquidity support facility would require effective regional economic surveillance, which in turn could serve as a basis for meaningful policy dialogue on regional issues. A regional mechanism – including regional surveillance and policy dialogue needed for a credible and effective liquidity facility – is meant to address regional issues of common interest, such as yen–won volatility, yuan–ASEAN currency issues and a joint response to US dollar depreciation. Such a regional mechanism would clearly complement the existing global mechanism, centered around IMF surveillance and the Group of 20 (G20) policy dialogue, where for example US dollar–yuan or euro–yuan issues might be discussed along with their global implications.

Tight, systematic coordination of exchange rate and monetary policies

The third step for concrete exchange rate policy coordination is the launch of greater systematic exchange rate and monetary policy coordination to create a regional monetary anchor. Two approaches are possible: the European approach and the parallel currency approach (Eichengreen 2006). Under the European approach, a common basket peg similar to the snake or exchange rate mechanism (ERM) could be introduced. All currencies would become freely flexible vis-à-vis external currencies, such as the US dollar and the euro, but maintain intraregional stability through the joint stabilization of individual currencies with respect to the ACU. The mechanism should include clearly defined, transparent monetary policy and intervention rules so as to provide a credible monetary anchor within East Asia as well as a fully elaborated short-term liquidity support arrangement, which would be large and speedy enough for frequent interventions in the region's currency markets. The AMCF will become the clearinghouse of frequent interventions as well as the issuer of official ACUs. Fiscal policy rules may also be designed to lend credibility to the exchange rate stabilization scheme.

The parallel currency approach could be introduced in the absence of strong political will. This approach involves the issuance of an ACU as a parallel legal tender together with national currencies, the issuance of ACU-denominated bonds, and the establishment of a clearing and settlement system for ACU transactions. In the longer run, as the volume of ACU transactions increases, the ACU could develop into the sole legal tender within the region.[17] The centralized reserve pool could then be converted into an Asian central bank.

A practical approach is to take a multi-track, multi-speed approach, whereby economies ready for deeper policy coordination would begin the formal process of policy coordination while others prepare to join later. A group of economies that are sufficiently integrated – such as Japan and Korea; the PRC and Hong Kong, China; or Singapore, Malaysia and

Brunei Darussalam – and with sufficient political commitment, may wish at this stage to initiate subregional currency stabilization schemes or even single-currency regimes. Each subregional group could intensify exchange rate and monetary policy coordination while allowing the possibility for others to join them subsequently. Over time these groups may start negotiations to integrate into a larger monetary zone.

9.4.3 Political Will and Further Steps

The success of any regional arrangement crucially depends on the strength of political commitment. In this connection, some authors have argued that, in an analogy to the case of individual economies, regional exchange rate pegs are dangerous in the absence of the requisite political commitment (Bayoumi et al. 2000; Eichengreen and Bayoumi 1999). These and other similar views, however, seem to overstate the case for the required degree of political commitment for the type of regional arrangement being proposed. It is true that any regional arrangement would involve a series of political decisions that constitute an intergovernmental agreement. However, in our proposal, once an agreement is reached on the composition of the ACU and there is a broad commitment to use the basket of currencies as a reference, everything else would be left to the discretion of the individual national authorities. This is not very different from most of the exchange rate arrangements currently in place, except that the US dollar is replaced by a common basket as the anchor currency.

Even so, this scheme will require a more organized framework of coordination for regional policy surveillance and consultation as time goes on (Kawai and Takagi 2005b). To the extent that the purpose of regional monetary policy coordination is, first and foremost, to stabilize intraregional exchange rates, there must ideally be a mechanism of ensuring that no country jeopardizes this objective by taking unilateral action that is completely out of line with those pursued in the rest of the region. As the action of any single member affects the value of the basket, there must necessarily be a mechanism to subject that action to the scrutiny of the other participating countries.

As the region becomes more integrated and hence more prepared, in terms of both economic criteria and political climate, for a more permanent commitment to creating economic and monetary union, greater efforts must be made to build requisite institutions. What lies ahead can only be a matter of speculation at this stage. Deeper macroeconomic policy coordination will be possible only with strong political leadership from the region's policymakers, especially in Japan and the PRC, and a well-articulated vision for what Asia should be like in the middle of the twenty-first century. Although few see it as feasible over the next few decades, the benefits of intraregional exchange rate stability, and even a common currency, may well increase over time, as the economies of the region continue to integrate and become more interdependent.

9.5 CONCLUSION

East Asia has seen rapid market-driven economic integration through trade, foreign direct investment and finance. This market-led integration has made regional exchange rate management an increasingly important policy agenda for the regional economies. While extraregional exchange rate flexibility is often required as a tool of sound macroeconomic management, especially in view of the large global payments imbalances and large capital inflows, intraregional exchange rate stability has become highly desirable for the increasingly integrated region. There is strong empirical evidence to show that exchange rate stability is critical to promoting intraregional trade, especially in parts and components, upon which the region's manufacturing production activities depend.

The pressure for continued correction of the global payments imbalance, robust economic recovery from the global financial crisis, and ultra-loose monetary policy pursued by the US Federal Reserve in the post-crisis period will likely cause significant US dollar depreciation. The global financial crisis, moreover, has highlighted the need to expand intraregional trade in final goods within the region. Increased regional exchange rate stability, within the context of a region-wide free trade agreement, should help to create a larger market for the region's own goods and services, by promoting cross-border investment, particularly in infrastructure, which is receiving increasing attention not only as an engine of growth but also as a productive way of recycling the region's savings.

The immediate step in exchange rate policy coordination would be for the region's economies to discuss exchange rate issues as part of enhanced economic surveillance, for which the ACU will be a useful reference tool. Initially, use can be made of an SDR-plus currency basket consisting of the US dollar, the euro, the UK pound and the ACU. Greater political support for economic policy coordination could eventually lead to further institutional integration capable of supporting intraregional exchange rate stability based on the ACU alone through an Asian version of the ERM. For this purpose substantial convergence will have to be achieved across economies in the region in terms of economic, financial, and structural conditions; performance; and policies.

To support exchange rate policy coordination, the region's economies must make greater efforts to strengthen regional financial cooperation: the CMIM, the ERPD process and the ABMI. Once the region implements the CMIM with sufficient capacity to conduct regional economic surveillance and to formulate independent adjustment policy, its lending operations can be delinked from IMF programs. Only then will the facility establish itself as an independent regional monetary fund. The recent creation of the AMRO is an important step in this direction. Much work remains, however, to strengthen collaboration between the region's finance ministers and central bank governors as well as to harmonize the region's financial sector supervisors and capital market regulators.

NOTES

1. Malaysia's adoption of a US dollar peg in September 1998 may have prompted Singapore and other neighboring countries to strengthen their currency stability against the US dollar.
2. Japan subsequently refrained from intervening in the foreign exchange market altogether until 15 September 2010 when, in an attempt to counter the appreciation pressure on the yen, it sold over 2 trillion yen in exchange for US dollars. This was a one-time action, however, likely prompted by increasing concerns over the negative impact of yen appreciation.
3. The IMF's recent review of the 'stability of the overall system of exchange rates', however, delivers a more nuanced message: 'For non systemically important countries, the choice of exchange rate regime can be tailored to their particular economic challenges, with the proviso that those opting for less flexible regimes should ensure strong macroeconomic fundamentals to minimize the risk of (potentially contagious) crises'. See IMF (2009).
4. We considered the following moving average (MA) representation of a structural VAR model for an East Asian economy:

$$\Delta \ln Y_t = \sum \phi_{1j} u_{t-j} + \sum \phi_{2j} v_{t-j} + \sum \phi_{3j} w_{t-j} + \sum \phi_{4j} x_{t-j} \quad (9.1)$$

$$\Delta \ln E_t = \sum \lambda_{1j} u_{t-j} + \sum \lambda_{2j} v_{t-j} + \sum \lambda_{3j} w_{t-j} + \sum \lambda_{4j} x_{t-j} \quad (9.2)$$

$$\Delta \ln P_t = \sum \eta_{1j} u_{t-j} + \sum \eta_{2j} v_{t-j} + \sum \eta_{3j} w_{t-j} + \sum \eta_{4j} x_{t-j} \quad (9.3)$$

where $\Delta \ln Y_t$, $\Delta \ln E_t$ and $\Delta \ln P_t$ are, respectively, the first differences in the natural logarithms of relative real output, the real effective exchange rate and the relative price level; x_t is an unspecified set of exogenous variables affecting the VAR system; and u_t, v_t and w_t are, respectively, macroeconomic fundamental shocks to relative real output growth, the rate of change in the real effective exchange rate, and relative price inflation. Here, relative real output is defined as the country's real GDP relative to the world's real GDP, the real effective exchange rate is defined as the country's real exchange rate vis-à-vis the world, and the relative price level is defined as the country's GDP deflator relative to the world's GDP deflator, where the relevant world variables are given by the weighted average of the United States (with the weight of 0.4), Japanese (0.3) and European Union (0.3) variables; the EU variables are in turn given by the weighted averages of the relevant variables for its members, with the GDP shares in 1990. In defining the real effective exchange rate, GDP deflators are used as the relevant price measures. Data frequency is annual and the sample period is 1970–1998 for all economies except the PRC and 1979–1998 for the PRC.

5. On the other hand, to the extent that purchasing power parity is more likely to hold in the long run, uncertainty associated with exchange rate volatility may have a smaller role to play in investment decisions.
6. If FDI is directed towards the production of domestic sales, greater exchange rate uncertainty may cause local production to replace exports to that market, thus increasing FDI flows. If FDI is directed towards the production of exports, exchange rate uncertainty increases the riskiness of that particular host country as a production base. See Ito et al. (1996) and Benassy-Quere et al. (2001).
7. Dixit and Pindyck (1994) argued that the net present value (NPV) rule should be modified to include the cost of waiting, so that the NPV of a project may be given by the present value of expected returns less the value of the option to invest later.
8. Theoretically, investment can rise or fall with greater exchange rate uncertainty. The types of industries more likely to benefit from exchange rate uncertainty are those with few alternative uses and little scrap value or with large entry costs. In contrast, the types of industries whose investment is likely to benefit from greater exchange rate stability are those with high scrap value but a low opportunity cost of waiting. Based on the estimation of aggregate investment equations for five major advanced economies, Darby et al. (1999) found significantly negative coefficients for exchange rate volatility.
9. According to McKinnon (2000), this was not optimal, however, because fluctuations in the yen–dollar rate caused boom and bust cycles for Japan and East Asian emerging economies; he called the yen–dollar rate the 'loose cannon in the pre-1997 East-Asian exchange rate regime'.
10. Benassy-Quere (1999) considered the case for coordinated action in the context of conflicting exchange rate objectives. Suppose that the authorities of two identical East Asian competitor economies are faced with a trade-off between stabilizing the debt-weighted effective exchange rate (with a higher share of the yen but no share for the other competitor economy's currency) and the trade-weighted effective exchange rate (with a lower share of the yen and a positive share for the other competitor economy's currency). In this case, it is shown that a cooperative solution is superior to the Nash equilibrium, because cooperation can allow the share of the yen to increase by making the determination of the bilateral exchange rate independent of considerations of competitiveness. Cooperation thus stabilizes the debt-weighted effective exchange rate with little loss in trade-weighted effective exchange rate stability.

    Ogawa and Ito (2002) also highlighted the benefit of policy coordination in the context of the choice of currency basket weights. Starting with the observation that the optimal weight depended on the weights adopted by a neighboring economy, they show in an extreme case that, if one economy adopted a dollar peg, the other economy might also need to adopt a dollar peg, and vice versa, with the dollar peg becoming the Nash equilibrium. Alternatively, a basket peg could become a Nash equilibrium, if both economies considered adopting one. Which of the Nash equilibria would be chosen depends on inertia and rational calculation. Both economies would be better off, if the decision to move to a Pareto dominant situation – that is, adoption of a basket peg – were made simultaneously.
11. See also Kenen (1994) and Hamada and Kawai (1997). Kawai and Takagi (2005b) also discuss these issues.
12. In Europe, the European Monetary Cooperation Fund administered three lending facilities.
13. The ACU could also be developed for invoicing trade-related transactions and serving as a denomination for local currency bond issues. See Kawai (2009).
14. In the future, divergence indicators based on ACU indexes could be used to induce

policy changes to reduce large exchange rate divergences across regional currencies. In this case, deciding on the ACU weights could assume an additional economic and political dimension as each economy attempts to maximize its degree of freedom in the regional exchange rate arrangement. For example, if the weight of currency A is 100 percent, the central bank of country A has full monetary autonomy; if it is zero, the country's central bank must passively accept the stance of monetary policy determined by the rest of the region. So each economy likely has an incentive to maximize its currency weight in the basket.

15. Although Singapore uses the exchange rate as a monetary policy instrument, other economies may choose policy interest rates or monetary aggregates to pursue non-inflationary economic growth.
16. Kawai (2008) estimates that 20 percent collective depreciation of all East Asian currencies would entail an appreciation of only 9 percent in effective terms even if all economies outside the region maintained the nominal value of their currencies against the US dollar.
17. The appeal of the 'parallel currency' approach is dictated more by economic forces (that is, market forces) than by politics. This is consistent with the greater emphasis placed by East Asian economies on market-led rather than policy-led integration. It also accommodates the fact that the East Asian political context is very different from that of Europe. An underlying commitment to political solidarity drove the transition to a monetary union in Europe. Europe also considered the parallel currency approach, but it was abandoned in favor of the Maastricht process because of the strong political commitment that existed at the time.

REFERENCES

Aghevli, B.B., M.S. Khan and P.J. Montiel (1991), 'Exchange rate policy in developing countries: some analytical issues', Occasional Paper 78 (March), Washington, DC: IMF.

Aizenman, J., M.D. Chinn and H. Ito (2008), 'Assessing the emerging global financial architecture: measuring the trilemma's configurations over time', NBER Working Paper No. 14533.

Aizenman, J., M.D. Chinn and H. Ito (2010), 'The emerging global financial architecture: tracing and evaluating new patterns of the trilemma configuration', *Journal of International Money and Finance*, **29** (4), 615–41.

Arize, A., T. Osang and D. Slottje (2000), 'Exchange rate volatility and foreign trade: evidence from thirteen LDCs', *Journal of Business and Economics Statistics*, **18** (January), 10–17.

Asian Development Bank (ADB) (2008), *Emerging Asian Regionalism: A Partnership for Shared Prosperity*, Manila: Asian Development Bank.

Bayoumi, T., B. Eichengreen and P. Mauro (2000), 'On regional monetary arrangements for ASEAN', *Journal of the Japanese and International Economies*, **14** (June), 121–48.

Benassy-Quere, A. (1999), 'Optimal pegs for East Asian currencies', *Journal of the Japanese and International Economies*, **13** (March), 44–60.

Benassy-Quere, A., L. Fontagne and A. Lahreche-Revil (2001), 'Exchange-rate strategies in the competition for attracting foreign direct investment', *Journal of the Japanese and International Economies*, **15** (2) 178–98.

Caballero, R.J. and V. Corbo (1989), 'The effect of real exchange rate uncertainty on exports: empirical evidence', *World Bank Economic Review*, **3** (May), 263–78.

Calvo, G.A. and C.M. Reinhart (2005), 'Fixing for your life', in Guillermo Calvo (ed), *Emerging Capital Markets in Turmoil: Bad Luck or Bad Policy?*, Cambridge, MA: MIT Press, pp. 357–402.

Darby, J., A. Hughes Hallett, J. Ireland and L. Piscitelli (1999), 'The impact of exchange rate uncertainty on the level of investment', *Economic Journal*, **109** (March), C55–67.

Dixit, A.K. and R.S. Pindyck (1994), *Investment under Uncertainty*, Princeton, NJ: Princeton University Press.

Dornbusch, R. and Y.C. Park (1999), 'Flexibility or nominal anchors?', in Stefan Collignon, Jean Pisani-Ferry and Yung Chul Park (eds), *Exchange Rate Policies in Emerging Asian Countries*, London, UK and New York, USA: Routledge, pp. 3–34.

Eichengreen, B. (1999), *Toward a New International Financial Architecture: A Practical Post-Asia Agenda*, Washington, DC: Institute for International Economics.

Eichengreen, B. (2006), 'The parallel-currency approach to Asian monetary integration', *American Economic Review*, **96** (2), 432–36.

Eichengreen, B. and T. Bayoumi (1999), 'Is Asia an optimum currency area?', in Stefan Collignon, Jean Pisani-Ferry and Yung Chul Park (eds), *Exchange Rate Policies in Emerging Asian Countries*, London, UK and New York, USA: Routledge, pp. 347–66.

Fischer, S. (2001), 'Exchange rate regimes: is the bipolar view correct?', *Journal of Economic Perspectives*, **15** (Spring), 3–24.

Frankel, J.A. (1999), 'No single currency regime is right for all countries or at all times', Essays in International Finance, No. 215 (August), Princeton, NJ: Princeton University.

Fukuda, S. and Y. Kon (2010), 'Macroeconomic impacts of foreign exchange reserve accumulation: theory and international evidence', ADBI Working Paper Series, No. 197, Tokyo: Asian Development Bank Institute.

Glick, R., M. Hutchison and R. Moreno (1999), 'Is pegging the exchange rate a cure for inflation? East Asian experiences', in Richard J. Sweeney, Clas G. Wihlborg and Thomas Willett (eds), *Exchange Rate Policies for Emerging Market Economies*, Boulder, CO: Westview Press, pp. 165–93.

Hamada, K. and M. Kawai (1997), 'International economic policy coordination: theory and policy implications', in M.U. Fratianni, D. Salvatore and J. von Hagen (eds), *Handbook of Comparative Economic Policies, Vol. 5: Macroeconomic Policy in Open Economies*, Westport, CT: Greenwood Press, pp. 87–147.

Hattari, R. and R.S. Rajan (2008), 'Sources of FDI flows to developing Asia: the roles of distance and time zones', ADBI Working Paper Series, No. 117, Tokyo: Asian Development Bank Institute.

Hayakawa, K. and F. Kimura (2008), 'The effect of exchange rate volatility on international trade in East Asia', Discussion Paper Series, ERIA-DP-2008-03, Jakarta: Economic Research Institute for ASEAN and East Asia.

Honohan, P. and P.R. Lane (1999), 'Pegging to the dollar and the euro', *International Finance*, **2** (3), 379–410.

Independent Evaluation Office (IEO) (2007), *IMF Exchange Rate Policy Advice*, Washington, DC: IMF.

International Monetary Fund (IMF) (2009), *Toward a Stable System of Exchange Rates*, Washington, DC: IMF.

International Monetary Fund (IMF) (2010), *Annual Report on Exchange Arrangements and Exchange Restrictions*, Washington, DC: IMF.
Ito, T., P. Isard, S. Symansky and T. Bayoumi (1996), 'Exchange rate movements and their impact on trade and investment in the APEC region', Occasional Paper, **145** (December), Washington, DC: IMF.
Kawai, M. (2008), 'Toward a regional exchange rate regime in East Asia', *Pacific Economic Review*, **13** (1), 83–103.
Kawai, M. (2009), 'An Asian currency unit for regional exchange-rate policy coordination', in Duck-Koo Chung and Barry Eichengreen (eds), *Fostering Monetary and Financial Cooperation in East Asia*, Singapore: Word Scientific, pp. 73–112.
Kawai, M. and S. Takagi (2005a), 'Strategy for a regional exchange rate arrangement in East Asia: analysis, review, and proposal', *Global Economic Review*, **34** (March), pp. 21–64.
Kawai, M. and S. Takagi (2005b), 'Towards regional monetary cooperation in East Asia: lessons from other parts of the world', *International Journal of Finance and Economics*, **8** (April), 97–116.
Kenen, P.B. (1994), *The International Economy*, 3rd edition, Cambridge: Cambridge University Press.
Kumar, R. and R. Dhawan (1991), 'Exchange rate volatility and Pakistan's exports to the developed world, 1974–85', *World Development*, **19** (September),1225–40.
McKenzie, M.D. (1999), 'The impact of exchange rate volatility on international trade flows', *Journal of Economic Surveys*, **13** (February), 71–106.
McKinnon, R.I. (2000), 'The East Asian dollar standard, life after death?', *Economic Notes*, **29** (February), 31–82.
Obstfeld, M. and K. Rogoff (1995), 'The mirage of fixed exchange rates', *Journal of Economic Perspectives*, **9** (Fall), 73–96.
Ogawa, E. and T. Ito (2002), 'On the desirability of a regional basket currency arrangement', *Journal of the Japanese and International Economies*, **16**, 317–34.
Takagi, S. (1988), 'A basket peg policy: operational issues for developing countries', *World Development*, **16** (February), 271–79.
Takagi, S. (1989), 'An alternative approach to the divergence indicator in the European monetary system', *De Economist*, **137** (3), 360–66.
Takagi, S. (1999), 'The yen and its East Asian neighbors, 1980–1995: cooperation or competition', in Takatoshi Ito and Anne O. Krueger (eds), *Changes in Exchange Rates in Rapidly Developing Countries: Theory, Practice, and Policy Issues*, Chicago, IL: University of Chicago Press, pp. 185–207.
Takagi, S. and I. Kozuru (2010), 'Output and price linkages in Asia's post-crisis macroeconomic interdependence', *Singapore Economic Review*, **55** (March), 59–81.
Thorbecke, W. (2008), 'The effect of exchange rate volatility on fragmentation in East Asia: evidence from the electronics industry', *Journal of the Japanese and International Economies*, **22**, 535–44.
Tsangarides, C. (2010), 'Crisis and recovery: role of the exchange rate regime in emerging market countries', IMF Working Paper 10/242, Washington, DC: IMF.
Williamson, J. (1982), 'A survey of the literature on the optimal peg', *Journal of Development Economics*, **11** (August), 39–61.
Williamson, J. (1999), 'The case for a common basket peg for East Asian currencies', in Stefan Collignon, Jean Pisani-Ferry and Yung Chul Park (eds),

Exchange Rate Policies in Emerging Asian Countries, London, UK and New York, USA: Routledge, pp. 327–43.
Williamson, J. (2001), 'The case for a basket, band and crawl (BBC) regime for East Asia', in David Gruen and John Simon (eds), *Future Directions for Monetary Policies in East Asia*, Sydney: Reserve Bank of Australia, pp. 96–111.

Index

Titles of publications are shown in *italics*.